LYNCHBURG COLLEGE
SYMPOSIUM READINGS

CLASSICAL SELECTIONS ON GREAT ISSUES

SERIES TWO
VOLUME IV

# FAITH AND MORALS

Plato
Aristotle
Aurelius
Dostoyevsky
Merton
Hopkins
Niebuhr
Bellah
James
Matthew



UNIVERSITY
PRESS OF
AMERICA

LANHAM • NEW YORK • LONDON

SERIES TWO

# SYMPOSIUM READINGS

Lynchburg College in Virginia

Compiled and Edited by the
following faculty members of Lynchburg College:

Kenneth E. Alrutz, A.M., University of Pennsylvania; Assistant Professor of English

Virginia B. Berger, M.A., Harvard University; Associate Professor of Music

Anne Marshall Huston, Ed.D., University of Virginia; Associate Professor of Education

James L. Campbell, Ph.D., University of Virginia; Associate Professor of English

Robert L. Frey, Ph.D., University of Minnesota; Professor of History

James A. Huston, Ph.D., New York University; Dean of the College, Professor of History and International Relations

Shannon McIntyre Jordan, Ph.D., University of Georgia; Instructor in Philosophy

Jan G. Linn, D.Min., Christian Theological Seminary; Associate Professor, College Chaplain

Peggy S. Pittas, M.A., Dalhousie University; Associate Professor of Psychology

Clifton W. Potter, Jr., Ph.D., University of Virginia; Professor of History

Julius A. Sigler, Ph.D., University of Virginia; Professor of Physics

Phillip H. Stump, Ph.D., University of California at Los Angeles; Assistant Professor of History

Thomas C. Tiller, Ph.D., Florida State University; Dean of Student Affairs, Professor of Education

**University Press of America,™ Inc.**

4720 Boston Way
Lanham, MD 20706

3 Henrietta Street
London WC2E 8LU England



Printed in the United States of America

**Library of Congress Cataloging in Publication Data**
Main entry under title:

Faith and morals.

(Classical selections on great issues; series 2, vol. 4)
1. Ethics–Addresses, essays, lectures. 2. Religion–Addresses, essays, lectures. I. Plato. II. Lynchburg College. III. Series.

| | | |
|---|---|---|
| BJ1012.F33 | 170 | 81–71948 |
| ISBN 0–8191–2301–3 | | AACR2 |
| ISBN 0–8191–2302–1 (pbk.) | | |

ACKNOWLEDGEMENTS

The following copyrighted materials have been used with the permission of the copyright holders:

From *The Book of Job*, Revised Standard Version, Thomas Nelson & Sons, Division of Christian Education & Ministry of the National Council of the Churches of Christ in the U.S.A., c.1952.

From *The Gospel According to Matthew,* The New English Bible, The Delegates of the Oxford University Press and The Syndics of the Cambridge University Press, c.1961.

From *The Seven Storey Mountain* by Thomas Merton. c.1948, Harcourt, Brace Jovanovich, Inc.

From *Moral Man and Immoral Society* by Reinhold Niebuhr. c.1932, Charles Scribner's Sons.

From *Beyond Belief,* "Civil Religion in America" by Robert N. Bellah. c.1970, American Academy of Arts and Sciences and the Author.

From *National Institute for Campus Ministries Journal,* "Biblical Religion and Social Science in the Modern World" by Robert N. Bellah. c.1981, National Institute for Campus Ministries.

The authors acknowledge with appreciation the permissions granted by these holders of the respective copyrights.

# INTRODUCTION TO VOLUME IV

Significant issues always have an ethical dimension. What is the nature of goodness? What is justice? What is the good life and how does one achieve it? What constitutes right and wrong? These are questions that challenge the best minds in every generation.

Moral and ethical queries often do not have clearcut answers. But the readings in this theme provide a wide variety of possible solutions that will challenge the reader to formulate his own answers while seeking to understand better the issues.

CONTENTS

## INTRODUCTION TO VOLUME IV

Significant issues always have an ethical dimension. What is the nature of goodness? What is justice? What is the good life and how does one achieve it? What constitutes right and wrong? These are questions that challenge the best minds in every generation.

Moral and ethical queries often do not have clearcut answers. But the readings in this theme provide a wide variety of possible solutions that will challenge the reader to formulate his own answers while seeking to understand better the issues.

Plato, THE REPUBLIC (Trans. by Benjamin Jowett)

1. How would you meet Glaucon's argument for injustice?

2. What is the point of the story of Gyges?

3. On what basis did Socrates suggest that Glaucon's dog was a "fine philosopher"? Do you agree?

4. If Plato's illustration in Book VI of the eye which sees by means of light from the sun is one side of an equation, how do you arrange the soul, science and truth as well as the idea of good to form the other side?

5. What are the themes of the allegory of the cave? Locate the pertinent passages for the support of your answer.

6. Why do philosophers make the best rulers? Or do they?

*The Republic* of Plato (c.427-c.347 B.C.) has been interpreted as a model both for an ideal government and for the soul. The following excerpts illustrate some of the most basic, but important, aspects of moral life.

# THE REPUBLIC

## PLATO

### BOOK II

With these words I was thinking that I had made an end of the discussion; but the end, in truth, proved to be only a beginning. For Glaucon, who is always the most pugnacious of men, was dissatisfied at Thrasymachus' retirement; he wanted to have the battle out. So he said to me: Socrates, do you wish really to persuade us, or only to seem to have persuaded us, that to be just is always better than to be unjust?

I should wish really to persuade you, I replied, if I could.

Then you certainly have not succeeded. Let me ask you now:—How would you arrange goods—are there not some which we welcome for their own sakes, and independently of their consequences, as, for example, harmless pleasures and enjoyments, which delight us at the time, although nothing follows from them?

I agree in thinking that there is such a class, I replied.

Is there not also a second class of goods, such as knowledge, sight, health, which are desirable not only in themselves, but also for their results?

Certainly, I said.

And would you not recognize a third class, such as gymnastic, and the care of the sick, and the physician's art; also the various ways of money-making—these do us good but we regard them as disagreeable; and no one would choose them for their own sakes, but only for the sake of some reward or result which flows from them?

There is, I said, this third class also. But why do you ask?

Because I want to know in which of the three classes you would place justice?

In the highest class, I replied,—among those goods which he who would be happy desires both for their own sake and for the sake of their results.

Then the many are of another mind; they think that justice is to be reckoned in the troublesome class, among goods which are to be pursued for the sake of rewards and of reputation, but in themselves are disagreeable and rather to be avoided.

I know, I said, that this is their manner of thinking, and that this was the thesis which Thrasymachus was maintaining just now, when he censured justice and praised injustice. But I am too stupid to be convinced by him.

I wish, he said, that you would hear me as well as him, and then I shall see whether you and I agree. For Thrasymachus seems to me, like a snake, to have been charmed by your voice sooner than he ought to have been; but to my mind the nature of justice and injustice have not yet been made clear. Setting aside their rewards and results, I want to know what they are in themselves, and how they inwardly work in the soul. If you please, then, I will revive the argument of Thrasymachus. And first I will speak of the nature and origin of justice according to the common view of them. Secondly, I will show that all men who practise justice do so against their will, of necessity, but not as a good. And thirdly, I will argue that there is reason in this view, for the life of the unjust is after all better far than the life of the just—if what they say is true, Socrates, since I myself am not of their opinion. But still I acknowledge that I am perplexed when I hear the voices of Thrasymachus and myriads of others dinning in my ears; and, on the other hand, I have never yet heard the superiority of justice to injustice maintained by any one in a satisfactory way. I want to hear justice praised in respect of itself; then I shall be satisfied, and you are the person from whom I think that I am most likely to hear this; and therefore I will praise the unjust life to the utmost of my power, and my manner of speaking will indicate the manner in which I desire to hear you too praising justice and censuring injustice. Will you say whether you approve of my proposal?

Indeed I do; nor can I imagine any theme about which a man of sense would oftener wish to converse.

I am delighted, he replied, to hear you say so, and shall begin by speaking, as I proposed, of the nature and origin of justice.

They say that to do injustice is, by nature, good; to suffer injustice, evil; but that the evil is greater than the good. And so when men have both done and suffered injustice and have had experience of both, not being able to avoid the one and obtain the other, they think that they had better agree among themselves to have neither; hence there arise laws and mutual covenants; and that which is ordained by law is termed by them lawful and just. This they affirm to be the origin and nature of justice;—it is a mean or compromise, between the best of all, which is to do injustice and not be punished, and the worst of all, which is to suffer injustice without the power of retaliation; and justice, being at a middle point between the two, is tolerated not as a good, but as the lesser evil, and honoured by reason of the inability of men to do injustice. For no man who is worthy to be called a man would ever submit to such an agreement if he were able to resist; he would be mad if he did. Such is the received account, Socrates, of the nature and origin of justice.

Now that those who practise justice do so involuntarily and because they have not the power to be unjust will best appear if we imagine something of this kind: having given both to the just and the unjust power to do what they will, let us watch and see whither desire will lead them; then we shall discover in the very act the just and unjust man to be proceeding along the same road, following their interest, which all natures deem to be their good, and are only diverted into the path of justice by the force of law. The liberty which we are supposing may be most completely given to them in the form of such a power as is said to have been possessed by Gyges[1] the ancestor of Croesus the Lydian.[1] According to the tradition, Gyges was a shepherd in the service of the king of Lydia; there was a great storm, and an earthquake made an opening in the earth at the place where he was feeding his flock. Amazed at the sight, he descended into the opening, where, among other marvels, he beheld a hollow brazen horse, having doors, at which he stooping and looking in saw a dead body of stature, as appeared to him, more than human, and having nothing on but a gold ring; this he took from the finger of the dead and reascended. Now the shepherds met together, according to custom, that they might send their monthly report about the flocks to the king; into their assembly he came having the ring on his finger, and as he was sitting among them he chanced to turn the collet of the ring inside his hand, when instantly he became invisible to the rest of the company and they began to speak of him as if he were no longer present. He was astonished at this, and again touching the ring he turned the collet outwards and reappeared; he made several trials of the ring, and always with the same result—when he turned the collet inwards he became invisible, when outwards he reappeared. Whereupon he contrived to be chosen one of the messengers who were sent to the court; where as soon as he arrived he seduced the queen, and with her help conspired against the king and slew him, and took the kingdom. Suppose now that there were two such magic rings, and the just put on one of them and the unjust the other; no man can be imagined to be of such an iron nature that he would stand fast in justice. No man would keep his hands off what was not his own when he could safely take what he liked out of the market, or go into houses and lie with any one at his pleasure, or

---

[1]Reading **Γυγῃ τῷ Κροίσου τοῦ Λυδοῦ προγόνῳ.**

kill or release from prison whom he would, and in all respects be like a God among men. Then the actions of the just would be as the actions of the unjust; they would both come at last to the same point. And this we may truly affirm to be a great proof that a man is just, not willingly or because he thinks that justice is any good to him individually, but of necessity, for wherever any one thinks that he can safely be unjust, there he is unjust. For all men believe in their hearts that injustice is far more profitable to the individual than justice, and he who argues as I have been supposing, will say that they are right. If you could imagine any one obtaining this power of becoming invisible, and never doing any wrong or touching what was another's, he would be thought by the lookers-on to be a most wretched idiot, although they would praise him to one another's faces, and keep up appearances with one another from a fear that they too might suffer injustice. Enough of this.

Now, if we are to form a real judgment of the life of the just and unjust, we must isolate them; there is no other way; and how is the isolation to be effected? I answer: Let the unjust man be entirely unjust, and the just man entirely just; nothing is to be taken away from either of them, and both are to be perfectly furnished for the work of their respective lives. First, let the unjust be like other distinguished masters of craft; like the skilful pilot or physician, who knows intuitively his own powers and keeps within their limits, and who, if he fails at any point, is able to recover himself. So let the unjust make his unjust attempts in the right way, and lie hidden if he means to be great in his injustice (he who is found out is nobody): for the highest reach of injustice is, to be deemed just when you are not. Therefore I say that in the perfectly unjust man we must assume the most perfect injustice; there is to be no deduction, but we must allow him, while doing the most unjust acts, to have acquired the greatest reputation for justice. If he has taken a false step he must be able to recover himself; he must be one who can speak with effect, if any of his deeds come to light, and who can force his way where force is required by his courage and strength, and command of money and friends. And at his side let us place the just man in his nobleness and simplicity, wishing, as Aeschylus says, to be and not to seem good. There must be no seeming, for if he seem to be just he will be honoured and rewarded, and then we shall not know whether he is just for the sake of justice or for the sake of honours and rewards; therefore, let him be clothed in justice only, and have no other covering; and he must be imagined in a state of life the opposite of the former. Let him be the best of men, and let him be thought the worst; then he will have been put to the proof; and we shall see whether he will be affected by the fear of infamy and its consequences. And let him continue thus to the hour of death; being just and seeming to be unjust. When both have reached the uttermost extreme, the one of justice and the other of injustice, let judgment be given which of them is the happier of the two.

Heavens! my dear Glaucon, I said, how energetically you polish them up for the decision, first one and then the other, as if they were two statues.

I do my best, he said. And now that we know what they are like there is no difficulty in tracing out the sort of life which awaits either of them. This I will proceed to describe; but as you may think the description a little too coarse, I ask you to suppose, Socrates, that the words which follow are not mine.—Let me put them into the mouths of the eulogists of injustice: They will tell you that the just man who is thought unjust will be scourged, racked, bound—will have his eyes burnt out; and, at last, after suffering every kind of evil, he will be impaled: Then he will understand that he ought to seem only, and not to be, just; the words of Aeschylus may be more truly spoken of the unjust than of the just. For the unjust is pursuing a reality; he does not live with a view to appearances—he wants to be really unjust and not to seem only:—

"His mind has a soil deep and fertile,
Out of which spring his prudent counsels."[2]

In the first place, he is thought just, and therefore bears rule in the city; he can marry whom he will, and give in marriage to whom he will; also he can trade and deal where he likes, and always to his own advantage, because he has no misgivings about injustice; and at every contest, whether in public or private, he gets the better of his antagonists, and gains at their expense, and is rich, and out of his gains he can benefit his friends, and harm his enemies; moreover, he can offer sacrifices, and dedicate gifts to the gods abundantly and magnificently, and can honour the gods or any man whom he wants to honour in a far better style than the just, and therefore he is likely to be dearer than they are to the gods. And thus, Socrates, gods and men are said to unite in making the life of the unjust better than the life of the just.

I was going to say something in answer to Glaucon, when Adeimantus, his brother, interposed: Socrates, he said, you do not suppose that there is nothing more to be urged?

Why, what else is there? I answered.

The strongest point of all has not been even mentioned, he replied.

Well, then, according to the proverb, "Let brother help brother"—if he fails in any part do you assist him; although I must confess that Glaucon has already said quite enough to lay me in the dust, and take from me the power of helping justice.

Nonsense, he replied. But let me add something more: There is another side to Glaucon's argument about the praise and censure of justice and injustice, which is equally required in order to bring out what I believe to be his meaning. Parents and tutors are always telling their sons and their wards that they are to be just; but why? not for the sake of justice, but for the sake of character and reputation; in the hope of

[2]Seven against Thebes, 574.

obtaining for him who is reputed just some of those offices, marriages, and the like which Glaucon has enumerated among the advantages accruing to the unjust from the reputation of justice. More, however, is made of appearances by this class of persons than by the others; for they throw in the good opinion of the gods, and will tell you of a shower of benefits which the heavens, as they say, rain upon the pious; and this accords with the testimony of the noble Hesiod and Homer, the first of whom says, that the gods make the oaks of the just—

"To bear acorns at their summit, and bees in the middle;
And the sheep are bowed down with the weight of their fleeces,"[3]

and many other blessings of a like kind are provided for them. And Homer has a very similar strain; for he speaks of one whose fame is—

"As the fame of some blameless king who, like a god,
Maintains justice; to whom the black earth brings forth
Wheat and barley, whose trees are bowed with fruit,
And his sheep never fail to bear, and the sea gives him fish."[4]

Still grander are the gifts of heaven which Musaeus and his son[5] vouchsafe to the just; they take them down into the world below, where they have the saints lying on couches at a feast, everlastingly drunk, crowned with garlands; their idea seems to be that an immortality of drunkenness is the highest meed of virtue. Some extend their rewards yet further; the posterity, as they say, of the faithful and just shall survive to the third and fourth generation. This is the style in which they praise justice. But about the wicked there is another strain; they bury them in a slough in Hades, and

[3]Hesiod, Works and Days, 230.
[4]Homer, Od. xix. 109.
[5]Eumolpus.

make them carry water in a sieve; also while they are yet living they bring them to infamy, and inflict upon them the punishments which Glaucon described as the portion of the just who are reputed to be unjust; nothing else does their invention supply. Such is their manner of praising the one and censuring the other.

Once more, Socrates, I will ask you to consider another way of speaking about justice and injustice, which is not confined to the poets, but is found in prose writers. The universal voice of mankind is always declaring that justice and virtue are honourable, but grievous and toilsome; and that the pleasures of vice and injustice are easy of attainment, and are only censured by law and opinion. They say also that honesty is for the most part less profitable than dishonesty; and they are quite ready to call wicked men happy, and to honour them both in public and private when they are rich or in any other way influential, while they despise and overlook those who may be weak and poor, even though acknowledging them to be better than the others. But most extraordinary of all is their mode of speaking about virtue and the gods: they say that the gods apportion calamity and misery to many good men, and good and happiness to the wicked. And mendicant prophets go to rich men's doors and persuade them that they have a power committed to them by the gods of making an atonement for a man's own or his ancestor's sins by sacrifices or charms, with rejoicings and feasts; and they promise to harm an enemy, whether just or unjust, at a small cost; with magic arts and incantations binding heaven, as they say, to execute their will. And the poets are the authorities to whom they appeal, now smoothing the path of vice with the words of Hesiod:—

"Vice may be had in abundance without trouble; the way is smooth and her dwelling-place is near. But before virtue the gods have set toil,"[6]

[6]Hesiod, Works and Days, 287.

and a tedious and uphill road: then citing Homer as a witness that the gods may be influenced by men; for he also says:—

"The gods, too, may be turned from their purpose; and men pray to them and avert their wrath by sacrifices and soothing entreaties, and by libations and the odour of fat, when they have sinned and transgressed."[7]

And they produce a host of books written by Musaeus and Orpheus, who were children of the Moon and the Muses—that is what they say—according to which they perform their ritual, and persuade not only individuals, but whole cities, that expiations and atonements for sin may be made by sacrifices and amusements which fill a vacant hour, and are equally at the service of the living and the dead; the latter sort they call mysteries, and they redeem us from the pains of hell, but if we neglect them no one knows what awaits us.

He proceeded: And now when the young hear all this said about virtue and vice, and the way in which gods and men regard them, how are their minds likely to be affected, my dear Socrates,—those of them, I mean, who are quickwitted, and, like bees on the wing, light on every flower, and from all that they hear are prone to draw conclusions as to what manner of persons they should be and in what way they should walk if they would make the best of life? Probably the youth will say to himself in the words of Pindar—

"Can I by justice or by crooked ways of deceit ascend a loftier tower which may be a fortress to me all my days?"

For what men say is that, if I am really just and am not also thought just, profit there is none, but the pain and loss on the other hand are unmistakable. But if, though unjust, I acquire the reputation of justice, a heavenly life is promised to me. Since then, as philosophers prove, appearance tyran-

[7]Homer, Iliad, ix. 493.

nizes over truth and is lord of happiness, to appearance I must devote myself. I will describe around me a picture and shadow of virtue to be the vestibule and exterior of my house; behind I will trail the subtle and crafty fox, as Archilochus, greatest of sages, recommends. But I hear some one exclaiming that the concealment of wickedness is often difficult; to which I answer, Nothing great is easy. Nevertheless, the argument indicates this, if we would be happy, to be the path along which we should proceed. With a view to concealment we will establish secret brotherhoods and political clubs. And there are professors of rhetoric who teach the art of persuading courts and assemblies; and so, partly by persuasion and partly by force, I shall make unlawful gains and not be punished. Still I hear a voice saying that the gods cannot be deceived, neither can they be compelled. But what if there are no gods? or, suppose them to have no care of human things—why in either case should we mind about concealment? And even if there are gods, and they do care about us, yet we know of them only from tradition and the genealogies of the poets; and these are the very persons who say that they may be influenced and turned by "sacrifices and soothing entreaties and by offerings." Let us be consistent then, and believe both or neither. If the poets speak truly, why then we had better be unjust, and offer of the fruits of injustice; for if we are just, although we may escape the vengeance of heaven, we shall lose the gains of injustice; but, if we are unjust, we shall keep the gains, and by our sinning and praying, and praying and sinning, the gods will be propitiated, and we shall not be punished. "But there is a world below in which either we or our posterity will suffer for our unjust deeds." Yes, my friend, will be the reflection, but there are mysteries and atoning deities, and these have great power. That is what mighty cities declare; and the children of the gods, who were their poets and prophets, bear a like testimony.

On what principle, then, shall we any longer choose justice rather than the worst injustice? when, if we only unite the latter with a deceitful regard to appearances, we shall fare to our mind both with gods and men, in life and after death, as the most numerous and the highest authorities tell us. Knowing all this, Socrates, how can a man who has any superiority of mind or person or rank or wealth, be willing to honour justice; or indeed to refrain from laughing when he hears justice praised? And even if there should be some one who is able to disprove the truth of my words, and who is satisfied that justice is best, still he is not angry with the unjust, but is very ready to forgive them, because he also knows that men are not just of their own free will; unless, peradventure, there be some one whom the divinity within him may have inspired with a hatred of injustice, or who has attained knowledge of the truth—but no other man. He only blames injustice who, owing to cowardice or age or some weakness, has not the power of being unjust. And this is proved by the fact that when he obtains the power, he immediately becomes unjust as far as he can be.

The cause of all this, Socrates, was indicated by us at the beginning of the argument, when my brother and I told you how astonished we were to find that of all the professing panegyrists of justice—beginning with the ancient heroes of whom any memorial has been preserved to us, and ending with the men of our own time—no one has ever blamed injustice or praised justice except with a view to the glories, honours, and benefits which flow from them. No one has ever adequately described either in verse or prose the true essential nature of either of them abiding in the soul, and invisible to any human or divine eye; or shown that of all the things of a man's soul which he has within him, justice is the greatest good, and injustice the greatest evil. Had this been the universal strain, had you sought to persuade us of this from our youth upwards, we should not have been on the watch to keep one another from doing wrong, but every one would have been his own watchman, because afraid, if he did wrong, of harbouring in himself the greatest of evils. I dare say that Thrasymachus and others would seriously hold the language which I have been merely repeating, and words even stronger than these about justice and injustice, grossly, as I conceive, perverting their true nature. But I speak in this vehement manner, as I must frankly confess to you, because I want to hear from you the opposite side; and I would ask you to show not only the superiority which justice has over injustice, but what effect they have on the possessor of them which makes the one to be a good and the other an evil to him. And please, as Glaucon requested of you, to exclude reputations; for unless you take away from each of them his true reputation and add on the false, we shall say that you do not praise justice, but the appearance of it; we shall think that you are only exhorting us to keep injustice dark, and that you really agree with Thrasymachus in thinking that justice is another's good and the interest of the stronger, and that injustice is a man's own profit and interest, though injurious to the weaker. Now as you have admitted that justice is one of that highest class of goods which are desired indeed for their results, but in a far greater degree for their own sakes—like sight or hearing or knowledge or health, or any other real and natural and not merely conventional good—I would ask you in your praise of justice to regard one point only: I mean the essential good and evil which justice and injustice work in the possessors of them. Let others praise justice and censure injustice, magnifying the rewards and honours of the one and abusing the other; that is a manner of arguing which, coming from them, I am ready to tolerate, but from you who have spent your whole life in the consideration of this question, unless I hear the contrary from your own lips, I expect something better. And therefore, I say, not only prove to us that justice is better than injustice, but show what they either of them do to the possessor of them, which makes the one to be a good and the other an evil, whether seen or unseen by gods and men.

I had always admired the genius of Glaucon and Adeimantus, but on hearing these words I was quite delighted, and said: Sons of an illustrious father, that was not a bad begining of the Elegiac verses which the admirer of Glaucon made in honour of you after you had distinguished yourselves at the battle of Megara:—

"Sons of Ariston," he sang, "divine offspring of an illustrious hero."

The epithet is very appropriate, for there is something truly divine in being able to argue as you have done for the superiority of injustice, and remaining unconvinced by your own arguments. And I do believe that you are not convinced —this I infer from your general character, for had I judged only from your speeches I should have mistrusted you. But now, the greater my confidence in you, the greater is my difficulty in knowing what to say. For I am in a strait between two; on the one hand I feel that I am unequal to the task; and my inability is brought home to me by the fact that you were not satisfied with the answer which I made to Thrasymachus, proving, as I thought, the superiority which justice has over injustice. And yet I cannot refuse to help, while breath and speech remain to me; I am afraid that there would be an impiety in being present when justice is evil spoken of and not lifting up a hand in her defence. And therefore I had best give such help as I can.

Glaucon and the rest entreated me by all means not to let the question drop, but to proceed in the investigation. They wanted to arrive at the truth, first, about the nature of justice and injustice, and secondly, about their relative advantages. I told them, what I really thought, that the enquiry would be of a serious nature, and would require very good eyes. Seeing then, I said, that we are no great wits, I think that we had better adopt a method which I may illustrate thus; suppose that a short-sighted person had been asked by some one to read small letters from a distance; and it occurred to some one else that they might be found in another place which was larger and in which the letters were larger—if they were the same and he could read the larger letters first, and then proceed to the lesser—this would have been thought a rare piece of good fortune.

Very true, said Adeimantus; but how does the illustration apply to our enquiry?

I will tell you, I replied; justice, which is the subject of our enquiry, is, as you know, sometimes spoken of as the virtue of an individual, and sometimes as the virtue of a State.

True, he replied.

And is not a State larger than an individual?

It is.

Then in the larger the quantity of justice is likely to be larger and more easily discernible. I propose therefore that we enquire into the nature of justice and injustice, first as they appear in the State, and secondly in the individual, proceeding from the greater to the lesser and comparing them.

That, he said, is an excellent proposal.

And if we imagine the State in process of creation, we shall see the justice and injustice of the State in process of creation also.

I dare say.

When the State is completed there may be a hope that the object of our search will be more easily discovered.

Yes, far more easily.

But ought we to attempt to construct one? I said; for to do so, as I am inclined to think, will be a very serious task. Reflect therefore.

I have reflected, said Adeimantus, and am anxious that you should proceed.

A State, I said, arises, as I conceive, out of the needs of mankind; no one is self-sufficing, but all of us have many wants. Can any other origin of a State be imagined?

There can be no other.

Then, as we have many wants, and many persons are needed to supply them, one takes a helper for one purpose and another for another; and when these partners and helpers are gathered together in one habitation the body of inhabitants is termed a State.

True, he said.

And they exchange with one another, and one gives, and another receives, under the idea that the exchange will be for their good.

Very true.

Then, I said, let us begin and create in idea a State; and yet the true creator is necessity, who is the mother of our invention.

Of course, he replied.

Now the first and greatest of necessities is food, which is the condition of life and existence.

Certainly.

The second is a dwelling, and the third clothing and the like.

True.

And now let us see how our city will be able to supply this great demand: We may suppose that one man is a husbandman, another a builder, some one else a weaver—shall we add to them a shoemaker, or perhaps some other purveyor to our bodily wants?

Quite right.

The barest notion of a State must include four or five men.

Clearly.

And how will they proceed? Will each bring the result of his labours into a common stock?—the individual husbandman, for example, producing for four, and labouring four times as long and as much as he need in the provision of food with which he supplies others as well as himself; or will he have nothing to do with others and not be at the trouble of producing for them, but provide for himself alone a fourth of the food in a fourth of the time, and in the remaining three-fourths of his time be employed in making a house or a coat or a pair of shoes, having no partnership with others, but supplying himself all his own wants?

Adeimantus thought that he should aim at producing food only and not at producing everything.

Probably, I replied, that would be the better way; and

when I hear you say this, I am myself reminded that we are not all alike; there are diversities of natures among us which are adapted to different occupations.

Very true.

And will you have a work better done when the workman has many occupations, or when he has only one?

When he has only one.

Further, there can be no doubt that a work is spoilt when not done at the right time?

No doubt.

For business is not disposed to wait until the doer of the business is at leisure; but the doer must follow up what he is doing, and make the business his first object.

He must.

And if so, we must infer that all things are produced more plentifully and easily and of a better quality when one man does one thing which is natural to him and does it at the right time, and leaves other things.

Undoubtedly.

Then more than four citizens will be required; for the husbandman will not make his own plough or mattock, or other implements of agriculture, if they are to be good for anything. Neither will the builder make his tools—and he too needs many; and in like manner the weaver and shoemaker.

True.

Then carpenters, and smiths, and many other artisans, will be sharers in our little State, which is already beginning to grow?

True.

Yet even if we add neatherds, shepherds, and other herdsmen, in order that our husbandmen may have oxen to plough with, and builders as well as husbandmen may have draught cattle, and curriers and weavers fleeces and hides,—still our State will not be very large.

That is true; yet neither will it be a very small State which contains all these.

Then, again, there is the situation of the city—to find a place where nothing need be imported is wellnigh impossible.

Impossible.

Then there must be another class of citizens who will bring the required supply from another city?

There must.

But if the trader goes empty-handed, having nothing which they require who will supply his need, he will come back empty-handed.

That is certain.

And therefore what they produce at home must be not only enough for themselves, but such both in quantity and quality as to accommodate those from whom their wants are supplied.

Very true.

Then more husbandmen and more artisans will be required?

They will.

Not to mention the importers and exporters, who are called merchants?

Yes.

Then we shall want merchants?

We shall.

And if merchandise is to be carried over the sea, skilful sailors will also be needed, and in considerable numbers?

Yes, in considerable numbers.

Then, again, within the city, how will they exchange their productions? To secure such an exchange was, as you will remember, one of our principal objects when we formed them into a society and constituted a State.

Clearly they will buy and sell.

Then they will need a market-place, and a money-token for purposes of exchange.

Certainly.

Suppose now that a husbandman, or an artisan, brings some production to market, and he comes at a time when there is no one to exchange with him,—is he to leave his calling and sit idle in the market-place?

Not at all; he will find people there who, seeing the want, undertake the office of salesmen. In well-ordered states they are commonly those who are the weakest in bodily strength, and therefore of little use for any other purpose; their duty is to be in the market, and to give money in exchange for goods to those who desire to sell and to take money from those who desire to buy.

This want, then, creates a class of retail-traders in our State. Is not "retailer" the term which is applied to those who sit in the market-place engaged in buying and selling, while those who wander from one city to another are called merchants?

Yes, he said.

And there is another class of servants, who are intellectually hardly on the level of companionship; still they have plenty of bodily strength for labour, which accordingly they sell, and are called, if I do not mistake, hirelings, hire being the name which is given to the price of their labour.

True.

Then hirelings will help to make up our population?

Yes.

And now, Adeimantus, is our State matured and perfected?

I think so.

Where, then, is justice, and where is injustice, and in what part of the State did they spring up?

Probably in the dealings of these citizens with one another. I cannot imagine that they are more likely to be found any where else.

I dare say that you are right in your suggestion, I said; we had better think the matter out, and not shrink from the enquiry.

Let us then consider, first of all, what will be their way of life, now that we have thus established them. Will they not produce corn, and wine, and clothes, and shoes, and build houses for themselves? And when they are housed, they will work, in summer, commonly, stripped and barefoot, but in winter substantially clothed and shod. They will feed on barley-meal and flour of wheat, baking and kneading them, making noble cakes and loaves; these they will serve up on a mat of reeds or on clean leaves, themselves reclining the while upon beds strewn with yew or myrtle. And they and their children will feast, drinking of the wine which they have made, wearing garlands on their heads, and hymning the praises of the gods, in happy converse with one another. And they will take care that their families do not exceed their means; having an eye to poverty or war.

But, said Glaucon, interposing, you have not given them a relish to their meal.

True, I replied, I had forgotten; of course they must have a relish—salt, and olives, and cheese, and they will boil roots and herbs such as country people prepare; for a dessert we shall give them figs, and peas, and beans; and they will roast myrtle-berries and acorns at the fire, drinking in moderation. And with such a diet they may be expected to live in peace and health to a good old age, and bequeath a similar life to their children after them.

Yes, Socrates, he said, and if you were providing for a city of pigs, how else would you feed the beasts?

But what would you have, Glaucon? I replied.

Why, he said, you should give them the ordinary conveniences of life. People who are to be comfortable are accustomed to lie on sofas, and dine off tables, and they should have sauces and sweets in the modern style.

Yes, I said, now I understand: the question which you would have me consider is, not only how a State, but how a luxurious State is created; and possibly there is no harm in this, for in such a State we shall be more likely to see how justice and injustice originate. In my opinion the true and healthy constitution of the State is the one which I have described. But if you wish also to see a State at fever-heat, I have no objection. For I suspect that many will not be satisfied with the simpler way of life. They will be for adding sofas, and tables, and other furniture; also dainties, and perfumes, and incense, and courtesans, and cakes, all these not of one sort only, but in every variety; we must go beyond the necessaries of which I was at first speaking, such as houses, and clothes, and shoes: the arts of the painter and the embroiderer will have to be set in motion, and gold and ivory and all sorts of materials must be procured.

True, he said.

Then we must enlarge our borders; for the original healthy State is no longer sufficient. Now will the city have to fill and swell with a multitude of callings which are not required by any natural want; such as the whole tribe of hunters and actors, of whom one large class have to do with forms and colours; another will be the votaries of music—poets and their attendant train of rhapsodists, players, dancers, contractors; also makers of divers kinds of articles, including women's dresses. And we shall want more servants. Will not tutors be also in request, and nurses wet and dry, tirewomen and barbers, as well as confectioners and cooks; and swineherds, too, who were not needed and therefore had no place in the former edition of our State, but are needed now? They must not be forgotten: and there will be animals of many other kinds, if people eat them.

Certainly.

And living in this way we shall have much greater need of physicians than before?

Much greater.

And the country which was enough to support the original inhabitants will be too small now, and not enough?

Quite true.

Then a slice of our neighbours' land will be wanted by us for pasture and tillage, and they will want a slice of ours, if, like ourselves, they exceed the limit of necessity, and give themselves up to the unlimited accumulation of wealth?

That, Socrates, will be inevitable.

And so we shall go to war, Glaucon. Shall we not?

Most certainly, he replied.

Then, without determining as yet whether war does good or harm, thus much we may affirm, that now we have discovered war to be derived from causes which are also the causes of almost all the evils in States, private as well as public.

Undoubtedly.

And our State must once more enlarge; and this time the enlargement will be nothing short of a whole army, which will have to go out and fight with the invaders for all that we have, as well as for the things and persons whom we were describing above.

Why? he said; are they not capable of defending themselves?

No, I said; not if we were right in the principle which was acknowledged by all of us when we were framing the State: the principle, as you will remember, was that one man cannot practise many arts with success.

Very true, he said.

But is not war an art?

Certainly.

And an art requiring as much attention as shoemaking?

Quite true.

And the shoemaker was not allowed by us to be a husbandman, or a weaver, or a builder—in order that we might have our shoes well made; but to him and to every other worker was assigned one work for which he was by nature fitted, and at that he was to continue working all his life long and at no other; he was not to let opportunities slip, and then he would become a good workman. Now nothing can be more important than that the work of a soldier should be well done. But is war an art so easily acquired that a man may be a warrior who is also a husbandman, or shoemaker, or other artisan; although no one in the world would be a good dice or draught player who merely took up the game as a recreation, and had not from his earliest years devoted himself to this and nothing else? No tools will make a man a skilled workman, or master of defence, nor be of any use to him who has not learned how to handle them, and has never bestowed any attention upon them. How then will he who takes up a shield or other implement of war become a good fighter all in a day, whether with heavy-armed or any other kind of troops?

Yes, he said, the tools which would teach men their own use would be beyond price.

And the higher the duties of the guardian, I said, the more time, and skill, and art, and application will be needed by him?

No doubt, he replied.

Will he not also require natural aptitude for his calling?

Certainly.

Then it will be our duty to select, if we can, natures which are fitted for the task of guarding the city?

It will.

And the selection will be no easy matter, I said; but we must be brave and do our best.

We must.

Is not the noble youth very like a well-bred dog in respect of guarding and watching?

What do you mean?

I mean that both of them ought to be quick to see, and swift to overtake the enemy when they see him; and strong too if, when they have caught him, they have to fight with him.

All these qualities, he replied, will certainly be required by them.

Well, and your guardian must be brave if he is to fight well?

Certainly.

And is he likely to be brave who has no spirit, whether horse or dog or any other animal? Have you never observed how invincible and unconquerable is spirit and how the presence of it makes the soul of any creature to be absolutely fearless and indomitable?

I have.

Then now we have a clear notion of the bodily qualities which are required in the guardian.

True.

And also of the mental ones; his soul is to be full of spirit?

Yes.

But are not these spirited natures apt to be savage with one another, and with everybody else?

A difficulty by no means easy to overcome, he replied.

Whereas, I said, they ought to be dangerous to their enemies, and gentle to their friends; if not, they will destroy themselves without waiting for their enemies to destroy them.

True, he said.

What is to be done then? I said; how shall we find a gentle nature which has also a great spirit, for the one is the contradiction of the other?

True.

He will not be a good guardian who is wanting in either of these two qualities; and yet the combination of them appears to be impossible; and hence we must infer that to be a good guardian is impossible.

I am afraid that what you say is true, he replied.

Here feeling perplexed I began to think over what had preceded.—My friend, I said, no wonder that we are in a perplexity; for we have lost sight of the image which we had before us.

What do you mean? he said.

I mean to say that there do exist natures gifted with those opposite qualities.

And where do you find them?

Many animals, I replied, furnish examples of them; our friend the dog is a very good one: you know that well-bred dogs are perfectly gentle to their familiars and acquaintances, and the reverse to strangers.

Yes, I know.

Then there is nothing impossible or out of the order of nature in our finding a guardian who has a similar combination of qualities?

Certainly not.

Would not he who is fitted to be a guardian, besides the spirited nature, need to have the qualities of a philosopher?

I do not apprehend your meaning.

The trait of which I am speaking, I replied, may be also seen in the dog, and is remarkable in the animal.

What trait?

Why, a dog, whenever he sees a stranger, is angry; when an acquaintance, he welcomes him, although the one has never done him any harm, nor the other any good. Did this never strike you as curious?

The matter never struck me before; but I quite recognise the truth of your remark.

And surely this instinct of the dog is very charming;—your dog is a true philosopher.

Why?

Why, because he distinguishes the face of a friend and of an enemy only by the criterion of knowing and not knowing. And must not an animal be a lover of learning who determines what he likes and dislikes by the test of knowledge and ignorance?

Most assuredly.

And is not the love of learning the love of wisdom, which is philosophy?

They are the same, he replied.

And may we not say confidently of man also, that he who is likely to be gentle to his friends and acquaintances, must by nature be a lover of wisdom and knowledge?

That we may safely affirm.

Then he who is to be a really good and noble guardian of the State will require to unite in himself philosophy and spirit and swiftness and strength?

Undoubtedly.

Then we have found the desired natures; and now that we have found them, how are they to be reared and educated? Is not this an enquiry which may be expected to throw light on the greater enquiry which is our final end—How do justice and injustice grow up in States? for we do not want either to omit what is to the point or to draw out the argument to an inconvenient length.

Adeimantus thought that the enquiry would be of great service to us.

Then, I said, my dear friend, the task must not be given up, even if somewhat long.

Certainly not.

Come then, and let us pass a leisure hour in story-telling, and our story shall be the education of our heroes.

By all means.

And what shall be their education? Can we find a better than the traditional sort?—and this has two divisions, gymnastic for the body, and music for the soul.

True.

Shall we begin education with music, and go on to gymnastic afterwards?

By all means.

And when you speak of music, do you include literature or not?

I do.

And literature may be either true or false?

Yes.

And the young should be trained in both kinds, and we begin with the false?

I do not understand your meaning, he said.

You know, I said, that we begin by telling children stories which, though not wholly destitute of truth, are in the main fictitious; and these stories are told them when they are not of an age to learn gymnastics.

Very true.

That was my meaning when I said that we must teach music before gymnastics.

Quite right, he said.

You know also that the beginning is the most important part of any work, especially in the case of a young and tender thing; for that is the time at which the character is being formed and the desired impression is more readily taken.

Quite true.

And shall we just carelessly allow children to hear any casual tales which may be devised by casual persons, and to receive into their minds ideas for the most part the very opposite of those which we should wish them to have when they are grown up?

We cannot.

Then the first thing will be to establish a censorship of the writers of fiction, and let the censors receive any tale of fiction which is good, and reject the bad; and we will desire mothers and nurses to tell their children the authorised ones only. Let them fashion the mind with such tales, even more fondly than they mould the body with their hands; but most of those which are now in use must be discarded.

Of what tales are you speaking? he said.

You may find a model of the lesser in the greater, I said; for they are necessarily of the same type, and there is the same spirit in both of them.

Very likely, he replied; but I do not as yet know what you would term the greater.

Those, I said, which are narrated by Homer and Hesiod, and the rest of the poets, who have ever been the great storytellers of mankind.

But which stories do you mean, he said; and what fault do you find with them?

A fault which is most serious, I said; the fault of telling a lie, and, what is more, a bad lie.

But when is this fault committed?

Whenever an erroneous representation is made of the nature of gods and heroes,—as when a painter paints a portrait not having the shadow of a likeness to the original.

Yes, he said, that sort of thing is certainly very blameable; but what are the stories which you mean?

First of all, I said, there was that greatest of all lies, in high places, which the poet told about Uranus, and which was a bad lie too,—I mean what Hesiod says that Uranus did, and how Cronus retaliated on him.[8] The doings of Cronus, and the sufferings which in turn his son inflicted upon him, even if they were true, ought certainly not to be lightly told to young and thoughtless persons; if possible, they had better be buried in silence. But if there is an absolute necessity for their mention, a chosen few might hear them in a mystery, and they should sacrifice not a common [Eleusinian] pig, but some huge and unprocurable victim; and then the number of the hearers will be very few indeed.

Why, yes, said he, those stories are extremely objectionable.

Yes, Adeimantus, they are stories not to be repeated in our State; the young man should not be told that in committing the worst of crimes he is far from doing anything outrageous; and that even if he chastises his father when he does wrong, in whatever manner, he will only be following the example of the first and greatest among the gods.

I entirely agree with you, he said; in my opinion those stories are quite unfit to be repeated.

Neither, if we mean our future guardians to regard the habit of quarrelling among themselves as of all things the basest, should any word be said to them of the wars in heaven, and of the plots and fightings of the gods against one another, for they are not true. No, we shall never mention the battles of the giants, or let them be embroidered on garments; and we shall be silent about the innumerable other quarrels of gods and heroes with their friends and relatives. If they would only believe us we would tell them that quarrelling is unholy, and that never up to this time has there been any quarrel between citizens; this is what old men and old women should begin by telling children; and when they grow up, the poets also should be told to compose for them in a similar spirit.[8a] But the narrative of Hephaestus binding Hera his mother, or how on another occasion Zeus sent him flying for

---

[8]Hesiod, Theogony, 154, 459.

[8a]Placing the comma afer γραυσί, and not after γιγνομένοις.

taking her part when she was being beaten, and all the battles of the gods in Homer—these tales must not be admitted into our State, whether they are supposed to have an allegorical meaning or not. For a young person cannot judge what is allegorical and what is literal; anything that he receives into his mind at that age is likely to become indelible and unalterable; and therefore it is most important that the tales which the young first hear should be models of virtuous thoughts.

There you are right, he replied; but if any one asks where are such models to be found and of what tales are you speaking—how shall we answer him?

I said to him, You and I, Adeimantus, at this moment are not poets, but founders of a State: now the founders of a State ought to know the general forms in which poets should cast their tales, and the limits which must be observed by them, but to make the tales is not their business.

Very true, he said; but what are these forms of theology which you mean?

Something of this kind, I replied:—God is always to be represented as he truly is, whatever be the sort of poetry, epic, lyric or tragic, in which the representation is given.

Right.

And he is not truly good? and must he not be represented as such?

Certainly.

And no good thing is hurtful?

No, indeed.

And that which is not hurtful hurts not?

Certainly not.

And that which hurts not does no evil?

No.

And can that which does no evil be a cause of evil?

Impossible.

And the good is advantageous?

Yes.

And therefore the cause of well-being?

Yes.

It follows therefore that the good is not the cause of all things, but of the good only?

Assuredly.

Then God, if he be good, is not the author of all things, as the many assert, but he is the cause of a few things only, and not of most things that occur to men. For few are the goods of human life, and many are the evils, and the good is to be attributed to God alone; of the evils the causes are to be sought elsewhere, and not in him.

That appears to me to be most true, he said.

Then we must not listen to Homer or to any other poet who is guilty of the folly of saying that two casks

> "Lie at the threshold of Zeus, full of lots, one of good, the other of evil lots,"[9]

and that he to whom Zeus gives a mixture of the two

> "Sometimes meets with evil fortune, at other times with good;"

but that he to whom is given the cup of unmingled ill,

> "Him wild hunger drives o'er the beauteous earth."

And again—

> "Zeus, who is the dispenser of good and evil to us."

And if any one asserts that the violation of oaths and treaties, which was really the work of Pandarus,[10] was brought about by Athene and Zeus, or that the strife and contention of the gods was instigated by Themis and Zeus,[11] he shall not have our approval; neither will we allow our young men to hear the words of Aeschylus, that

> "God plants guilt among men when he desires utterly to destroy a house."

---

[9]Iliad xxiv. 527.
[10]Iliad ii. 69.
[11]Ib. xx.

And if a poet writes of the sufferings of Niobe—the subject of the tragedy in which these iambic verses occur—or of the house of Pelops, or of the Trojan war or on any similar theme, either we must not permit him to say that these are the works of God, or if they are of God, he must devise some explanation of them such as we are seeking; he must say that God did what was just and right, and they were the better for being punished; but that those who are punished are miserable, and that God is the author of their misery—the poet is not to be permitted to say; though he may say that the wicked are miserable because they require to be punished, and are benefited by receiving punishment from God; but that God being good is the author of evil to any one is to be strenuously denied, and not to be said or sung or heard in verse or prose by any one whether old or young in any well-ordered commonwealth. Such a fiction is suicidal, ruinous, impious.

I agree with you, he replied, and am ready to give my assent to the law.

Let this then be one of our rules and principles concerning the gods to which our poets and reciters will be expected to conform—that God is not the author of all things, but of good only.

That will do, he said.

And what do you think of a second principle? Shall I ask you whether God is a magician, and of a nature to appear insidiously now in one shape, and now in another—sometimes himself changing and passing into many forms, sometimes deceiving us with the semblance of such transformations; or is he one and the same immutably fixed in his own proper image?

I cannot answer you, he said, without more thought.

Well, I said; but if we suppose a change in anything, that change must be effected either by the thing itself, or by some other thing?

Most certainly.

And things which are at their best are also least liable to

be altered or discomposed; for example, when healthiest and strongest, the human frame is least liable to be affected by meats and drinks, and the plant which is in the fullest vigour also suffers least from winds or the heat of the sun or any similar causes.

Of course.

And will not the bravest and wisest soul be least confused or deranged by any external influence?

True.

And the same principle, as I should suppose, applies to all composite things—furniture, houses, garments: when good and well made, they are least altered by time and circumstances.

Very true.

Then everything which is good, whether made by art or nature, or both, is least liable to suffer change from without?

True.

But surely God and the things of God are in every way perfect?

Of course they are.

Then he can hardly be compelled by external influence to take many shapes?

He cannot.

But may he not change and transform himself?

Clearly, he said, that must be the case if he is changed at all.

And will he then change himself for the better and fairer, or for the worse and more unsightly?

If he change at all he can only change for the worse, for we cannot suppose him to be deficient either in virtue or beauty.

Very true, Adeimantus; but then, would any one, whether God or man, desire to make himself worse?

Impossible.

Then it is impossible that God should ever be willing to change; being, as is supposed, the fairest and best that is conceivable, every God remains absolutely and for ever in his own form.

That necessarily follows, he said, in my judgment.

Then, I said, my dear friend, let none of the poets tell us that

"The gods, taking the disguise of strangers from other lands, walk up and down cities in all sorts of forms;"[12]

and let no one slander Proteus and Thetis, neither let any one, either in tragedy or in any other kind of poetry, introduce Hera disguised in the likeness of a priestess asking an alms

"For the life-giving daughters of Inachus the river of Argos;"

—let us have no more lies of that sort. Neither must we have mothers under the influence of the poets scaring their children with a bad version of these myths—telling how certain gods, as they say, "Go about by night in the likeness of so many strangers and in divers forms;" but let them take heed lest they make cowards of their children, and at the same time speak blasphemy against the gods.

Heaven forbid, he said.

But although the gods are themselves unchangeable, still by witchcraft and deception they may make us think that they appear in various forms?

Perhaps, he replied.

Well, but can you imagine that God will be willing to lie, whether in word or deed, or to put forth a phantom of himself?

I cannot say, he replied.

Do you not know, I said, that the true lie, if such an expression may be allowed, is hated of gods and men?

What do you mean? he said.

I mean that no one is willingly deceived in that which is the truest and highest part of himself, or about the truest

---

[12]Hom. Od. xvii. 485.

and highest matters; there, above all, he is most afraid of a lie having possession of him.

Still, he said, I do not comprehend you.

The reason is, I replied, that you attribute some profound meaning to my words; but I am only saying that deception, or being deceived or uninformed about the highest realities in the highest part of themselves, which is the soul, and in that part of them to have and to hold the lie, is what mankind least like;—that, I say, is what they utterly detest.

There is nothing more hateful to them.

And, as I was just now remarking, this ignorance in the soul of him who is deceived may be called the true lie; for the lie in words is only a kind of imitation and shadowy image of a previous affection of the soul, not pure unadulterated falsehood. Am I not right?

Perfectly right.

The true lie is hated not only by the gods, but also by men?

Yes.

Whereas the lie in words is in certain cases useful and not hateful; in dealing with enemies—that would be an instance; or again, when those whom we call our friends in a fit of madness or illusion are going to do some harm, then it is useful and is a sort of medicine or preventive; also in the tales of mythology, of which we were just now speaking—because we do not know the truth about ancient times, we make falsehood as much like truth as we can, and so turn it to account.

Very true, he said.

But can any of these reasons apply to God? Can we suppose that he is ignorant of antiquity, and therefore has recourse to invention?

That would be ridiculous, he said.

Then the lying poet has no place in our idea of God?

I should say not.

Or perhaps he may tell a lie because he is afraid of enemies?

That is inconceivable.

But he may have friends who are senseless or mad?

But no mad or senseless person can be a friend of God.

Then no motive can be imagined why God should lie?

None whatever.

Then the superhuman and divine is absolutely incapable of falsehood?

Yes.

Then is God perfectly simple and true both in word and deed;[13] he changes not; he deceives not, either by sign or word, by dream or waking vision.

Your thoughts, he said, are the reflection of my own.

You agree with me then, I said, that this is the second type or form in which we should write and speak about divine things. The gods are not magicians who transform themselves, neither do they deceive mankind in any way.

I grant that.

Then, although we are admirers of Homer, we do not admire the lying dream which Zeus sends to Agamemnon; neither will we praise the verses of Aeschylus in which Thetis says that Apollo at her nuptials

"Was celebrating in song her fair progeny whose days were to be long, and to know no sickness. And when he had spoken of my lot as in all things blessed of heaven he raised a note of triumph and cheered my soul. And I thought that the word of Phoebus, being divine and full of prophecy, would not fail. And now he himself who uttered the strain, he who was present at the banquet, and who said this—he it is who has slain my son."[14]

These are the kind of sentiments about the gods which will arouse our anger; and he who utters them shall be refused a chorus; neither shall we allow teachers to make use of them in the instruction of the young, meaning, as we do, that our guardians, as far as men can be, should be true worshippers of the gods and like them.

---

[13]Omitting κατὰ φαντασίας.

[14]From a lost play.

I entirely agree, he said, in these principles, and promise to make them my laws.

## BOOK VI

And thus, Glaucon, after the argument has gone a weary way, the true and the false philosophers have at length appeared in view.

I do not think, he said, that the way could have been shortened.

I suppose not, I said; and yet I believe that we might have had a better view of both of them if the discussion could have been confined to this one subject and if there were not many other questions awaiting us, which he who desires to see in what respect the life of the just differs from that of the unjust must consider.

And what is the next question? he asked.

Surely, I said, the one which follows next in order. Inasmuch as philosophers only are able to grasp the eternal and unchangeable, and those who wander in the region of the many and variable are not philosophers, I must ask you which of the two classes should be the rulers of our State?

And how can we rightly answer that question?

Whichever of the two are best able to guard the laws and institutions of our State—let them be our guardians.

Very good.

Neither, I said, can there be any question that the guardian who is to keep anything should have eyes rather than no eyes?

There can be no question of that.

And are not those who are verily and indeed wanting in the knowledge of the true being of each thing, and who have in their souls no clear pattern, and are unable as with a painter's eye to look at the absolute truth and to that original to repair, and having perfect vision of the other world to order the laws about beauty, goodness, justice in this, if not already ordered, and to guard and preserve the order of them —are not such persons, I ask, simply blind?

Truly, he replied, they are much in that condition.

And shall they be our guardians when there are others who, besides being their equals in experience and falling short of them in no particular of virtue, also know the very truth of each thing?

There can be no reason, he said, for rejecting those who have this greatest of all great qualities; they must always have the first place unless they fail in some other respect.

Suppose then, I said, that we determine how far they can unite this and the other excellences.

By all means.

In the first place, as we began by observing, the nature of the philosopher has to be ascertained. We must come to an understanding about him, and, when we have done so, then, if I am not mistaken, we shall also acknowledge that such an union of qualities is possible, and that those in whom they are united, and those only, should be rulers in the State.

What do you mean?

Let us suppose that philosophical minds always love knowledge of a sort which shows them the eternal nature not varying from generation and corruption.

Agreed.

And further, I said, let us agree that they are lovers of all true being; there is no part whether greater or less, or more or less honourable, which they are willing to renounce; as we said before of the lover and the man of ambition.

True.

And if they are to be what we were describing, is there not another quality which they should also possess?

What quality?

Truthfulness: they will never intentionally receive into their mind falsehood, which is their detestation, and they will love the truth.

Yes, that may be safely affirmed of them.

"May be," my friend, I replied, is not the word; say rather "must be affirmed:" for he whose nature is amorous of anything cannot help loving all that belongs or is akin to the object of his affections.

Right, he said.

And is there anything more akin to wisdom than truth?

How can there be?

Can the same nature be a lover of wisdom and a lover of falsehood?

Never.

The true lover of learning then must from his earliest youth, as far as in him lies, desire all truth?

Assuredly.

But then again, as we know by experience, he whose desires are strong in one direction will have them weaker in others; they will be like a stream which has been drawn off into another channel.

True.

He whose desires are drawn towards knowledge in every form will be absorbed in the pleasures of the soul, and will hardly feel bodily pleasure—I mean, if he be a true philosopher and not a sham one.

That is most certain.

Such an one is sure to be temperate and the reverse of covetous; for the motives which make another man desirous of having and spending, have no place in his character.

Very true.

Another criterion of the philosophical nature has also to be considered.

What is that?

There should be no secret corner of illiberality; nothing can be more antagonistic than meanness to a soul which is ever longing after the whole of things both divine and human.

Most true, he replied.

Then how can he who has magnificence of mind and is the spectator of all time and all existence, think much of human life?

He cannot.

Or can such an one account death fearful?

No indeed.

Then the cowardly and mean nature has no part in true philosophy?

Certainly not.

Or again: can he who is harmoniously constituted, who is not covetous or mean, or a boaster, or a coward—can he, I say, ever be unjust or hard in his dealings?

Impossible.

Then you will soon observe whether a man is just and gentle, or rude and unsociable; these are the signs which distinguish even in youth the philosophical nature from the unphilosophical.

True.

There is another point which should be remarked.

What point?

Whether he has or has not a pleasure in learning; for no one will love that which gives him pain, and in which after much toil he makes little progress.

Certainly not.

And again, if he is forgetful and retains nothing of what he learns, will he not be an empty vessel?

That is certain.

Labouring in vain, he must end in hating himself and his fruitless occupation?

Yes.

Then a soul which forgets cannot be ranked among genuine philosophic natures; we must insist that the philosopher should have a good memory?

Certainly.

And once more, the inharmonious and unseemly nature can only tend to disproportion?

Undoubtedly.

And do you consider truth to be akin to proportion or to disproportion?

To proportion.

Then, besides other qualities, we must try to find a naturally well-proportioned and gracious mind, which will move spontaneously towards the true being of everything.

Certainly.

Well, and do not all these qualities, which we have been enumerating, go together, and are they not, in a manner, necessary to a soul, which is to have a full and perfect participation of being?

They are absolutely necessary, he replied.

And must not that be a blameless study which he only can pursue who has the gift of a good memory, and is quick to learn,—noble, gracious, the friend of truth, justice, courage, temperance, who are his kindred?

The god of jealousy himself, he said, could find no fault with such a study.

And to men like him, I said, when perfected by years and education, and to these only you will entrust the State.

Here Adeimantus interposed and said: To these statements, Socrates, no one can offer a reply; but when you talk in this way, a strange feeling passes over the minds of your hearers: They fancy that they are led astray a little at each step in the argument, owing to their own want of skill in asking and answering questions; these littles accumulate, and at the end of the discussion they are found to have sustained a mighty overthrow and all their former notions appear to be turned upside down. And as unskilful players of draughts are at last shut up by their more skilful adversaries and have no piece to move, so they too find themselves shut up at last; for they have nothing to say in this new game of which words are the counters; and yet all the time they are in the right. The observation is suggested to me by what is now occurring. For any one of us might say, that although in words he is not able to meet you at each step of the argument, he sees as a fact that the votaries of philosophy, when they carry on the study, not only in youth as a part of education, but as the pursuit of their maturer years, most of them become strange monsters, not to say utter rogues, and that those who may be considered the best of them are made useless to the world by the very study which you extol.

Well, and do you think that those who say so are wrong?

I cannot tell, he replied; but I should like to know what is your opinion.

Hear my answer; I am of opinion that they are quite right.

Then how can you be justified in saying that cities will not cease from evil until philosophers rule in them, when philosophers are acknowledged by us to be of no use to them?

You ask a question, I said, to which a reply can only be given in a parable.

Yes, Socrates; and that is a way of speaking to which you are not at all accustomed, I suppose.

I perceive, I said, that you are vastly amused at having plunged me into such a hopeless discussion; but now hear the parable, and then you will be still more amused at the meagreness of my imagination: for the manner in which the best men are treated in their own States is so grievous that no single thing on earth is comparable to it; and therefore, if I am to plead their cause, I must have recourse to fiction, and put together a figure made up of many things, like the fabulous unions of goats and stags which are found in pictures. Imagine then a fleet or a ship in which there is a captain who is taller and stronger than any of the crew, but he is a little deaf and has a similar infirmity in sight, and his knowledge of navigation is not much better. The sailors are quarrelling with one another about the steering—every one is of opinion that he has a right to steer, though he has never learned the art of navigation and cannot tell who taught him or when he learned, and will further assert that it cannot be taught, and they are ready to cut in pieces any one who says the contrary. They throng about the captain, begging and praying him to commit the helm to them; and if at any time they do not prevail, but others are preferred to them, they kill the others or throw them overboard, and having first chained up the noble captain's senses with drink or some narcotic drug, they mutiny and take possession of the ship and make free with the stores; thus, eating and drinking, they proceed on their voyage in such a manner as might be expected of them. Him who is their partisan and cleverly aids them in their plot for getting the ship out of the captain's hands into their own whether by force or persuasion, they compliment with the name of sailor, pilot, able seaman, and abuse the other sort of man, whom they call a good-for-nothing; but that the true pilot must pay attention to the year and seasons and sky and stars and winds, and whatever else belongs to his art, if he intends to be really qualified for the command of a ship, and that he must and will be the steerer, whether other people like or not—the possibility of this union of authority with the steerer's art has never seriously entered into their thoughts or been made part of their calling.[15] Now in vessels which are in a state of mutiny and by sailors who are mutineers, how will the true pilot be regarded? Will he not be called by them a prater, a star-gazer, a good-for-nothing?

Of course, said Adeimantus.

Then you will hardly need, I said, to hear the interpretation of the figure, which describes the true philosopher in his relation to the State; for you understand already.

Certainly.

Then suppose you now take this parable to the gentleman who is surprised at finding that philosophers have no honour in their cities; explain it to him and try to convince him that their having honour would be far more extraordinary.

I will.

Say to him, that, in deeming the best votaries of philosophy to be useless to the rest of the world, he is right; but also tell him to attribute their uselessness to the fault of those who will not use them, and not to themselves. The pilot should not humbly beg the sailors to be commanded by him—that is not the order of nature; neither are "the wise to go to the

---

[15]Or, applying ὅπως δὲ κυβερνήσει to the mutineers, "But only understanding (ἐπαίοντας) that he (the mutinous pilot) must rule in spite of other people, never considering that there is an art of command which may be practised in combination with the pilot's art."

doors of the rich"—the ingenious author of this saying told a lie—but the truth is, that, when a man is ill, whether he be rich or poor, to the physician he must go, and he who wants to be governed, to him who is able to govern. The ruler who is good for anything ought not to beg his subjects to be ruled by him; although the present governors of mankind are of a different stamp; they may be justly compared to the mutinous sailors, and the true helmsman to those who are called by them good-for-nothings and star-gazers.

Precisely so, he said.

For these reasons, and among men like these, philosophy, the noblest pursuit of all, is not likely to be much esteemed by those of the opposite faction; not that the greatest and most lasting injury is done to her by her opponents, but by her own professing followers, the same of whom you suppose the accuser to say, that the greater number of them are arrant rogues, and the best are useless; in which opinion I agreed.

Yes.

And the reason why the good are useless has now been explained?

True.

Then shall we proceed to show that the corruption of the majority is also unavoidable, and that this is not to be laid to the charge of philosophy any more than the other?

By all means.

And let us ask and answer in turn, first going back to the description of the gentle and noble nature. Truth, as you will remember, was his leader, whom he followed always and in all things; failing in this, he was an imposter, and had no part or lot in true philosophy.

Yes, that was said.

Well, and is not this one quality, to mention no others, greatly at variance with present notions of him?

Certainly, he said.

And have we not a right to say in his defence, that the true lover of knowledge is always striving after being—that is his nature; he will not rest in the multiplicity of individuals which is an appearance only, but will go on—the keen edge will not be blunted, nor the force of his desire abate until he have attained the knowledge of the true nature of every essence by a sympathetic and kindred power in the soul, and by that power drawing near and mingling and becoming incorporate with very being, having begotten mind and truth, he will have knowledge and will live and grow truly, and then, and not till then, will he cease from his travail.

Nothing, he said, can be more just than such a description of him.

And will the love of a lie be any part of a philosopher's nature? Will he not utterly hate a lie?

He will.

And when truth is the captain, we cannot suspect any evil of the band which he leads?

Impossible.

Justice and health of mind will be of the company, and temperance will follow after?

True, he replied.

Neither is there any reason why I should again set in array the philosopher's virtues, as you will doubtless remember that courage, magnificence, apprehension, memory, were his natural gifts. And you objected that, although no one could deny what I then said, still, if you leave words and look at facts, the persons who are thus described are some of them manifestly useless, and the greater number utterly depraved; we were then led to enquire into the grounds of these accusations, and have now arrived at the point of asking why are the majority bad, which question of necessity brought us back to the examination and definition of the true philosopher.

Exactly.

And we have next to consider the corruptions of the philosophic nature, why so many are spoiled and so few escape spoiling—I am speaking of those who were said to be useless but not wicked—and, when we have done with them, we will speak of the imitators of philosophy, what manner of men are they who aspire after a profession which is above them and of which they are unworthy, and then, by their manifold inconsistencies, bring upon philosophy, and upon all philosophers, that universal reprobation of which we speak.

What are these corruptions? he said.

I will see if I can explain them to you. Every one will admit that a nature having in perfection all the qualities which we required in a philosopher, is a rare plant which is seldom seen among men.

Rare indeed.

And what numberless and powerful causes tend to destroy these rare natures!

What causes?

In the first place there are their own virtues, their courage, temperance, and the rest of them, every one of which praiseworthy qualities (and this is a most singular circumstance) destroys and distracts from philosophy the soul which is the possessor of them.

That is very singular, he replied.

Then there are all the ordinary goods of life—beauty, wealth, strength, rank, and great connections in the State—you understand the sort of things—these also have a corrupting and distracting effect.

I understand; but I should like to know more precisely what you mean about them.

Grasp the truth as a whole, I said, and in the right way; you will then have no difficulty in apprehending the preceding remarks, and they will no longer appear strange to you.

And how am I to do so? he asked.

Why, I said, we know that all germs or seeds, whether vegetable or animal, when they fail to meet with proper nutriment or climate or soil, in proportion to their vigour, are all the more sensitive to the want of a suitable environment, for evil is a greater enemy to what is good than what is not.

Very true.

There is reason in supposing that the finest natures, when under alien conditions, receive more injury than the inferior, because the contrast is greater.

Certainly.

And may we not say, Adeimantus, that the most gifted minds, when they are ill-educated, become pre-eminently bad? Do not great crimes and the spirit of pure evil spring out of a fulness of nature ruined by education rather than from any inferiority, whereas weak natures are scarcely capable of any very great good or very great evil?

There I think that you are right.

And our philosopher follows the same analogy—he is like a plant which, having proper nurture, must necessarily grow and mature into all virtue, but, if sown and planted in an alien soil, becomes the most noxious of all weeds, unless he be preserved by some divine power. Do you really think, as people so often say, that our youth are corrupted by Sophists, or that private teachers of the art corrupt them in any degree worth speaking of? Are not the public who say these things the greatest of all Sophists? And do they not educate to perfection young and old, men and women alike, and fashion them after their own hearts?

When is this accomplished? he said.

When they meet together, and the world sits down at an assembly, or in a court of law, or a theatre, or a camp, or in any other popular resort, and there is a great uproar, and they praise some things which are being said or done, and blame other things, equally exaggerating both, shouting and clapping their hands, and the echo of the rocks and the place in which they are assembled redoubles the sound of the praise or blame—at such a time will not a young man's heart, as they say, leap within him? Will any private training enable him to stand firm against the overwhelming flood of popular opinion? or will he be carried away by the stream? Will he not have the notions of good and evil which the public in general have—he will do as they do, and as they are, such will he be?

Yes, Socrates; necessity will compel him.

And yet, I said, there is a still greater necessity, which has not been mentioned.

What is that?

The gentle force of attainder or confiscation or death, which, as you are aware, these new Sophists and educators, who are the public, apply when their words are powerless.

Indeed they do; and in right good earnest.

Now what opinion of any other Sophist, or of any private person, can be expected to overcome in such an unequal contest?

None, he replied.

No, indeed, I said, even to make the attempt is a great piece of folly; there neither is, nor has been, nor is ever likely to be, any different type of character which has had no other training in virtue but that which is supplied by public opinion[16]—I speak, my friend, of human virtue only; what is more than human, as the proverb says, is not included: for I would not have you ignorant that, in the present evil state of governments, whatever is saved and comes to good is saved by the power of God, as we may truly say.

I quite assent, he replied.

Then let me crave your assent also to a further observation.

What are you going to say?

Why, that all those mercenary individuals, whom the many call Sophists and whom they deem to be their adversaries, do, in fact, teach nothing but the opinion of the many, that is to say, the opinions of their assemblies; and this is their wisdom. I might compare them to a man who should study the tempers and desires of a mighty strong beast who is fed by him—he would learn how to approach and handle him, also at what times and from what causes he is dangerous or the reverse, and what is the meaning of his several cries, and

[16] Or, taking παρὰ in another sense, "trained to virtue on their principles."

by what sounds, when another utters them, he is soothed or infuriated; and you may suppose further, that when, by continually attending upon him, he has become perfect in all this, he calls his knowledge wisdom, and makes of it a system or art, which he proceeds to teach, although he has no real notion of what he means by the principles or passions of which he is speaking, but calls this honourable and that dishonourable, or good or evil, or just or unjust, all in accordance with the tastes and tempers of the great brute. Good he pronounces to be that in which the beast delights and evil to be that which he dislikes; and he can give no other account of them except that the just and noble are the necessary, having never himself seen, and having no power of explaining to others the nature of either, or the difference between them, which is immense. By heaven, would not such an one be a rare educator?

Indeed he would.

And in what way does he who thinks that wisdom is the discernment of the tempers and tastes of the motley multitude, whether in painting or music, or, finally, in politics, differ from him whom I have been describing? For when a man consorts with the many, and exhibits to them his poem or other work of art or the service which he has done the State, making them his judges[17] when he is not obliged, the so-called necessity of Diomede will oblige him to produce whatever they praise. And yet the reasons are utterly ludicrous which they give in confirmation of their own notions about the honourable and good. Did you ever hear any of them which were not?

No, nor am I likely to hear.

You recognise the truth of what I have been saying? Then let me ask you to consider further whether the world will ever be induced to believe in the existence of absolute beauty rather than of the many beautiful, or of the absolute in each kind rather than of the many in each kind?

[17]Putting a comma after τῶν ἀναγκαίων.

Certainly not.

Then the world cannot possibly be a philosopher?

Impossible.

And therefore philosophers must inevitably fall under the censure of the world?

They must.

And of individuals who consort with the mob and seek to please them?

That is evident.

Then, do you see any way in which the philosopher can be preserved in his calling to the end? and remember what we were saying of him, that he was to have quickness and memory and courage and magnificence—these were admitted by us to be the true philosopher's gifts.

Yes.

Will not such an one from his early childhood be in all things first among all, especially if his bodily endowments are like his mental ones?

Certainly, he said.

And his friends and fellow-citizens will want to use him as he gets older for their own purposes?

No question.

Falling at his feet, they will make requests to him and do him honour and flatter him, because they want to get into their hands now, the power which he will one day possess.

That often happens, he said.

And what will a man such as he is be likely to do under such circumstances, especially if he be a citizen of a great city, rich and noble, and a tall proper youth? Will he not be full of boundless aspirations, and fancy himself able to manage the affairs of Hellenes and of barbarians, and having got such notions into his head will he not dilate and elevate himself in the fulness of vain pomp and senseless pride?

To be sure he will.

Now, when he is in this state of mind, if some one gently comes to him and tells him that he is a fool and must get understanding, which can only be got by slaving for it, do you think that, under such adverse circumstances, he will be easily induced to listen?

Far otherwise.

And even if there be some one who through inherent goodness or natural reasonableness has had his eyes opened a little and is humbled and taken captive by philosophy, how will his friends behave when they think that they are likely to lose the advantage which they were hoping to reap from his companionship? Will they not do and say anything to prevent him from yielding to his better nature and to render his teacher powerless, using to this end private intrigues as well as public prosecutions?

There can be no doubt of it.

And how can one who is thus circumstanced ever become a philosopher?

Impossible.

Then were we not right in saying that even the very qualities which make a man a philosopher may, if he be ill-educated, divert him from philosophy, no less than riches and their accompaniments and the other so-called goods of life?

We were quite right.

Thus, my excellent friend, is brought about all that ruin and failure which I have been describing of the natures best adapted to the best of all pursuits; they are natures which we maintain to be rare at any time; this being the class out of which come the men who are the authors of the greatest evil to States and individuals; and also of the greatest good when the tide carries them in that direction; but a small man never was the doer of any great thing either to individuals or to States.

That is most true, he said.

And so philosophy is left desolate, with her marriage rite incomplete: for her own have fallen away and forsaken her, and while they are leading a false and unbecoming life, other unworthy persons, seeing that she has no kinsmen to be her protectors, enter in and dishonour her; and fasten upon her the reproaches which, as you say, her reprovers utter, who affirm of her votaries that some are good for nothing, and that the greater number deserve the severest punishment.

That is certainly what people say.

Yes; and what else would you expect, I said, when you think of the puny creatures who, seeing this land open to them—a land well stocked with fair names and showy titles—like prisoners running out of prison into a sanctuary, take a leap out of their trades into philosophy; those who do so being probably the cleverest hands at their own miserable crafts? For, although philosophy be in this evil case, still there remains a dignity about her which is not to be found in the arts. And many are thus attracted by her whose natures are imperfect and whose souls are maimed and disfigured by their meannesses, as their bodies are by their trades and crafts. Is not this unavoidable?

Yes.

Are they not exactly like a bald little tinker who has just got out of durance and come into a fortune; he takes a bath and puts on a new coat, and is decked out as a bridegroom going to marry his master's daughter, who is left poor and desolate?

A most exact parallel.

What will be the issue of such marriages? Will they not be vile and bastard?

There can be no question of it.

And when persons who are unworthy of education approach philosophy and make an alliance with her who is a rank above them what sort of ideas and opinions are likely to be generated? Will they not be sophisms captivating to the ear,[18] having nothing in them genuine, or worthy of or akin to true wisdom?

No doubt, he said.

Then, Adeimantus, I said, the worthy disciples of philosophy will be but a small remnant: perchance some noble and well-educated person, detained by exile in her service, who in the absence of corrupting influences remains devoted

---

[18] Or "will they not deserve to be called sophisms," . . . .

to her; or some lofty soul born in a mean city, the politics of which he contemns and neglects; and there may be a gifted few who leave the arts, which they justly despise, and come to her;—or peradventure there are some who are restrained by our friend Theages' bridle; for everything in the life of Theages conspired to divert him from philosophy; but ill-health kept him away from politics. My own case of the internal sign is hardly worth mentioning, for rarely, if ever, has such a monitor been given to any other man. Those who belong to this small class have tasted how sweet and blessed a possession philosophy is, and have also seen enough of the madness of the multitude; and they know that no politician is honest, nor is there any champion of justice at whose side they may fight and be saved. Such an one may be compared to a man who has fallen among wild beasts—he will not join in the wickedness of his fellows, but neither is he able singly to resist all their fierce natures, and therefore seeing that he would be of no use to the State or to his friends, and reflecting that he would have to throw away his life without doing any good either to himself or others, he holds his peace, and goes his own way. He is like one who, in the storm of dust and sleet which the driving wind hurries along, retires under the shelter of a wall; and seeing the rest of mankind full of wickedness, he is content, if only he can live his own life and be pure from evil or unrighteousness, and depart in peace and good-will, with bright hopes.

Yes, he said, and he will have done a great work before he departs.

A great work—yes; but not the greatest, unless he find a State suitable to him; for in a State which is suitable to him, he will have a larger growth and be the saviour of his country, as well as of himself.

The causes why philosophy is in such an evil name have now been sufficiently explained: the injustice of the charges against her has been shown—is there anything more which you wish to say?

Nothing more on that subject, he replied; but I should like

to know which of the governments now existing is in your opinion the one adapted to her.

Not any of them, I said; and that is precisely the accusation which I bring against them—not one of them is worthy of the philosophic nature, and hence that nature is warped and enstranged;—as the exotic seed which is sown in a foreign land becomes denaturalized, and is wont to be overpowered and to lose itself in the new soil, even so this growth of philosophy, instead of persisting, degenerates and receives another character. But if philosophy ever finds in the State that perfection which she herself is, then will be seen that she is in truth divine, and that all other things, whether natures of men or institutions, are but human;—and now, I know, that you are going to ask, What that State is.

No, he said; there you are wrong, for I was going to ask another question—whether it is the State of which we are the founders and inventors, or some other?

Yes, I replied, ours in most respects; but you may remember my saying before, that some living authority would always be required in the State having the same idea of the constitution which guided you when as legislator you were laying down the laws.

That was said, he replied.

Yes, but not in a satisfactory manner; you frightened us by interposing objections, which certainly showed that the discussion would be long and difficult; and what still remains is the reverse of easy.

What is there remaining?

The question how the study of philosophy may be so ordered as not to be the ruin of the State: All great attempts are attended with risk; "hard is the good," as men say.

Still, he said, let the point be cleared up, and the enquiry will then be complete.

I shall not be hindered, I said, by any want of will, but, if at all, by a want of power: my zeal you may see for yourselves; and please to remark in what I am about to say how boldly and unhesitatingly I declare that States should pursue philosophy, not as they do now, but in a different spirit.

In what manner?

At present, I said, the students of philosophy are quite young; beginning when they are hardly past childhood, they devote only the time saved from moneymaking and housekeeping to such pursuits; and even those of them who are reputed to have most of the philosophic spirit, when they come within sight of the great difficulty of the subject, I mean dialectic, take themselves off. In after life when invited by some one else, they may, perhaps, go and hear a lecture, and about this they make much ado, for philosophy is not considered by them to be their proper business: at last, when they grow old, in most cases they are extinguished more truly than Heracleitus' sun, inasmuch as they never light up again.[19]

But what ought to be their course?

Just the opposite. In childhood and youth their study, and what philosophy they learn, should be suited to their tender years: during this period while they are growing up towards manhood, the chief and special care should be given to their bodies that they may have them to use in the service of philosophy; as life advances and the intellect begins to mature, let them increase the gymnastics of the soul; but when the strength of our citizens fails and is past civil and military duties, then let them range at will and engage in no serious labour, as we intend them to live happily here, and to crown this life with a similar happiness in another.

How truly in earnest you are, Socrates! he said; I am sure of that; and yet most of your hearers, if I am not mistaken, are likely to be still more earnest in their opposition to you, and will never be convinced; Thrasymachus least of all.

Do not make a quarrel, I said, between Thrasymachus and me, who have recently become friends, although, indeed, we were never enemies; for I shall go on striving to the utmost until I either convert him and other men, or do something

[19]Heracleitus said that the sun was extinguished every evening and relighted every morning.

which may profit them against the day when they live again, and hold the like discourse in another state of existence.

You are speaking of a time which is not very near.

Rather, I replied, of a time which is as nothing in comparison with eternity. Nevertheless, I do not wonder that the many refuse to believe; for they have never seen that of which we are now speaking realized; they have seen only a conventional imitation of philosophy, consisting of words artificially brought together, not like these of ours having a natural unity. But a human being who in word and work is perfectly moulded, as far as he can be, into the proportion and likeness of virtue—such a man ruling in a city which bears the same image, they have never yet seen, neither one nor many of them—do you think that they ever did?

No indeed.

No, my friend, and they have seldom, if ever, heard free and noble sentiments; such as men utter when they are earnestly and by every means in their power seeking after truth for the sake of knowledge, while they look coldly on the subtleties of controversy, of which the end is opinion and strife, whether they meet with them in the courts of law or in society.

They are strangers, he said, to the words of which you speak.

And this was what we foresaw, and this was the reason why truth forced us to admit, not without fear and hesitation, that neither cities nor States nor individuals will ever attain perfection until the small class of philosophers whom we termed useless but not corrupt are providentially compelled, whether they will or not, to take care of the State, and until a like necessity be laid on the State to obey them;[20] or until kings, or if not kings, the sons of kings or princes, are divinely inspired with a true love of true philosophy. That either or both of these alternatives are impossible, I see no reason to

[20]Reading κατηκόῳ or κατηκόοις .

affirm: if they were so, we might indeed be justly ridiculed as dreamers and visionaries. Am I not right?

Quite right.

If then, in the countless ages of the past, or at the present hour in some foreign clime which is far away and beyond our ken, the perfected philosopher is or has been or hereafter shall be compelled by a superior power to have the charge of the State, we are ready to assert to the death, that this our constitution has been, and is—yea, and will be whenever the Muse of Philosophy is queen. There is no impossibility in all this; that there is a difficulty, we acknowledge ourselves.

My opinion agrees with yours, he said.

But do you mean to say that this is not the opinion of the multitude?

I should imagine not, he replied.

O my friend, I said, do not attack the multitude: they will change their minds, if, not in an aggressive spirit, but gently and with the view of soothing them and removing their dislike of over-education, you show them your philosophers as they really are and describe as you were just now doing their character and profession, and then mankind will see that he of whom you are speaking is not such as they supposed—if they view him in this new light, they will surely change their notion of him, and answer in another strain.[21] Who can be at enmity with one who loves them, who that is himself gentle and free from envy will be jealous of one in whom there is no jealousy? Nay, let me answer for you, that in a few this harsh temper may be found but not in the majority of mankind.

I quite agree with you, he said.

And do you not also think, as I do, that the harsh feeling which the many entertain towards philosophy originates in

[21]Reading ἦ καὶ ἐὰν οὕτω θεῶνται without a question, and ἀλλοίαν τοι: or, retaining the question and taking ἀλλοίαν δόξαν in a new sense: "Do you mean to say really that, viewing him in this light, they will be of another mind from yours, and answer in another strain?"

the pretenders, who rush in uninvited, and are always abusing them, and finding fault with them, who make persons instead of things the theme of their conversation? and nothing can be more unbecoming in philosophers than this.

It is most unbecoming.

For he, Adeimantus, whose mind is fixed upon true being, has surely no time to look down upon the affairs of earth, or to be filled with malice and envy, contending against men; his eye is ever directed towards things fixed and immutable, which he sees neither injuring nor injured by one another, but all in order moving according to reason; these he imitates, and to these he will, as far as he can, conform himself. Can a man help imitating that with which he holds reverential converse?

Impossible.

And the philosopher holding converse with the divine order, becomes orderly and divine, as far as the nature of man allows; but like every one else, he will suffer from detraction.

Of course.

And if a necessity be laid upon him of fashioning, not only himself, but human nature generally, whether in States or individuals, into that which he beholds elsewhere, will he, think you, be an unskilful artificer of justice, temperance, and every civil virtue?

Anything but unskilful.

And if the world perceives that what we are saying about him is the truth, will they be angry with philosophy? Will they disbelieve us, when we tell them that no State can be happy which is not designed by artists who imitate the heavenly pattern?

They will not be angry if they understand, he said. But how will they draw out the plan of which you are speaking?

They will begin by taking the State and the manners of men, from which, as from a tablet, they will rub out the picture, and leave a clean surface. This is no easy task. But whether easy or not, herein will lie the difference between them and every other legislator,—they will have nothing to do either with individual or State, and will inscribe no laws, until they have either found, or themselves made, a clean surface.

They will be very right, he said.

Having effected this, they will proceed to trace an outline of the constitution?

No doubt.

And when they are filling in the work, as I conceive, they will often turn their eyes upwards and downwards: I mean that they will first look at absolute justice and beauty and temperance, and again at the human copy; and will mingle and temper the various elements of life into the image of a man; and thus they will conceive according to that other image, which, when existing among men, Homer calls the form and likeness of God.

Very true, he said.

And one feature they will erase, and another they will put in, until they have made the ways of men, as far as possible, agreeable to the ways of God?

Indeed, he said, in no way could they make a fairer picture.

And now, I said, are we beginning to persuade those whom you described as rushing at us with might and main, that the painter of constitutions is such an one as we are praising; at whom they were so very indignant because to his hands we committed the State; and are they growing a little calmer at what they have just heard?

Much calmer, if there is any sense in them.

Why, where can they still find any ground for objection? Will they doubt that the philosopher is a lover of truth and being?

They would not be so unreasonable.

Or that his nature, being such as we have delineated, is akin to the highest good?

Neither can they doubt this.

But again, will they tell us that such a nature, placed under favourable circumstances, will not be perfectly good and wise if any ever was? Or will they prefer those whom we have rejected?

Surely not.

Then will they still be angry at our saying, that, until philosophers bear rule, States and individuals will have no rest from evil, nor will this our imaginary State ever be realized?

I think that they will be less angry.

Shall we assume that they are not only less angry but quite gentle, and that they have been converted and for very shame, if for no other reason, cannot refuse to come to terms?

By all means, he said.

Then let us suppose that the reconciliation has been effected. Will any one deny the other point, that there may be sons of kings or princes who are by nature philosophers?

Surely no man, he said.

And when they have come into being will any one say that they must of necessity be destroyed; that they can hardly be saved is not denied even by us; but that in the whole course of ages no single one of them can escape—who will venture to affirm this?

Who indeed!

But, said I, one is enough; let there be one man who has a city obedient to his will, and he might bring into existence the ideal polity about which the world is so incredulous.

Yes, one is enough.

The ruler may impose the laws and institutions which we have been describing, and the citizens may possibly be willing to obey them?

Certainly.

And that others should approve, of what we approve, is no miracle or impossibility?

I think not.

But we have sufficiently shown, in what has preceded, that all this, if only possible, is assuredly for the best.

We have.

And now we say not only that our laws, if they could be

enacted, would be for the best, but also that the enactment of them, though difficult, is not impossible.

Very good.

And so with pain and toil we have reached the end of one subject, but more remains to be discussed;—how and by what studies and pursuits will the saviours of the constitution be created, and at what ages are they to apply themselves to their several studies?

Certainly.

I omitted the troublesome business of the possession of women, and the procreation of children, and the appointment of the rulers, because I knew that the perfect State would be eyed with jealousy and was difficult of attainment; but that piece of cleverness was not of much service to me, for I had to discuss them all the same. The women and children are now disposed of, but the other question of the rulers must be investigated from the very beginning. We were saying, as you will remember, that they were to be lovers of their country, tried by the test of pleasures and pains, and neither in hardships, nor in dangers, nor at any other critical moment were to lose their patriotism—he was to be rejected who failed, but he who always came forth pure, like gold tried in the refiner's fire, was to be made a ruler, and to receive honours and rewards in life and after death. This was the sort of thing which was being said, and then the argument turned aside and veiled her face; not liking to stir the question which has now arisen.

I perfectly remember, he said.

Yes, my friend, I said, and I then shrank from hazarding the bold word; but now let me dare to say—that the perfect guardian must be a philosopher.

Yes, he said, let that be affirmed.

And do not suppose that there will be many of them; for the gifts which were deemed by us to be essential rarely grow together; they are mostly found in shreds and patches.

What do you mean? he said.

You are aware, I replied, that quick intelligence, memory,

sagacity, cleverness, and similar qualities, do not often grow together, and that persons who possess them and are at the same time high-spirited and magnanimous are not so constituted by nature as to live orderly and in a peaceful and settled manner; they are driven any way by their impulses, and all solid principle goes out of them.

Very true, he said.

On the other hand, those steadfast natures which can better be depended upon, which in a battle are impregnable to fear and immovable, are equally immovable when there is anything to be learned; they are always in a torpid state, and are apt to yawn and go to sleep over any intellectual toil.

Quite true.

And yet we were saying that both qualities were necessary in those to whom the higher education is to be imparted, and who are to share in any office or command.

Certainly, he said.

And will they be a class which is rarely found?

Yes, indeed.

Then the aspirant must not only be tested in those labours and dangers and pleasures which we mentioned before, but there is another kind of probation which we did not mention —he must be exercised also in many kinds of knowledge, to see whether the soul will be able to endure the highest of all, or will faint under them, as in any other studies and exercises.

Yes, he said, you are quite right in testing him. But what do you mean by the highest of all knowledge?

You may remember, I said, that we divided the soul into three parts; and distinguished the several natures of justice, temperance, courage, and wisdom?

Indeed, he said, if I had forgotten, I should not deserve to hear more.

And do you remember the word of caution which preceded the discussion of them?

To what do you refer?

We were saying, if I am not mistaken, that he who wanted to see them in their perfect beauty must take a longer and more circuitous way, at the end of which they would appear; but that we could add on a popular exposition of them on a level with the discussion which had preceded. And you replied that such an exposition would be enough for you, and so the enquiry was continued in what to me seemed to be a very inaccurate manner; whether you were satisfied or not, it is for you to say.

Yes, he said, I thought and the others thought that you gave us a fair measure of truth.

But, my friend, I said, a measure of such things which in any degree falls short of the whole truth is not fair measure; for nothing imperfect is the measure of anything, although persons are too apt to be contented and think that they need search no further.

Not an uncommon case when people are indolent.

Yes, I said; and there cannot be any worse fault in a guardian of the State and of the laws.

True.

The guardian then, I said, must be required to take the longer circuit, and toil at learning as well as at gymnastics, or he will never reach the highest knowledge of all which, as we were just now saying, is his proper calling.

What, he said, is there a knowledge still higher than this—higher than justice and the other virtues?

Yes, I said, there is. And of the virtues too we must behold not the outline merely, as at present—nothing short of the most finished picture should satisfy us. When little things are elaborated with an infinity of pains, in order that they may appear in their full beauty and utmost clearness, how ridiculous that we should not think the highest truths worthy of attaining the highest accuracy!

A right noble thought[22]; but do you suppose that we shall refrain from asking you what is this highest knowledge?

Nay, I said, ask if you will; but I am certain that you have heard the answer many times, and now you either do not un-

[22]Or separating καὶ μάλα from ἄξιον, "True, he said, and a noble thought"; or ἄξιον τὸ διανόημα may be a gloss.

derstand me or, as I rather think, you are disposed to be troublesome; for you have often been told that the idea of good is the highest knowledge, and that all other things become useful and advantageous only by their use of this. You can hardly be ignorant that of this I was about to speak, concerning which, as you have often heard me say, we know so little; and, without which, any other knowledge or possession of any kind will profit us nothing. Do you think that the possession of all other things is of any value if we do not possess the good? or the knowledge of all other things if we have no knowledge of beauty and goodness?

Assuredly not.

You are further aware that most people affirm pleasure to be the good, the the finer sort of wits say it is knowledge?

Yes.

And you are aware too that the latter cannot explain what they mean by knowledge, but are obliged after all to say knowledge of the good?

How ridiculous!

Yes, I said, that they should begin by reproaching us with our ignorance of the good, and then presume our knowledge of it—for the good they define to be knowledge of the good, just as if we understand them when they use the term "good" —this is of course ridiculous.

Most true, he said.

And those who make pleasure their good are in equal perplexity; for they are compelled to admit that there are bad pleasures as well as good.

Certainly.

And therefore to acknowledge that bad and good are the same?

True.

There can be no doubt about the numerous difficulties in which this question is involved.

There can be none.

Further, do we not see that many are willing to do or to have or to seem to be what is just and honourable without the reality; but no one is satisfied with the appearance of good—the reality is what they seek; in the case of the good, appearance is despised by every one.

Very true, he said.

Of this then, which every soul of man pursues and makes the end of all his actions, having a presentiment that there is such an end, and yet hesitating because neither knowing the nature nor having the same assurance of this as of other things, and therefore losing whatever good there is in other things,—of a principle such and so great as this ought the best men in our State, to whom everything is entrusted, to be in the darkness of ignorance?

Certainly not, he said.

I am sure, I said, that he who does not know how the beautiful and the just are likewise good will be but a sorry guardian of them; and I suspect that no one who is ignorant of the good will have a true knowledge of them.

That, he said, is a shrewd suspicion of yours.

And if we only have a guardian who has this knowledge our State will be perfectly ordered?

Of course, he replied; but I wish that you would tell me whether you conceive this supreme principle of the good to be knowledge or pleasure, or different from either?

Aye, I said, I knew all along that a fastidious gentleman[28] like you would not be contented with the thoughts of other people about these matters.

True, Socrates; but I must say that one who like you has passed a lifetime in the study of philosophy should not be always repeating the opinions of others, and never telling his own.

Well, but has any one a right to say positively what he does not know?

---

[28]Reading ἀνὴρ καλός : or reading ἀνὴρ καλῶς, "I quite well knew from the very first, that you, &c."

Not, he said, with the assurance of positive certainty; he has no right to do that: but he may say what he thinks, as a matter of opinion.

And do you not know, I said, that all mere opinions are bad, and the best of them blind? You would not deny that those who have any true notion without intelligence are only like blind men who feel their way along the road?

Very true.

And do you wish to behold what is blind and crooked and base, when others will tell you of brightness and beauty?

Still, I must implore you, Socrates, said Glaucon, not to turn away just as you are reaching the goal; if you will only give such an explanation of the good as you have already given of justice and temperance and the other virtues, we shall be satisfied.

Yes, my friend, and I shall be at least equally satisfied, but I cannot help fearing that I shall fail, and that my indiscreet zeal will bring ridicule upon me. No, sweet sirs, let us not at present ask what is the actual nature of the good, for to reach what is now in my thoughts would be an effort too great for me. But of the child of the good who is likest him, I would fain speak, if I could be sure that you wished to hear—otherwise, not.

By all means, he said, tell us about the child, and you shall remain in our debt for the account of the parent.

I do indeed wish, I replied, that I could pay, and you receive, the account of the parent, and not, as now, of the offspring only; take, however, this latter by way of interest,[24] and at the same time have a care that I do not render a false account, although I have no intention of deceiving you.

Yes, we will take all the care that we can: proceed.

Yes, I said, but I must first come to an understanding with you, and remind you of what I have mentioned in the course of this discussion, and at many other times.

What?

---

[24] A play upon τόκος which means both "offspring" and "interest."

The old story, that there is a many beautiful and a many good, and so of other things which we describe and define; to all of them "many" is applied.

True, he said.

And there is an absolute beauty and an absolute good, and of other things to which the term "many" is applied there is an absolute; for they may be brought under a single idea, which is called the essence of each.

Very true.

The many, as we say, are seen but not known, and the ideas are known but not seen.

Exactly.

And what is the organ with which we see the visible things?

The sight, he said.

And with the hearing, I said, we hear, and with the other senses perceive the other objects of sense?

True.

But have you remarked that sight is by far the most costly and complex piece of workmanship which the artificer of the senses ever contrived?

No, I never have, he said.

Then reflect: has the ear or voice need of any third or additional nature in order that the one may be able to hear and the other to be heard?

Nothing of the sort.

No, indeed, I replied; and the same is true of most, if not all, the other senses—you would not say that any of them requires such an addition?

Certainly not.

But you see that without the addition of some other nature there is no seeing or being seen?

How do you mean?

Sight being, as I conceive, in the eyes, and he who has eyes wanting to see; colour being also present in them, still unless there be a third nature specially adapted to the purpose, the owner of the eyes will see nothing and the colours will be invisible.

Of what nature are you speaking?

Of that which you term light, I replied.

True, he said.

Noble, then, is the bond which links together sight and visibility, and great beyond other bonds by no small difference of nature; for light is their bond, and light is no ignoble thing?

Nay, he said, the reverse of ignoble.

And which, I said, of the gods in heaven would you say was the lord of this element? Whose is that light which makes the eye to see perfectly and the visible to appear?

You mean the sun, as you and all mankind say.

May not the relation of sight to this deity be described as follows?

How?

Neither sight nor the eye in which sight resides is the sun?

No.

Yet of all the organs of sense the eye is the most like the sun?

By far the most like.

And the power which the eye possesses is a sort of effluence which is dispensed from the sun?

Exactly.

Then the sun is not sight, but the author of sight who is recognised by sight.

True, he said.

And this is he whom I call the child of the good, whom the good begat in his own likeness, to be in the visible world, in relation to sight and the things of sight, what the good is in the intellectual world in relation to mind and the things of mind.

Will you be a little more explicit? he said.

Why, you know, I said, that the eyes, when a person directs them towards objects on which the light of day is no longer shining, but the moon and stars only, see dimly, and are nearly blind; they seem to have no clearness of vision in them?

Very true.

But when they are directed towards objects on which the sun shines, they see clearly and there is sight in them?

Certainly.

And the soul is like the eye: when resting upon that on which truth and being shine, the soul perceives and understands and is radiant with intelligence; but when turned towards the twilight of becoming and perishing, then she has opinion only, and goes blinking about, and is first of one opinion and then of another, and seems to have no intelligence?

Just so.

Now, that which imparts truth to the known and the power of knowing to the knower is what I would have you term the idea of good, and this you will deem to be the cause of science,[25] and of truth in so far as the latter becomes the subject of knowledge; beautiful too, as are both truth and knowledge, you will be right in esteeming this other nature as more beautiful than either; and, as in the previous instance, light and sight may be truly said to be like the sun, and yet not to be the sun, so in this other sphere, science and truth may be deemed to be like the good, but not the good; the good has a place of honour yet higher.

What a wonder of beauty that must be, he said, which is the author of science and truth, and yet surpasses them in beauty; for you surely cannot mean to say that pleasure is the good?

God forbid, I replied; but may I ask you to consider the image in another point of view?

In what point of view?

You would say, would you not, that the sun is not only the author of visibility in all visible things, but of generation and nourishment and growth, though he himself is not generation?

Certainly.

---

[25]Reading διανοοῦ.

In like manner the good may be said to be not only the author of knowledge to all things known, but of their being and essence, and yet the good is not essence, but far exceeds essence in dignity and power.

Glaucon said, with a ludicrous earnestness: By the light of heaven, how amazing!

Yes, I said, and the exaggeration may be set down to you; for you made me utter my fancies.

And pray continue to utter them; at any rate let us hear if there is anything more to be said about the similitude of the sun.

Yes, I said, there is a great deal more.

Then omit nothing, however slight.

I will do my best, I said; but I should think that a great deal will have to be omitted.

You have to imagine, then, that there are two ruling powers, and that one of them is set over the intellectual world, the other over the visible. I do not say heaven, lest you should fancy that I am playing upon the name (οὐρανός, ὁρατός). May I suppose that you have this distinction of the visible and intelligible fixed in your mind?

I have.

Now take a line which has been cut into two unequal[26] parts, and divide each of them again in the same proportion, and suppose the two main divisions to answer, one to the visible and the other to the intelligible, and then compare the subdivisions in respect of their clearness and want of clearness, and you will find that the first section in the sphere of the visible consists of images. And by images I mean, in the first place, shadows, and in the second place, reflections in water and in solid, smooth and polished bodies and the like: Do you understand?

Yes, I understand.

Imagine, now, the other section, of which this is only the

---

[26]Reading ἄνισα.

resemblance, to include the animals which we see, and everything that grows or is made.

Very good.

Would you not admit that both the sections of this division have different degrees of truth, and that the copy is to the original as the sphere of opinion is to the sphere of knowledge?

Most undoubtedly.

Next proceed to consider the manner in which the sphere of the intellectual is to be divided.

In what manner?

Thus:—There are two subdivisions, in the lower of which the soul uses the figures given by the former division as images; the enquiry can only be hypothetical, and instead of going upwards to a principle descends to the other end; in the higher of the two, the soul passes out of hypotheses, and goes up to a principle which is above hypotheses, making no use of images[27] as in the former case, but proceeding only in and through the ideas themselves.

I do not quite understand your meaning, he said.

Then I will try again; you will understand me better when I have made some preliminary remarks. You are aware that students of geometry, arithmetic, and the kindred sciences assume the odd and the even and the figures and three kinds of angles and the like in their several branches of science; these are their hypotheses, which they and every body are supposed to know, and therefore they do not deign to give any account of them either to themselves or others; but they begin with them, and go on until they arrive at last, and in a consistent manner, at their conclusion?

Yes, he said, I know.

And do you not know also that although they make use of the visible forms and reason about them, they are thinking not of these, but of the ideals which they resemble; not of the figures which they draw, but of the absolute square and the absolute diameter, and so on—the forms which they draw

---

[27]Reading *ὧνπερ ἐκεῖνο εἰκόνων*.

or make, and which have shadows and reflections in water of their own, are converted by them into images, but they are really seeking to behold the things themselves, which can only be seen with the eye of the mind?

That is true.

And of this kind I spoke as the intelligible, although in the search after it the soul is compelled to use hypotheses; not ascending to a first principle, because she is unable to rise above the region of hypothesis, but employing the objects of which the shadows below are resemblances in their turn as images, they having in relation to the shadows and reflections of them a greater distinctness, and therefore a higher value.

I understand, he said, that you are speaking of the province of geometry and the sister arts.

And when I speak of the other division of the intelligible, you will understand me to speak of that other sort of knowledge which reason herself attains by the power of dialectic, using the hypotheses not as first principles, but only as hypotheses—that is to say, as steps and points of departure into a world which is above hypotheses, in order that she may soar beyond them to the first principle of the whole; and clinging to this and then to that which depends on this, by successive steps she descends again without the aid of any sensible object, from ideas, through ideas, and in ideas she ends.

I understand you, he replied; not perfectly, for you seem to me to be describing a task which is really tremendous; but, at any rate, I understand you to say that knowledge and being, which the science of dialectic contemplates, are clearer than the notions of the arts, as they are termed, which proceed from hypotheses only: these are also contemplated by the understanding, and not by the senses: yet, because they start from hypotheses and do not ascend to a principle, those who contemplate them appear to you not to exercise the higher reason upon them, although when a first principle is added to them they are cognizable by the higher reason. And the habit which is concerned with geometry and the cognate sciences I suppose that you would term understanding and not reason, as being intermediate between opinion and reason.

You have quite conceived my meaning, I said; and now, corresponding to these four divisions, let there be four faculties in the soul—reason answering to the highest, understanding to the second, faith (or conviction) to the third, and perception of shadows to the last—and let there be a scale of them, and let us suppose that the several faculties have clearness in the same degree that their objects have truth.

I understand, he replied, and give my assent, and accept your arrangement.

# BOOK VII

And now, I said, let me show in a figure how far our nature is enlightened or unenlightened: — Behold! human beings living in an underground den, which has a mouth open towards the light and reaching all along the den; here they have been from their childhood, and have their legs and necks chained so that they can not move, and can only see before them, being prevented by the chains from turning round their heads. Above and behind them a fire is blazing at a distance, and between the fire and the prisoners there is a raised way; and you will see, if you look, a low wall built along the way, like the screen which marionette players have in front of them, over which they show the puppets.

I see.

And do you see, I said, men passing along the wall carrying all sorts of vessels, and statues and figures of animals made of wood and stone and various materials, which appear over the wall? Some of them are talking, others silent.

You have shown me a strange image, and they are strange prisoners.

Like ourselves, I replied; and they see only their own shadows, or the shadows of one another, which the fire throws on the opposite wall of the cave?

True, he said; how could they see anything but the shadows if they were never allowed to move their heads?

And of the objects which are being carried in like manner they would only see the shadows?

Yes, he said.

And if they were able to converse with one another, would they not suppose that they were naming what was actually before them? [1]

Very true.

And suppose further that the prison had an echo which came from the other side, would they not be sure to fancy when one of the passers-by spoke that the voice which they heard came from the passing shadow?

No question, he replied.

To them, I said, the truth would be literally nothing but the shadows of the images.

That is certain.

And now look again, and see what will naturally follow if the prisoners are released and disabused of their error. At first, when any of them is liberated and compelled suddenly to stand up and turn his neck round and walk and look towards the light, he will suffer sharp pains; the glare will distress him, and he will be unable to see the realities of which in his former state he had seen the shadows; and then conceive some one saying to him, that what he saw before was an illusion, but that now, when he is approaching nearer to being and his eye is turned towards more real existence, he has a clearer vision, — what will be his reply? And you may further imagine that his instructor is pointing to the objects as they pass and requiring him to name them, — will he not be perplexed? Will he not fancy that the shadows which he formerly saw are truer than the objects which are now shown to him?

Far truer.

And if he is compelled to look straight at the light, will he not have a pain in his eyes which will make him

[1] Reading παρόντα.

turn away to take refuge in the objects of vision which he can see, and which he will conceive to be in reality clearer than the things which are now being shown to him?

True, he said.

And suppose once more, that he is reluctantly dragged up a steep and rugged ascent, and held fast until he is forced into the presence of the sun himself, is he not likely to be pained and irritated? When he approaches the light his eyes will be dazzled, and he will not be able to see anything at all of what are now called realities.

Not all in a moment, he said.

He will require to grow accustomed to the sight of the upper world. And first he will see the shadows best, next the reflections of men and other objects in the water, and then the objects themselves; then he will gaze upon the light of the moon and the stars and the spangled heaven; and he will see the sky and the stars by night better than the sun or the light of the sun by day?

Certainly.

Last of all he will be able to see the sun, and not mere reflections of him in the water, but he will see him in his own proper place, and not in another; and he will contemplate him as he is.

Certainly.

He will then proceed to argue that this is he who gives the season and the years, and is the guardian of all that is in the visible world, and in a certain way the cause of all things which he and his fellows have been accustomed to behold?

Clearly, he said, he would first see the sun and then reason about him.

And when he remembered his old habitation, and the wisdom of the den and his fellow-prisoners, do you not suppose that he would felicitate himself on the change, and pity them?

Certainly, he would.

And if they were in the habit of conferring honors among themselves on those who were quickest to observe the passing shadows and to remark which of them went before, and which followed after, and which were together; and who were therefore best able to draw conclusions as to the future, do you think that he would care for such honors and glories, or envy the possessors of them? Would he not say with Homer,

> "Better to be the poor servant of a poor master,"

and to endure anything, rather than think as they do and live after their manner?

Yes, he said, I think that he would rather suffer anything than entertain these false notions and live in this miserable manner.

Imagine once more, I said, such an one coming suddenly out of the sun to be replaced in his old situation: would he not be certain to have his eyes full of darkness?

To be sure, he said.

And if there were a contest, and he had to compete in measuring the shadows with the prisoners who had never moved out of the den, while his sight was still weak, and before his eyes had become steady (and the time which would be needed to acquire this new habit of sight might be very considerable), would he not be ridiculous? Men would say of him that up he went and down he came without his eyes; and that it was better not even to think of ascending; and if any one tried to loose another and lead him up to the light, let them only catch the offender, and they would put him to death.

No question, he said.

This entire allegory, I said, you may now append, dear Glaucon, to the previous argument; the prison-house is the world of sight, the light of the fire is the sun, and you will not misapprehend me if you interpret the journey upwards to be the ascent of the soul into the intellectual world according to my poor belief, which, at your desire, I have expressed—whether rightly or wrongly God knows. But, whether true or false, my opinion is that in the world of knowledge the idea of good appears last of all, and is seen only with an effort; and, when seen, is also inferred to be the universal author of all things beautiful and right, parent of light and of the lord of light in this visible world, and the immediate source of reason and truth in the intellectual; and that this is the power upon which he who would act rationally either in public or private life must have his eye fixed.

I agree, he said, as far as I am able to understand you.

Moreover, I said, you must not wonder that those who attain to this beatific vision are unwilling to descend to human affairs; for their souls are ever hastening into the upper world where they desire to dwell; which desire of theirs is very natural, if our allegory may be trusted.

Yes, very natural.

And is there anything surprising in one who passes from divine contemplations to the evil state of man, misbehaving himself in a ridiculous manner; if, while his eyes are blinking and before he has become accustomed to the surrounding darkness, he is compelled to fight in courts of law, or in other places, about the images or the shadows of images of justice, and is endeavoring to meet the conceptions of those who have never yet seen absolute justice?

Anything but surprising, he replied.

Any one who has common sense will remember that the bewilderments of the eyes are of two kinds, and arise from two causes, either from coming out of the light or from going into the light, which is true of the mind's eye, quite as much as of the bodily eye; and he who remembers this when he sees any one whose vision is perplexed and weak, will not be too ready to laugh; he will first ask whether that soul of man has come out of the brighter life, and is unable to see because unaccustomed to the dark, or having turned from darkness to the day is dazzled by excess of light. And he will count the one happy in his condition and state of being, and he will pity the other; or, if he have a mind to laugh at the soul which comes from below into the light, there will be more reason in this than in the laugh which greets him who returns from above out of the light into the den.

That, he said, is a very just distinction.

But then, if I am right, certain professors of education must be wrong when they say that they can put a knowledge into the soul which was not there before, like sight into blind eyes.

They undoubtedly say this, he replied.

Whereas, our argument shows that the power and capacity of learning exists in the soul already; and that just as the eye was unable to turn from darkness to light without the whole body, so too the instrument of knowledge can only by the movement of the whole soul be turned from the world of becoming into that of being, and learn by degrees to endure the sight of being, and of the brightest and best of being, or in other words, of the good.

Very true.

And must there not be some art which will effect conversion in the easiest and quickest manner; not implanting the faculty of sight, for that exists already, but has been turned in the wrong direction, and is looking away from the truth?

Yes, he said, such an art may be presumed.

And whereas the other so-called virtues of the soul seem to be akin to bodily qualities, for even when they are not originally innate they can be implanted later by habit and exercise, the virtue of wisdom more than anything else contains a divine element which always remains, and by this conversion is rendered useful and profitable; or, on the other hand, hurtful and useless. Did you never observe the narrow intelligence flashing from the keen eye of a clever rogue — how eager he is, how clearly his paltry soul sees the way to his end; he is the reverse of blind, but his keen eye-sight is forced into the service of evil, and he is mischievous in proportion to his cleverness?

Very true, he said.

But what if there had been a circumcision of such natures in the days of their youth; and they had been severed from those sensual pleasures, such as eating and drinking, which, like leaden weights, were attached to them at their birth, and which drag them down and turn the vision of their souls upon the things that are below — if, I say, they had been released from these impediments and turned in the opposite direction, the very same faculty in them would have seen the truth as keenly as they see what their eyes are turned to now.

Very likely.

Yes, I said; and there is another thing which is likely, or rather a necessary inference from what has preceded, that neither the uneducated and uninformed of the truth, nor yet those who never make an end of their education, will be able ministers of State; not the former, because they have no single aim of duty which is the rule of all their actions, private as well as public; nor the latter, because they will not act at all except upon compulsion, fancying that they are already dwelling apart in the islands of the blest.

Very true, he replied.

Then, I said, the business of us who are the founders of the State will be to compel the best minds to attain that knowledge which we have already shown to be the greatest of all — they must continue to ascend until they arrive at the good; but when they have ascended and seen enough we must not allow them to do as they do now.

What do you mean?

I mean that they remain in the upper world: but this must not be allowed; they must be made to descend again among the prisoners in the den, and partake of their labors and honors, whether they are worth having or not.

But is not this unjust? he said; ought we to give them a worse life, when they might have a better?

You have again forgotten, my friend, I said, the intention of the legislator, who did not aim at making any one class in the State happy above the rest; the happiness was to be in the whole State, and he held the citizens together by persuasion and necessity, making them benefactors of the State, and therefore benefactors of one another; to this end he created them, not to please themselves, but to be his instruments in binding up the State.

True, he said, I had forgotten.

Observe, Glaucon, that there will be no injustice in compelling our philosophers to have a care and providence of others; we shall explain to them that in other States, men of their class are not obliged to share in the toils of politics: and this is reasonable.

for they grow up at their own sweet will, and the government would rather not have them. Being self-taught, they can not be expected to show any gratitude for a culture which they have never received. But we have brought you into the world to be rulers of the hive, kings of yourselves and of the other citizens, and have educated you far better and more perfectly than they have been educated, and you are better able to share in the double duty. Wherefore each of you, when his turn comes, must go down to the general underground abode, and get the habit of seeing in the dark. When you have acquired the habit, you will see ten thousand times better than the inhabitants of the den, and you will know what the several images are, and what they represent, because you have seen the beautiful and just and good in their truth. And thus our State, which is also yours, will be a reality, and not a dream only, and will be administered in a spirit unlike that of other States, in which men fight with one another about shadows only and are distracted in the struggle for power, which in their eyes is a great good. Whereas the truth is that the State in which the rulers are most reluctant to govern is always the best and most quietly governed, and the State in which they are most eager, the worst.

Quite true, he replied.

And will our pupils, when they hear this, refuse to take their turn at the toils of State, when they are allowed to spend the greater part of their time with one another in the heavenly light?

Impossible, he answered; for they are just men, and the commands which we impose upon them are just; there can be no doubt that every one of them will take office as a stern necessity, and not after the fashion of our present rulers of State.

Yes, my friend, I said; and there lies the point. You must contrive for your future rulers another and a better life than that of a ruler, and then you may have a well-ordered State; for only in the State which offers this, will they rule who are truly rich, not in silver and gold, but in virtue and wisdom, which are the true blessings of life. Whereas if they go to the administration of public affairs, poor and hungering after their own private advantage, thinking that hence they are to snatch the chief good, order there can never be; for they will be fighting about office, and the civil and domestic broils which thus arise will be the ruin of the rulers themselves and of the whole State.

Most true, he replied.

And the only life which looks down upon the life of political ambition is that of true philosophy. Do you know of any other?

Indeed, I do not, he said.

And those who govern ought not to be lovers of the task? For, if they are, there will be rival lovers, and they will fight.

No question.

Who then are those whom we shall compel to be guardians? Surely they will be the men who are wisest about affairs of State, and by whom the State is best administered, and who at the same time have other honors and another and a better life than that of politics?

Aristotle, NICOMACHEAN ETHICS (Trans. by Martin Ostwald)

1. Do you agree with Aristotle that all human activity aims at a good end? Why or why not?

2. Explain the Aristotelian concept of happiness. Do you believe that this happiness is the highest good to be sought?

3. What is Aristotle's understanding of the good?

4. Is happiness a gift of the god(s), or is it the result of virtuous activity? Explain.

5. Distinguish between intellectual and moral virtue.

6. Explain Aristotle's "golden mean" and how it is central to his ethical system.

7. How does Aristotle's system of ethics differ from Plato's?

Aristotle's (c.384-c.322 B.C.) treatment of the moral life was more systematic than that of his teacher, Plato. His *Ethics*, which is dedicated to his son, Nicomachus, aims at the achievement of virtue.

# NICOMACHEAN ETHICS

## ARISTOTLE

### BOOK I

1 Every art and every inquiry, and similarly every action and pursuit, is thought to aim at some good; and for this reason the good has rightly been declared[1] to be that at which all things aim. But a certain difference is found among ends; some are activities, others are products apart from the activities that produce them. Where there are ends apart from the actions, it is the nature of the products to be better than the activities. Now, as there are many actions, arts, and sciences, their ends also are many; the end of the medical art is health, that of shipbuilding a vessel, that of strategy victory, that of economics wealth. But where such arts fall under a single capacity—as bridle-making and the other arts concerned with the equipment of horses fall under the art of riding, and this and every military action under strategy, in the same way other arts fall under yet others—in all of these the ends of the master arts are to be preferred to all the subordinate ends; for it is for the sake of the former that the latter are pursued. It makes no difference whether the activities themselves are the ends of the actions, or something else apart from the activities, as in the case of the sciences just mentioned.

2 If, then, there is some end of the things we do, which we desire for its own sake (everything else being desired for the

[1]Perhaps by Eudoxus; Cf. $1172^b$ 9.

sake of this), and if we do not choose everything for the sake of something else (for at that rate the process would go on to infinity, so that our desire would be empty and vain), clearly this must be the good and the chief good. Will not the knowledge of it, then, have a great influence on life? Shall we not, like archers who have a mark to aim at, be more likely to hit upon what is right? If so, we must try, in outline at least to determine what it is, and of which of the sciences or capacities it is the object. It would seem to belong to the most authoritative art and that which is most truly the master art. And politics appears to be of this nature; for it is this that ordains which of the sciences should be studied in a state, and which each class of citizens should learn and up to what point they should learn them; and we see even the most highly esteemed of capacities to fall under this, e. g. strategy, economics, rhetoric; now, since politics uses the rest of the sciences, and since, again, it legislates as to what we are to do and what we are to abstain from, the end of this science must include those of the others, so that this end must be the good for man. For even if the end is the same for a single man and for a state, that of the state seems at all events something greater and more complete whether to attain or to preserve; though it is worth while to attain the end merely for one man, it is finer and more godlike to attain it for a nation or for city-states. These, then, are the ends at which our inquiry aims, since it is political science, in one sense of that term.

3 Our discussion will be adequate if it has as much clearness as the subject-matter admits of, for precision is not to be sought for alike in all discussions, any more than in all the products of the crafts. Now fine and just actions, which political science investigates, admit of much variety and fluctuation of opinion, so that they may be thought to exist only by convention, and not by nature. And goods also give rise to a similar fluctuation because they bring harm to many people; for before now men have been undone by reason of

their wealth, and others by reason of their courage. We must be content, then, in speaking of such subjects and with such premisses to indicate the truth roughly and in outline, and in speaking about things which are only for the most part true and with premisses of the same kind to reach conclusions that are no better. In the same spirit, therefore, should each type of statement be *received;* for it is the mark of an educated man to look for precision in each class of things just so far as the nature of the subject admits; it is evidently equally foolish to accept probable reasoning from a mathematician and to demand from a rhetorician scientific proofs.

Now each man judges well the things he knows, and of these he is a good judge. And so the man who has been educated in a subject is a good judge of that subject, and the man who has received an all-round education is a good judge in general. Hence a young man is not a proper hearer of lectures on political science; for he is inexperienced in the actions that occur in life, but its discussions start from these and are about these; and, further, since he tends to follow his passions, his study will be vain and unprofitable, because the end aimed at is not knowledge but action. And it makes no difference whether he is young in years or youthful in character; the defect does not depend on time, but on his living, and pursuing each successive object, as passion directs. For to such persons, as to the incontinent, knowledge brings no profit; but to those who desire and act in accordance with a rational principle knowledge about such matters will be of great benefit.

These remarks about the student, the sort of treatment to be expected, and the purpose of the inquiry, may be taken as our preface.

4 Let us resume our inquiry and state, in view of the fact that all knowledge and every pursuit aims at some good, what it is that we say political science aims at and what is the highest of all goods achievable by action. Verbally there is very general agreement; for both the general run of men

and people of superior refinement say that it is happiness, and identify living well and doing well with being happy; but with regard to what happiness is they differ, and the many do not give the same account as the wise. For the former think it is some plain and obvious thing, like pleasure, wealth, or honour; they differ, however, from one another—and often even the same man identifies it with different things, with health when he is ill, with wealth when he is poor; but, conscious of their ignorance, they admire those who proclaim some great ideal that is above their comprehension. Now some thought that apart from these many goods there is another which is self-subsistent and causes the goodness of all these as well. To examine all the opinions that have been held were perhaps somewhat fruitless; enough to examine those that are most prevalent or that seem to be arguable.

Let us not fail to notice, however, that there is a difference between arguments from and those to the first principles. For Plato, too, was right in raising this question and asking, as he used to do, "are we on the way from or to the first principles?"[2] There is a difference, as there is in a race-course between the course from the judges to the turning-point and the way back. For, while we must begin with what is known, things are objects of knowledge in two senses—some to us, some without qualification. Presumably, then, *we* must begin with things known to *us*. Hence any one who is to listen intelligently to lectures about what is noble and just and, generally, about the subjects of political science must have been brought up in good habits. For the fact is the starting-point, and if this is sufficiently plain to him, he will not at the start need the reason as well; and the man who has been well brought up has or can easily get starting-points. And as for him who neither has nor can get them, let him hear the words of Hesiod:

---

[2]Cf. *Rep.* 511 B.

Far best is he who knows all things himself;
Good, he that hearkens when men counsel right;
But he who neither knows, nor lays to heart
Another's wisdom, is a useless wight.

5 Let us, however, resume our discussion from the point at which we digressed. To judge from the lives that men lead, most men, and men of the most vulgar type, seem (not without some ground) to identify the good, or happiness, with pleasure; which is the reason why they love the life of enjoyment. For there are, we may say, three prominent types of life—that just mentioned, the political, and thirdly the contemplative life. Now the mass of mankind are evidently quite slavish in their tastes, preferring a life suitable to beasts, but they get some ground for their view from the fact that many of those in high places share the tastes of Sardanapalus. A consideration of the prominent types of life shows that people of superior refinement and of active disposition identify happiness with honour; for this is, roughly speaking, the end of the political life. But it seems too superficial to be what we are looking for, since it is thought to depend on those who bestow honour rather than on him who receives it, but the good we divine to be something proper to a man and not easily taken from him. Further, men seem to pursue honour in order that they may be assured of their goodness; at least it is by men of practical wisdom that they seek to be honoured, and among those who know them, and on the ground of their virtue; clearly, then, according to them, at any rate, virtue is better. And perhaps one might even suppose this to be, rather than honour, the end of the political life. But even this appears somewhat incomplete; for possession of virtue seems actually compatible with being asleep, or with lifelong inactivity, and, further, with the greatest sufferings and misfortunes; but a man who was living so no one would call happy, unless he were maintaining a thesis at all costs. But enough of this; for the subject has been sufficiently treated even in the current discus-

sions. Third comes the contemplative life, which we shall consider later.

The life of money-making is one undertaken under compulsion, and wealth is evidently not the good we are seeking; for it is merely useful and for the sake of something else. And so one might rather take the aforenamed objects to be ends; for they are loved for themselves. But it is evident that not even these are ends; yet many arguments have been thrown away in support of them. Let us leave this subject, then.

6 We had perhaps better consider the universal good and discuss thoroughly what is meant by it, although such an inquiry is made an uphill one by the fact that the Forms have been introduced by friends of our own. Yet it would perhaps be thought to be better, indeed to be our duty, for the sake of maintaining the truth even to destroy what touches us closely, especially as we are philosophers or lovers of wisdom; for, while both are dear, piety requires us to honour truth above our friends.

The men who introduced this doctrine did not posit Ideas of classes within which they recognized priority and posteriority (which is the reason why they did not maintain the existence of an Idea embracing all numbers); but the term "good" is used both in the category of substance and in that of quality and in that of relation, and that which is *per se*, i.e. substance, is prior in nature to the relative (for the latter is like an offshoot and accident of being); so that there could not be a common Idea set over all these goods. Further, since "good" has as many senses as "being" (for it is predicated both in the category of substance, as of God and of reason, and in quality, i. e. of the virtues, and in quantity, i. e. of that which is moderate, and in relation, i. e. of the useful, and in time, i. e. of the right opportunity, and in place, i. e. of the right locality and the like), clearly it cannot be something universally present in all cases and single; for then it could not have been predicated in all the categories but in one only. Further, since of the things answering to one Idea there is one science, there would have been one science of all the goods; but as it is there are many sciences even of the things that fall under one category, e. g. of opportunity, for opportunity in war is studied by strategists and in disease by medicine, and the moderate in food is studied by medicine and in exercise by the science of gymnastics. And one might ask the question, what in the world they *mean* by "a thing itself," if (as is the case) in "man himself" and in a particular man the account of man is one and the same. For in so far as they are man, they will in no respect differ; and if this is so, neither will "good itself" and particular goods, in so far as they are good. But again it will not be good any the more for being eternal, since that which lasts long is no whiter than that which perishes in a day. The Pythagoreans seem to give a more plausible account of the good, when they place the one in the column of goods; and it is they that Speusippus seems to have followed.

But let us discuss these matters elsewhere; an objection to what we have said, however, may be discerned in the fact that the Platonists have not been speaking about *all* goods, and that the goods that are pursued and loved for themselves are called good by reference to a single Form, while those which tend to produce or to preserve these somehow or to prevent their contraries are called so by reference to these, and in a secondary sense. Clearly, then, goods must be spoken of in two ways, and some must be good in themselves, the others by reason of these. Let us separate, then, things good in themselves from things useful, and consider whether the former are called good by reference to a single Idea. What sort of goods would one call good in themselves? Is it those that are pursued even when isolated from others, such as intelligence, sight, and certain pleasures and honours? Certainly, if we pursue these also for the sake of something else, yet one would place them among things good in themselves. Or is nothing other than the Idea of good good in itself? In that case the Form will be empty. But if the things we have named are also things good in themselves, the account of the good will have to appear as something identical in them all, as that of whiteness is identical in snow and in white lead. But of honour, wisdom, and pleasure, just in respect of their goodness, the accounts are distinct and diverse. The good, therefore, is not some common element answering to one Idea.

But what then do we mean by the good? It is surely not like the things that only chance to have the same name. Are goods one, then, by being derived from one good or by all contributing to one good, or are they rather one by analogy? Certainly as sight is in the body, so is reason in the soul, and so on in other cases. But perhaps these subjects had better be dismissed for the present; for perfect precision about them would be more appropriate to another branch of philosophy. And similarly with regard to the Idea; even if there is some one good which is universally predicable of goods or is capable of separate and independent existence, clearly it could not be achieved or attained by man; but we are now seeking something attainable. Perhaps, however, some one might think it worth while to recognize this with a view to the goods that *are* attainable and achievable; for having this as a sort of pattern we shall know better the goods that are good for us, and if we know them shall attain them. This argument has some plausibility, but seems to clash with the procedure of the sciences; for all of these, though they aim at some good and seek to supply the deficiency of it, leave on one side the knowledge of *the* good. Yet that all the exponents of the arts should be ignorant of, and should not even seek, so great an aid is not probable. It is hard, too, to see how a weaver or a carpenter will be benefited in regard to his own craft by knowing this "good itself," or how the man who has viewed the Idea itself will be a better doctor or general thereby. For a doctor seems not even to study health in this way, but the health of man, or perhaps rather the health of a particular man; it is individuals that he is healing. But enough of these topics.

7 Let us again return to the good we are seeking, and ask what it can be. It seems different in different actions and arts; it is different in medicine, in strategy, and in the other arts likewise. What then is the good of each? Surely that for whose sake everything else is done. In medicine this is health, in strategy victory, in architecture a house, in any other sphere something else, and in every action and pursuit the end; for it is for the sake of this that all men do whatever else they do. Therefore, if there is an end for all that we do, this will be the good achievable by action, and if there are more than one, these will be the goods achievable by action.

So the argument has by a different course reached the same point; but we must try to state this even more clearly. Since there are evidently more than one end, and we choose some of these (e. g. wealth, flutes, and in general instruments) for the sake of something else, clearly not all ends are final ends; but the chief good is evidently something final. Therefore, if there is only one final end, this will be what we are seeking, and if there are more than one, the most final of these will be what we are seeking. Now we call that which is in itself worthy of pursuit more final than that which is worthy of pursuit for the sake of something else, and that which is never desirable for the sake of something else more final than the things that are desirable both in themselves and for the sake of that other thing, and therefore we call final without qualification that which is always desirable in itself and never for the sake of something else.

Now such a thing happiness, above all else, is held to be; for this we choose always for itself and never for the sake of something else, but honour, pleasure, reason, and every virtue we choose indeed for themselves (for if nothing resulted from them we should still choose each of them), but we choose them also for the sake of happiness, judging that by means of them we shall be happy. Happiness, on the other hand, no one chooses for the sake of these, nor, in general, for anything other than itself.

From the point of view of self-sufficiency the same result

seems to follow; for the final good is thought to be self-sufficient. Now by self-sufficient we do not mean that which is sufficient for a man by himself, for one who lives a solitary life, but also for parents, children, wife, and in general for his friends and fellow citizens, since man is born for citizenship. But some limit must be set to this; for if we extend our requirement to ancestors and descendants and friends' friends we are in for an infinite series. Let us examine this question, however, on another occasion; the self-sufficient we now define as that which when isolated makes life desirable and lacking in nothing; and such we think happiness to be; and further we think it most desirable of all things, without being counted as one good thing among others—if it were so counted it would clearly be made more desirable by the addition of even the least of goods; for that which is added becomes an excess of goods, and of goods the greater is always more desirable. Happiness, then, is something final and self-sufficient, and is the end of action.

Presumably, however, to say that happiness is the chief good seems a platitude, and a clearer account of what it is is still desired. This might perhaps be given, if we could first ascertain that function of man. For just as for a flute-player, a sculptor, or any artist, and, in general, for all things that have a function or activity, the good and the "well" is thought to reside in the function, so would it seem to be for man, if he has a function. Have the carpenter, then, and the tanner certain functions or activities, and has man none? Is he born without a function? Or as eye, hand, foot, and in general each of the parts evidently has a function, may one lay it down that man similarly has a function apart from all these? What then can this be? Life seems to be common even to plants, but we are seeking what is peculiar to man. Let us exclude, therefore, the life of nutrition and growth. Next there would be a life of perception, but *it* also seems to be common even to the horse, the ox, and every animal. There remains, then, an active life of the element that has a rational principle; of this, one part has such a principle in the sense of being obedient to one, the other in the sense of possessing one and exercising thought. And, as "life of the rational element" also has two meanings, we must state that life in the sense of activity is what we mean; for this seems to be the more proper sense of the term. Now if the function of man is an activity of soul which follows or implies a rational principle, and if we say "a so-and-so" and "a good so-and-so" have a function which is the same in kind, e. g. a lyre-player and a good lyre-player, and so without qualification in all cases, eminence in respect of goodness being added to the name of the function (for the function of a lyre-player is to play the lyre, and that of a good lyre-player is to do so well): if this is the case, [and we state the function of man to be a certain kind of life, and this to be an activity or actions of the soul implying a rational principle, and the function of a good man to be the good and noble performance of these, and if any action is well performed when it is performed in accordance with the appropriate excellence: if this is the case,] human good turns out to be activity of soul in accordance with virtue, and if there are more than one virtue, in accordance with the best and most complete.

But we must add "in a complete life." For one swallow does not make a summer, nor does one day; and so too one day, or a short time, does not make a man blessed and happy.

Let this serve as an outline of the good; for we must presumably first sketch it roughly, and then later fill in the details. But it would seem that any one is capable of carrying on and articulating what has once been well outlined, and that time is a good discoverer or partner in such a work; to which facts the advances of the arts are due; for any one can add what is lacking. And we must also remember what has been said before, and not look for precision in all things alike, but in each class of things such precision as accords with the subject-matter, and so much as is appropriate to the inquiry. For a carpenter and a geometer investigate the right angle in different ways; the former does so in so far as the right angle is useful for his work, while the latter inquires what it is or what sort of thing it is; for he is a spectator of the truth. We must act in the same way, then, in all other matters as well, that our main task may not be subordinated to minor questions. Nor must we demand the cause in all matters alike; it is enough in some cases that the *fact* be well established, as in the case of the first principles; the fact is the primary thing or first principle. Now of first principles we see some by induction, some by perception, some by a certain habituation, and others too in other ways. But each set of principles we must try to investigate in the natural way, and we must take pains to state them definitely, since they have a great influence on what follows. For the beginning is thought to be more than half of the whole, and many of the questions we ask are cleared up by it.

8 We must consider it, however, in the light not only of our conclusion and our premisses, but also of what is commonly said about it; for with a true view all the data harmonize, but with a false one the facts soon clash. Now goods have been divided into three classes, and some are described as external, others as relating to soul or to body; we call those that relate to soul most properly and truly goods, and physical actions and activities we class as relating to soul. Therefore our account must be sound, at least according to this view, which is an old one and agreed on by philosophers. It is correct also in that we identify the end with certain actions and activities; for thus it falls among goods of the soul and not among external goods. Another belief which harmonizes with our account is that the happy man lives well and does well; for we have practically defined happiness as a sort of good life and good action. The characteristics that are looked for in happiness seem also, all of them, to belong to what we have defined happiness as being. For some identify happiness with virtue, some with practical wisdom, others with a kind of philosophic wisdom, others with these, or one of these, accompanied by pleasure or not without pleasure; while others include also external prosperity. Now some of

these views have been held by many men and men of old, others by a few eminent persons; and it is not probable that either of these should be entirely mistaken, but rather that they should be right in at least some one respect or even in most respects.

With those who identify happiness with virtue or some one virtue our account is in harmony; for to virtue belongs virtuous activity. But it makes, perhaps, no small difference whether we place the chief good in possession or in use, in state of mind or in activity. For the state of mind may exist without producing any good result, as in a man who is asleep or in some other way quite inactive, but the activity cannot; for one who has the activity will of necessity be acting, and acting well. And as in the Olympic Games it is not the most beautiful and the strongest that are crowned but those who compete (for it is some of these that are victorious), so those who act win, and rightly win, the noble and good things in life.

Their life is also in itself pleasant. For pleasure is a state of *soul,* and to each man that which he is said to be a lover of is pleasant; e. g. not only is a horse pleasant to the lover of horses, and a spectacle to the lover of sights, but also in the same way just acts are pleasant to the lover of justice and in general virtuous acts to the lover of virtue. Now for most men their pleasures are in conflict with one another because these are not by nature pleasant, but the lovers of what is noble find pleasant the things that are by nature pleasant; and virtuous actions are such, so that these are pleasant for such men as well as in their own nature. Their life, therefore, has no further need of pleasure as a sort of adventitious charm, but has its pleasure in itself. For, besides what we have said, the man who does not rejoice in noble actions is not even good; since no one would call a man just who did not enjoy acting justly, nor any man liberal who did not enjoy liberal actions; and similarly in all other cases. If this is so, virtuous actions must be in themselves pleasant. But they are also *good* and *noble,* and have each of these attributes in the highest degree, since the good man judges well about these attributes; his judgment is such as we have described.[8] Happiness then is the best, noblest, and most pleasant thing in the world, and these attributes are not severed as in the inscription at Delos—

> Most noble is that which is justest, and best is health;
> But pleasantest is it to win what we love.

For all these properties belong to the best activities; and these, or one—the best—of these, we identify with happiness.

Yet evidently, as we said, it needs the external goods as well; for it is impossible, or not easy, to do noble acts without the proper equipment. In many actions we use friends and riches and political power as instruments; and there are some things the lack of which takes the lustre from happiness, as good birth, goodly children, beauty; for the man who is very ugly in appearance or ill-born or solitary and childless is not very likely to be happy, and perhaps a man would be still less likely if he had thoroughly bad children or friends or had lost good children or friends by death. As we said, then, happiness seems to need this sort of prosperity in addition; for which reason some identify happiness with good fortune, though others identify it with virtue.

9 For this reason also the question is asked, whether happiness is to be acquired by learning or by habituation or some other sort of training, or comes in virtue of some divine providence or again by chance. Now if there is *any* gift of the gods to men, it is reasonable that happiness should be god-given, and most surely god-given of all human things inasmuch as it is the best. But this question would perhaps be more appropriate to another inquiry; happiness seems, however, even if it is not god-sent but comes as a result of virtue and some process of learning or training, to be among the most god-like things; for that which is the prize and end of

[8] i. e., he judges that virtuous actions are good and noble in the highest degree.

virtue seems to be the best thing in the world, and something godlike and blessed.

It will also on this view be very generally shared; for all who are not maimed as regards their potentiality for virtue may win it by a certain kind of study and care. But if it is better to be happy thus than by chance, it is reasonable that the facts should be so, since everything that depends on the action of nature is by nature as good as it can be, and similarly everything that depends on art or any rational cause, and especially if it depends on the best of all causes. To entrust to chance what is greatest and most noble would be a very defective arrangement.

The answer to the question we are asking is plain also from the definition of happiness; for it has been said to be a virtuous activity of soul, of a certain kind. Of the remaining goods, some must necessarily pre-exist as conditions of happiness, and others are naturally co-operative and useful as instruments. And this will be found to agree with what we said at the outset; for we stated the end of political science to be the best end, and political science spends most of its pains on making the citizens to be of a certain character, viz. good and capable of noble acts.

It is natural, then, that we call neither ox nor horse nor any other of the animals happy; for none of them is capable of sharing in such activity. For this reason also a boy is not happy; for he is not yet capable of such acts, owing to his age; and boys who are called happy are being congratulated by reason of the hopes we have for them. For there is required, as we said, not only complete virtue but also a complete life, since many changes occur in life, and all manner of chances, and the most prosperous may fall into great misfortunes in old age, as is told of Priam in the Trojan Cycle; and one who has experienced such chances and has ended wretchedly no one calls happy.

10 Must no one at all, then, be called happy while he lives; must we, as Solon says, see the end? Even if we are to

lay down this doctrine, is it also the case that a man *is* happy when he is *dead*? Or is not this quite absurd, especially for us who say that happiness is an activity? But if we do not call the dead man happy, and if Solon does not mean this, but that one can then safely *call* a man blessed as being at last beyond evils and misfortunes, this also affords matter for discussion; for both evil and good are thought to exist for a dead man, as much as for one who is alive but not aware of them; e. g. honours and dishonours and the good or bad fortunes of children and in general of descendants. And this also presents a problem; for though a man has lived happily up to old age and has had a death worthy of his life, many reverses may befall his descendants—some of them may be good and attain the life they deserve, while with others the opposite may be the case; and clearly too the degrees of relationship between them and their ancestors may vary indefinitely. It would be odd, then, if the dead man were to share in these changes and become at one time happy, at another wretched; while it would also be odd if the fortunes of the descendants did not for *some* time have *some* effect on the happiness of their ancestors.

But we must return to our first difficulty; for perhaps by a consideration of it our present problem might be solved. Now if we must see the end and only then call a man happy, not as being happy but as having been so before, surely this is a paradox, that when he is happy the attribute that belongs to him is not to be truly predicated of him because we do not wish to call living men happy, on account of the changes that may befall them, and because we have assumed happiness to be something permanent and by no means easily changed, while a single man may suffer many turns of fortune's wheel. For clearly if we were to keep pace with his fortunes, we should often call the same man happy and again wretched, making the happy man out to be a "chameleon and insecurely based." Or is this keeping pace with his fortunes quite wrong? Success or failure in life does not depend on these, but human life, as we said, needs these as mere additions, while virtuous activities or their opposites are what constitute happiness or the reverse.

The question we have now discussed confirms our definition. For no function of man has so much permanence as virtuous activities (these are thought to be more durable even than knowledge of the sciences), and of these themselves the most valuable are more durable because those who are happy spend their life most readily and most continuously in these; for this seems to be the reason why we do not forget them. The attribute in question,[4] then, will belong to the happy man, and he will be happy throughout his life; for always, or by preference to everything else, he will be engaged in virtuous action and contemplation, and he will bear the chances of life most nobly and altogether decorously, if he is "truly good" and "foursquare beyond reproach."[5]

Now many events happen by chance, and events differing in importance; small pieces of good fortune or of its opposite clearly do not weigh down the scales of life one way or the other, but a multitude of great events if they turn out well will make life happier (for not only are they themselves such as to add beauty to life, but the way a man deals with them may be noble and good), while if they turn out ill they crush and maim happiness; for they both bring pain with them and hinder many activities. Yet even in these nobility shines through, when a man bears with resignation many great misfortunes, not through insensibility to pain but through nobility and greatness of soul.

If activities are, as we said, what gives life its character, no happy man can become miserable; for he will never do the acts that are hateful and mean. For the man who is truly good and wise, we think, bears all the chances of life becomingly and always makes the best of circumstances, as a good general makes the best military use of the army at his command and a good shoemaker makes the best shoes out of the hides that are given him; and so with all other craftsmen. And if this

---

[4]Durability.
[5]Simonides.

is the case, the happy man can never become miserable—though he will not reach *blessedness,* if he meet with fortunes like those of Priam.

Nor, again, is he many-coloured and changeable; for neither will he be moved from his happy state easily or by any ordinary misadventures, but only by many great ones, nor, if he has had many great misadventures, will he recover his happiness in a short time, but if at all, only in a long and complete one in which he has attained many splendid successes.

Why then should we not say that he is happy who is active in accordance with complete virtue and is sufficiently equipped with external goods, not for some chance period but throughout a complete life? Or must we add "and who is destined to live thus and die as befits his life"? Certainly the future is obscure to us, while happiness, we claim, is an end and something in every way final. If so, we shall call happy those among living men in whom these conditions are, and are to be, fulfilled—but happy *men.* So much for these questions.

11 That the fortunes of descendants and of all a man's friends should not affect his happiness at all seems a very unfriendly doctrine, and one opposed to the opinions men hold; but since the events that happen are numerous and admit of all sorts of difference, and some come more near to us and others less so, it seems a long—nay, an infinite—task to discuss each in detail; a general outline will perhaps suffice. If, then, as some of a man's own misadventures have a certain weight and influence on life while others are, as it were, lighter, so too there are differences among the misadventures of our friends taken as a whole, and it makes a difference whether the various sufferings befall the living or the dead (much more even than whether lawless and terrible deeds are presupposed in a tragedy or done on the stage), this difference also must be taken into account; or rather, perhaps, the fact that doubt is felt whether the dead share in any good or evil. For it seems, from these considerations, that even if anything

whether good or evil penetrates to them, it must be something weak and negligible, either in itself or for them, or if not, at least it must be such in degree and kind as not to make happy those who are not happy nor to take away their blessedness from those who are. The good or bad fortunes of friends, then, seem to have some effects on the dead, but effects of such a kind and degree as neither to make the happy unhappy nor to produce any other change of the kind.

12 These questions having been definitely answered, let us consider whether happiness is among the things that are praised or rather among the things that are prized; for clearly it is not to be placed among *potentialities*. Everything that is praised seems to be praised because it is of a certain kind and is related somehow to something else; for we praise the just or brave man and in general both the good man and virtue itself because of the actions and functions involved, and we praise the strong man, the good runner, and so on, because he is of a certain kind and is related in a certain way to something good and important. This is clear also from the praises of the gods; for it seems absurd that the gods should be referred to our standard, but this *is* done because praise involves a reference, as we said, to something else. But if praise is for things such as we have described, clearly what applies to the best things is not praise, but something greater and better, as is indeed obvious; for what we do to the gods and the most godlike of men is to call them blessed and happy. And so too with good *things;* no one praises happiness as he does justice, but rather calls it blessed, as being something more divine and better.

Eudoxus also seems to have been right in his method of advocating the supremacy of pleasure; he thought that the fact that, though a good, it is not praised indicated it to be better than the things that are praised, and that this is what God and the good are; for by reference to these all other things are judged. *Praise* is appropriate to virtue, for as a result of virtue men tend to do noble deeds; but *encomia* are bestowed on acts, whether of the body or of the soul. But perhaps nicety in these matters is more proper to those who have made a study of encomia; to us it is clear from what has been said that happiness is among the things that are prized and perfect. It seems to be so also from the fact that it is a first principle; for it is for the sake of this that we all do all that we do, and the first principle and cause of goods is, we claim, something prized and divine.

13 Since happiness is an activity of soul in accordance with perfect virtue, we must consider the nature of virtue; for perhaps we shall thus see better the nature of happiness. The true student of politics, too, is thought to have studied virtue above all things; for he wishes to make his fellow citizens good and obedient to the laws. As an example of this we have the lawgivers of the Cretans and the Spartans, and any others of the kind that there may have been. And if this inquiry belongs to political science, clearly the pursuit of it will be in accordance with our original plan. But clearly the virtue we must study is human virtue; for the good we were seeking was human good and the happiness human happiness. By human virtue we mean not that of the body but that of the soul; and happiness also we call an activity of soul. But if this is so, clearly the student of politics must know somehow the facts about soul, as the man who is to heal the eyes or the body as a whole must know about the eyes or the body; and all the more since politics is more prized and better than medicine; but even among doctors the best educated spend much labour on acquiring knowledge of the body. The student of politics, then, must study the soul, and must study it with these objects in view, and do so just to the extent which is sufficient for the questions we are discussing; for further precision is perhaps something more laborious than our purposes require.

Some things are said about it, adequately enough, even in the discussions outside our school, and we must use these; e. g. that one element in the soul is irrational and one has a rational principle. Whether these are separated as the parts of the body or of anything divisible are, or are distinct by definition but by nature inseparable, like convex and concave in the circumference of a circle, does not affect the present question.

Of the irrational element one division seems to be widely distributed, and vegetative in its nature, I mean that which causes nutrition and growth; for it is this kind of power of the soul that one must assign to all nurslings and to embryos, and this same power to full-grown creatures; this is more reasonable than to assign some different power to them. Now the excellence of this seems to be common to all species and not specifically human; for this part or faculty seems to function most in sleep, while goodness and badness are least manifest in sleep (whence comes the saying that the happy are no better off than the wretched for half their lives; and this happens naturally enough, since sleep is an inactivity of the soul in that respect in which it is called good or bad), unless perhaps to a small extent some of the movements actually penetrate to the soul, and in this respect the dreams of good men are better than those of ordinary people. Enough of this subject, however; let us leave the nutritive faculty alone, since it has by its nature no share in human excellence.

There seems to be also another irrational element in the soul—one which in a sense, however, shares in a rational principle. For we praise the rational principle of the continent man and of the incontinent, and the part of their soul that has such a principle, since it urges them aright and towards the best objects; but there is found in them also another element naturally opposed to the rational principle, which fights against and resists that principle. For exactly as paralysed limbs when we intend to move them to the right turn on the contrary to the left, so is it with the soul; the impulses of incontinent people move in contrary directions. But while in the body we see that which moves astray, in the soul we do not. No doubt, however, we must none the less suppose that in the soul too there is something contrary to the rational principle, resisting and opposing it. In what sense it is distinct from the other elements does not concern us. Now even this seems to have a share in a rational principle, as we said; at any rate in the continent man it obeys the rational principle —and presumably in the temperate and brave man it is still more obedient; for in him it speaks, on all matters, with the same voice as the rational principle.

Therefore the irrational element also appears to be twofold. For the vegetative element in no way shares in a rational principle, but the appetitive, and in general the desiring element in a sense shares in it, in so far as it listens to and obeys it; this is the sense in which we speak of "taking account" of one's father or one's friends, not that in which we speak of "accounting" for a mathematical property. That the irrational element is in some sense persuaded by a rational principle is indicated also by the giving of advice and by all reproof and exhortation. And if this element also must be said to have a rational principle, that which has a rational principle (as well as that which has not) will be twofold, one subdivision having it in the strict sense and in itself, and the other having a tendency to obey as one does one's father.

Virtue too is distinguished into kinds in accordance with this difference; for we say that some of the virtues are intellectual and others moral, philosophic wisdom and understanding and practical wisdom being intellectual, liberality and temperance moral. For in speaking about a man's character we do not say that he is wise or has understanding but that he is good-tempered or temperate; yet we praise the wise man also with respect to his state of mind; and of states of mind we call those which merit praise virtues.

## BOOK II

1 Virtue, then, being of two kinds, intellectual and moral, intellectual virtue in the main owes both its birth and its

growth to teaching (for which reason it requires ex[illegible] and time), while moral virtue comes about as a result [illegible] whence also its name *ethike* is one that is formed by [illegible] variation from the word *ethos* (habit). From this it is also plain that none of the moral virtues arises in us by nature; for nothing that exists by nature can form a habit contrary to its nature. For instance the stone which by nature moves downwards cannot be habituated to move upwards, not even if one tries to train it by throwing it up ten thousand times; nor can fire be habituated to move downwards, nor can anything else that by nature behaves in one way be trained to behave in another. Neither by nature, then, nor contrary to nature do the virtues arise in us; rather we are adapted by nature to receive them, and are made perfect by habit.

Again, of all the things that come to us by nature we first acquire the potentiality and later exhibit the activity (this is plain in the case of the senses; for it was not by often seeing or often hearing that we got these senses, but on the contrary we had them before we used them, and did not come to have them by using them); but the virtues we get by first exercising them, as also happens in the case of the arts as well. For the things we have to learn before we can do them, we learn by doing them, e. g. men become builders by building and lyre-players by playing the lyre; so too we become just by doing just acts, temperate by doing temperate acts, brave by doing brave acts.

This is confirmed by what happens in states; for legislators make the citizens good by forming habits in them, and this is the wish of every legislator, and those who do not effect it miss their mark, and it is in this that a good constitution differs from a bad one.

Again, it is from the same causes and by the same means that every virtue is both produced and destroyed, and similarly every art; for it is from playing the lyre that both good and bad lyre-players are produced. And the corresponding statement is true of builders and of all the rest; men will be good or bad builders as a result of building well or badly.

For if this were not so, there would have been no need of a teacher, but all men would have been born good or bad at their craft. This, then, is the case with the virtues also; by doing the acts that we do in our transactions with other men we become just or unjust, and by doing the acts that we do in the presence of danger, and being habituated to feel fear or confidence, we become brave or cowardly. The same is true of appetites and feelings of anger; some men become temperate and good-tempered, others self-indulgent and irascible, by behaving in one way or the other in the appropriate circumstances. Thus, in one word, states of character arise out of like activities. This is why the activities we exhibit must be of a certain kind; it is because the states of character correspond to the differences between these. It makes no small difference, then, whether we form habits of one kind or of another from our very youth; it makes a very great difference, or rather *all* the difference.

2 Since, then, the present inquiry does not aim at theoretical knowledge like the others (for we are inquiring not in order to know what virtue is, but in order to become good, since otherwise our inquiry would have been of no use), we must examine the nature of actions, namely how we ought to do them; for these determine also the nature of the states of character that are produced, as we have said. Now, that we must act according to the right rule is a common principle and must be assumed—it will be discussed later, i. e. both what the right rule is, and how it is related to the other virtues. But this must be agreed upon beforehand, that the whole account of matters of conduct must be given in outline and not precisely, as we said at the very beginning that the accounts we demand must be in accordance with the subject-matter; matters concerned with conduct and questions of what is good for us have no fixity, any more than matters of health. The general account being of this nature, the account of particular cases is yet more lacking in exactness; for they do not fall under any art or precept but the

agents themselves must in each case consider what is appropriate to the occasion, as happens also in the art of medicine or of navigation.

But though our present account is of this nature we must give what help we can. First, then, let us consider this, that it is the nature of such things to be destroyed by defect and excess, as we see in the case of strength and of health (for to gain light on things imperceptible we must use the evidence of sensible things); both excessive and defective exercise destroys the strength, and similarly drink or food which is above or below a certain amount destroys the health, while that which is proportionate both produces and increases and preserves it. So too is it, then, in the case of temperance and courage and the other virtues. For the man who flies from and fears everything and does not stand his ground against anything becomes a coward, and the man who fears nothing at all but goes to meet every danger becomes rash; and similarly the man who indulges in every pleasure and abstains from none becomes self-indulgent, while the man who shuns every pleasure, as boors do, becomes in a way insensible; temperance and courage, then, are destroyed by excess and defect, and preserved by the mean.

But not only are the sources and causes of their origination and growth the same as those of their destruction, but also the sphere of their actualization will be the same; for this is also true of the things which are more evident to sense, e. g. of strength; it is produced by taking much food and undergoing much exertion, and it is the strong man that will be most able to do these things. So too is it with the virtues; by abstaining from pleasures we become temperate, and it is when we have become so that we are most able to abstain from them; and similarly too in the case of courage; for by being habituated to despise things that are terrible and to stand our ground against them we become brave, and it is when we have become so that we shall be most able to stand our ground against them.

3 We must take as a sign of states of character the pleasure or pain that ensues on acts; for the man who abstains from bodily pleasures and delights in this very fact is temperate, while the man who is annoyed at it is self-indulgent, and he who stands his ground against things that are terrible and delights in this or at least is not pained is brave, while the man who is pained is a coward. For moral excellence is concerned with pleasures and pains; it is on account of the pleasure that we do bad things, and on account of the pain that we abstain from noble ones. Hence we ought to have been brought up in a particular way from our very youth, as Plato says, so as both to delight in and to be pained by the things that we ought; for this is the right education.

Again, if the virtues are concerned with actions and passions, and every passion and every action is accompanied by pleasure and pain, for this reason also virtue will be concerned with pleasures and pains. This is indicated also by the fact that punishment is inflicted by these means; for it is a kind of cure, and it is the nature of cures to be effected by contraries.

Again, as we said but lately, every state of soul has a nature relative to and concerned with the kind of things by which it tends to be made worse or better; but it is by reason of pleasures and pains that men become bad, by pursuing and avoiding these—either the pleasures and pains they ought not—or when they ought not or as they ought not, or by going wrong in one of the other similar ways that may be distinguished. Hence men[6] even define the virtues as certain states of impassivity and rest; not well, however, because they speak absolutely, and do not say "as one ought" and "as one ought not" and "when one ought or ought not," and the other things that may be added. We assume, then, that this kind of excellence tends to do what is best with regard to pleasures and pains, and vice does the contrary.

The following facts also may show us that virtue and vice are concerned with these same things. There being three

[6]Probably Speusippus is referred to.

objects of choice and three of avoidance, the noble, the advantageous, the pleasant, and their contraries, the base, the injurious, the painful, about all of these the good man tends to go right and the bad man to go wrong, and especially about pleasure; for this is common to the animals, and also it accompanies all objects of choice; for even the noble and the advantageous appear pleasant.

Again, it has grown up with us all from our infancy; this is why it is difficult to rub off this passion, engrained as it is in our life. And we measure even our actions, some of us more and others less, by the rule of pleasure and pain. For this reason, then, our whole inquiry must be about these; for to feel delight and pain rightly or wrongly has no small effect on our actions.

Again, it is harder to fight with pleasure than with anger, to use Heraclitus' phrase, but both art and virtue are always concerned with what is harder; for even the good is better when it is harder. Therefore for this reason also the whole concern both of virtue and of political science is with pleasures and pains; for the man who uses these well will be good, he who uses them badly bad.

That virtue, then, is concerned with pleasures and pains, and that by the acts from which it arises it is both increased and, if they are done differently, destroyed, and that the acts from which it arose are those in which it actualizes itself—let this be taken as said.

4 The question might be asked, what we mean by saying that we must become just by doing just acts, and temperate by doing temperate acts; for if men do just and temperate acts, they are already just and temperate, exactly as, if they do what is in accordance with the laws of grammar and of music, they are grammarians and musicians.

Or is this not true even of the arts? It is possible to do something that is in accordance with the laws of grammar, either by chance or at the suggestion of another. A man will be a grammarian then, only when he has both done something grammatical and done it grammatically; and this means doing it in accordance with the grammatical knowledge in himself.

Again, the case of the arts and that of the virtues are not similar; for the products of the arts have their goodness in themselves, so that it is enough that they should have a certain character, but if the acts that are in accordance with the virtues have themselves a certain character it does not follow that they are done justly or temperately. The agent also must be in a certain condition when he does them; in the first place he must have knowledge, secondly he must choose the acts, and choose them for their own sakes, and thirdly his action must proceed from a firm and unchangeable character. These are not reckoned in as conditions of the possession of the arts, except the bare knowledge; but as a condition of the possession of the virtues knowledge has little or no weight, while the other conditions count not for a little but for everything, i. e. the very conditions which result from often doing just and temperate acts.

Actions, then, are called just and temperate when they are such as the just or the temperate man would do; but it is not the man who does these that is just and temperate, but the man who also does them *as* just and temperate men do them. It is well said, then, that it is by doing just acts that the just man is produced, and by doing temperate acts the temperate man; without doing these no one would have even a prospect of becoming good.

But most people do not do these, but take refuge in theory and think they are being philosophers and will become good in this way, behaving somewhat like patients who listen attentively to their doctors, but do none of the things they are ordered to do. As the latter will not be made well in body by such a course of treatment, the former will not be made well in soul by such a course of philosophy.

5 Next we must consider what virtue is. Since things that are found in the soul are of three kinds—passions, faculties,

states of character, virtue must be one of these. By passions I mean appetite, anger, fear, confidence, envy, joy, friendly feeling, hatred, longing, emulation, pity, and in general the feelings that are accompanied by pleasure or pain; by faculties the things in virtue of which we are said to be capable of feeling these, e. g. of becoming angry or being pained or feeling pity; by states of character the things in virtue of which we stand well or badly with reference to the passions, e. g. with reference to anger we stand badly if we feel it violently or too weakly, and well if we feel it moderately; and similarly with reference to the other passions.

Now neither the virtues nor the vices are *passions*, because we are not called good or bad on the ground of our passions, but are so called on the ground of our virtues and our vices, and because we are neither praised nor blamed for our passions (for the man who feels fear or anger is not praised, nor is the man who simply feels anger blamed, but the man who feels it in a certain way), but for our virtues and our vices we *are* praised or blamed.

Again, we feel anger and fear without choice, but the virtues are modes of choice or involve choice. Further, in respect of the passions we are said to be moved, but in respect of the virtues and the vices we are said not to be moved but to be disposed in a particular way.

For these reasons also they are not *faculties;* for we are neither called good nor bad, nor praised nor blamed, for the simple capacity of feeling the passions again, we have the faculties by nature, but we are not made good or bad by nature; we have spoken of this before.

If, then, the virtues are neither passions nor faculties, all that remains is that they should be *states of character.*

Thus we have stated what virtue is in respect of its genus.

6 We must, however, not only describe virtue as a state of character, but also say what sort of state it is. We may remark, then, that every virtue or excellence both brings into good condition the thing of which it is the excellence and

makes the work of that thing be done well; e. g. the excellence of the eye makes both the eye and its work good; for it is by the excellence of the eye that we see well. Similarly the excellence of the horse makes a horse both good in itself and good at running and at carrying its rider and at awaiting the attack of the enemy. Therefore, if this is true in every case, the virtue of man also will be the state of character which makes a man good and which makes him do his own work well.

How this is to happen we have stated already, but it will be made plain also by the following consideration of the specific nature of virtue. In everything that is continuous and divisible it is possible to take more, less, or an equal amount, and that either in terms of the thing itself or relatively to us; and the equal is an intermediate between excess and defect. By the intermediate in the object I mean that which is equidistant from each of the extremes, which is one and the same for all men; by the intermediate relatively to us that which is neither too much nor too little—and this is not one, nor the same for all. For instance, if ten is many and two is few, six is the intermediate, taken in terms of the object; for it exceeds and is exceeded by an equal amount; this is intermediate according to arithmetical proportion. But the intermediate relatively to us is not to be taken so; if ten pounds are too much for a particular person to eat and two too little, it does not follow that the trainer will order six pounds; for this also is perhaps too much for the person who is to take it, or too little—too little for Milo,[7] too much for the beginner in athletic exercises. The same is true of running and wrestling. Thus a master of any art avoids excess and defect, but seeks the intermediate and chooses this—the intermediate not in the object but relatively to us.

If it is thus, then, that every art does its work well—by looking to the intermediate and judging its works by this standard (so that we often say of good works of art that it is not possible either to take away or to add anything, imply-

[7]A famous wrestler.

ing that excess and defect destroy the goodness of works of art, while the mean preserves it; and good artists, as we say, look to this in their work), and if, further, virtue is more exact and better than any art, as nature also is, then virtue must have the quality of aiming at the intermediate. I mean moral virtue; for it is this that is concerned with passions and actions, and in these there is excess, defect, and the intermediate. For instance, both fear and confidence and appetite and anger and pity and in general pleasure and pain may be felt both too much and too little, and in both cases not well; but to feel them at the right times, with reference to the right objects, towards the right people, with the right motive, and in the right way, is what is both intermediate and best, and this is characteristic of virtue. Similarly with regard to actions also there is excess, defect, and the intermediate. Now virtue is concerned with passions and actions, in which excess is a form of failure, and so is defect, while the intermediate is praised and is a form of success; and being praised and being successful are both characteristics of virtue. Therefore virtue is a kind of mean, since, as we have seen, it aims at what is intermediate.

Again, it is possible to fail in many ways (for evil belongs to the class of the unlimited, as the Pythagoreans conjectured, and good to that of the limited), while to succeed is possible only in one way (for which reason also one is easy and the other difficult—to miss the mark easy, to hit it difficult); for these reasons also, then, excess and defect are characteristic of vice, and the mean of virtue;

> For men are good in but one way, but bad in many.

Virtue, then, is a state of character concerned with choice, lying in a mean, i. e. the mean relative to us, this being determined by a rational principle, and by that principle by which the man of practical wisdom would determine it. Now it is a mean between two vices, that which depends on excess and that which depends on defect; and again it is a mean because the vices respectively fall short of or exceed what is right in both passions and actions, while virtue both finds and chooses that which is intermediate. Hence in respect of its substance and the definition which states its essence virtue is a mean, with regard to what is best and right an extreme.

But not every action nor every passion admits of a mean; for some have names that already imply badness, e. g. spite, shamelessness, envy, and in the case of actions adultery, theft, murder; for all of these and suchlike things imply by their names that they are themselves bad, and not the excesses or deficiencies of them. It is not possible, then, ever to be right with regard to them; one must always be wrong. Nor does goodness or badness with regard to such things depend on committing adultery with the right woman, at the right time, and in the right way, but simply to do any of them is to go wrong. It would be equally absurd, then, to expect that in unjust, cowardly, and voluptuous action there should be a mean, an excess, and a deficiency; for at that rate there would be a mean of excess and of deficiency, an excess of excess, and a deficiency of deficiency. But as there is no excess and deficiency of temperance and courage because what is intermediate is in a sense an extreme, so too of the actions we have mentioned there is no mean nor any excess and deficiency, but however they are done they are wrong; for in general there is neither a mean of excess and deficiency, nor excess and deficiency of a mean.

7 We must, however, not only make this general statement, but also apply it to the individual facts. For among statements about conduct those which are general apply more widely, but those which are particular are more genuine, since conduct has to do with individual cases, and our statements must harmonize with the facts in these cases. We may take these cases from our table. With regard to feelings of fear and confidence courage is the mean; of the people who exceed, he who exceeds in fearlessness has no name (many of the states have no name), while the man who exceeds in confidence is rash, and he who exceeds in fear and falls short in

confidence is a coward. With regard to pleasures and pains—not all of them, and not so much with regard to the pains—the mean is temperance, the excess self-indulgence. Persons deficient with regard to the pleasures are not often found; hence such persons also have received no name. But let us call them "insensible."

With regard to giving and taking of money the mean is liberality, the excess and the defect prodigality and meanness. In these actions people exceed and fall short in contrary ways; the prodigal exceeds in spending and falls short in taking, while the mean man exceeds in taking and falls short in spending. (At present we are giving a mere outline or summary, and are satisfied with this; later these states will be more exactly determined.) With regard to money there are also other dispositions—a mean, magnificence (for the magnificent man differs from the liberal man; the former deals with large sums, the latter with small ones), an excess, tastelessness and vulgarity, and a deficiency, niggardliness; these differ from the states opposed to liberality, and the mode of their difference will be stated later.

With regard to honour and dishonour the mean is proper pride, the excess is known as a sort of "empty vanity," and the deficiency is undue humility; and as we said liberality was related to magnificence, differing from it by dealing with small sums, so there is a state similarly related to proper pride, being concerned with small honours while that is concerned with great. For it is possible to desire honour as one ought, and more than one ought, and less, and the man who exceeds in his desires is called ambitious, the man who falls short unambitious, while the intermediate person has no name. The dispositions also are nameless, except that that of the ambitious man is called ambition. Hence the people who are at the extremes lay claim to the middle place; and we ourselves sometimes call the intermediate person ambitious and sometimes unambitious, and sometimes praise the ambitious man and sometimes the unambitious. The reason of our doing this will be stated in what follows; but now let us speak of the remaining states according to the method which has been indicated.

With regard to anger also there is an excess, a deficiency, and a mean. Although they can scarcely be said to have names, yet since we call the intermediate person good-tempered let us call the mean good temper; of the persons at the extremes let the one who exceeds be called irascible, and his vice irascibility, and the man who falls short an inirascible sort of person, and the deficiency inirascibility.

There are also three other means, which have a certain likeness to one another, but differ from one another: for they are all concerned with intercourse in words and actions, but differ in that one is concerned with truth in this sphere, the other two with pleasantness; and of this one kind is exhibited in giving amusement, the other in all the circumstances of life. We must therefore speak of these too, that we may the better see that in all things the mean is praiseworthy, and the extremes neither praiseworthy nor right, but worthy of blame. Now most of these states also have no names, but we must try, as in the other cases, to invent names ourselves so that we may be clear and easy to follow. With regard to truth, then, the intermediate is a truthful sort of person and the mean may be called truthfulness, while the pretence which exaggerates is boastfulness and the person characterized by it a boaster, and that which understates is mock modesty and the person characterized by it mock-modest. With regard to pleasantness in the giving of amusement the intermediate person is ready-witted and the disposition ready wit, the excess is buffoonery and the person characterized by it a buffoon, while the man who falls short is a sort of boor and his state is boorishness. With regard to the remaining kind of pleasantness, that which is exhibited in life in general, the man who is pleasant in the right way is friendly and the mean is friendliness, while the man who exceeds is an obsequious person if he has no end in view, a flatterer if he is aiming at his own advantage, and the man who falls short and is unpleasant in all circumstances is a quarrelsome and surly sort of person.

There are also means in the passions and concerned with the passions; since shame is not a virtue, and yet praise is extended to the modest man. For even in these matters one man is said to be intermediate, and another to exceed, as for instance the bashful man who is ashamed of everything; while he who falls short or is not ashamed of anything at all is shameless, and the intermediate person is modest. Righteous indignation is a mean between envy and spite, and these states are concerned with the pain and pleasures that are felt at the fortunes of our neighbours; the man who is characterized by righteous indignation is pained at undeserved good fortune, the envious man, going beyond him, is pained at all good fortune, and the spiteful man falls so far short of being pained that he even rejoices. But these states there will be an opportunity of describing elsewhere; with regard to justice, since it has not one simple meaning, we shall, after describing the other states, distinguish its two kinds and say how each of them is a mean; and similarly we shall treat also of the rational virtues.

8 There are three kinds of disposition, then, two of them vices, involving excess and deficiency respectively, and one a virtue, viz. the mean, and all are in a sense opposed to all; for the extreme states are contrary both to the intermediate state and to each other, and the intermediate to the extremes; as the equal is greater relatively to the less, less relatively to the greater, so the middle states are excessive relatively to the deficiencies, deficient relatively to the excesses, both in passions and in actions. For the brave man appears rash relatively to the coward, and cowardly relatively to the rash man; and similarly the temperate man appears self-indulgent relatively to the insensible man, insensible relatively to the self-indulgent, and the liberal man prodigal relatively to the mean man, mean relatively to the prodigal. Hence also the people at the extremes push the intermediate man each over to the other,

and the brave man is called rash by the coward, cowardly by the rash man, and correspondingly in the other cases.

These states being thus opposed to one another, the greatest contrariety is that of the extremes to each other, rather than to the intermediate; for these are further from each other than from the intermediate, as the great is further from the small and the small from the great than both are from the equal. Again, to the intermediate some extremes show a certain likeness, as that of rashness to courage and that of prodigality to liberality; but the extremes show the greatest unlikeness to each other; now contraries are defined as the things that are furthest from each other, so that things that are further apart are more contrary.

To the mean in some cases the deficiency, in some the excess is more opposed; e. g. it is not rashness, which is an excess, but cowardice, which is a deficiency, that is more opposed to courage, and not insensibility, which is a deficiency, but self-indulgence, which is an excess, that is more opposed to temperance. This happens from two reasons, one being drawn from the thing itself; for because one extreme is nearer and liker to the intermediate, we oppose not this but rather its contrary to the intermediate. E. g., since rashness is thought liker and nearer to courage, and cowardice more unlike, we oppose rather the latter to courage; for things that are further from the intermediate are thought more contrary to it. This, then, is one cause, drawn from the thing itself; another is drawn from ourselves; for the things to which we ourselves more naturally tend seem more contrary to the intermediate. For instance, we ourselves tend more naturally to pleasures, and hence are more easily carried away towards self-indulgence than towards propriety. We describe as contrary to the mean, then, rather the directions in which we more often go to great lengths; and therefore self-indulgence, which is an excess, is the more contrary to temperance.

9 That moral virtue is a mean, then, and in what sense it is so, and that it is a mean between two vices, the one involv-

ing excess, the other deficiency, and that it is such because its character is to aim at what is intermediate in passions and in actions, has been sufficiently stated. Hence also it is no easy task to be good. For in everything it is no easy task to find the middle, e. g. to find the middle of a circle is not for every one but for him who knows; so, too, any one can get angry—that is easy—or give or spend money; but to do this to the right person, to the right extent, at the right time, with the right motive, and in the right way, *that* is not for every one, nor is it easy; wherefore goodness is both rare and laudable and noble.

Hence he who aims at the intermediate must first depart from what is the more contrary to it, as Calypso advises—

Hold the ship out beyond that surf and spray.[8]

For of the extremes one is more erroneous, one less so; therefore, since to hit the mean is hard in the extreme, we must as a second best, as people say, take the least of the evils; and this will be done best in the way we describe.

But we must consider the things towards which we ourselves also are easily carried away; for some of us tend to one thing, some to another; and this will be recognizable from the pleasure and the pain we feel. We must drag ourselves away to the contrary extreme; for we shall get into the intermediate state by drawing well away from error, as people do in straightening sticks that are bent.

Now in everything the pleasant or pleasure is most to be guarded against; for we do not judge it impartially. We ought, then, to feel towards pleasure as the elders of the people felt towards Helen, and in all circumstances repeat their saying; for if we dismiss pleasure thus we are less likely to go astray. It is by doing this, then (to sum the matter up) that we shall best be able to hit the mean.

But this is no doubt difficult, and especially in individual

[8]*Od.* xii. 219f. (Mackail's trans.). But it was Circe who gave the advice (xii. 108), and the actual quotation is from Odysseus' orders to his steersman.

cases; for it is not easy to determine both how and with whom and on what provocation and how long one should be angry; for we too sometimes praise those who fall short and call them good-tempered, but sometimes we praise those who get angry and call them manly. The man, however, who deviates little from goodness is not blamed, whether he do so in the direction of the more or of the less, but only the man who deviates more widely; for *he* does not fail to be noticed. But up to what point and to what extent a man must deviate before he becomes blameworthy it is not easy to determine by reasoning, any more than anything else that is perceived by the senses; such things depend on particular facts, and the decision rests with perception. So much, then, is plain, that the intermediate state is in all things to be praised, but that we must incline sometimes towards the excess, sometimes towards the deficiency; for so shall we most easily hit the mean and what is right.

## BOOK III

1 Since virtue is concerned with passions and actions, and on voluntary passions and actions praise and blame are bestowed, on those that are involuntary pardon, and sometimes also pity, to distinguish the voluntary and the involuntary is presumably necessary for those who are studying the nature of virtue, and useful also for legislators with a view to the assigning both of honours and of punishments.

Those things, then, are thought involuntary, which take place under compulsion or owing to ignorance; and that is compulsory of which the moving principle is outside, being a principle in which nothing is contributed by the person who is acting or is feeling the passion, e. g. if he were to be carried somewhere by a wind, or by men who had him in their power.

But with regard to the things that are done from fear of

greater evils or for some noble object (e. g. if a tyrant were to order one to do something base, having one's parents and children in his power, and if one did the action they were to be saved, but otherwise would be put to death), it may be debated whether such actions are involuntary or voluntary. Something of the sort happens also with regard to the throwing of goods overboard in a storm; for in the abstract no one throws goods away voluntarily, but on condition of its securing the safety of himself and his crew any sensible man does so. Such actions, then, are mixed, but are more like voluntary actions; for they are worthy of choice at the time when they are done, and the end of an action is relative to the occasion. Both the terms, then, "voluntary" and "involuntary," must be used with reference to the moment of action. Now the man acts voluntarily; for the principle that moves the instrumental parts of the body in such actions is in him, and the things of which the moving principle is in a man himself are in his power to do or not to do. Such actions, therefore, are voluntary, but in the abstract perhaps involuntary; for no one would choose any such act in itself.

For such actions men are sometimes even praised, when they endure something base or painful in return for great and noble objects gained; in the opposite case they are blamed, since to endure the greatest indignities for no noble end or for a trifling end is the mark of an inferior person. On some actions praise indeed is not bestowed, but pardon is, when one does what he ought not under pressure which overstrains human nature and which no one could withstand. But some acts, perhaps, we cannot be forced to do, but ought rather to face death after the most fearful sufferings; for the things that "forced" Euripides' Alcmaeon to slay his mother seem absurd. It is difficult sometimes to determine what should be chosen at what cost, and what should be endured in return for what gain, and yet more difficult to abide by our decisions; for as a rule what is expected is painful, and what we are forced to do is base, whence praise and blame are bestowed on those who have been compelled or have not.

What sort of acts, then, should be called compulsory? We answer that without qualification actions are so when the cause is in the external circumstances and the agent contributes nothing. But the things that in themselves are involuntary, but now and in return for these gains are worthy of choice, and whose moving principle is in the agent, are in themselves involuntary, but now and in return for these gains voluntary. They are more like voluntary acts; for actions are in the class of particulars, and the particular acts here are voluntary. What sort of things are to be chosen, and in return for what, it is not easy to state; for there are many differences in the particular cases.

But if some one were to say that pleasant and noble objects have a compelling power, forcing us from without, all acts would be for him compulsory; for it is for these objects that all men do everything they do. And those who act under compulsion and unwillingly act with pain, but those who do acts for their pleasantness and nobility do them with pleasure; it is absurd to make external circumstances responsible, and not oneself, as being easily caught by such attractions, and to make oneself responsible for noble acts but the pleasant objects responsible for base acts. The compulsory, then, seems to be that whose moving principle is outside, the person compelled contributing nothing.

Everything that is done by reason of ignorance is *not* voluntary; it is only what produces pain and repentance that is *in*voluntary. For the man who has done something owing to ignorance, and feels not the least vexation at his action, has not acted voluntarily, since he did not know what he was doing, nor yet involuntarily, since he is not pained. Of people, then, who act by reason of ignorance he who repents is thought an involuntary agent, and the man who does not repent may, since he is different, be called a not voluntary agent; for, since he differs from the other, it is better that he should have a name of his own.

Acting by reason of ignorance seems also to be different from acting *in* ignorance; for the man who is drunk or in a rage is thought to act as a result not of ignorance but of one of the causes mentioned, yet not knowingly but in ignorance.

Now every wicked man is ignorant of what he ought to do and what he ought to abstain from, and it is by reason of error of this kind that men become unjust and in general bad; but the term "involuntary" tends to be used not if a man is ignorant of what is to his advantage—for it is not mistaken purpose that causes involuntary action (it leads rather to wickedness), nor ignorance of the universal (for *that* men are *blamed*), but ignorance of particulars, i. e. of the circumstances of the action and the objects with which it is concerned. For it is on these that both pity and pardon depend, since the person who is ignorant of any of these acts involuntarily.

Perhaps it is just as well, therefore, to determine their nature and number. A man may be ignorant, then, of who he is, what he is doing, what or whom he is acting on, and sometimes also what (e. g. what instrument) he is doing it with, and to what end (e. g. he may think his act will conduce to some one's safety), and how he is doing it (e. g. whether gently or violently). Now of all of these no one could be ignorant unless he were mad, and evidently also he could not be ignorant of the agent; for how could he not know himself? But of what he is doing a man might be ignorant, as for instance people say "it slipped out of their mouths as they were speaking," or "they did not know it was a secret," as Aeschylus said of the mysteries, or a man might say he "let it go off when he merely wanted to show its working," as the man did with the catapult. Again, one might think one's son was an enemy, as Merope did, or that a pointed spear had a button on it, or that a stone was pumice-stone; or one might give a man a draught to save him, and really kill him; or one might want to touch a man, as people do in sparring, and really wound him. The ignorance may relate, then, to any of these things, i. e. of the circumstances of the action, and the man who was ignorant of any of these is thought to have acted involuntarily, and especially if he was ignorant on the most important points; and these are thought to be the circumstances of the action and its end. Further, the doing of an act that is called involuntary in virtue of ignorance of this sort must be painful and involve repentance.

Since that which is done under compulsion or by reason of ignorance is involuntary, the voluntary would seem to be that of which the moving principle is in the agent himself, he being aware of the particular circumstances of the action. Presumably acts done by reason of anger or appetite are not rightly called involuntary.[9] For in the first place, on that showing none of the other animals will act voluntarily, nor will children; and secondly, is it meant that we do not do voluntarily *any* of the acts that are due to appetite or anger, or that we do the noble acts voluntarily and the base acts involuntarily? Is not this absurd, when one and the same thing is the cause? But it would surely be odd to describe as involuntary the things one ought to desire; and we ought both to be angry at certain things and to have an appetite for certain things, e. g. for health and for learning. Also what is involuntary is thought to be painful, but what is in accordance with appetite is thought to be pleasant. Again, what is the difference in respect of involuntariness between errors committed upon calculation and those committed in anger? Both are to be avoided, but the irrational passions are thought not less human than reason is, and therefore also the actions which proceed from anger or appetite are the man's actions. It would be odd, then, to treat them as involuntary.

2 Both the voluntary and the involuntary having been delimited, we must next discuss choice; for it is thought to be most closely bound up with virtue and to discriminate characters better than actions do.

Choice, then, seems to be voluntary, but not the same thing as the voluntary; the latter extends more widely. For both children and the lower animals share in voluntary action, but

[9]A reference to Pl. *Laws* 863 B, ff., where anger and appetite are coupled with ignorance as sources of wrong action.

not in choice, and acts done on the spur of the moment we describe as voluntary, but not as chosen.

Those who say it is appetite or anger or wish or a kind of opinion do not seem to be right. For choice is not common to irrational creatures as well, but appetite and anger are. Again, the incontinent man acts with appetite, but not with choice; while the continent man on the contrary acts with choice, but not with appetite. Again, appetite is contrary to choice, but not appetite to appetite. Again, appetite relates to the pleasant and the painful, choice neither to the painful nor to the pleasant.

Still less is it anger; for acts due to anger are thought to be less than any others objects of choice.

But neither is it wish, though it seems near to it; for choice cannot relate to impossibles, and if any one said he chose them he would be thought silly; but there may be a wish even for impossibles, e. g. for immortality. And wish may relate to things that could in no way be brought about by one's own efforts, e. g. that a particular actor or athlete should win in a competition; but no one chooses such things, but only the things that he thinks could be brought about by his own efforts. Again, wish relates rather to the end, choice to the means; for instance, we wish to be healthy, but we choose the acts which will make us healthy, and we wish to be happy and say we do, but we cannot well say we choose to be so; for, in general, choice seems to relate to the things that are in our own power.

For this reason, too, it cannot be opinion; for opinion is thought to relate to all kinds of things, no less to eternal things and impossible things than to things in our own power; and it is distinguished by its falsity or truth, not by its badness or goodness, while choice is distinguished rather by these.

Now with opinion in general perhaps no one even says it is identical. But it is not identical even with any kind of opinion; for by choosing what is good or bad we are men of a certain character, which we are not by holding certain opinions. And we choose to get or avoid something good or bad, but we have opinions about what a thing is or whom it is good for or how it is good for him; we can hardly be said to opine to get or avoid anything. And choice is praised for being related to the right object rather than for being rightly related to it, opinion for being truly related to its object. And we choose what we best know to be good, but we opine what we do not quite know; and it is not the same people that are thought to make the best choices and to have the best opinions, but some are thought to have fairly good opinions, but by reason of vice to choose what they should not. If opinion precedes choice or accompanies it, that makes no difference; for it is not this that we are considering, but whether it is *identical* with some kind of opinion.

What, then, or what kind of thing is it, since it is none of the things we have mentioned? It seems to be voluntary, but not all that is voluntary to be an object of choice. Is it, then, what has been decided on by previous deliberation? At any rate choice involves a rational principle and thought. Even the name seems to suggest that it is what is chosen before other things.

3 Do we deliberate about everything, and is everything a possible subject of deliberation, or is deliberation impossible about some things? We ought presumably to call not what a fool or a madman would deliberate about, but what a sensible man would deliberate about, a subject of deliberation. Now about eternal things no one deliberates, e. g. about the material universe or the incommensurability of the diagonal and the side of a square. But no more do we deliberate about the things that involve movement but always happen in the same way, whether of necessity or by nature or from any other cause, e. g. the solstices and the risings of the stars; nor about things that happen now in one way, now in another, e. g. droughts and rains; nor about chance events, like the finding of treasure. But we do not deliberate even about all human affairs; for instance, no Spartan deliberates about the best

constitution for the Scythians. For none of these things can be brought about by our own efforts.

We deliberate about things that are in our power and can be done; and these are in fact what is left. For nature, necessity, and chance are thought to be causes, and also reason and everything that depends on man. Now every class of men deliberates about the things that can be done by their own efforts. And in the case of exact and self-contained sciences there is no deliberation, e. g. about the letters of the alphabet (for we have no doubt how they should be written); but the things that are brought about by our own efforts, but not always in the same way, are the things about which we deliberate, e. g. questions of medical treatment or of money-making. And we do so more in the case of the art of navigation than in that of gymnastics, inasmuch as it has been less exactly worked out, and again about other things in the same ratio, and more also in the case of the arts than in that of the sciences; for we have more doubt about the former. Deliberation is concerned with things that happen in a certain way for the most part, but in which the event is obscure, and with things in which it is indeterminate. We call in others to aid us in deliberation on important questions, distrusting ourselves as not being equal to deciding.

We deliberate not about ends but about means. For a doctor does not deliberate whether he shall heal, nor an orator whether he shall persuade, nor a statesman whether he shall produce law and order, nor does any one else deliberate about his end. They assume the end and consider how and by what means it is to be attained; and if it seems to be produced by several means they consider by which it is most easily and best produced, while if it is achieved by one only they consider how it will be achieved by this and by what means *this* will be achieved, till they come to the first cause, which in the order of discovery is last. For the person who deliberates seems to investigate and analyse in the way described as though he were analysing a geometrical construction[10] (not all investigation appears to be deliberation—for instance mathematical investigations—but all deliberation is investigation), and what is last in the order of analysis seems to be first in the order of becoming. And if we come on an impossibility, we give up the search, e. g. if we need money and this cannot be got; but if a thing appears possible we try to do it. By "possible" things I mean things that might be brought about by our own efforts; and these in a sense include things that can be brought about by the efforts of our friends, since the moving principle is in ourselves. The subject of investigation is sometimes the instruments, sometimes the uses of them; and similarly in the other cases—sometimes the means, sometimes the mode of using it or the means of bringing it about. It seems, then, as has been said, that man is a moving principle of actions; now deliberation is about the things to be done by the agent himself, and actions are for the sake of things other than themselves. For the end cannot be a subject of deliberation, but only the means; nor indeed can the particular facts be a subject of it, as whether this is bread or has been baked as it should; for these are matters of perception. If we are to be always deliberating, we shall have to go on to infinity.

The same thing is deliberated upon and is chosen, except that the object of choice is already determinate, since it is that which has been decided upon as a result of deliberation that is the object of choice. For every one ceases to inquire how he is to act when he has brought the moving principle back to himself and to the ruling part of himself; for this is what chooses. This is plain also from the ancient constitutions, which Homer represented; for the kings announced their choices to the people. The object of choice being one of the things in our own power which is desired after deliberation, choice will be deliberate desire of things in our own

---

[10]Aristotle has in mind the method of discovering the solution of a geometrical problem. The problem being to construct a figure of a certain kind, we suppose it constructed and then analyse it to see if there is some figure by constructing which we can construct the required figure, and so on till we come to a figure which our existing knowledge enables us to construct.

power; for when we have decided as a result of deliberation, we desire in accordance with our deliberation.

We may take it, then, that we have described choice in outline, and stated the nature of its objects and the fact that it is concerned with means.

4 That *wish* is for the end has already been stated; some think it is for the good, others for the apparent good. Now those who say that the good is the object of wish must admit in consequence that that which the man who does not choose aright wishes for is not an object of wish (for if it is to be so, it must also be good; but it was, if it so happened, bad); while those who say the apparent good is the object of wish must admit that there is no natural object of wish, but only what seems good to each man. Now different things appear good to different people, and, if it so happens, even contrary things.

If these consequences are unpleasing, are we to say that absolutely and in truth the good is the object of wish, but for each person the apparent good; that that which is in truth an object of wish is an object of wish to the good man, while any chance thing may be so to the bad man, as in the case of bodies also the things that are in truth wholesome are wholesome for bodies which are in good condition, while for those that are diseased other things are wholesome—or bitter or sweet or hot or heavy, and so on; since the good man judges each class of things rightly, and in each the truth appears to him? For each state of character has its own ideas of the noble and the pleasant, and perhaps the good man differs from others most by seeing the truth in each class of things, being as it were the norm and measure of them. In most things the error seems to be due to pleasure; for it appears a good when it is not. We therefore choose the pleasant as a good, and avoid pain as an evil.

5 The end, then, being what we wish for, the means what we deliberate about and choose, actions concerning means

must be according to choice and voluntary. Now the exercise of the virtues is concerned with means. Therefore virtue also is in our own power, and so too vice. For where it is in our power to act it is also in our power not to act, and *vice versa;* so that, if to act, where this is noble, is in our power, not to act, which will be base, will also be in our power, and if not to act, where this is noble, is in our power, to act, which will be base, will also be in our power. Now if it is in our power to do noble or base acts, and likewise in our power not to do them, and this was what being good or bad meant, then it is in our power to be virtuous or vicious.

The saying that "no one is voluntarily wicked nor involuntarily happy" seems to be partly false and partly true; for no one is involuntarily happy, but wickedness *is* voluntary. Or else we shall have to dispute what has just been said, at any rate, and deny that man is a moving principle or begetter of his actions as of children. But if these facts are evident and we cannot refer actions to moving principles other than those in ourselves, the acts whose moving principles are in us must themselves also be in our power and voluntary.

Witness seems to be borne to this both by individuals in their private capacity and by legislators themselves; for these punish and take vengeance on those who do wicked acts (unless they have acted under compulsion or as a result of ignorance for which they are not themselves responsible), while they honour those who do noble acts, as though they meant to encourage the latter and deter the former. But no one is encouraged to do the things that are neither in our power nor voluntary; it is assumed that there is no gain in being persuaded not to be hot or in pain or hungry or the like, since we shall experience these feelings none the less. Indeed, we punish a man for his very ignorance, if he is thought responsible for the ignorance, as when penalties are doubled in the case of drunkenness; for the moving principle is in the man himself, since he had the power of not getting drunk and his getting drunk was the cause of his ignorance. And we punish those who are ignorant of anything in the laws that they ought to know and that it is not difficult, and so too in the case of anything else that they are thought to be ignorant of through carelessness; we assume that it is in their power not to be ignorant, since they have the power of taking care.

But perhaps a man is the kind of man not to take care. Still they are themselves by their slack lives responsible for becoming men of that kind, and men make themselves responsible for being unjust or self-indulgent, in the one case by cheating and in the other by spending their time in drinking bouts and the like; for it is activities exercised on particular objects that make the corresponding character. This is plain from the case of people training for any contest or action; they practise the activity the whole time. Now not to know that it is from the exercise of activities on particular objects that states of character are produced is the mark of a thoroughly senseless person. Again, it is irrational to suppose that a man who acts unjustly does not wish to be unjust or a man who acts self-indulgently to be self-indulgent. But if *without* being ignorant a man does the things which will make him unjust, he will be unjust voluntarily. Yet it does not follow that if he wishes he will cease to be unjust and will be just. For neither does the man who is ill become well on those terms. We may suppose a case in which he is ill voluntarily, through living incontinently and disobeying his doctors. In that case it was *then* open to him not to be ill, but not now, when he has thrown away his chance, just as when you have let a stone go it is too late to recover it; but yet it was in your power to throw it, since the moving principle was in you. So, too, to the unjust and to the self-indulgent man it was open at the beginning not to become men of this kind, and so they are unjust and self-indulgent voluntarily; but now that they have become so it is not possible for them not to be so.

But not only are the vices of the soul voluntary, but those of the body also for some men, whom we accordingly blame; while no one blames those who are ugly by nature, we blame those who are so owing to want of exercise and care. So it is, too, with respect to weakness and infirmity; no one would reproach a man blind from birth or by disease or from a blow, but rather pity him, while every one would blame a man who was blind from drunkenness or some other form of self-indulgence. Of vices of the body, then, those in our own power are blamed, those not in our power are not. And if this be so, in the other cases also the vices that are blamed must be in our own power.

Now some one may say that all men desire the apparent good, but have no control over the appearance, but the end appears to each man in a form answering to his character. We reply that if each man is somehow responsible for his state of mind, he will also be himself somehow responsible for the appearance; but if not, no one is responsible for his own evil-doing, but every one does evil acts through ignorance of the end, thinking that by these he will get what is best, and the aiming at the end is not self-chosen but one must be born with an eye, as it were, by which to judge rightly and choose what is truly good, and he is well endowed by nature who is well endowed with this. For it is what is greatest and most noble, and what we cannot get or learn from another, but must have just such as it was when given us at birth, and to be well and nobly endowed with this will be perfect and true excellence of natural endowment. If this is true, then, how will virtue be more voluntary than vice? To both men alike, the good and the bad, the end appears and is fixed by nature or however it may be, and it is by referring everything else to this that men do whatever they do.

Whether, then, it is not by nature that the end appears to each man such as it does appear, but something also depends on him, or the end is natural but because the good man adopts the means voluntarily virtue is voluntary, vice also will be none the less voluntary; for in the case of the bad man there is equally present that which depends on himself in his actions even if not in his end. If, then, as is asserted, the virtues are voluntary (for we are ourselves somehow partly responsible for our states of character, and it is by being persons of a certain kind that we assume the end to be so and so), the vices also will be voluntary; for the same is true of them.

With regard to the virtues in *general* we have stated their genus in outline, viz. that they are means and that they are states of character, and that they tend, and by their own nature, to the doing of the acts by which they are produced, and that they are in our power and voluntary, and act as the right rule prescribes. But actions and states of character are not voluntary in the same way; for we are masters of our actions from the beginning right to the end, if we know the particular facts, but though we control the beginning of our states of character the gradual progress is not obvious, any more than it is in illnesses, because it was in our power, however, to act in this way or not in this way, therefore the states are voluntary.

Let us take up the several virtues, however, and say which they are and what sort of things they are concerned with and how they are concerned with them; at the same time it will become plain how many they are. And first let us speak of courage.

6 That it is a mean with regard to feelings of fear and confidence has already been made evident; and plainly the things we fear are terrible things, and these are, to speak without qualification, evils; for which reason people even define fear as expectation of evil. Now we fear all evils, e. g. disgrace, poverty, disease, friendlessness, death, but the brave man is not thought to be concerned with all; for to fear some things is even right and noble, and it is base not to fear them —e. g. disgrace; he who fears this is good and modest, and he who does not is shameless. He is, however, by some people called brave, by a transference of the word to a new meaning; for he has in him something which is like the brave man, since the brave man also is a fearless person. Poverty and disease we perhaps ought not to fear, nor in general the things that do not proceed from vice and are not due to a

man himself. But not even the man who is fearless of these is brave. Yet we apply the word to him also in virtue of a similarity; for some who in the dangers of war are cowards are liberal and are confident in face of the loss of money. Nor is a man a coward if he fears insult to his wife and children or envy or anything of the kind; nor brave if he is confident when he is about to be flogged. With what sort of terrible things, then, is the brave man concerned? Surely with the greatest; for no one is more likely than he to stand his ground against what is awe-inspiring. Now death is the most terrible of all things; for it is the end, and nothing is thought to be any longer either good or bad for the dead. But the brave man would not seem to be concerned even with death in *all* circumstances, e. g. at sea or in disease. In what circumstances, then? Surely in the noblest. Now such deaths are those in battle; for these take place in the greatest and noblest danger. And these are correspondingly honoured in city-states and at the courts of monarchs. Properly, then, he will be called brave who is fearless in face of a noble death, and of all emergencies that involve death; and the emergencies of war are in the highest degree of this kind. Yet at sea also, and in disease; the brave man is fearless, but not in the same way as the seamen; for he has given up hope of safety, and is disliking the thought of death in this shape, while they are hopeful because of their experience. At the same time, we show courage in situations where there is the opportunity of showing prowess or where death is noble; but in these forms of death neither of these conditions is fulfilled.

7 What is terrible is not the same for all men; but we say there are things terrible even beyond human strength. These, then, are terrible to every one—at least to every sensible man; but the terrible things that are *not* beyond human strength differ in magnitude and degree, and so too do the things that inspire confidence. Now the brave man is as dauntless as man may be. Therefore, while he will fear even the things

that are not beyond human strength, he will face them as he ought and as the rule directs, for honour's sake; for this is the end of virtue. But it is possible to fear these more, or less, and again to fear things that are not terrible as if they were. Of the faults that are committed one consists in fearing what one should not, another in fearing as we should not, another in fearing when we should not, and so on; and so too with respect to the things that inspire confidence. The man, then, who faces and who fears the right things and from the right motive, in the right way and at the right time, and who feels confidence under the corresponding conditions, is brave; for the brave man feels and acts according to the merits of the case and in whatever way the rule directs. Now the end of every activity is conformity to the corresponding state of character. This is true, therefore, of the brave man as well as of others. But courage is noble. Therefore the end also is noble; for each thing is defined by its end. Therefore it is for a noble end that the brave man endures and acts as courage directs.

Of those who go to excess he who exceeds in fearlessness has no name (we have said previously that many states of character have no names), but he would be a sort of madman or insensible person if he feared nothing, neither earthquakes nor the waves, as they say the Celts do not; while the man who exceeds in confidence about what really is terrible is rash. The rash man, however, is also thought to be boastful and only a pretender to courage; at all events, as the brave man *is* with regard to what is terrible, so the rash man wishes to *appear;* and so he imitates him in situations where he can. Hence also most of them are a mixture of rashness and cowardice; for, while in these situations they display confidence, they do not hold their ground against what is really terrible. The man who exceeds in fear is a coward; for he fears both what he ought not and as he ought not, and all the similar characterizations attach to him. He is lacking also in confidence; but he is more conspicuous for his excess of fear in painful situations. The coward, then, is a despairing sort of person; for he fears everything. The brave man, on the other hand, has the opposite disposition; for confidence is the mark of a hopeful disposition. The coward, the rash man, and the brave man, then, are concerned with the same objects but are differently disposed towards them; for the first two exceed and fall short, while the third holds the middle, which is the right, position; and rash men are precipitate, and wish for dangers beforehand but draw back when they are in them, while brave men are keen in the moment of action, but quiet beforehand.

As we have said, then, courage is a mean with respect to things that inspire confidence or fear, in the circumstances that have been stated; and it chooses or endures things because it is noble to do so, or because it is base not to do so. But to die to escape from poverty or love or anything painful is not the mark of a brave man, but rather of a coward; for it is softness to fly from what is troublesome, and such a man endures death not because it is noble but to fly from evil.

8 Courage, then, is something of this sort, but the name is also applied to five other kinds. (1) First comes the courage of the citizen-soldier; for this is most like true courage. Citizen-soldiers seem to face dangers because of the penalties imposed by the laws and the reproaches they would otherwise incur, and because of the honours they win by such action; and therefore those peoples seem to be bravest among whom cowards are held in dishonour and brave men in honour. This is the kind of courage that Homer depicts, e. g. in Diomede and in Hector:

> First will Polydamas be to heap reproach on me then;

and

> For Hector one day 'mid the Trojans shall utter his vaulting harangue:
> "Afraid was Tydeides, and fled from my face."

This kind of courage is most like to that which we described earlier, because it is due to virtue; for it is due to shame and to desire of a noble object (i. e. honour) and avoidance of disgrace, which is ignoble. One might rank in the same class even those who are compelled by their rulers; but they are inferior, inasmuch as they do what they do not from shame but from fear, and to avoid not what is disgraceful but what is painful; for their masters compel them, as Hector[11] does:

But if I shall spy any dastard that cowers far from the fight,
Vainly will such an one hope to escape from the dogs.

And those who give them their posts, and beat them if they retreat, do the same, and so do those who draw them up with trenches or something of the sort behind them; all of these apply compulsion. But one ought to be brave not under compulsion but because it is noble to be so.

(2) Experience with regard to particular facts is also thought to be courage; this is indeed the reason why Socrates thought courage was knowledge. Other people exhibit this quality in other dangers, and professional soldiers exhibit it in the dangers of war; for there seem to be many empty alarms in war, of which these have had the most comprehensive experience; therefore they seem brave, because the others do not know the nature of the facts. Again, their experience makes them most capable in attack and in defence, since they can use their arms and have the kind that are likely to be best both for attack and for defence; therefore they fight like armed men against unarmed or like trained athletes against amateurs; for in such contests too it is not the bravest men that fight best, but those who are strongest and have their bodies in the best condition. Professional soldiers turn cowards, however, when the danger puts too great a strain on them and they are inferior in numbers and equipment; for they are the first to fly, while citizen-forces die at their posts,

---

[11]Aristotle's quotation is more like *Il.* ii. 391-3, where Agamemnon speaks, than xv. 348-51, where Hector speaks.

as in fact happened at the temple of Hermes.[12] For to the latter flight is disgraceful and death is preferable to safety on those terms; while the former from the very beginning faced the danger on the assumption that they were stronger, and when they know the facts they fly, fearing death more than disgrace; but the brave man is not that sort of person.

(3) Passion also is sometimes reckoned as courage; those who act from passion, like wild beasts rushing at those who have wounded them, are thought to be brave, because brave men also are passionate; for passion above all things is eager to rush on danger, and hence Homer's "put strength into his passion"[13] and "aroused their spirit and passion"[14] and "hard he breathed panting"[15] and "his blood boiled."[15a] For all such expressions seem to indicate the stirring and onset of passion. Now brave men act for honour's sake, but passion aids them; while wild beasts act under the influence of pain; for they attack because they have been wounded or because they are afraid, since if they are in a forest they do not come near one. Thus they are not brave because, driven by pain and passion, they rush on danger without foreseeing any of the perils, since at that rate even asses would be brave when they are hungry; for blows will not drive them from their food; and lust also makes adulterers do many daring things. [Those creatures are not brave, then, which are driven on to danger by pain or passion.] The "courage" that is due to passion seems to be the most natural, and to be courage if choice and motive be added.

Men, then, as well as beasts, suffer pain when they are angry, and are pleased when they exact their revenge; those who fight for these reasons, however, are pugnacious but not brave; for they do not act for honour's sake nor as the rule directs, but from strength of feeling; they have, however, something akin to courage.

---

[12]The reference is to a battle at Coronea in the Sacred War, *c.* 353 B. C., in which the Phocians defeated the citizens of Coronea and some Boeotian regulars.

[13]This is a conflation of *Il.* xi. 11 or xiv. 151 and xvi. 529.

[14]Cf. *Il.* v. 470, xv. 232, 594.

[15]Cf. *Od.* xxiv. 318 f.

[15a]The phrase does not occur in Homer; it is found in Theocr. xx. 15.

(4) Nor are sanguine people brave; for they are confident in danger only because they have conquered often and against many foes. Yet they closely resemble brave men, because both are confident; but brave men are confident for the reasons stated earlier, while these are so because they think they are the strongest and can suffer nothing. (Drunken men also behave in this way; they become sanguine.) When their adventures do not succeed, however, they run away; but it was the mark of a brave man to face things that are, and seem, terrible for a man, because it is noble to do so and disgraceful not to do so. Hence also it is thought the mark of a braver man to be fearless and undisturbed in sudden alarms than to be so in those that are foreseen; for it must have proceeded more from a state of character, because less from preparation; acts that are foreseen may be chosen by calculation and rule, but sudden actions must be in accordance with one's state of character.

(5) People who are ignorant of the danger also appear brave, and they are not far removed from those of a sanguine temper, but are inferior inasmuch as they have no self-reliance while these have. Hence also the sanguine hold their ground for a time; but those who have been deceived about the facts fly if they know or suspect that these are different from what they supposed, as happened to the Argives when they fell in with the Spartans and took them for Sicyonians.[16]

9 ❧ We have, then, described the character both of brave men and of those who are thought to be brave.

Though courage is concerned with feelings of confidence and of fear, it is not concerned with both alike, but more with the things that inspire fear; for he who is undisturbed in face of these and bears himself as he should towards these is more truly brave than the man who does so towards the things that inspire confidence. It is for facing what is painful, then, as has been said, that men are called brave. Hence also courage involves pain and is justly praised; for it is harder to face

[16]At the Long Walls of Corinth, 392 B. C. Cf. Xen. *Hell.* iv. 4. 10.

what is painful than to abstain from what is pleasant. Yet the end which courage sets before it would seem to be pleasant, but to be concealed by the attending circumstances, as happens also in athletic contests; for the end at which boxers aim is pleasant—the crown and the honours—but the blows they take are distressing to flesh and blood, and painful, and so is their whole exertion; and because the blows and the exertions are many the end, which is but small, appears to have nothing pleasant in it. And so, if the case of courage is similar, death and wounds will be painful to the brave man and against his will, but he will face them because it is noble to do so or because it is base not to do so. And the more he is possessed of virtue in its entirety and the happier he is, the more he will be pained at the thought of death; for life is best worth living for such a man, and he is knowingly losing the greatest goods, and this is painful. But he is none the less brave, and perhaps all the more so, because he chooses noble deeds of war at that cost. It is not the case, then, with all the virtues that the exercise of them is pleasant, except in so far as it reaches its end. But it is quite possible that the best soldiers may be not men of this sort but those who are less brave but have no other good; for these are ready to face danger, and they sell their life for trifling gains.

So much, then, for courage; it is not difficult to grasp its nature in outline, at any rate, from what has been said.

After courage let us speak of temperance; for these seem to be the virtues of the irrational parts.

10 We have said that temperance is a mean with regard to pleasures (for it is less, and not in the same way, concerned with pains); self-indulgence also is manifested in the same sphere. Now, therefore, let us determine with what sort of pleasures they are concerned. We may assume the distinction between bodily pleasures and those of the soul, such as love of honour and love of learning; for the lover of each of these delights in that of which he is a lover, the body being in no

way affected, but rather the mind; but men who are concerned with such pleasures are called neither temperate nor self-indulgent. Nor, again, are those who are concerned with the other pleasures that are not bodily; for those who are fond of hearing and telling stories and who spend their days on anything that turns up are called gossips, but not self-indulgent, nor are those who are pained at the loss of money or of friends.

Temperance must be concerned with bodily pleasures, but not all even of these; for those who delight in objects of vision, such as colours and shapes and painting, are called neither temperate nor self-indulgent; yet it would seem possible to delight even in these either as one should or to excess or to a deficient degree.

And so too is it with objects of hearing; no one calls those who delight extravagantly in music or acting self-indulgent, nor those who do so as they ought temperate.

Nor do we apply these names to those who delight in odour, unless it be incidentally; we do not call those self-indulgent who delight in the odour of apples or roses or incense, but rather those who delight in the odour of unguents or of dainty dishes; for self-indulgent people delight in these because these remind them of the objects of their appetite. And one may see even other people, when they are hungry, delighting in the smell of food; but to delight in this kind of thing is the mark of the self-indulgent man; for these are objects of appetite to him.

Nor is there in animals other than man any pleasure connected with these senses, except incidentally. For dogs do not delight in the scent of hares, but in the eating of them, but the scent told them the hares were there; nor does the lion delight in the lowing of the ox, but in eating it; but he perceived by the lowing that it was near, and therefore appears to delight in the lowing; and similarly he does not delight because he sees "a stag or a wild goat,"[17] but because he is

[17] *Il.* iii. 24.

going to make a meal of it. Temperance and self-indulgence, however, are concerned with the kind of pleasures that the other animals share in, which therefore appear slavish and brutish; these are touch and taste. But even of taste they appear to make little or no use; for the business of taste is the discriminating of flavours, which is done by wine-tasters and people who season dishes; but they hardly take pleasure in making these discriminations, or at least self-indulgent people do not, but in the actual enjoyment, which in all cases comes through touch, both in the case of food and in that of drink and in that of sexual intercourse. This is why a certain gourmand prayed that his throat might become longer than a crane's, implying that it was the contact that he took pleasure in. Thus the sense with which self-indulgence is connected is the most widely shared of the senses; and self-indulgence would seem to be justly a matter of reproach, because it attaches to us not as men but as animals. To delight in such things, then, and to love them above all others, is brutish. For even of the pleasures of touch the most liberal have been eliminated, e. g. those produced in the gymnasium by rubbing and by the consequent heat; for the contact characteristic of the self-indulgent man does not affect the whole body but only certain parts.

11 Of the appetites some seem to be common, others to be peculiar to individuals and acquired; e. g. the appetite for food is natural, since every one who is without it craves for food or drink, and sometimes for both, and for love also (as Homer says)[18] if he is young and lusty; but not every one craves for this or that kind of nourishment or love, nor for the same things. Hence such craving appears to be our very own. Yet it has of course something natural about it; for different things are pleasant to different kinds of people, and some things are more pleasant to every one than chance objects. Now in the natural appetites few go wrong, and only in one direction, that of excess; for to eat or drink whatever

[18] *Il.* xxiv. 130.

offers itself till one is surfeited is to exceed the natural amount, since natural appetite is the replenishment of one's deficiency. Hence these people are called belly-gods, this implying that they fill their belly beyond what is right. It is people of entirely slavish character that become like this. But with regard to the pleasures peculiar to individuals many people go wrong and in many ways. For while the people who are "fond of so and so" are so called because they delight either in the wrong things, or more than most people do, or in the wrong way, the self-indulgent exceed in all three ways; they both delight in some things that they ought not to delight in (since they are hateful), and if one ought to delight in some of the things they delight in, they do so more than one ought and than most men do.

Plainly, then, excess with regard to pleasures is self-indulgence and is culpable; with regard to pains one is not, as in the case of courage, called temperate for facing them or self-indulgent for not doing so, but the self-indulgent man is so called because he is pained more than he ought at not getting pleasant things (even his pain being caused by pleasure), and the temperate man is so called because he is not pained at the absence of what is pleasant and at his abstinence from it.

The self-indulgent man, then, craves for all pleasant things or those that are most pleasant, and is led by his appetite to choose these at the cost of everything else; hence he is pained both when he fails to get them and when he is merely craving for them (for appetite involves pain); but it seems absurd to be pained for the sake of pleasure. People who fall short with regard to pleasures and delight in them less than they should are hardly found; for such insensibility is not human. Even the other animals distinguish different kinds of food and enjoy some and not others; and if there is any one who finds nothing pleasant and nothing more attractive than anything else, he must be something quite different from a man; this sort of person has not received a name because he hardly occurs. The temperate man occupies a middle position with regard to these objects. For he neither enjoys the things that the self-indulgent man enjoys most—but rather dislikes them—nor in general the things that he should not, nor anything of this sort to excess, nor does he feel pain or craving when they are absent, or does so only to a moderate degree, and not more than he should, nor when he should not, and so on; but the things that, being pleasant, make for health or for good condition, he will desire moderately and as he should, and also other pleasant things if they are not hindrances to these ends, or contrary to what is noble, or beyond his means. For he who neglects these conditions loves such pleasures more than they are worth, but the temperate man is not that sort of person, but the sort of person that the right rule prescribes.

12 Self-indulgence is more like a voluntary state than cowardice. For the former is actuated by pleasure, the latter by pain, of which the one is to be chosen and the other to be avoided; and pain upsets and destroys the nature of the person who feels it, while pleasure does nothing of the sort. Therefore self-indulgence is more voluntary. Hence also it is more a matter of reproach; for it is easier to become accustomed to its objects, since there are many things of this sort in life, and the process of habituation to them is free from danger, while with terrible objects the reverse is the case. But cowardice would seem to be voluntary in a different degree from its particular manifestations; for it is itself painless, but in these we are upset by pain, so that we even throw down our arms and disgrace ourselves in other ways; hence our acts are even thought to be done under compulsion. For the self-indulgent man, on the other hand, the particular acts are voluntary (for he does them with craving and desire), but the whole state is less so; for no one craves to be self-indulgent.

The name self-indulgence is applied also to childish faults; for they bear a certain resemblance to what we have been considering. Which is called after which, makes no difference to our present purpose; plainly, however, the later is called after the earlier. The transference of the name seems not a bad one; for that which desires what is base and which develops quickly ought to be kept in a chastened condition, and these characteristics belong above all to appetite and to the child, since children in fact live at the beck and call of appetite, and it is in them that the desire for what is pleasant is strongest. If, then, it is not going to be obedient and subject to the ruling principle, it will go to great lengths; for in an irrational being the desire for pleasure is insatiable even if it tries every source of gratification, and the exercise of appetite increases its innate force, and if appetites are strong and violent they even expel the power of calculation. Hence they should be moderate and few, and should in no way oppose the rational principle—and this is what we call an obedient and chastened state—and as the child should live according to the direction of his tutor, so the appetitive element should live according to rational principle. Hence the appetitive element in a temperate man should harmonize with the rational principle; for the noble is the mark at which both aim, and the temperate man craves for the things he ought, as he ought, and when he ought; and this is what rational principle directs.

Here we conclude our account of temperance.

## BOOK IV

1 Let us speak next of liberality. It seems to be the mean with regard to wealth; for the liberal man is praised not in respect of military matters, nor of those in respect of which the temperate man is praised, nor of judicial decisions, but with regard to the giving and taking of wealth, and especially in respect of giving. Now by "wealth" we mean all the things whose value is measured by money. Further, prodigality and meanness are excesses and defects with regard to wealth; and meanness we always impute to those who care more than they ought for wealth, but we sometimes apply the word

"prodigality" in a complex sense; for we call those men prodigals who are incontinent and spend money on self-indulgence. Hence also they are thought the poorest characters; for they combine more vices than one. Therefore the application of the word to them is not its proper use; for a "prodigal" means a man who has a single evil quality, that of wasting his substance; since a prodigal is one who is being ruined by his own fault, and the wasting of substance is thought to be a sort of ruining of oneself, life being held to depend on possession of substance.

This, then, is the sense in which we take the word "prodigality." Now the things that have a use may be used either well or badly; and riches is a useful thing; and everything is used best by the man who has the virtue concerned with it; riches, therefore, will be used best by the man who has the virtue concerned with wealth; and this is the liberal man. Now spending and giving seem to be the using of wealth; taking and keeping rather the possession of it. Hence it is more the mark of the liberal man to give to the right people than to take from the right sources and not to take from the wrong. For it is more characteristic of virtue to do good than to have good done to one, and more characteristic to do what is noble than not to do what is base; and it is not hard to see that giving implies doing good and doing what is noble, and taking implies having good done to one or not acting basely. And gratitude is felt towards him who gives, not towards him who does not take, and praise also is bestowed more on him. It is easier, also, not to take than to give; for men are apter to give away their own too little than to take what is another's. Givers, too, are called liberal; but those who do not take are not praised for liberality but rather for justice; while those who take are hardly praised at all. And the liberal are almost the most loved of all virtuous characters, since they are useful; and this depends on their giving.

Now virtuous actions are noble and done for the sake of the noble. Therefore the liberal man, like other virtuous men, will give for the sake of the noble, and rightly; for he will give to the right people, the right amounts, and at the right time, with all the other qualifications that accompany right giving; and that too with pleasure or without pain; for that which is virtuous is pleasant or free from pain—least of all will it be painful. But he who gives to the wrong people or not for the sake of the noble but for some other cause, will be called not liberal but by some other name. Nor is he liberal who gives with pain; for he would prefer the wealth to the noble act, and this is not characteristic of a liberal man. But no more will the liberal man take from wrong sources; for such taking is not characteristic of the man who sets no store by wealth. Nor will he be a ready asker; for it is not characteristic of a man who confers benefits to accept them lightly. But he will take from the right sources, e. g. from his own possessions, not as something noble but as a necessity, that he may have something to give. Nor will he neglect his own property, since he wishes by means of this to help others. And he will refrain from giving to anybody and everybody, that he may have something to give to the right people, at the right time, and where it is noble to do so. It is highly characteristic of a liberal man also to go to excess in giving, so that he leaves too little for himself; for it is the nature of a liberal man not to look to himself. The term "liberality" is used relatively to a man's substance; for liberality resides not in the multitude of the gifts but in the state of character of the giver, and this is relative to the giver's substance. There is therefore nothing to prevent the man who gives less from being the more liberal man, if he has less to give. Those are thought to be more liberal who have not made their wealth but inherited it; for in the first place they have no experience of want, and secondly all men are fonder of their own productions, as are parents and poets. It is not easy for the liberal man to be rich, since he is not apt either at taking or at keeping, but at giving away, and does not value wealth for its own sake but as a means to giving. Hence comes the charge that is brought against fortune, that those who deserve riches most get it least. But it is not unreasonable that it should turn out so; for he cannot have wealth, any more than anything else, if he does not take pains to have it. Yet he will not give to the wrong people nor at the wrong time, and so on; for he would no longer be acting in accordance with liberality, and if he spent on these objects he would have nothing to spend on the right objects. For, as has been said, he is liberal who spends according to his substance and on the right objects; and he who exceeds is prodigal. Hence we do not call despots prodigal; for it is thought not easy for them to give and spend beyond the amount of their possessions. Liberality, then, being a mean with regard to giving and taking of wealth, the liberal man will both give and spend the right amounts and on the right objects, alike in small things and in great, and that with pleasure; he will also take the right amounts and from the right sources. For, the virtue being a mean with regard to both, he will do both as he ought; since this sort of taking accompanies proper giving, and that which is not of this sort is contrary to it, and accordingly the giving and taking that accompany each other are present together in the same man, while the contrary kinds evidently are not. But if he happens to spend in a manner contrary to what is right and noble, he will be pained, but moderately and as he ought; for it is the mark of virtue both to be pleased and to be pained at the right objects and in the right way. Further, the liberal man is easy to deal with in money matters; for he can be got the better of, since he sets no store by money, and is more annoyed if he has not spent something that he ought than pained if he has spent something that he ought not, and does not agree with the saying of Simonides.

The prodigal errs in these respects also; for he is neither pleased nor pained at the right things or in the right way; this will be more evident as we go on. We have said that prodigality and meanness are excesses and deficiencies, and in two things, in giving and in taking; for we include spending under giving. Now prodigality exceeds in giving and not taking, and falls short in taking, while meanness falls short in giving, and exceeds in taking, except in small things.

The characteristics of prodigality are not often combined; for it is not easy to give to all if you take from none; private persons soon exhaust their substance with giving, and it is to these that the name of prodigals is applied—though a man of this sort would seem to be in no small degree better than a mean man. For he is easily cured both by age and by poverty, and thus he may move towards the middle state. For he has the characteristics of the liberal man, since he both gives and refrains from taking, though he does neither of these in the right manner or well. Therefore if he were brought to do so by habituation or in some other way, he would be liberal; for he will then give to the right people, and will not take from the wrong sources. This is why he is thought to have not a bad character; it is not the mark of a wicked or ignoble man to go to excess in giving and not taking, but only of a foolish one. The man who is prodigal in this way is thought much better than the mean man both for the aforesaid reasons and because he benefits many while the other benefits no one, not even himself.

But most prodigal people, as has been said, also take from the wrong sources, and are in this respect mean. They become apt to take because they wish to spend and cannot do this easily; for their possessions soon run short. Thus they are forced to provide means from some other source. At the same time, because they care nothing for honour, they take recklessly and from any source; for they have an appetite for giving, and they do not mind how or from what source. Hence also their giving is not liberal; for it is not noble, nor does it aim at nobility, nor is it done in the right way; sometimes they make rich those who should be poor, and will give nothing to people of respectable character, and much to flatterers or those who provide them with some other pleasure. Hence also most of them are self-indulgent; for they spend lightly and waste money on their indulgences, and incline towards pleasures because they do not live with view to what is noble.

The prodigal man, then, turns into what we have described

if he is left untutored, but if he is treated with care he will arrive at the intermediate and right state. But meanness is both incurable (for old age and every disability is thought to make men mean) and more innate in men than prodigality; for most men are fonder of getting money than of giving. It also extends widely, and is multiform, since there seem to be many kinds of meanness.

For it consists in two things, deficiency in giving and excess in taking, and is not found complete in all men but is sometimes divided; some men go to excess in taking, others fall short in giving. Those who are called by such names as "miserly," "close," "stingy," all fall short in giving, but do not covet the possessions of others nor wish to get them. In some this is due to a sort of honesty and avoidance of what is disgraceful (for some seem, or at least profess, to hoard their money for this reason, that they may not some day be forced to do something disgraceful; to this class belong the cheeseparer and every one of the sort; he is so called from his excess of unwillingness to give anything); while others again keep their hands off the property of others from fear, on the ground that it is not easy, if one takes the property of others oneself, to avoid having one's own taken by them; they are therefore content neither to take nor to give.

Others again exceed in respect of taking by taking anything and from any source, e. g. those who ply sordid trades, pimps and all such people, and those who lend small sums and at high rates. For all of these take more than they ought and from wrong sources. What is common to them is evidently sordid love of gain; they all put up with a bad name for the sake of gain, and little gain at that. For those who made great gains but from wrong sources, and not the right gains, e. g. despots when they sack cities and spoil temples, we do not call mean but rather wicked, impious, and unjust. But the gamester and the footpad [and the highwayman] belong to the class of the mean, since they have a sordid love of gain. For it is for gain that both of them ply their craft and endure the disgrace of it.

## 3

Marcus Aurelius, MEDITATIONS (Trans. by George Long)

1. Do the *Meditations* reflect a respect for all of life? Explain.

2. To what extent might Aurelius agree with the modern adage, "Pick yourself up by your own bootstraps"?

3. Identify the highest ideals Aurelius says should be chosen for one's life.

4. What roles does the mind play in the good life, according to Aurelius?

5. From what you have read in the *Meditations*, what role do the gods play in the human condition?

6. How would you describe Aurelius' attitude toward life?

7. What advice do you think Aurelius would give to the freshman class here at Lynchburg College?

Marcus Aurelius (121-180) reigned as Roman Emperor from 167 to 180. He died of an infection while fighting the barbarians who threatened his empire. It was on these campaigns that he wrote his *Meditations*. Marcus Aurelius believed in a system of philosophy called Stoicism; its influence on him is discernable in the *Meditations*.

# THE MEDITATIONS OF MARCUS AURELIUS ANTONINUS

## II

BEGIN the morning by saying to thyself, I shall meet with the busybody, the ungrateful, arrogant, deceitful, envious, unsocial. All these things happen to them by reason of their ignorance of what is good and evil. But I who have seen the nature of the good that it is beautiful and of the bad that it is ugly, and the nature of him who does wrong, that it is akin to me, not [only] of the same blood or seed, but that it participates in [the same] intelligence and [the same] portion of the divinity, I can neither be injured by any of them, for no one can fix on me what is ugly, nor can I be angry with my kinsman, nor hate him. For we are made for co-operation, like feet, like hands, like eyelids, like the rows of the upper and lower teeth. To act against one another then is contrary to nature; and it is acting against one another to be vexed and to turn away.

2. Whatever this is that I am, it is a little flesh and breath, and the ruling part. Throw away thy books; no longer distract thyself: it is not allowed; but as if thou wast now dying, despise the flesh, it is blood and bones and a network, a contexture of nerves, veins and arteries. See the breath also, what kind of a thing it is; air, and not always the same, but every moment sent out and again sucked in. The third then is the ruling part: consider thus: Thou art an old man; no longer let this be a slave, no longer be pulled by the strings like a puppet to unsocial movements, no longer be either dissatisfied with thy present lot, or shrink from the future.

3. All that is from the gods is full of providence. That which is from fortune is not separated from nature or without an interweaving and involution with the things which are ordered by Providence. From thence all things flow; and there is besides necessity, and that which is for the advantage of the whole universe, of which thou art a part. But that is good for every part of nature which the nature of the whole brings, and what serves to maintain this nature. Now the universe is preserved, as by the changes of the elements, so by the changes of things compounded of the elements. Let these principles be enough for thee; let them always be fixed opinions. But cast away the thirst after books, that thou mayest not die murmuring, but cheerfully, truly, and from thy heart thankful to the gods.

4. Remember how long thou hast been putting off these things, and how often thou hast received an opportunity from the gods, and yet dost not use it. Thou must now at last perceive of what universe thou art a part, and of what administrator of the universe thy existence is an efflux, and that a limit of time is fixed for thee, which if thou dost not use for clearing away the clouds from thy mind, it will go and thou wilt go, and it will never return.

5. Every moment think steadily as a Roman and a man to do what thou hast in hand with perfect and simple dignity, and feeling of affection, and freedom, and justice; and to give thyself relief from all other thoughts. And thou wilt give thyself relief, if thou doest every act of thy life as if it were the last, laying aside all carelessness and passionate aversion from the commands of reason, and all hypocrisy, and self-love, and discontent with the portion which has been given to thee. Thou seest how few the things are, the which if a man lays hold of, he is able to live a life which flows in quiet, and is like the existence of the gods; for the gods on their part will require nothing more from him who observes these things.

6. Do wrong to thyself, do wrong to thyself, my soul; but thou wilt no longer have the opportunity of honouring thyself. Every man's life is sufficient. But thine is nearly finished, though thy soul reverences not itself, but places thy felicity in the souls of others.

7. Do the things external which fall upon thee distract thee? Give thyself time to learn something new and good, and cease to be whirled around. But then thou must also avoid being carried about the other way. For those too are triflers who have wearied themselves in life by their activity, and yet have no object to which to direct every movement, and, in a word, all their thoughts.

8. Through not observing what is in the mind of another a man has seldom been seen to be unhappy; but those who do not observe the movements of their own minds must of necessity be unhappy.

9. This thou must always bear in mind, what is the nature of the whole, and what is my nature, and how this is related to that, and what kind of a part it is of what kind of a whole; and that there is no one who hinders thee from always doing and saying the things which are according to the nature of which thou art a part.

10. Theophrastus, in his comparison of bad acts—such a comparison as one would make in accordance with the common notions of mankind—says, like a true philosopher, that the offences which are committed through desire are more blamable than those which are committed through anger. For he who is excited by anger seems to turn away from reason with a certain pain and unconscious contraction; but he who offends through desire, being overpowered by pleasure, seems to be in a manner more intemperate and more womanish

in his offences. Rightly then, and in a way worthy of philosophy, he said that the offence which is committed with pleasure is more blamable than that which is committed with pain; and on the whole the one is more like a person who has been first wronged and through pain is compelled to be angry; but the other is moved by his own impulse to do wrong, being carried toward doing something by desire.

11. Since it is possible that thou mayest depart from life this very moment, regulate every act and thought accordingly. But to go away from among men, if there are gods, is not a thing to be afraid of, for the gods will not involve thee in evil; but if indeed they do not exist, or if they have no concern about human affairs, what is it to me to live in a universe devoid of gods or devoid of providence? But in truth they do exist, and they do care for human things, and they have put all the means in man's power to enable him not to fall into real evils. And as to the rest, if there was anything evil, they would have provided for this also, that it should be altogether in a man's power not to fall into it. Now, that which does not make a man worse, how can it make a man's life worse? But neither through ignorance, nor having the knowledge, but not the power to guard against or correct these things, is it possible that the nature of the universe has overlooked them; nor is it possible that it has made so great a mistake, either through want of power or want of skill, that good and evil should happen indiscriminately to the good and the bad. But death certainly, and life, honour and dishonour, pain and pleasure, all these things equally happen to good men and bad, being things which make us neither better nor worse. Therefore they are neither good nor evil.

12. How quickly all these things disappear, in the universe the bodies themselves, but in time the remembrance of them; what is the nature of all sensible things, and particularly those which attract with the bait of pleasure or terrify by pain, or are noised about by vapoury fame; how worthless, and contemptible, and sordid, and perishable, and dead they are—all this it is the part of the intellectual faculty to observe. To observe, too, who these are whose opinions and voices give reputation; what death is, and the fact that, if a man looks at it in itself, and by the abstractive power of reflection resolves

into their parts all the things which present themselves to the imagination in it, he will then consider it to be nothing else than an operation of nature; and if any one is afraid of an operation of nature he is a child. This, however, is not only an operation of nature, but it is also a thing which conduces to the purposes of nature. To observe, too, how man comes near to the Deity, and by what part of him, and when this part of man is so disposed (vi. 28).

13. Nothing is more wretched than a man who traverses everything in a round, and pries into things beneath the earth, as the poet says, and seeks by conjecture what is in the minds of his neighbours, without perceiving that it is sufficient to attend to the dæmon within him, and to reverence it sincerely. And reverence of the dæmon consists in keeping it pure from passion and thoughtlessness, and dissatisfaction with what comes from gods and men. For the things from the gods merit veneration for their excellence; and the things from men should be dear to us by reason of kinship; and sometimes even, in a manner, they move our pity by reason of men's ignorance of good and bad; this defect being not less than that which deprives us of the power of distinguishing things that are white and black.

14. Though thou shouldest be going to live three thousand years, and as many times ten thousand years, still remember that no man loses any other life than this which he now lives, nor lives any other than this which he now loses. The longest and shortest are thus brought to the same. For the present is the same to all, though that which perishes is not the same; and so that which is lost appears to be a mere moment. For a man cannot lose either the past or the future: for what a man has not, how can any one take this from him? These two things then thou must bear in mind: the one, that all things from eternity are of like forms and come round in a circle, and that it makes no difference whether a man shall see the same things during a hundred years or two hundred, or an infinite time; and the second, that the longest liver and he who will die soonest lose just the same. For the present is the only thing of which a man can be deprived, if it is true that this is the only thing which he has, and that a man cannot lose a thing if he has it not.

15. Remember that all is opinion. For what was said by the Cynic

Monimus is manifest: and manifest too is the use of what was said, if a man receives what may be got out of it as far as it is true.

16. The soul of man does violence to itself, first of all when it becomes an abscess and, as it were, a tumour on the universe, so far as it can. For to be vexed at anything which happens is a separation of ourselves from nature, in some part of which the natures of all other things are contained. In the next place, the soul does violence to itself when it turns away from any man, or even moves towards him with the intention of injuring, such as are the souls of those who are angry. In the third place, the soul does violence to itself when it is overpowered by pleasure or by pain. Fourthly, when it plays a part, and does or says anything insincerely and untruly. Fifthly, when it allows any act of its own and any movement to be without an aim, and does anything thoughtlessly and without considering what it is, it being right that even the smallest things be done with reference to an end; and the end of rational animals is to follow the reason and the law of the most ancient city and polity.

17. Of human life the time is a point, and the substance is in a flux, and the perception dull, and the composition of the whole body subject to putrefaction, and the soul of a whirl, and fortune hard to divine, and fame a thing devoid of judgment. And, to say all in a word, everything which belongs to the body is a stream, and what belongs to the soul is a dream and vapour, and life is a warfare and a stranger's sojourn, and after-fame is oblivion. What, then, is that which is able to conduct a man? One thing, and only one—philosophy. But this consists in keeping the dæmon within a man free from violence and unharmed, superior to pains and pleasures, doing nothing without a purpose, nor yet falsely and with hypocrisy, not feeling the need of another man's doing or not doing anything; and besides, accepting all that happens, and all that is allotted, as coming from thence, wherever it is, from whence he himself came; and, finally, waiting for death with a cheerful mind, as being nothing else than a dissolution of the elements of which every living being is compounded. But if there is no harm to the elements themselves in each continually changing into another, why should a man have any apprehension about the change and dissolution of all the elements? For

it is according to nature, and nothing is evil which is according to nature.

This in Carnuntum.

## III

WE ought to consider not only that our life is daily wasting away and a smaller part of it is left, but another thing also must be taken into the account, that if a man should live longer it is quite uncertain whether the understanding will still continue sufficient for the comprehension of things, and retain the power of contemplation which strives to acquire the knowledge of the divine and the human. For if he shall begin to fall into dotage, perspiration and nutrition and imagination and appetite, and whatever else there is of the kind, will not fail; but the power of making use of ourselves, and filling up the measure of our duty, and clearly separating all appearances, and considering whether a man should now depart from life, and whatever else of the kind absolutely requires a disciplined reason, all this is already extinguished. We must make haste then, not only because we are daily nearer to death, but also because the conception of things and the understanding of them cease first.

2. We ought to observe also that even the things which follow after the things which are produced according to nature contain something pleasing and attractive. For instance, when bread is baked some parts are split at the surface, and these parts which thus open, and have a certain fashion contrary to the purpose of the baker's art, are beautiful in a manner, and in a peculiar way excite a desire for eating. And again, figs, when they are quite ripe, gape open, and in the ripe olives the very circumstance of their being near to rottenness adds a peculiar beauty to the fruit. And the ears of corn bending down, and the lion's eyebrows, and the foam which flows from the mouth of wild boars, and many other things—though they are far from being beautiful, if a man should examine them severally—still, because they are consequent upon the things which are formed by nature, help to adorn them, and they please the mind; so that if a man should have a feeling and deeper insight with respect to the things which are

produced in the universe, there is hardly one of those which follow by way of consequence which will not seem to him to be in a manner disposed so as to give pleasure. And so he will see even the real gaping jaws of wild beasts with no less pleasure than those which painters and sculptors show by imitation; and in an old woman and an old man he will be able to see a certain maturity and comeliness; and the attractive loveliness of young persons he will be able to look on with chaste eyes; and many such things will present themselves, not pleasing to every man, but to him only who has become truly familiar with nature and her works.

3. Hippocrates after curing many diseases himself fell sick and died. The Chaldæi foretold the deaths of many, and then fate caught them too. Alexander, and Pompeius, and Caius Cæsar, after so often completely destroying whole cities, and in battle cutting to pieces many ten thousands of cavalry and infantry, themselves too at last departed from life. Heraclitus, after so many speculations on the conflagration of the universe, was filled with water internally and died smeared all over with mud. And lice destroyed Democritus; and other lice killed Socrates. What means all this? Thou hast embarked, thou hast made the voyage, thou art come to shore; get out. If indeed to another life, there is no want of gods, not even there. But if to a state without sensation, thou wilt cease to be held by pains and pleasures, and to be a slave to the vessel which is as much inferior as that which serves it is superior; for the one is intelligence and deity; the other is earth and corruption.

4. Do not waste the remainder of thy life in thoughts about others, when thou dost not refer thy thoughts to some object of common utility. For thou losest the opportunity of doing something else when thou hast such thoughts as these, What is such a person doing, and why, and what is he saying, and what is he thinking of, and what is he contriving, and whatever else of the kind makes us wander away from the observation of our own ruling power. We ought then to check in the series of our thoughts everything that is without a purpose and useless, but most of all the overcurious feeling and the malignant; and a man should use himself to think of those things only about which if one should suddenly ask, What hast thou now in thy thoughts? with perfect openness thou mightest immediately

answer, This or That; so that from thy words it should be plain that everything in thee is simple and benevolent, and such as befits a social animal, one that cares not for thoughts about pleasure or sensual enjoyments at all, nor has any rivalry or envy and suspicion, or anything else for which thou wouldst blush if thou shouldst say that thou hadst it in thy mind. For the man who is such and no longer delays being among the number of the best, is like a priest and minister of the gods, using too the [deity] which is planted within him, which makes the man uncontaminated by pleasure, unharmed by any pain, untouched by any insult, feeling no wrong, a fighter in the noblest fight, one who cannot be overpowered by any passion, dyed deep with justice, accepting with all his soul everything which happens and is assigned to him as his portion; and not often, nor yet without great necessity and for the general interest, imagining what another says, or does, or thinks. For it is only what belongs to himself that he makes the matter for his activity; and he constantly thinks of that which is allotted to himself out of the sum total of things, and he makes his own acts fair, and he is persuaded that his own portion is good. For the lot which is assigned to each man is carried along with him and carries him along with it. And he remembers also that every rational animal is his kinsman, and that to care for all men is according to man's nature; and a man should hold on to the opinion not of all but of those only who confessedly live according to nature. But as to those who live not so, he always bears in mind what kind of men they are both at home and from home, both by night and by day, and what they are, and with what men they live an impure life. Accordingly, he does not value at all the praise which comes from such men, since they are not even satisfied with themselves.

5. Labour not unwillingly, nor without regard to the common interest, nor without due consideration, nor with distraction; nor let studied ornament set off thy thoughts, and be not either a man of many words, or busy about too many things. And further, let the deity which is in thee be the guardian of a living being, manly and of ripe age, and engaged in matter political, and a Roman, and a ruler, who has taken his post like a man waiting for the signal which summons him from life, and ready to go, having need neither of oath nor of any man's testimony. Be cheerful also, and seek not

external help nor the tranquillity which others give. A man then must stand erect, not be kept erect by others.

6. If thou findest in human life anything better than justice, truth, temperance, fortitude, and, in a word, anything better than thy own mind's self-satisfaction in the things which it enables thee to do according to right reason, and in the condition that is assigned to thee without thy own choice; if, I say, thou seest anything better than this, turn to it with all thy soul, and enjoy that which thou hast found to be the best. But if nothing appears to be better than the deity which is planted in thee, which has subjected to itself all thy appetites, and carefully examines all the impressions, and, as Socrates said, has detached itself from the persuasions of sense, and has submitted itself to the gods, and cares for mankind; if thou findest everything else smaller and of less value than this, give place to nothing else, for if thou dost once diverge and incline to it, thou wilt no longer without distraction be able to give the preference to that good thing which is thy proper possession and thy own; for it is not right that anything of any other kind, such as praise from the many, or power, or enjoyment of pleasure, should come into competition with that which is rationally and politically [or, practically] good. All these things, even though they may seem to adapt themselves [to the better things] in a small degree, obtain the superiority all at once, and carry us away. But do thou, I say, simply and freely choose the better, and hold to it.—But that which is useful is the better.—Well then, if it is only useful to thee as a rational being, keep to it; but if it is only useful to thee as an animal, say so, and maintain thy judgment without arrogance; only take care that thou makest the inquiry by a sure method.

7. Never value anything as profitable to thyself which shall compel thee to break thy promise, to lose thy self-respect, to hate any man, to suspect, to curse, to act the hypocrite, to desire anything which needs walls and curtains: for he who has preferred to everything else his own intelligence and dæmon and the worship of its excellence, acts no tragic part, does not groan, will not need either solitude or much company; and, what is chief of all, he will live without either pursuing or flying from [death]; but whether for a longer or a shorter time he shall have the soul inclosed in the body, he cares not at all; for even if he must depart immediately, he will go as readily as if he

were going to do anything else which can be done with decency and order; taking care of this only all through life, that his thoughts turn not away from anything which belongs to an intelligent animal and a member of a civil community.

8. In the mind of one who is chastened and purified thou wilt find no corrupt matter, nor impurity, nor any sore skinned over. Nor is his life incomplete when fate overtakes him, as one may say of an actor who leaves the stage before ending and finishing the play. Besides, there is in him nothing servile, nor affected, nor too closely bound [to other things], nor yet detached [from other things], nothing worthy of blame, nothing which seeks a hiding-place.

9. Reverence the faculty which produces opinion. On this faculty it entirely depends whether there shall exist in thy ruling part any opinion inconsistent with nature and the constitution of the rational animal. And this faculty promises freedom from hasty judgment, and friendship towards men, and obedience to the gods.

10. Throwing away then all things, hold to these only which are few; and besides bear in mind that every man lives only this present time, which is an indivisible point, and that all the rest of his life is either past or it is uncertain. Short then is the time which every man lives, and small the nook of the earth where he lives; and short too the longest posthumous fame, and even this only continued by a succession of poor human beings, who will very soon die, and who know not even themselves, much less him who died long ago.

11. To the aids which have been mentioned let this one still be added:—Make for thyself a definition or description of the thing which is presented to thee, so as to see distinctly what kind of a thing it is in its substance, in its nudity, in its complete entirety, and tell thyself its proper name, and the names of the things of which it has been compounded, and into which it will be resolved. For nothing is so productive of elevation of mind as to be able to examine methodically and truly every object which is presented to thee in life, and always to look at things so as to see at the same time what kind of universe this is, and what kind of use everything performs in it, and what value everything has with reference to the whole, and what with reference to man, who is a citizen of the highest city, of which all other cities are like families; what each thing is, and of what it

is composed, and how long it is the nature of this thing to endure which now makes an impression on me, and what virtue I have need of with respect to it, such as gentleness, manliness, truth, fidelity, simplicity, contentment, and the rest. Wherefore, on every occasion a man should say: This comes from God; and this is according to the apportionment and spinning of the thread of destiny, and suchlike coincidence and chance; and this is from one of the same stock and a kinsman and partner, one who knows not however what is according to his nature. But I know; for this reason I behave towards him according to the natural law of fellowship with benevolence and justice. At the same time however in things indifferent I attempt to ascertain the value of each.

12. If thou workest at that which is before thee, following right reason seriously, vigorously, calmly, without allowing anything else to distract thee, but keeping thy divine part pure, as if thou shouldst be bound to give it back immediately; if thou holdest to this, expecting nothing, fearing nothing, but satisfied with thy present activity according to nature, and with heroic truth in every word and sound which thou utterest, thou wilt live happy. And there is no man who is able to prevent this.

13. As physicians have always their instruments and knives ready for cases which suddenly require their skill, so do thou have principles ready for the understanding of things divine and human, and doing everything, even the smallest, with a recollection of the bond which unites the divine and human to one another. For neither wilt thou do anything well which pertains to man without at the same time having a reference to things divine; nor the contrary.

14. No longer wander at hazard; for neither wilt thou read thy own memoirs, nor the acts of the ancient Romans and Hellenes, and the selections from books which thou wast reserving for thy old age. Hasten then to the end which thou hast before thee, and, throwing away idle hopes, come to thy own aid, if thou carest at all for thyself, while it is in thy power.

15. They know not how many things are signified by the words stealing, sowing, buying, keeping quiet, seeing what ought to be done; for this is not effected by the eyes, but by another kind of vision.

16. Body, soul, intelligence: to the body belong sensations, to the soul appetites, to the intelligence principles. To receive the impressions of forms by means of appearances belongs even to animals; to be pulled by the strings of desire belongs both to wild beasts and to men who have made themselves into women, and to a Phalaris and a Nero: and to have the intelligence that guides to the things which appear suitable belongs also to those who do not believe in the gods, and who betray their country, and do their impure deeds when they have shut the doors. If then everything else is common to all that I have mentioned, there remains that which is peculiar to the good man, to be pleased and content with what happens, and with the thread which is spun for him; and not to defile the divinity which is planted in his breast, nor disturb it by a crowd of images, but to preserve it tranquil, following it obediently as a god, neither saying anything contrary to the truth, nor doing anything contrary to justice. And if all men refuse to believe that he lives a simple, modest, and contented life, he is neither angry with any of them, nor does he deviate from the way which leads to the end of life, to which a man ought to come pure, tranquil, ready to depart, and without any compulsion perfectly reconciled to his lot.

## IV

THAT which rules within, when it is according to nature, is so affected with respect to the events which happen, that it always easily adapts itself to that which is possible and is presented to it. For it requires no definite material, but it moves towards its purpose, under certain conditions however; and it makes a material for itself out of that which opposes it, as fire lays hold of what falls into it, by which a small light would have been extinguished: but when the fire is strong, it soon appropriates to itself the matter which is heaped on it, and consumes it, and rises higher by means of this very material.

2. Let no act be done without a purpose, nor otherwise than according to the perfect principles of art.

3. Men seek retreats for themselves, houses in the country, seashores, and mountains; and thou too art wont to desire such things

very much. But this is altogether a mark of the most common sort of men, for it is in thy power whenever thou shalt choose to retire into thyself. For nowhere, either with more quiet or more freedom from trouble, does a man retire than into his own soul, particularly when he has within him such thoughts that by looking into them he is immediately in perfect tranquillity; and I affirm that tranquillity is nothing else than the good ordering of the mind. Constantly then give to thyself this retreat, and renew thyself; and let thy principles be brief and fundamental, which, as soon as thou shalt recur to them, will be sufficient to cleanse the soul completely, and to send thee back free from all discontent with the things to which thou returnest. For with what art thou discontented? With the badness of men? Recall to thy mind this conclusion, that rational animals exist for one another, and that to endure is a part of justice, and that men do wrong involuntarily; and consider how many already, after mutual enmity, suspicion, hatred, and fighting, have been stretched dead, reduced to ashes; and be quiet at last.—But perhaps thou art dissatisfied with that which is assigned to thee out of the universe.—Recall to thy recollection this alternative; either there is providence or atoms [fortuitous concurrence of things]; or remember the arguments by which it has been proved that the world is a kind of political community [and be quiet at last].—But perhaps corporeal things will still fasten upon thee.—Consider then further that the mind mingles not with the breath, whether moving gently or violently, when it has once drawn itself apart and discovered its own power, and think also of all that thou hast heard and assented to about pain and pleasure [and be quiet at last].—But perhaps the desire of the thing called fame will torment thee.—See how soon everything is forgotten, and look at the chaos of infinite time on each side of [the present], and the emptiness of applause, and the changeableness and want of judgment in those who pretend to give praise, and the narrowness of the space within which it is circumscribed [and be quiet at last]. For the whole earth is a point, and how small a nook in it is this thy dwelling, and how few are there in it, and what kind of people are they who will praise thee.

This then remains: Remember to retire into this little territory of thy own, and, above all, do not distract or strain thyself, but be free, and look at things as a man, as a human being, as a citizen, as a mortal. But among the things readiest to thy hand to which thou shalt turn, let there be these, which are two. One is that things do not touch the soul, for they are external and remain immovable; but our perturbations come only from the opinion which is within. The other is that all these things, which thou seest, change immediately and will no longer be; and constantly bear in mind how many of these changes thou hast already witnessed. The universe is transformation: life is opinion.

4. If our intellectual part is common, the reason also, in respect of which we are rational beings, is common: if this is so, common also is the reason which commands us what to do, and what not to do; if this is so, there is a common law also; if this is so, we are fellow-citizens; if this is so, we are members of some political community; if this is so, the world is in a manner a state. For of what other common political community will any one say that the whole human race are members? And from thence, from this common political community comes also our very intellectual faculty and reasoning faculty and our capacity for law; or whence do they come? For as my earthly part is a portion given to me from certain earth, and that which is watery from another element, and that which is hot and fiery from some peculiar source (for nothing comes out of that which is nothing, as nothing also returns to non-existence), so also the intellectual part comes from some source.

5. Death is such as generation is, a mystery of nature; a composition out of the same elements, and a decomposition into the same; and altogether not a thing of which any man should be ashamed, for it is not contrary to [the nature of] a reasonable animal, and not contrary to the reason of our constitution.

6. It is natural that these things should be done by such persons, it is a matter of necessity; and if a man will not have it so, he will not allow the fig-tree to have juice. But by all means bear this in mind, that within a very short time both thou and he will be dead; and soon not even your names will be left behind.

7. Take away thy opinion, and then there is taken away the complaint, "I have been harmed." Take away the complaint, "I have been harmed," and the harm is taken away.

8. That which does not make a man worse than he was, also does not make his life worse, nor does it harm him either from without or from within.

9. The nature of that which is [universally] useful has been compelled to do this.

10. Consider that everything which happens, happens justly, and if thou observest carefully, thou wilt find it to be so. I do not say only with respect to the continuity of the series of things, but with respect to what is just, and as if it were done by one who assigns to each thing its value. Observe then as thou hast begun; and whatever thou doest, do it in conjunction with this, the being good, and in the sense in which a man is properly understood to be good. Keep to this in every action.

11. Do not have such an opinion of things as he has who does thee wrong, or such as he wishes thee to have, but look at them as they are in truth.

12. A man should always have these two rules in readiness; the one, to do only whatever the reason of the ruling and legislating faculty may suggest for the use of men; the other, to change thy opinion, if there is any one at hand who sets thee right and moves thee from any opinion. But this change of opinion must proceed only from a certain persuasion, as of what is just or of common advantage, and the like, not because it appears pleasant or brings reputation.

13. Hast thou reason? I have.—Why then dost not thou use it? For if this does its own work, what else dost thou wish?

14. Thou hast existed as a part. Thou shalt disappear in that which produced thee; but rather thou shalt be received back into its seminal principle by transmutation.

15. Many grains of frankincense on the same altar: one falls before, another falls after; but it makes no difference.

16. Within ten days thou wilt seem a god to those to whom thou art now a beast and an ape, if thou wilt return to thy principles and the worship of reason.

17. Do not act as if thou wert going to live ten thousand years. Death hangs over thee. While thou livest, while it is in thy power, be good.

18. How much trouble he avoids who does not look to see what

his neighbour says or does or thinks, but only to what he does himself, that it may be just and pure; or, as Agathon says, look not round at the depraved morals of others, but run straight along the line without deviating from it.

19. He who has a vehement desire for posthumous fame does not consider that every one of those who remember him will himself also die very soon; then again also they who have succeeded them, until the whole remembrance shall have been extinguished as it is transmitted through men who foolishly admire and perish. But suppose that those who will remember are even immortal, and that the remembrance will be immortal, what then is this to thee? And I say not, what is it to the dead? but, what is it to the living? What is praise, except indeed so far as it has a certain utility? For thou now rejectest unseasonably the gift of nature, clinging to something else. . . .

20. Everything which is in any way beautiful is beautiful in itself, and terminates in itself, not having praise as part of itself. Neither worse then nor better is a thing made by being praised. I affirm this also of the things which are called beautiful by the vulgar; for example, material things and works of art. That which is really beautiful has no need of anything; not more than law, not more than truth, not more than benevolence or modesty. Which of these things is beautiful because it is praised, or spoiled by being blamed? Is such a thing as an emerald made worse than it was, if it is not praised? or gold, ivory, purple, a lyre, a little knife, a flower, a shrub?

21. If souls continue to exist, how does the air contain them from eternity?—But how does the earth contain the bodies of those who have been buried from time so remote? For as here the mutation of these bodies after a certain continuance, whatever it may be, and their dissolution make room for other dead bodies; so the souls which are removed into the air after subsisting for some time are transmuted and diffused, and assume a fiery nature by being received into the seminal intelligence of the universe, and in this way make room for the fresh souls which come to dwell there. And this is the answer which a man might give on the hypothesis of souls continuing to exist. But we must not only think of the number of

bodies which are thus buried, but also of the number of animals which are daily eaten by us and the other animals. For what a number is consumed, and thus in a manner buried in the bodies of those who feed on them! And nevertheless this earth receives them by reason of the changes [of these bodies] into blood, and the transformations into the aërial or the fiery element.

What is the investigation into the truth in this matter? The division into that which is material and that which is the cause of form [the formal] (vii. 29).

22. Do not be whirled about, but in every movement have respect to justice, and on the occasion of every impression maintain the faculty of comprehension [or understanding].

23. Everything harmonizes with me which is harmonious to thee, O Universe. Nothing for me is too early nor too late, which is in due time for thee. Everything is fruit to me which thy seasons bring, O Nature: from thee are all things, in thee are all things, to thee all things return. The poet says, Dear city of Cecrops; and wilt not thou say, Dear city of Zeus?

24. Occupy thyself with few things, says the philosopher, if thou wouldst be tranquil.—But consider if it would not be better to say, Do what is necessary, and whatever the reason of the animal which is naturally social requires, and as it requires. For this brings not only the tranquillity which comes from doing well, but also that which comes from doing few things. For the greatest part of what we say and do being unnecessary, if a man takes this away, he will have more leisure and less uneasiness. Accordingly on every occasion a man should ask himself, Is this one of the unnecessary things? Now a man should take away not only unnecessary acts but also unnecessary thoughts, for thus superfluous acts will not follow after.

25. Try how the life of the good man suits thee, the life of him who is satisfied with his portion out of the whole, and satisfied with his own just acts and benevolent disposition.

26. Hast thou seen those things? Look also at these. Do not disturb thyself. Make thyself all simplicity. Does any one do wrong? It is to himself that he does the wrong. Has anything happened to thee? Well, out of the universe from the beginning everything

which happens has been apportioned and spun out to thee. In a word, thy life is short. Thou must turn to profit the present by the aid of reason and justice. Be sober in thy relaxation.

27. Either it is a well arranged universe or a chaos huddled together, but still a universe. But can a certain order subsist in thee, and disorder in the All? And this, too, when all things are so separated and diffused and sympathetic.

28. A black character, a womanish character, a stubborn character, bestial, childish, animal, stupid, counterfeit, scurrilous, fraudulent, tyrannical.

29. If he is a stranger to the universe who does not know what is in it, no less is he a stranger who does not know what is going on in it. He is a runaway, who flies from social reason; he is blind, who shuts the eyes of the understanding; he is poor, who has need of another, and has not from himself all things which are useful for life. He is an abscess on the universe, who withdraws and separates himself from the reason of our common nature through being displeased with the things which happen, for the same nature produces this, and has produced thee too; he is a piece rent asunder from the state, who tears his own soul from that of reasonable animals, which is one.

30. The one is a philosopher without a tunic, and the other without a book: here is another half naked: Bread I have not, he says, and I abide by reason. And I do not get the means of living out of my learning, and I abide [by my reason].

31. Love the art, poor as it may be, which thou hast learned, and be content with it; and pass through the rest of life like one who has intrusted to the gods with his whole soul all that he has, making thyself neither the tyrant nor the slave of any man.

32. Consider, for example, the times of Vespasian. Thou wilt see all these things, people marrying, bringing up children, sick, dying, warring, feasting, trafficking, cultivating the ground, flattering, obstinately arrogant, suspecting, plotting, wishing for some to die, grumbling about the present, loving, heaping up treasure, desiring consulship, kingly power. Well, then, that life of these people no longer exists at all. Again, remove to the times of Trajan. Again, all is the same. Their life, too, is gone. In like manner view also

the other epochs of time and of whole nations, and see how many after great efforts soon fell and were resolved into the elements. But chiefly thou shouldst think of those whom thou hast thyself known distracting themselves about idle things, neglecting to do what was in accordance with their proper constitution, and to hold firmly to this and to be content with it. And herein it is necessary to remember that the attention given to everything has its proper value and proportion. For thus thou wilt not be dissatisfied, if thou appliest thyself to smaller matters no further than is fit.

33. The words which were formerly familiar are now antiquated; so also the names of those who were famed of old, are now in a manner antiquated: Camillus, Cæso, Volesus, Leonnatus, and a little after also Scipio and Cato, then Augustus, then also Hadrianus and Antoninus. For all things soon pass away and become a mere tale, and complete oblivion soon buries them. And I say this of those who have shone in a wondrous way. For the rest, as soon as they have breathed out their breath, they are gone, and no man speaks of them. And, to conclude the matter, what is even an eternal remembrance? A mere nothing. What, then, is that about which we ought to employ our serious pains? This one thing, thoughts just, and acts social, and words which never lie, and a disposition which gladly accepts all that happens, as necessary, as usual, as flowing from a principle and source of the same kind.

34. Willingly give thyself up to Clotho [one of the fates], allowing her to spin thy thread into whatever things she pleases.

35. Everything is only for a day, both that which remembers and that which is remembered.

36. Observe constantly that all things take place by change, and accustom thyself to consider that the nature of the Universe loves nothing so much as to change the things which are and to make new things like them. For everything that exists is in a manner the seed of that which will be. But thou art thinking only of seeds which are cast into the earth or into a womb: but this is a very vulgar notion.

37. Thou wilt soon die, and thou art not yet simple, nor free from perturbations, nor without suspicion of being hurt by external things, nor kindly disposed towards all; nor dost thou yet place wisdom only in acting justly.

38. Examine men's ruling principles, even those of the wise, what kind of things they avoid, and what kind they pursue.

39. What is evil to thee does not subsist in the ruling principle of another; nor yet in any turning and mutation of thy corporeal covering. Where is it then? It is in that part of thee in which subsists the power of forming opinions about evils. Let this power then not form [such] opinions, and all is well. And if that which is nearest to it, the poor body, is cut, burnt, filled with matter and rottenness, nevertheless let the part which forms opinions about these things be quiet, that is, let it judge that nothing is either bad or good which can happen equally to the bad man and the good. For that which happens equally to him who lives contrary to nature and to him who lives according to nature, is neither according to nature nor contrary to nature.

40. Constantly regard the universe as one living being, having one substance and one soul; and observe how all things have reference to one perception, the perception of this one living being; and how all things act with one movement; and how all things are the cooperating causes of all things which exist; observe too the continuous spinning of the thread and the contexture of the web.

41. Thou art a little soul bearing about a corpse, as Epictetus used to say (I. c. 19).

42. It is no evil for things to undergo change, and no good for things to subsist in consequence of change.

43. Time is like a river made up of the events which happen, and a violent stream; for as soon as a thing has been seen, it is carried away, and another comes in its place, and this will be carried away too.

44. Everything which happens is as familiar and well known as the rose in spring and the fruit in summer; for such is disease, and death, and calumny, and treachery, and whatever else delights fools or vexes them.

45. In the series of things those which follow are always aptly fitted to those which have gone before; for this series is not like a mere enumeration of disjointed things, which has only a necessary sequence, but it is a rational connection: and as all existing things are arranged together harmoniously, so the things which come into

existence exhibit no mere succession, but a certain wonderful relationship (vi. 38; vii. 9; vii. 75, note).

46. Always remember the saying of Heraclitus, that the death of earth is to become water, and the death of water is to become air, and the death of air is to become fire, and reversely. And think too of him who forgets whither the way leads, and that men quarrel with that with which they are most constantly in communion, the reason which governs the universe; and the things which they daily meet with seem to them strange: and consider that we ought not to act and speak as if we were asleep, for even in sleep we seem to act and speak; and that we ought not, like children who learn from their parents, simply to act and speak as we have been taught.

47. If any god told thee that thou shalt die to-morrow, or certainly on the day after to-morrow, thou wouldst not care much whether it was on the third day or on the morrow, unless thou wast in the highest degree mean-spirited—for how small is the difference?—so think it no great thing to die after as many years as thou canst name rather than to-morrow.

48. Think continually how many physicians are dead after often contracting their eyebrows over the sick; and how many astrologers after predicting with great pretensions the deaths of others; and how many philosophers after endless discourses on death or immortality; how many heroes after killing thousands; and how many tyrants who have used their power over men's lives with terrible insolence as if they were immortal; and how many cities are entirely dead, so to speak, Helice and Pompeii and Herculaneum, and others innumerable. Add to the reckoning all whom thou hast known, one after another. One man after burying another has been laid out dead, and another buries him; and all this in a short time. To conclude, always observe how ephemeral and worthless human things are, and what was yesterday a little mucus, to-morrow will be a mummy or ashes. Pass then through this little space of time conformably to nature, and end thy journey in content, just as an olive falls off when it is ripe, blessing nature who produced it, and thanking the tree on which it grew.

49. Be like the promontory against which the waves continually break, but it stands firm and tames the fury of the water around it.

Unhappy am I, because this has happened to me.—Not so, but Happy am I, though this has happened to me, because I continue free from pain, neither crushed by the present nor fearing the future. For such a thing as this might have happened to every man; but every man would not have continued free from pain on such an occasion. Why, then, is that rather a misfortune than this a good fortune? And dost thou in all cases call that a man's misfortune, which is not a deviation from man's nature? And does a thing seem to thee to be a deviation from man's nature, when it is not contrary to the will of man's nature? Well, thou knowest the will of nature. Will then this which has happened prevent thee from being just, magnanimous, temperate, prudent, secure against inconsiderate opinions and falsehood; will it prevent thee from having modesty, freedom, and everything else, by the presence of which man's nature obtains all that is its own? Remember, too, on every occasion which leads thee to vexation to apply this principle: not that this is a misfortune, but that to bear it nobly is good fortune.

50. It is a vulgar but still a useful help towards contempt of death, to pass in review those who have tenaciously stuck to life. What more then have they gained than those who have died early? Certainly they lie in their tombs somewhere at last, Cadicianus, Fabius, Julianus, Lepidus, or any one else like them, who have carried out many to be buried, and then were carried out themselves. Altogether the interval is small [between birth and death]; and consider with how much trouble, and in company with what sort of people, and in what a feeble body this interval is laboriously passed. Do not then consider life a thing of any value. For look to the immensity of time behind thee, and to the time which is before thee, another boundless space. In this infinity then what is the difference between him who lives three days and him who lives three generations?

51. Always run to the short way; and the short way is the natural: accordingly say and do everything in conformity with the soundest reason. For such a purpose frees a man from trouble, and warfare, and all artifice and ostentatious display.

## V

IN THE morning when thou risest unwillingly, let this thought be present—I am rising to the work of a human being. Why then am I dissatisfied if I am going to do the things for which I exist and for which I was brought into the world? Or have I been made for this, to lie in the bedclothes and keep myself warm?—But this is more pleasant.—Dost thou exist then to take thy pleasure, and not at all for action or exertion? Dost thou not see the little plants, the little birds, the ants, the spiders, the bees working together to put in order their several parts of the universe? And art thou unwilling to do the work of a human being, and dost thou not make haste to do that which is according to thy nature?—But it is necessary to take rest also.—It is necessary: however nature has fixed bounds to this too: she has fixed bounds both to eating and drinking, and yet thou goest beyond these bounds, beyond what is sufficient; yet in thy acts it is not so, but thou stoppest short of what thou canst do. So thou lovest not thyself, for if thou didst, thou wouldst love thy nature and her will. But those who love their several arts exhaust themselves in working at them unwashed and without food; but thou valuest thy own nature less than the turner values the turning art, or the dancer the dancing art, or the lover of money values his money, or the vainglorious man his little glory. And such men, when they have a violent affection to a thing, choose neither to eat nor to sleep rather than to perfect the things which they care for. But are the acts which concern society more vile in thy eyes and less worthy of thy labour?

2. How easy it is to repel and to wipe away every impression which is troublesome or unsuitable, and immediately to be in all tranquillity.

3. Judge every word and deed which are according to nature to be fit for thee; and be not diverted by the blame which follows from any people, nor by their words, but if a thing is good to be done or said, do not consider it unworthy of thee. For those persons have their peculiar leading principle and follow their peculiar movement; which things do not thou regard, but go straight on, following thy own nature and the common nature; and the way of both is one.

4. I go through the things which happen according to nature until I shall fall and rest, breathing out my breath into that element out of which I daily draw it in, and falling upon that earth out of which my father collected the seed, and my mother the blood, and my nurse the milk; out of which during so many years I have been supplied with food and drink; which bears me when I tread on it and abuse it for so many purposes.

5. Thou sayest, men cannot admire the sharpness of thy wits.—Be it so; but there are many other things of which thou canst not say, I am not formed for them by nature. Show those qualities then which are altogether in thy power: sincerity, gravity, endurance of labour, aversion to pleasure, contentment with thy portion and with few things, benevolence, frankness, no love of superfluity, freedom from trifling magnanimity. Dost thou not see how many qualities thou art immediately able to exhibit, in which there is no excuse of natural incapacity and unfitness, and yet thou still remainest voluntarily below the mark? or art thou compelled through being defectively furnished by nature to murmur, and to be stingy, and to flatter, and to find fault with thy poor body, and to try to please men, and to make great display, and to be restless in thy mind? No, by the gods: but thou mightest have been delivered from these things long ago. Only if in truth thou canst be charged with being rather slow and dull of comprehension, thou must exert thyself about this also, not neglecting it nor yet taking pleasure in thy dullness.

6. One man, when he has done a service to another, is ready to set it down to his account as a favour conferred. Another is not ready to do this, but still in his own mind he thinks of the man as his debtor, and he knows what he has done. A third in a manner does not even know what he has done, but he is like a vine which has produced grapes, and seeks for nothing more after it has once produced its proper fruit. As a horse when he has run, a dog when he has tracked the game, a bee when it has made the honey, so a man when he has done a good act, does not call out for others to come and see, but he goes on to another act, as a vine goes on to produce again the grapes in season.—Must a man then be one of these, who in a manner act thus without observing it?—Yes.—But this very thing is necessary, the observation of what a man is doing; for it may be

said, it is characteristic of the social animal to perceive that he is working in a social manner, and indeed to wish that his social partner also should perceive it.—It is true what thou sayest, but thou dost not rightly understand what is now said; and for this reason thou wilt become one of those of whom I spoke before, for even they are misled by a certain show of reason. But if thou wilt choose to understand the meaning of what is said, do not fear that for this reason thou wilt omit any social act.

7. A prayer of the Athenians: Rain, rain, O dear Zeus, down on the plowed fields of the Athenians and on the plains.—In truth we ought not to pray at all, or we ought to pray in this simple and noble fashion.

8. Just as we must understand when it is said, That Æsculapius prescribed to this man horse-exercise, or bathing in cold water, or going without shoes, so we must understand it when it is said, That the nature of the universe prescribed to this man disease or mutilation or loss or anything else of the kind. For in the first case prescribed means something like this: he prescribed this for this man as a thing adapted to procure health; and in the second case it means, That which happens to [or suits] every man is fixed in a manner for him suitably to his destiny. For this is what we mean when we say that things are suitable to us, as the workmen say of squared stones in walls or the pyramids, that they are suitable, when they fit them to one another in some kind of connection. For there is altogether one fitness [harmony]. And as the universe is made up out of all bodies to be such a body as it is, so out of all existing causes necessity [destiny] is made up to be such a cause as it is. And even those who are completely ignorant understand what I mean, for they say, It [necessity, destiny] brought this to such a person.—This then was brought and this was prescribed to him. Let us then receive these things, as well as those which Æsculapius prescribes. Many, as a matter of course, even among his prescriptions, are disagreeable, but we accept them in the hope of health. Let the perfecting and accomplishment of the things, which the common nature judges to be good, be judged by thee to be of the same kind as thy health. And so accept everything which happens,

even if it seem disagreeable, because it leads to this, to the health of the universe and to the prosperity and felicity of Zeus [the universe]. For he would not have brought on any man what he has brought, if it were not useful for the whole. Neither does the nature of anything, whatever it may be, cause anything which is not suitable to that which is directed by it. For two reasons, then, it is right to be content with that which happens to thee; the one, because it was done for thee and prescribed for thee, and in a manner had reference to thee, originally from the most ancient causes spun with thy destiny; and the other, because even that which comes severally to every man is to the power which administers the universe a cause of felicity and perfection, nay even of its very continuance. For the integrity of the whole is mutilated, if thou cuttest off anything whatever from the conjunction and the continuity either of the parts or of the causes. And thou dost cut off, as far as it is in thy power, when thou art dissatisfied, and in a manner triest to put anything out of the way.

9. Be not disgusted, nor discouraged, nor dissatisfied, if thou dost not succeed in doing everything according to right principles; but when thou hast failed, return back again, and be content if the greater part of what thou doest is consistent with man's nature, and love this to which thou returnest; and do not return to philosophy as if she were a master, but act like those who have sore eyes and apply a bit of sponge and egg, or as another applies a plaster, or drenching with water. For thus thou wilt not fail to obey reason and thou wilt repose in it. And remember that philosophy requires only the things which thy nature requires; but thou wouldst have something else which is not according to nature. It may be objected, Why, what is more agreeable than this [which I am doing]? But is not this the very reason why pleasure deceives us? And consider if magnanimity, freedom, simplicity, equanimity, piety are not more agreeable. For what is more agreeable than wisdom itself, when thou thinkest of the security and the happy course of all things which depend on the faculty of understanding and knowledge?

10. Things are in such a kind of envelopment that they have seemed to philosophers, not a few nor those common philosophers,

altogether unintelligible; nay even to the Stoics themselves they seem difficult to understand. And all our assent is changeable; for where is the man who never changes? Carry thy thoughts then to the objects themselves, and consider how short-lived they are and worthless, and that they may be in the possession of a filthy wretch or a whore or a robber. Then turn to the morals of those who live with thee, and it is hardly possible to endure even the most agreeable of them, to say nothing of a man being hardly able to endure himself. In such darkness, then, and dirt, and in so constant a flux, both of substance and of time, and of motion, and of things moved, what there is worth being highly prized, or even an object of serious pursuit, I cannot imagine. But on the contrary it is a man's duty to comfort himself, and to wait for the natural dissolution and not to be vexed at the delay, but to rest in these principles only: the one, that nothing will happen to me which is not conformable to the nature of the universe; and the other, that it is in my power never to act contrary to my god and dæmon: for there is no man who will compel me to this.

11. About what am I now employing my own soul? On every occasion I must ask myself this question, and inquire, what have I now in this part of me which they call the ruling principle? and whose soul have I now? that of a child, or of a young man, or of a feeble woman, or of a tyrant, or of a domestic animal, or of a wild beast?

12. What kind of things those are which appear good to the many, we may learn even from this. For if any man should conceive certain things as being really good, such as prudence, temperance, justice, fortitude, he would not after having first conceived these endure to listen to anything which should not be in harmony with what is really good. But if a man has first conceived as good the things which appear to the many to be good, he will listen and readily receive as very applicable that which was said by the comic writer. Thus even the many perceive the difference. For were it not so, this saying would not offend and would not be rejected [in the first case], while we receive it when it is said of wealth, and of the means which further luxury and fame, as said fitly and wittily. Go on then and ask if we should value and think those things to be good, to which

after their first conception in the mind the words of the comic writer might be aptly applied—that he who has them, through pure abundance has not a place to ease himself in.

13. I am composed of the formal and the material; and neither of them will perish into non-existence, as neither of them came into existence out of non-existence. Every part of me then will be reduced by change into some part of the universe, and that again will change into another part of the universe, and so on forever. And by consequence of such a change I too exist, and those who begot me, and so on forever in the other direction. For nothing hinders us from saying so, even if the universe is administered according to definite periods [of revolution].

14. Reason and the reasoning art [philosophy] are powers which are sufficient for themselves and for their own works. They move then from a first principle which is their own, and they make their way to the end which is proposed to them; and this is the reason why such acts are named Catorthóseis or right acts, which word signifies that they proceed by the right road.

15. None of these things ought to be called a man's which do not belong to a man, as man. They are not required of a man, nor does man's nature promise them, nor are they the means of man's nature attaining its end. Neither then does the end of man lie in these things, nor yet that which aids to the accomplishment of this end, and that which aids toward this end is that which is good. Besides, if any of these things did belong to man, it would not be right for a man to despise them and to set himself against them; nor would a man be worthy of praise who showed that he did not want these things, nor would he who stinted himself in any of them be good, if indeed these things were good. But now the more of these things a man deprives himself of, or of other things like them, or even when he is deprived of any of them, the more patiently he endures the loss, just in the same degree he is a better man.

16. Such as are thy habitual thoughts, such also will be the character of thy mind; for the soul is dyed by the thoughts. Dye it then with a continuous series of such thoughts as these: for instance, that where a man can live, there he can also live well. But he must live in a palace—well then, he can also live well in a palace. And again,

consider that for whatever purpose each thing has been constituted, for this it has been constituted, and toward this it is carried; and its end is in that toward which it is carried; and where the end is, there also is the advantage and the good of each thing. Now the good for the reasonable animal is society; for that we are made for society has been shown above. Is it not plain that the inferior exist for the sake of the superior? but the things which have life are superior to those which have not life, and of those which have life the superior are those which have reason.

17. To seek what is impossible is madness: and it is impossible that the bad should not do something of this kind.

18. Nothing happens to any man which he is not formed by nature to bear. The same things happen to another, and either because he does not see that they have happened or because he would show a great spirit he is firm and remains unharmed. It is a shame then that ignorance and conceit should be stronger than wisdom.

19. Things themselves touch not the soul, not in the least degree; nor have they admission to the soul, nor can they turn or move the soul: but the soul turns and moves itself alone, and whatever judgments it may think proper to make, such it makes for itself the things which present themselves to it.

20. In one respect man is the nearest thing to me, so far as I must do good to men and endure them. But so far as some men make themselves obstacles to my proper acts, man becomes to me one of the things which are indifferent, no less than the sun or wind or a wild beast. Now it is true that these may impede my action, but they are no impediments to my affects and disposition, which have the power of acting conditionally and changing: for the mind converts and changes every hindrance to its activity into an aid; and so that which is a hindrance is made a furtherance to an act; and that which is an obstacle on the road helps us on this road.

21. Reverence that which is best in the universe; and this is that which makes use of all things and directs all things. And in like manner also reverence that which is best in thyself; and this is of the same kind as that. For in thyself also, that which makes use of everything else, is this, and thy life is directed by this.

22. That which does no harm to the state, does no harm to the

citizen. In the case of every appearance of harm apply this rule: if the state is not harmed by this, neither am I harmed. But if the state is harmed, thou must not be angry with him who does harm to the state. Show him where his error is.

23. Often think of the rapidity with which things pass by and disappear, both the things which are and the things which are produced. For substance is like a river in a continual flow, and the activities of things are in constant change, and the causes work in infinite varieties; and there is hardly anything which stands still. And consider this which is near to thee, this boundless abyss of the past and of the future in which all things disappear. How then is he not a fool who is puffed up with such things or plagued about them or makes himself miserable? for they vex him only for a time, and a short time.

24. Think of the universal substance, of which thou hast a very small portion; and of universal time, of which a short and indivisible interval has been assigned to thee; and of that which is fixed by destiny, and how small a part of it thou art.

25. Does another do me wrong? Let him look to it. He has his own disposition, his own activity. I now have what the universal nature wills me to have; and I do what my nature now wills me to do.

26. Let the part of thy soul which leads and governs be undisturbed by the movements in the flesh, whether of pleasure or of pain; and let it not unite with them, but let it circumscribe itself and limit those affects to their parts. But when these affects rise up to the mind by virtue of that other sympathy that naturally exists in a body which is all one, then thou must not strive to resist the sensation, for it is natural: but let not the ruling part of itself add to the sensation the opinion that it is either good or bad.

27. Live with the gods. And he does live with the gods who constantly shows to them that his own soul is satisfied with that which is assigned to him, and that it does all that the dæmon wishes, which Zeus hath given to every man for his guardian and guide, a portion of himself. And this is every man's understanding and reason.

28. Art thou angry with him whose arm-pits stink? art thou angry with him whose mouth smells foul? What good will this

anger do thee? He has such a mouth, he has such arm-pits: it is necessary that such an emanation must come from such things—but the man has reason, it will be said, and he is able, if he takes pains, to discover wherein he offends—I wish thee well of thy discovery. Well then, and thou hast reason: by thy rational faculty stir up his rational faculty; show him his error, admonish him. For if he listens, thou wilt cure him, and there is no need of anger. [Neither tragic actor nor whore.[1]]

29. As thou intendest to live when thou are gone out, . . . so it is in thy power to live here. But if men do not permit thee, then get away out of life, yet so as if thou wert suffering no harm. The house is smoky, and I quit it. Why dost thou think that this is any trouble? But so long as nothing of the kind drives me out, I remain, am free, and no man shall hinder me from doing what I choose; and I choose to do what is according to the nature of the rational and social animal.

30. The intelligence of the universe is social. Accordingly it has made the inferior things for the sake of the superior, and it has fitted the superior to one another. Thou seest how it has subordinated, co-ordinated and assigned to everything its proper portion, and has brought together into concord with one another the things which are the best.

31. How hast thou behaved hitherto to the gods, thy parents, brethren, children, teachers, to those who looked after thy infancy, to thy friends, kinsfolk, to thy slaves? Consider if thou hast hitherto behaved to all in such a way that this may be said of thee:

Never has wronged a man in deed or word.

And call to recollection both how many things thou hast passed through, and how many things thou hast been able to endure: and that the history of thy life is now complete, and thy service is ended: and how many beautiful things thou hast seen: and how many pleasures and pains thou hast despised; and how many things called honourable thou hast spurned; and to how many ill-minded folks thou hast shown a kind disposition.

32. Why do unskilled and ignorant souls disturb him who has skill and knowledge? What soul then has skill and knowledge?

[1]This sentence is imperfect or corrupt, or both.

That which knows beginning and end, and knows the reason which pervades all substance and through all time by fixed periods [revolutions] administers the universe.

33. Soon, very soon, thou wilt be ashes, or a skeleton, and either a name or not even a name; but name is sound and echo, and the things which are much valued in life are empty and rotten and trifling, and [like] little dogs biting one another, and little children quarrelling, laughing, and then straightway weeping. But fidelity and modesty and justice and truth are fled

> Up to Olympus from the wide-spread earth.
> *Hesiod, Works, etc.*, v. 197.

What then is there which still detains thee here? if the objects of sense are easily changed and never stand still, and the organs of perception are dull and easily receive false impressions; and the poor soul itself is an exhalation from blood. But to have good repute amid such a world as this is an empty thing. Why then dost thou not wait in tranquillity for thy end, whether it is extinction or removal to another state? And until that time comes, what is sufficient? Why, what else than to venerate the gods and bless them, and to do good to men, and to practise tolerance and self-restraint; but as to everything which is beyond the limits of the poor flesh and breath, to remember that this is neither thine nor in thy power.

34. Thou canst pass thy life in an equable flow of happiness, if thou canst go by the right way, and think and act in the right way. These two things are common both to the soul of God and to the soul of man, and to the soul of every rational being, not to be hindered by another; and to hold good to consist in the disposition to justice and the practice of it, and in this to let thy desire find its termination.

35. If this is neither my own badness, nor an effect of my own badness, and the common weal is not injured, why am I troubled about it? and what is the harm to the common weal?

36. Do not be carried along inconsiderately by the appearance of things, but give help [to all] according to thy ability and their fitness; and if they should have sustained loss in matters which are indifferent, do not imagine this to be a damage. For it is a bad

habit. But as the old man, when he went away, asked back his foster-child's top, remembering that it was a top, so do thou in this case also.

When thou art calling out on the Rostra, hast thou forgotten, man, what these things are? Yes; but they are objects of great concern to these people—wilt thou too then be made a fool for these things? I was once a fortunate man, but I lost it, I know not how. But fortunate means that a man has assigned to himself a good fortune; and a good fortune is good disposition of the soul, good emotions, good actions.

## VII

WHAT is badness? It is that which thou hast often seen. And on the occasion of everything which happens keep this in mind, that it is that which thou hast often seen. Everywhere up and down thou wilt find the same things, with which the old histories are filled, those of the middle ages and those of our own day; with which cities and houses are filled now. There is nothing new; all things are both familiar and short-lived.

2. How can our principles become dead, unless the impressions [thoughts] which correspond to them are extinguished? But it is in thy power continuously to fan these thoughts into a flame. I can have that opinion about anything, which I ought to have. If I can, why am I disturbed? The things which are external to my mind have no relation at all to my mind. Let this be the state of thy affects, and thou standest erect. To recover thy life is in thy power. Look at things again as thou didst use to look at them; for in this consists the recovery of thy life.

3. The idle business of show, plays on the stage, flocks of sheep, herds, exercises with spears, a bone to cast to little dogs, a bit of bread into fish-ponds, labourings of ants and burden-carrying, runnings about of frightened little mice, puppets pulled by strings—[all alike]. It is thy duty then in the midst of such things to show good humour and not a proud air; to understand, however, that every man is worth just so much as the things are worth about which he busies himself.

4. In discourse thou must attend to what is said, and in every movement thou must observe what is doing. And in the one thou shouldst see immediately to what end it refers, but in the other watch carefully what is the thing signified.

5. Is my understanding sufficient for this or not? If it is sufficient I use it for the work as an instrument given by the universal nature. But if it is not sufficient, then either I retire from the work and give

way to him who is able to do it better, unless there be some reason why I ought not to do so; or I do it as well as I can, taking to help me the man who with the aid of my ruling principle can do what is now fit and useful for the general good. For whatsoever either by myself or with another I can do, ought to be directed to this only, to that which is useful and well suited to society.

6. How many after being celebrated by fame have been given up to oblivion; and how many who have celebrated the fame of others have long been dead.

7. Be not ashamed to be helped; for it is thy business to do thy duty like a soldier in the assault on a town. How then, if being lame thou canst not mount up on the battlements alone, but with the help of another it is possible?

8. Let not future things disturb thee, for thou wilt come to them, if it shall be necessary, having with thee the same reason which now thou usest for present things.

9. All things are implicated with one another, and the bond is holy; and there is hardly anything unconnected with any other thing. For things have been co-ordinated, and they combine to form the same universe [order]. For there is one universe made up of all things, and one god who pervades all things, and one substance, and one law, [one] common reason in all intelligent animals, and one truth; if indeed there is also one perfection for all animals which are of the same stock and participate in the same reason.

10. Everything material soon disappears in the substance of the whole; and everything formal [causal] is very soon taken back into the universal reason; and the memory of everything is very soon overwhelmed in time.

11. To the rational animal the same act is according to nature and according to reason.

12. Be thou erect, or be made erect (iii. 5).

13. Just as it is with the members in those bodies which are united in one, so it is with rational beings which exist separate, for they have been constituted for one co-operation. And the perception of this will be more apparent to thee, if thou often sayest to thyself that I am a member [μέλος] of the system of rational beings. But if [using the letter *r*] thou sayest that thou art a part [μέρος], thou

dost not yet love men from thy heart; beneficence does not yet delight thee for its own sake; thou still doest it barely as a thing of propriety, and not yet as doing good to thyself.

14. Let there fall externally what will on the parts which can feel the effects of this fall. For those parts which have felt will complain, if they choose. But I, unless I think that what has happened is an evil, am not injured. And it is in my power not to think so.

15. Whatever any one does or says, I must be good, just as if the gold, or the emerald, or the purple were always saying this: Whatever any one does or says, I must be emerald and keep my colour.

16. The ruling faculty does not disturb itself; I mean, does not frighten itself or cause itself pain. But if any one else can frighten or pain it, let him do so. For the faculty itself will not by its own opinion turn into such ways. Let the body itself take care, if it can, that it suffer nothing, and let it speak, if it suffers. But the soul itself, that which is subject to fear, to pain, which has completely the power of forming an opinion about these things, will suffer nothing, for it will never deviate into such a judgment. The leading principle in itself wants nothing, unless it makes a want for itself; and therefore it is both free from perturbation and unimpeded, if it does not disturb and impede itself.

17. Eudæmonia [happiness] is a good dæmon, or a good thing. What then art thou doing here, O imagination? go away, I entreat thee by the gods, as thou didst come, for I want thee not. But thou art come according to thy old fashion. I am not angry with thee: only go away.

18. Is any man afraid of change? Why, what can take place without change? What then is more pleasing or more suitable to the universal nature? And canst thou take a bath unless the wood undergoes a change? And canst thou be nourished unless the food undergoes a change? And can anything else that is useful be accomplished without change? Dost thou not see then that for thyself also to change is just the same, and equally necessary for the universal nature?

19. Through the universal substance as through a furious torrent all bodies are carried, being by their nature united with and cooperating with the whole, as the parts of our body with one another.

How many a Chrysippus, how many a Socrates, how many an Epictetus has time already swallowed up? And let the same thought occur to thee with reference to every man and thing (v. 23; vi. 15).

20. One thing only troubles me, lest I should do something which the constitution of man does not allow, or in the way which it does not allow, or what it does not allow now.

21. Near is thy forgetfulness of all things; and near the forgetfulness of thee by all.

22. It is peculiar to man to love even those who do wrong. And this happens, if when they do wrong it occurs to thee that they are kinsmen, and that they do wrong through ignorance and unintentionally, and that soon both of you will die; and above all, that the wrong-doer has done thee no harm, for he has not made thy ruling faculty worse than it was before.

23. The universal nature out of the universal substance, as if it were wax, now moulds a horse, and when it has broken this up, it uses the material for a tree, then for a man, then for something else; and each of these things subsists for a very short time. But it is no hardship for the vessel to be broken up, just as there was none in its being fastened together (viii. 50).

24. A scowling look is altogether unnatural; when it is often assumed, the result is that all comeliness dies away, and at last is so completely extinguished that it cannot be again lighted up at all. Try to conclude from this very fact that it is contrary to reason. For if even the perception of doing wrong shall depart, what reason is there for living any longer?

25. Nature which governs the whole will soon change all things which thou seest, and out of their substance will make other things, and again other things from the substance of them, in order that the world may be ever new (xii. 23).

26. When a man has done thee any wrong, immediately consider with what opinion about good or evil he has done wrong. For when thou hast seen this, thou wilt pity him, and wilt neither wonder nor be angry. For either thou thyself thinkest the same thing to be good that he does, or another thing of the same kind. It is thy duty then to pardon him. But if thou dost not think such things to be good or

evil, thou wilt more readily be well-disposed to him who is in error.

27. Think not so much of what thou hast not as of what thou hast: but of the things which thou hast select the best, and then reflect how eagerly they would have been sought, if thou hadst them not. At the same time, however, take care that thou dost not through being so pleased with them accustom thyself to overvalue them, so as to be disturbed if ever thou shouldst not have them.

28. Retire into thyself. The rational principle which rules has this nature, that it is content with itself when it does what is just, and so secures tranquillity.

29. Wipe out the imagination. Stop the pulling of the strings. Confine thyself to the present. Understand well what happens either to thee or to another. Divide and distribute every object into the causal [formal] and the material. Think of thy last hour. Let the wrong which is done by a man stay there where the wrong was done (viii. 29).

30. Direct thy attention to what is said. Let thy understanding enter into the things that are doing and the things which do them (vii. 4).

31. Adorn thyself with simplicity and modesty and with indifference towards the things which lie between virtue and vice. Love mankind. Follow God. The poet says that Law rules all. And it is enough to remember that law rules all.[1]

32. About death: whether it is a dispersion, or a resolution into atoms, or annihilation, it is either extinction or change.

33. About pain: the pain which is intolerable carries us off; but that which lasts a long time is tolerable; and the mind maintains its own tranquillity by retiring into itself, and the ruling faculty is not made worse. But the parts which are harmed by pain, let them, if they can, give their opinion about it.

34. About fame: look at the minds [of those who seek fame], observe what they are, and what kind of things they avoid, and what kind of things they pursue. And consider that as the heaps of sand piled on one another hide the former sands, so in life the events which go before are soon covered by those which come after.

[1]The end of this section is unintelligible.

35. From Plato: the man who has an elevated mind and takes a view of all time and of all substance, dost thou suppose it possible for him to think that human life is anything great? It is not possible, he said. Such a man then will think that death also is no evil. Certainly not.

36. From Antisthenes: It is royal to do good and to be abused.

37. It is a base thing for the countenance to be obedient and to regulate and compose itself as the mind commands, and for the mind not to be regulated and composed by itself.

38. It is not right to vex ourselves at things,
For they care nought about it.

39. To the immortal gods and us give joy.

40. Life must be reaped like the ripe ears of corn:
One man is born; another dies.

41. If gods care not for me and for my children,
There is a reason for it.

42. For the good is with me, and the just.

43. No joining others in their wailing, no violent emotion.

44. From Plato: But I would make this man a sufficient answer, which is this: Thou sayest not well, if thou thinkest that a man who is good for anything at all ought to compute the hazard of life or death, and should not rather look to this only in all that he does, whether he is doing what is just or unjust, and the works of a good or a bad man.

45. For thus it is, men of Athens, in truth: wherever a man has placed himself thinking it the best place for him, or has been placed by a commander, there in my opinion he ought to stay and to abide the hazard, taking nothing into the reckoning, either death or anything else, before the baseness [of deserting his post].

46. But, my good friend, reflect whether that which is noble and good is not something different from saving and being saved; for as to a man living such or such a time, at least one who is really a man, consider if this is not a thing to be dismissed from the thoughts: and there must be no love of life: but as to these matters a man must intrust them to the deity and believe what the women say, that no man can escape his destiny, the next inquiry being how he may best live the time that he has to live.

47. Look round at the courses of the stars, as if thou wert going along with them; and constantly consider the changes of the elements into one another; for such thoughts purge away the filth of the terrene life.

48. This is a fine saying of Plato: That he who is discoursing about men should look also at earthly things as if he viewed them from some higher place; should look at them in their assemblies, armies, agricultural labours, marriages, treaties, births, deaths, noise of the courts of justice, desert places, various nations of barbarians, feasts, lamentations, markets, a mixture of all things and an orderly combination of contraries.

49. Consider the past; such great changes of political supremacies. Thou mayest foresee also the things which will be. For they will certainly be of like form, and it is not possible that they should deviate from the order of the things which take place now: accordingly to have contemplated human life for forty years is the same as to have contemplated it for ten thousand years. For what more wilt thou see?

50. That which has grown from the earth to the earth,
But that which has sprung from heavenly seed,
Back to the heavenly realms returns.

This is either a dissolution of the mutual involution of the atoms, or a similar dispersion of the unsentient elements.

51. With food and drinks and cunning magic arts
Turning the channel's course to 'scape from death.
The breeze which heaven has sent
We must endure, and toil without complaining.

52. Another may be more expert in casting his opponent; but he is not more social, nor more modest, nor better disciplined to meet all that happens, nor more considerate with respect to the faults of his neighbours.

53. Where any work can be done conformably to the reason which is common to gods and men, there we have nothing to fear; for where we are able to get profit by means of the activity which is successful and proceeds according to our constitution, there no harm is to be suspected.

54. Everywhere and at all times it is in thy power piously to

acquiesce in thy present condition, and to behave justly to those who are about thee, and to exert thy skill upon thy present thoughts, that nothing shall steal into them without being well examined.

55. Do not look around thee to discover other men's ruling principles, but look straight to this, to what nature leads thee, both the universal nature through the things which happen to thee, and thy own nature through the acts which must be done by thee. But every being ought to do that which is according to its constitution; and all other things have been constituted for the sake of rational beings, just as among irrational things the inferior for the sake of the superior, but the rational for the sake of one another.

The prime principle then in man's constitution is the social. And the second is not to yield to the persuasions of the body, for it is the peculiar office of the rational and intelligent motion to circumscribe itself, and never to be overpowered either by the motion of the senses or of the appetites, for both are animal; but the intelligent motion claims superiority and does not permit itself to be overpowered by the others. And with good reason, for it is formed by nature to use all of them. The third thing in the rational constitution is freedom from error and from deception. Let then the ruling principle holding fast to these things go straight on, and it has what is its own.

56. Consider thyself to be dead, and to have completed thy life up to the present time; and live according to nature the remainder which is allowed thee.

57. Love that only which happens to thee and is spun with the thread of thy destiny. For what is more suitable?

58. In everything which happens keep before thy eyes those to whom the same things happened, and how they were vexed, and treated them as strange things, and found fault with them: and now where are they? Nowhere. Why then dost thou too choose to act in the same way? and why dost thou not leave these agitations which are foreign to nature, to those who cause them and those who are moved by them? And why art thou not altogether intent upon the right way of making use of the things which happen to thee? for then thou wilt use them well, and they will be a material for thee [to work on]. Only attend to thyself, and resolve to be a good man in every act which thou doest; and remember . . .

59. Look within. Within is the fountain of good, and it will ever bubble up, if thou wilt ever dig.

60. The body ought to be compact, and to show no irregularity either in motion or attitude. For what the mind shows in the face by maintaining in it the expression of intelligence and propriety, that ought to be required also in the whole body. But all these things should be observed without affectation.

61. The art of life is more like the wrestler's art than the dancer's, in respect of this, that it should stand ready and firm to meet onsets which are sudden and unexpected.

62. Constantly observe who those are whose approbation thou wishest to have, and what ruling principles they possess. For then thou wilt neither blame those who offend involuntarily, nor wilt thou want their approbation, if thou lookest to the sources of their opinions and appetites.

63. Every soul, the philosopher says, is involuntarily deprived of truth; consequently in the same way it is deprived of justice and temperance and benevolence and everything of the kind. It is most necessary to bear this constantly in mind, for thus thou wilt be more gentle towards all.

64. In every pain let this thought be present, that there is no dishonour in it, nor does it make the governing intelligence worse, for it does not damage the intelligence either so far as the intelligence is rational or so far as it is social. Indeed in the case of most pains let this remark of Epicurus aid thee, that pain is neither intolerable nor everlasting, if thou bearest in mind that it has its limits, and if thou addest nothing to it in imagination: and remember this too, that we do not perceive that many things which are disagreeable to us are the same as pain, such as excessive drowsiness, and the being scorched by heat, and the having no appetite. When then thou art discontented about any of these things, say to thyself that thou art yielding to pain.

65. Take care not to feel towards the inhuman as they feel towards men.

66. How do we know if Telauges was not superior in character to Socrates? for it is not enough that Socrates died a more noble death, and disputed more skilfully with the sophists, and passed the night in

the cold with more endurance, and that when he was bid to arrest Leon of Salamis, he considered it more noble to refuse, and that he walked in a swaggering way in the streets—though as to this fact one may have great doubts if it was true. But we ought to inquire, what kind of a soul it was that Socrates possessed, and if he was able to be content with being just towards men and pious towards the gods, neither idly vexed on account of men's villainy, nor yet making himself a slave to any man's ignorance, nor receiving as strange anything that fell to his share out of the universal, nor enduring it as intolerable, nor allowing his understanding to sympathize with the affects of the miserable flesh.

67. Nature has not so mingled [the intelligence] with the composition of the body, as not to have allowed thee the power of circumscribing thyself and of bringing under subjection to thyself all that is thy own; for it is very possible to be a divine man and to be recognized as such by no one. Always bear this in mind; and another thing too, that very little indeed is necessary for living a happy life. And because thou hast despaired of becoming a dialectician and skilled in the knowledge of nature, do not for this reason renounce the hope of being both free and modest and social and obedient to God.

68. It is in thy power to live free from all compulsion in the greatest tranquillity of mind, even if all the world cry out against thee as much as they choose, and even if wild beasts tear in pieces the members of this kneaded matter which has grown around thee. For what hinders the mind in the midst of all this from maintaining itself in tranquillity, and in a just judgment of all surrounding things, and in a ready use of the objects which are presented to it, so that the judgment may say to the thing which falls under its observation: This thou art in substance [reality], though in men's opinion thou mayest appear to be of a different kind; and the use shall say to that which falls under the hand: Thou art the thing that I was seeking; for to me that which presents itself is always a material for virtue, both rational and political, and, in a word, for the exercise of art, which belongs to man or God. For everything which happens has a relationship either to God or man, and is neither new nor difficult to handle, but usual and apt matter to work on.

69. The perfection of moral character consists in this, in passing every day as the last, and in being neither violently excited, nor torpid, nor playing the hypocrite.

70. The gods who are immortal are not vexed because during so long a time they must tolerate continually men such as they are and so many of them bad; and besides this, they also take care of them in all ways. But thou, who art destined to end so soon, art thou wearied of enduring the bad, and this too when thou art one of them?

71. It is a ridiculous thing for a man not to fly from his own badness, which is indeed possible, but to fly from other men's badness, which is impossible.

72. Whatever the rational and political [social] faculty finds to be neither intelligent nor social, it properly judges to be inferior to itself.

73. When thou hast done a good act and another has received it, why dost thou still look for a third thing besides these, as fools do, either to have the reputation of having done a good act or to obtain a return?

74. No man is tired of receiving what is useful. But it is useful to act according to nature. Do not then be tired of receiving what is useful by doing it to others.

75. The nature of the All moved to make the universe. But now either everything that takes place comes by way of consequence or [continuity]; or even the chief things towards which the ruling power of the universe directs its own movement are governed by no rational principle. If this is remembered it will make thee more tranquil in many things (vi. 44; ix. 28).

# XII

ALL those things at which thou wishest to arrive by a circuitous road, thou canst have now, if thou dost not refuse them to thyself. And this means, if thou wilt take no notice of all the past, and trust the future to providence, and direct the present only conformably to piety and justice. Conformably to piety, that thou mayest be content with the lot which is assigned to thee, for nature designed it for thee and thee for it. Conformably to justice, that thou mayest always speak the truth freely and without disguise, and do the things which are agreeable to law and according to the worth of each. And let neither another man's wickedness hinder thee, nor opinion nor voice, nor yet the sensations of the poor flesh which has grown about thee; for the passive part will look to this. If then, whatever the time may be when thou shalt be near to thy departure, neglecting everything else thou shalt respect only thy ruling faculty and the divinity within thee, and if thou shalt be afraid not because thou must sometime cease to live, but if thou shalt fear never to have begun to live according to nature—then thou wilt be a man worthy of the universe which has produced thee, and thou wilt cease to be a stranger in thy native land, and to wonder at things which happen daily as if they were something unexpected, and to be dependent on this or that.

2. God sees the minds [ruling principles] of all men bared of the material vesture and rind and impurities. For with his intellec-

tual part alone he touches the intelligence only which has flowed and been derived from himself into these bodies. And if thou also usest thyself to do this, thou wilt rid thyself of thy much trouble. For he who regards not the poor flesh which envelops him, surely will not trouble himself by looking after raiment and dwelling and fame and suchlike externals and show.

3. The things are three of which thou art composed, a little body, a little breath [life], intelligence. Of these the first two are thine, so far as it is thy duty to take care of them; but the third alone is properly thine. Therefore, if thou shalt separate from thyself, that is, from thy understanding, whatever others do or say, and whatever thou hast done or said thyself, and whatever future things trouble thee because they may happen, and whatever in the body which envelops thee, or in the breath [life], which is by nature associated with the body, is attached to thee independent of thy will, and whatever the external circumfluent vortex whirls round, so that the intellectual power exempt from the things of fate can live pure and free by itself, doing what is just and accepting what happens and saying the truth: if thou wilt separate, I say, from this ruling faculty the things which are attached to it by the impressions of sense, and the things of time to come and of time that is past, and wilt make thyself like Empedocles' sphere—

All round, and in its joyous rest reposing;

and if thou shalt strive to live only what is really thy life, that is, the present, then thou wilt be able to pass that portion of life which remains for thee up to the time of thy death, free from perturbations, nobly, and obedient to thy own dæmon [to the god that is within thee] (ii. 13, 17; iii. 5, 6; xi. 12).

4. I have often wondered how it is that every man loves himself more than all the rest of men, but yet sets less value on his own opinion of himself than on the opinion of others. If then a god or a wise teacher should present himself to a man and bid him to think of nothing and to design nothing which he would not express as soon as he conceived it, he could not endure it even for a single day. So much more respect have we to what our neighbours shall think of us than to what we shall think of ourselves.

5. How can it be that the gods, after having arranged all things well and benevolently for mankind, have overlooked this alone, that some men and very good men, and men who, as we may say, have had most communion with the divinity, and through pious acts and religious observances have been most intimate with the divinity, when they have once died should never exist again, but should be completely extinguished?

But if this is so, be assured that if it ought to have been otherwise, the gods would have done it. For if it were just, it would also be possible; and if it were according to nature, nature would have had it so. But because it is not so, if in fact it is not so, be thou convinced that it ought not to have been so:—for thou seest even of thyself that in this inquiry thou art disputing with the deity; and we should not thus dispute with the gods, unless they were most excellent and most just;—but if this is so, they would not have allowed anything in the ordering of the universe to be neglected unjustly and irrationally.

6. Practise thyself even in the things which thou despairest of accomplishing. For even the left hand, which is ineffectual for all other things for want of practice, holds the bridle more vigorously than the right hand; for it has been practised in this.

7. Consider in what condition, both in body and soul, a man should be when he is overtaken by death; and consider the shortness of life, the boundless abyss of time, past and future, the feebleness of all matter.

8. Contemplate the formative principles [forms] of things bare of their coverings; the purposes of actions; consider what pain is, what pleasure is, and death, and fame; who is to himself the cause of his uneasiness; how no man is hindered by another; that everything is opinion.

9. In the application of thy principles thou must be like the pancratiast, not like the gladiator; for the gladiator lets fall the sword which he uses and is killed; but the other always has his hand, and needs to do nothing else than use it.

10. See what things are in themselves, dividing them into matter, form and purpose.

11. What a power man has to do nothing except what God will approve, and to accept all that God may give him.

12. With respect to that which happens conformably to nature, we ought to blame neither gods, for they do nothing wrong either voluntarily or involuntarily, nor men, for they do nothing wrong except involuntarily. Consequently we should blame nobody (ii. 11, 12, 13; vii. 62; viii. 17).

13. How ridiculous and what a stranger he is who is surprised at anything which happens in life.

14. Either there is a fatal necessity and invincible order, or a kind providence, or a confusion without a purpose and without a director (iv. 27). If then there is an invincible necessity, why dost thou resist? But if there is a providence which allows itself to be propitiated, make thyself worthy of the help of the divinity. But if there is a confusion without a governor, be content that in such a tempest thou hast in thyself a certain ruling intelligence. And even if the tempest carry thee away, let it carry away the poor flesh, the poor breath, everything else; for the intelligence at least it will not carry away.

15. Does the light of the lamp shine without losing its splendour until it is extinguished; and shall the truth which is in thee and justice and temperance be extinguished [before thy death]?

16. When a man has presented the appearance of having done wrong, [say], How then do I know if this is a wrongful act? And even if he has done wrong, how do I know that he has not condemned himself? and so this is like tearing his own face. Consider that he who would not have the bad man do wrong, is like the man who would not have the fig-tree to bear juice in the figs and infants to cry and the horse to neigh, and whatever else must of necessity be. For what must a man do who has such a character? If then thou art irritable, cure this man's disposition.

17. If it is not right, do not do it: if it is not true, do not say it. [For let thy efforts be.—][1]

18. In everything always observe what the thing is which produces for thee an appearance, and resolve it by dividing it into the

[1]There is something wrong here, or incomplete.

formal, the material, the purpose, and the time within which it must end.

19. Perceive at last that thou hast in thee something better and more divine than the things which cause the various effects, and as it were pull thee by the strings. What is there now in my mind? is it fear, or suspicion, or desire, or anything of the kind? (v. 11.)

20. First, do nothing inconsiderately, nor without a purpose. Second, make thy acts refer to nothing else than to a social end.

21. Consider that before long thou wilt be nobody and nowhere, nor will any of the things exist which thou now seest, nor any of those who are now living. For all things are formed by nature to change and be turned and to perish in order that other things in continuous succession may exist (ix. 28).

22. Consider that everything is opinion, and opinion is in thy power. Take away then, when thou choosest, thy opinion, and like a mariner, who has doubled the promontory, thou wilt find calm, everything stable, and a waveless bay.

23. Any one activity, whatever it may be, when it has ceased at its proper time, suffers no evil because it has ceased; nor he who has done this act, does he suffer any evil for this reason that the act has ceased. In like manner then the whole which consists of all the acts, which is our life, if it cease at its proper time, suffers no evil for this reason that it has ceased; nor he who has terminated this series at the proper time, has he been ill dealt with. But the proper time and the limit nature fixes, sometimes as in old age the peculiar nature of man, but always the universal nature, by the change of whose parts the whole universe continues ever young and perfect. And everything which is useful to the universal is always good and in season. Therefore the termination of life for every man is no evil, because neither is it shameful, since it is both independent of the will and not opposed to the general interest, but it is good, since it is seasonable and profitable to and congruent with the universal. For thus too he is moved by the deity who is moved in the same manner with the deity and moved towards the same things in his mind.

24. These three principles thou must have in readiness. In the things which thou doest do nothing either inconsiderately or otherwise than as justice herself would act; but with respect to what may

happen to thee from without, consider that it happens either by chance or according to providence, and thou must neither blame chance nor accuse providence. Second, consider what every being is from the seed to the time of its receiving a soul, and from the reception of a soul to the giving back of the same, and of what things every being is compounded and into what things it is resolved. Third, if thou shouldst suddenly be raised up above the earth, and shouldst look down on human beings, and observe the variety of them how great it is, and at the same time also shouldst see at a glance how great is the number of beings who dwell all around in the air and the æther, consider that as often as thou shouldst be raised up, thou wouldst see the same things, sameness of form and shortness of duration. Are these things to be proud of?

25. Cast away opinion: thou art saved. Who then hinders thee from casting it away?

26. When thou art troubled about anything, thou hast forgotten this, that all things happen according to the universal nature; and forgotten this, that a man's wrongful act is nothing to thee; and further thou hast forgotten this, that everything which happens, always happened so and will happen so, and now happens so everywhere; forgotten this too, how close is the kinship between a man and the whole human race, for it is a community, not of a little blood or seed, but of intelligence. And thou hast forgotten this too, that every man's intelligence is a god, and is an efflux of the deity; and forgotten this, that nothing is a man's own, but that his child and his body and his very soul came from the deity; forgotten this, that everything is opinion; and lastly thou hast forgotten that every man lives the present time only, and loses only this.

27. Constantly bring to thy recollection those who have complained greatly about anything, those who have been most conspicuous by the greatest fame or misfortunes or enmities or fortunes of any kind: then think where are they all now? Smoke and ash and a tale, or not even a tale. And let there be present to thy mind also everything of this sort, how Fabius Catullinus lived in the country, and Lucius Lupus in his gardens, and Stertinius at Baiæ, and Tiberius at Capreæ, and Velius Rufus [or Rufus at Velia]; and in fine think of the eager pursuit of anything conjoined with

pride; and how worthless everything is after which men violently strain; and how much more philosophical it is for a man in the opportunities presented to him to show himself just, temperate, obedient to the gods, and to do this with all simplicity: for the pride which is proud of its want of pride is the most intolerable of all.

28. To those who ask, Where hast thou seen the gods or how dost thou comprehend that they exist and so worshipest them? I answer, in the first place, they may be seen even with the eyes; in the second place, neither have I seen even my own soul and yet I honour it. Thus then with respect to the gods, from what I constantly experience of their power, from this I comprehend that they exist and I venerate them.

29. The safety of life is this, to examine everything all through, what it is itself, what is its material, what the formal part; with all thy soul to do justice and to say the truth. What remains except to enjoy life by joining one good thing to another so as not to leave even the smallest intervals between?

30. There is one light of the sun, though it is interrupted by walls, mountains, and other things infinite. There is one common substance, though it is distributed among countless bodies which have their several qualities. There is one soul, though it is distributed among infinite natures and individual circumscriptions [or individuals]. There is one intelligent soul, though it seems to be divided. Now in the things which have been mentioned all the other parts, such as those which are air and matter, are without sensation and have no fellowship: and yet even these parts the intelligent principle holds together, and the gravitation towards the same. But intellect in a peculiar manner tends to that which is of the same kin, and combines with it, and the feeling for communion is not interrupted.

31. What dost thou wish? to continue to exist? Well, dost thou wish to have sensation? movement? growth? and then again to cease to grow? to use thy speech? to think? What is there of all these things which seem to thee worth desiring? But if it is easy to set little value on all these things, turn to that which remains, which is to follow reason and god. But it is inconsistent with honouring reason and god to be troubled because by death a man will be deprived of the other things.

32. How small a part of the boundless and unfathomable time is assigned to every man! for it is very soon swallowed up in the eternal. And how small a part of the whole substance! and how small a part of the universal soul! and on what a small clod of the whole earth thou creepest! Reflecting on all this, consider nothing to be great, except to act as thy nature leads thee, and to endure that which the common nature brings.

33. How does the ruling faculty make use of itself? for all lies in this. But everything else, whether it is in the power of thy will or not, is only lifeless ashes and smoke.

34. This reflection is most adapted to move us to contempt of death, that even those who think pleasure to be a good and pain an evil still have despised it.

35. The man to whom that only is good which comes in due season, and to whom it is the same thing whether he has done more or fewer acts conformable to right reason, and to whom it makes no difference whether he contemplates the world for a longer or a shorter time—for this man neither is death a terrible thing (iii. 7; vi. 23; x. 20; xii. 23).

36. Man, thou hast been a citizen in this great state [the world]: what difference does it make to thee whether for five years [or three]? for that which is conformable to the laws is just for all. Where is the hardship then, if no tyrant nor yet an unjust judge sends thee away from the state, but nature who brought thee into it? the same as if a prætor who has employed an actor dismisses him from the stage.—"But I have not finished the five acts, but only three of them."—Thou sayest well, but in life the three acts are the whole drama; for what shall be a complete drama is determined by him who was once the cause of its composition, and now of its dissolution: but thou art the cause of neither. Depart then satisfied, for he also who releases thee is satisfied.

4

THE BOOK OF JOB (Revised Standard Version)

THE GOSPEL OF MATTHEW (New English Bible)

1. What did Satan bet that he could goad Job into doing? What did Job curse?

2. To what causes did Job's friends attribute his troubles? What advice did they each offer him? How did he respond?

3. What does God tell Job about his ability to understand God's ways? How does Job reply?

4. If the principal question of this book concerns the reason a righteous man is made to suffer, what answer is given?

5. Does Job demonstrate "the patience of Job"? Explain.

6. What image of God do you see in Job? What image of Satan do you see?

7. Who won the bet?

8. Does this story fit the frequently used outline of a state of perfection which is disturbed causing suffering and change but leading ultimately to adaptation and growth? Discuss in detail.

9. With what kind of blessedness or happiness do you think the Beatitudes are concerned?

10. According to the Sermon, what is virtuous behavior? What is the relationship between the Sermon and the Ten Commandments?

11. Compare the relationship of virtue and happiness in the Sermon with that of Aristotle's *Ethics*.

12. What does "turning the other cheek" mean to you? Is this teaching realistic in today's world?

13. Is there a difference in the application of the teachings of the Sermon to individuals and groups?

14. Is the Sermon an ethical statement for Christians which is not to be applied to society as a general ethic? If it could be applied to society in general, what effect would it have?

15. What would it mean for you to love your enemies?

16. What is the highest good according to the Sermon? How does it compare with Aristotle?

The book of Job, from the Old Testament, explores a wide range of issues related to the role of God in human suffering. The story can be understood as a parable. Thomas Carlyle called the book of Job "one of the grandest things ever written with a pen... It is our first, oldest statement of the never-ending problem - - man's destiny, and God's ways with him here on this earth... There is nothing written, I think, in the Bible or out of it, of equal literary merit."

## THE BOOK OF

# JOB

1 There was a man in the land of Uz, whose name was Job; and that man was blameless and upright, one who feared God, and turned away from evil. 2 There were born to him seven sons and three daughters. 3 He had seven thousand sheep, three thousand camels, five hundred yoke of oxen, and five hundred she-asses, and very many servants; so that this man was the greatest of all the people of the east. 4 His sons used to go and hold a feast in the house of each on his day; and they would send and invite their three sisters to eat and drink with them. 5 And when the days of the feast had run their course, Job would send and sanctify them, and he would rise early in the morning and offer burnt offerings according to the number of them all; for Job said, "It may be that my sons have sinned, and cursed God in their hearts." Thus Job did continually.

6 Now there was a day when the sons of God came to present themselves before the LORD, and Satan[a] also came among them. 7 The LORD said to Satan, "Whence have you come?" Satan answered the LORD, "From going to and fro on the earth, and from walking up and down on it." 8 And the LORD said to Satan, "Have you considered my servant Job, that there is none like him on the earth, a blameless and upright man, who fears God and turns away from evil?" 9 Then Satan answered the LORD, "Does Job fear God for nought? 10 Hast thou not put a hedge about him and his house and all that he has, on every side? Thou hast blessed the work of his hands, and his possessions have increased in the land. 11 But put forth thy hand now, and touch all that he has, and he will curse thee to thy face." 12 And the LORD said to Satan, "Behold, all that he has is in your power; only upon himself do not put forth your hand." So Satan went forth from the presence of the LORD.

13 Now there was a day when his sons and daughters were eating and drinking wine in their eldest brother's house; 14 and there came a messenger to Job, and said, "The oxen were plowing and the asses feeding beside them; 15 and the Sabe'ans fell upon them and took them, and slew the servants with the edge of the sword; and I alone have escaped to tell you." 16 While he was yet speaking, there came another, and said, "The fire of God fell from heaven and burned up the sheep and the servants, and consumed them; and I alone have escaped to tell you." 17 While he was yet speaking, there came another, and said, "The Chalde'ans formed three companies, and made a raid upon the camels and took them, and slew the servants with the edge of the sword; and I alone have escaped to tell you." 18 While he was yet speaking, there came another, and said, "Your sons and daughters were eating and drinking wine in their eldest brother's house; 19 and behold, a great wind came across the wilderness, and struck the four corners of the house, and it fell upon the young people, and they are dead; and I alone have escaped to tell you."

20 Then Job arose, and rent his robe, and shaved his head, and fell upon the ground, and worshiped. 21 And he said, "Naked I came from my mother's womb, and naked shall I return; the LORD gave, and the LORD has taken away; blessed be the name of the LORD."

22 In all this Job did not sin or charge God with wrong.

2 Again there was a day when the sons of God came to present

[a] Heb *the adversary*

themselves before the LORD, and Sa-
tan also came among them to present
himself before the LORD. 2 And the
LORD said to Satan, "Whence have
you come?" Satan answered the LORD,
"From going to and fro on the earth,
and from walking up and down on
it." 3 And the LORD said to Satan,
"Have you considered my servant
Job, that there is none like him on
the earth, a blameless and upright
man, who fears God and turns away
from evil? He still holds fast his
integrity, although you moved me
against him, to destroy him without
cause." 4 Then Satan answered the
LORD, "Skin for skin! All that a man
has he will give for his life. 5 But put
forth thy hand now, and touch his
bone and his flesh, and he will curse
thee to thy face." 6 And the LORD said
to Satan, "Behold, he is in your
power; only spare his life."

7 So Satan went forth from the
presence of the LORD, and afflicted
Job with loathsome sores from the
sole of his foot to the crown of his
head. 8 And he took a potsherd with
which to scrape himself, and sat
among the ashes. 9 Then his wife said
to him, "Do you still hold fast your
integrity? Curse God, and die."

10 But he said to her, "You speak
as one of the foolish women would
speak. Shall we receive good at the
hand of God, and shall we not re-
ceive evil?" In all this Job did not
sin with his lips.

11 Now when Job's three friends
heard of all this evil that had come
upon him, they came each from his
own place, Eli′phaz the Te′manite,
Bildad the Shuhite, and Zophar the
Na′amathite. They made an appoint-
ment together to come to condole
with him and comfort him. 12 And
when they saw him from afar, they
did not recognize him; and they raised
their voices and wept; and they rent
their robes and sprinkled dust upon
their heads toward heaven. 13 And
they sat with him on the ground
seven days and seven nights, and no
one spoke a word to him, for they saw
that his suffering was very great.

3 After this Job opened his mouth
and cursed the day of his birth.
2 And Job said:

3 "Let the day perish wherein I was born,
and the night which said,
'A man-child is conceived.'
4 Let that day be darkness!
May God above not seek it,
nor light shine upon it.
5 Let gloom and deep darkness claim it.
Let clouds dwell upon it;
let the blackness of the day terrify it.
6 That night—let thick darkness seize it!
let it not rejoice among the days of the year,
let it not come into the number of the months.
7 Yea, let that night be barren;
let no joyful cry be heard[b] in it.
8 Let those curse it who curse the day,
who are skilled to rouse up Levi-athan.
9 Let the stars of its dawn be dark;
let it hope for light, but have none,
nor see the eyelids of the morning;
10 because it did not shut the doors of my mother's womb,
nor hide trouble from my eyes.

11 "Why did I not die at birth,
come forth from the womb and expire?
12 Why did the knees receive me?
Or why the breasts, that I should suck?
13 For then I should have lain down and been quiet;
I should have slept; then I should have been at rest,
14 with kings and counselors of the earth
who rebuilt ruins for themselves.

[b] Heb *come*  3. 3-19: Jer. 20. 14-18.

15 or with princes who had gold,
who filled their houses with silver.
16 Or why was I not as a hidden untimely birth,
as infants that never see the light?
17 There the wicked cease from troubling,
and there the weary are at rest.
18 There the prisoners are at ease together;
they hear not the voice of the taskmaster.
19 The small and the great are there,
and the slave is free from his master.

20 "Why is light given to him that is in misery,
and life to the bitter in soul,
21 who long for death, but it comes not,
and dig for it more than for hid treasures;
22 who rejoice exceedingly,
and are glad, when they find the grave?
23 Why is light given to a man whose way is hid,
whom God has hedged in?
24 For my sighing comes as[c] my bread,
and my groanings are poured out like water.
25 For the thing that I fear comes upon me,
and what I dread befalls me.
26 I am not at ease, nor am I quiet;
I have no rest; but trouble comes."

4 Then Eli'phaz the Te'manite answered:
2 "If one ventures a word with you, will you be offended?
Yet who can keep from speaking?
3 Behold, you have instructed many,
and you have strengthened the weak hands.
4 Your words have upheld him who was stumbling,
and you have made firm the feeble knees.
5 But now it has come to you, and you are impatient;
it touches you, and you are dismayed.
6 Is not your fear of God your confidence,
and the integrity of your ways your hope?

7 "Think now, who that was innocent ever perished?
Or where were the upright cut off?
8 As I have seen, those who plow iniquity
and sow trouble reap the same.
9 By the breath of God they perish,
and by the blast of his anger they are consumed.
10 The roar of the lion, the voice of the fierce lion,
the teeth of the young lions, are broken.
11 The strong lion perishes for lack of prey,
and the whelps of the lioness are scattered.

12 "Now a word was brought to me stealthily,
my ear received the whisper of it.
13 Amid thoughts from visions of the night,
when deep sleep falls on men,
14 dread came upon me, and trembling,
which made all my bones shake.
15 A spirit glided past my face;
the hair of my flesh stood up.
16 It stood still,
but I could not discern its appearance.
A form was before my eyes;
there was silence, then I heard a voice:
17 'Can mortal man be righteous before[d] God?
can a man be pure before[d] his Maker?

[c] Heb *before* [d] Or *more than*

[18] Even in his servants he puts no
trust,
and his angels he charges with
error;
[19] how much more those who dwell in
houses of clay,
whose foundation is in the dust,
who are crushed before the moth.
[20] Between morning and evening they
are destroyed;
they perish for ever without any
regarding it.
[21] If their tent-cord is plucked up
within them,
do they not die, and that without
wisdom?'

5 "Call now; is there any one who
will answer you?
To which of the holy ones will
you turn?
[2] Surely vexation kills the fool,
and jealousy slays the simple.
[3] I have seen the fool taking root,
but suddenly I cursed his dwell-
ing.
[4] His sons are far from safety,
they are crushed in the gate,
and there is no one to deliver
them.
[5] His harvest the hungry eat,
and he takes it even out of
thorns;[e]
and the thirsty[f] pant after his[g]
wealth.
[6] For affliction does not come from
the dust,
nor does trouble sprout from the
ground;
[7] but man is born to trouble
as the sparks fly upward.

[8] "As for me, I would seek God,
and to God would I commit my
cause;
[9] who does great things and un-
searchable,
marvelous things without num-
ber:
[10] he gives rain upon the earth
and sends waters upon the fields;
[11] he sets on high those who are lowly,
and those who mourn are lifted
to safety.
[12] He frustrates the devices of the
crafty,
so that their hands achieve no
success.
[13] He takes the wise in their own
craftiness;
and the schemes of the wily are
brought to a quick end.
[14] They meet with darkness in the
daytime,
and grope at noonday as in the
night.
[15] But he saves the fatherless from
their mouth,[h]
the needy from the hand of the
mighty.
[16] So the poor have hope,
and injustice shuts her mouth.

[17] "Behold, happy is the man whom
God reproves;
therefore despise not the chasten-
ing of the Almighty.
[18] For he wounds, but he binds up;
he smites, but his hands heal.
[19] He will deliver you from six trou-
bles;
in seven there shall no evil touch
you.
[20] In famine he will redeem you from
death,
and in war from the power of
the sword.
[21] You shall be hid from the scourge
of the tongue,
and shall not fear destruction
when it comes.
[22] At destruction and famine you shall
laugh,
and shall not fear the beasts of
the earth.
[23] For you shall be in league with the
stones of the field,
and the beasts of the field shall
be at peace with you.
[24] You shall know that your tent is
safe,

[e] Heb obscure [f] Aquila Symmachus Syr Vg: Heb *snare* [g] Heb *their*
[h] Cn: Heb uncertain 5. 12-13: 1 Cor. 3. 19.

and you shall inspect your fold
and miss nothing.
25 You shall know also that your descendants shall be many,
and your offspring as the grass
of the earth.
26 You shall come to your grave in
ripe old age,
as a shock of grain comes up to
the threshing floor in its
season.
27 Lo, this we have searched out; it
is true.
Hear, and know it for your
good."[i]

## 6

Then Job answered:
2 "O that my vexation were
weighed,
and all my calamity laid in the
balances!
3 For then it would be heavier than
the sand of the sea;
therefore my words have been
rash.
4 For the arrows of the Almighty are
in me;
my spirit drinks their poison;
the terrors of God are arrayed
against me.
5 Does the wild ass bray when he has
grass,
or the ox low over his fodder?
6 Can that which is tasteless be eaten
without salt,
or is there any taste in the slime
of the purslane?[j]
7 My appetite refuses to touch them;
they are as food that is loathsome
to me.[k]

8 "O that I might have my request,
and that God would grant my
desire;
9 that it would please God to crush
me,
that he would let loose his hand
and cut me off!
10 This would be my consolation;
I would even exult[l] in pain unsparing;
for I have not denied the words
of the Holy One.
11 What is my strength, that I should
wait?
And what is my end, that I
should be patient?
12 Is my strength the strength of
stones,
or is my flesh bronze?
13 In truth I have no help in me,
and any resource is driven from
me.

14 "He who withholds[m] kindness
from a friend
forsakes the fear of the Almighty.
15 My brethren are treacherous as a
torrent-bed,
as freshets that pass away,
16 which are dark with ice,
and where the snow hides itself.
17 In time of heat they disappear;
when it is hot, they vanish from
their place.
18 The caravans turn aside from their
course;
they go up into the waste, and
perish.
19 The caravans of Tema look,
the travelers of Sheba hope.
20 They are disappointed because they
were confident;
they come thither and are confounded.
21 Such you have now become to
me;[n]
you see my calamity, and are
afraid.
22 Have I said, 'Make me a gift'?
Or, 'From your wealth offer a
bribe for me'?
23 Or, 'Deliver me from the adversary's hand'?
Or, 'Ransom me from the hand
of oppressors'?

24 "Teach me, and I will be silent;

[i] Heb *for yourself* [j] The meaning of the Hebrew word is uncertain [k] Heb obscure
[l] The meaning of the Hebrew word is uncertain [m] Syr Vg Compare Tg: Heb obscure
[n] Cn Compare Gk Syr: Heb obscure

make me understand how I have
erred.
25 How forceful are honest words!
But what does reproof from you
reprove?
26 Do you think that you can reprove
words,
when the speech of a despairing
man is wind?
27 You would even cast lots over the
fatherless,
and bargain over your friend.

28 "But now, be pleased to look at me;
for I will not lie to your face.
29 Turn, I pray, let no wrong be done.
Turn now, my vindication is at
stake.
30 Is there any wrong on my tongue?
Cannot my taste discern ca-
lamity?

7 "Has not man a hard service upon
earth,
and are not his days like the days
of a hireling?
2 Like a slave who longs for the
shadow,
and like a hireling who looks for
his wages,
3 so I am allotted months of empti-
ness,
and nights of misery are appor-
tioned to me.
4 When I lie down I say, 'When shall
I arise?'
But the night is long,
and I am full of tossing till the
dawn.
5 My flesh is clothed with worms and
dirt;
my skin hardens, then breaks
out afresh.
6 My days are swifter than a weaver's
shuttle,
and come to their end without
hope.

7 "Remember that my life is a breath;
my eye will never again see good.
8 The eye of him who sees me will
behold me no more;
while thy eyes are upon me, I
shall be gone.
9 As the cloud fades and vanishes,
so he who goes down to Sheol
does not come up;
10 he returns no more to his house,
nor does his place know him any
more.

11 "Therefore I will not restrain my
mouth;
I will speak in the anguish of my
spirit;
I will complain in the bitterness
of my soul.
12 Am I the sea, or a sea monster,
that thou settest a guard over me?
13 When I say, 'My bed will comfort
me,
my couch will ease my com-
plaint,'
14 then thou dost scare me with
dreams
and terrify me with visions,
15 so that I would choose strangling
and death rather than my bones.
16 I loathe my life; I would not live
for ever.
Let me alone, for my days are a
breath.
17 What is man, that thou dost make
so much of him,
and that thou dost set thy mind
upon him,
18 dost visit him every morning,
and test him every moment?
19 How long wilt thou not look away
from me,
nor let me alone till I swallow my
spittle?
20 If I sin, what do I do to thee, thou
watcher of men?
Why hast thou made me thy
mark?
Why have I become a burden to
thee?
21 Why dost thou not pardon my
transgression
and take away my iniquity?
For now I shall lie in the earth;
thou wilt seek me, but I shall not
be."

7. 17: Ps. 8. 4.

8 Then Bildad the Shuhite answered:
2 "How long will you say these things,
and the words of your mouth be a great wind?
3 Does God pervert justice?
Or does the Almighty pervert the right?
4 If your children have sinned against him,
he has delivered them into the power of their transgression.
5 If you will seek God
and make supplication to the Almighty,
6 if you are pure and upright,
surely then he will rouse himself for you
and reward you with a rightful habitation.
7 And though your beginning was small,
your latter days will be very great.

8 "For inquire, I pray you, of bygone ages,
and consider what the fathers have found;
9 for we are but of yesterday, and know nothing,
for our days on earth are a shadow.
10 Will they not teach you, and tell you,
and utter words out of their understanding?

11 "Can papyrus grow where there is no marsh?
Can reeds flourish where there is no water?
12 While yet in flower and not cut down,
they wither before any other plant.
13 Such are the paths of all who forget God;
the hope of the godless man shall perish.
14 His confidence breaks in sunder,
and his trust is a spider's web.[o]
15 He leans against his house, but it does not stand;
he lays hold of it, but it does not endure.
16 He thrives before the sun,
and his shoots spread over his garden.
17 His roots twine about the stoneheap;
he lives among the rocks.[p]
18 If he is destroyed from his place,
then it will deny him, saying, 'I have never seen you.'
19 Behold, this is the joy of his way;
and out of the earth others will spring.

20 "Behold, God will not reject a blameless man,
nor take the hand of evildoers.
21 He will yet fill your mouth with laughter,
and your lips with shouting.
22 Those who hate you will be clothed with shame,
and the tent of the wicked will be no more."

9 Then Job answered:
2 "Truly I know that it is so:
But how can a man be just before God?
3 If one wished to contend with him,
one could not answer him once in a thousand times.
4 He is wise in heart, and mighty in strength
—who has hardened himself against him, and succeeded?—
5 he who removes mountains, and they know it not,
when he overturns them in his anger;
6 who shakes the earth out of its place,
and its pillars tremble;
7 who commands the sun, and it does not rise;
who seals up the stars;
8 who alone stretched out the heavens,
and trampled the waves of the sea;[q]

[o] Heb *house* [p] Gk Vg: Heb uncertain [q] Or *trampled the back of the sea dragon*

9 who made the Bear and Orion,
the Plei'ades and the chambers of the south;
10 who does great things beyond understanding,
and marvelous things without number.
11 Lo, he passes by me, and I see him not;
he moves on, but I do not perceive him.
12 Behold, he snatches away; who can hinder him?
Who will say to him, 'What doest thou'?

13 "God will not turn back his anger;
beneath him bowed the helpers of Rahab.
14 How then can I answer him,
choosing my words with him?
15 Though I am innocent, I cannot answer him;
I must appeal for mercy to my accuser.[r]
16 If I summoned him and he answered me,
I would not believe that he was listening to my voice.
17 For he crushes me with a tempest,
and multiplies my wounds without cause;
18 he will not let me get my breath,
but fills me with bitterness.
19 If it is a contest of strength, behold him!
If it is a matter of justice, who can summon him?[s]
20 Though I am innocent, my own mouth would condemn me;
though I am blameless, he would prove me perverse.
21 I am blameless; I regard not myself;
I loathe my life.
22 It is all one; therefore I say,
he destroys both the blameless and the wicked.
23 When disaster brings sudden death,
he mocks at the calamity[t] of the innocent.
24 The earth is given into the hand of the wicked;
he covers the faces of its judges—
if it is not he, who then is it?

25 "My days are swifter than a runner;
they flee away, they see no good.
26 They go by like skiffs of reed,
like an eagle swooping on the prey.
27 If I say, 'I will forget my complaint,
I will put off my sad countenance, and be of good cheer,'
28 I become afraid of all my suffering,
for I know thou wilt not hold me innocent.
29 I shall be condemned;
why then do I labor in vain?
30 If I wash myself with snow,
and cleanse my hands with lye,
31 yet thou wilt plunge me into a pit,
and my own clothes will abhor me.
32 For he is not a man, as I am, that I might answer him,
that we should come to trial together.
33 There is no[u] umpire between us,
who might lay his hand upon us both.
34 Let him take his rod away from me,
and let not dread of him terrify me.
35 Then I would speak without fear of him,
for I am not so in myself.

10 "I loathe my life;
I will give free utterance to my complaint;
I will speak in the bitterness of my soul.
2 I will say to God, Do not condemn me;
let me know why thou dost contend against me.
3 Does it seem good to thee to oppress,
to despise the work of thy hands
and favor the designs of the wicked?

[r] Or *for my right* [s] Compare Gk: Heb *me*. The text of the verse is uncertain
[t] The meaning of the Hebrew word is uncertain [u] Another reading is *Would that there were*

[4] Hast thou eyes of flesh?
Dost thou see as man sees?
[5] Are thy days as the days of man,
or thy years as man's years,
[6] that thou dost seek out my iniquity
and search for my sin,
[7] although thou knowest that I am not guilty,
and there is none to deliver out of thy hand?
[8] Thy hands fashioned and made me;
and now thou dost turn about and destroy me.[v]
[9] Remember that thou hast made me of clay;[w]
and wilt thou turn me to dust again?
[10] Didst thou not pour me out like milk
and curdle me like cheese?
[11] Thou didst clothe me with skin and flesh,
and knit me together with bones and sinews.
[12] Thou hast granted me life and steadfast love;
and thy care has preserved my spirit.
[13] Yet these things thou didst hide in thy heart;
I know that this was thy purpose.
[14] If I sin, thou dost mark me,
and dost not acquit me of my iniquity.
[15] If I am wicked, woe to me!
If I am righteous, I cannot lift up my head,
for I am filled with disgrace
and look upon my affliction.
[16] And if I lift myself up,[x] thou dost hunt me like a lion,
and again work wonders against me;
[17] thou dost renew thy witnesses against me,
and increase thy vexation toward me;
thou dost bring fresh hosts against me.[y]

[18] "Why didst thou bring me forth from the womb?
Would that I had died before any eye had seen me,
[19] and were as though I had not been,
carried from the womb to the grave.
[20] Are not the days of my life few?[z]
Let me alone, that I may find a little comfort[a]
[21] before I go whence I shall not return,
to the land of gloom and deep darkness,
[22] the land of gloom[b] and chaos,
where light is as darkness."

11 Then Zophar the Na'amathite answered:
[2] "Should a multitude of words go unanswered,
and a man full of talk be vindicated?
[3] Should your babble silence men,
and when you mock, shall no one shame you?
[4] For you say, 'My doctrine is pure,
and I am clean in God's eyes.'
[5] But oh, that God would speak,
and open his lips to you,
[6] and that he would tell you the secrets of wisdom!
For he is manifold in understanding.[c]
Know then that God exacts of you less than your guilt deserves.

[7] "Can you find out the deep things of God?
Can you find out the limit of the Almighty?
[8] It is higher than heaven[d]—what can you do?
Deeper than Sheol—what can you know?

[v] Cn Compare Gk Syr: Heb *made me together round about and thou dost destroy me*
[w] Gk: Heb *like clay* [x] Syr: Heb *he lifts himself up*
[y] Cn Compare Gk: Heb *changes and a host are with me*
[z] Cn Compare Gk Syr: Heb *Are not my days few? Let him cease*
[a] Heb *brightens up* [b] Heb *gloom as darkness, deep darkness*
[c] Heb obscure [d] Heb *The heights of heaven*

[9] Its measure is longer than the earth,
and broader than the sea.
[10] If he passes through, and imprisons,
and calls to judgment, who can hinder him?
[11] For he knows worthless men;
when he sees iniquity, will he not consider it?
[12] But a stupid man will get understanding,
when a wild ass's colt is born a man.

[13] "If you set your heart aright,
you will stretch out your hands toward him.
[14] If iniquity is in your hand, put it far away,
and let not wickedness dwell in your tents.
[15] Surely then you will lift up your face without blemish;
you will be secure, and will not fear.
[16] You will forget your misery;
you will remember it as waters that have passed away.
[17] And your life will be brighter than the noonday;
its darkness will be like the morning.
[18] And you will have confidence, because there is hope;
you will be protected [e] and take your rest in safety.
[19] You will lie down, and none will make you afraid;
many will entreat your favor.
[20] But the eyes of the wicked will fail;
all way of escape will be lost to them,
and their hope is to breathe their last."

12 Then Job answered:
[2] "No doubt you are the people,
and wisdom will die with you.
[3] But I have understanding as well as you;
I am not inferior to you.
Who does not know such things as these?
[4] I am a laughingstock to my friends;
I, who called upon God and he answered me,
a just and blameless man, am a laughingstock.
[5] In the thought of one who is at ease there is contempt for misfortune;
it is ready for those whose feet slip.
[6] The tents of robbers are at peace,
and those who provoke God are secure,
who bring their god in their hand.[f]

[7] "But ask the beasts, and they will teach you;
the birds of the air, and they will tell you;
[8] or the plants of the earth,[g] and they will teach you;
and the fish of the sea will declare to you.
[9] Who among all these does not know
that the hand of the LORD has done this?
[10] In his hand is the life of every living thing
and the breath of all mankind.
[11] Does not the ear try words
as the palate tastes food?
[12] Wisdom is with the aged,
and understanding in length of days.

[13] "With God [h] are wisdom and might;
he has counsel and understanding.
[14] If he tears down, none can rebuild;
if he shuts a man in, none can open.
[15] If he withholds the waters, they dry up;
if he sends them out, they overwhelm the land.

[e] Or *you will look around* [f] Hebrew uncertain [g] Or *speak to the earth* [h] Heb *him*

16 With him are strength and wisdom;
the deceived and the deceiver are his.
17 He leads counselors away stripped,
and judges he makes fools.
18 He looses the bonds of kings,
and binds a waistcloth on their loins.
19 He leads priests away stripped,
and overthrows the mighty.
20 He deprives of speech those who are trusted,
and takes away the discernment of the elders.
21 He pours contempt on princes,
and looses the belt of the strong.
22 He uncovers the deeps out of darkness,
and brings deep darkness to light.
23 He makes nations great, and he destroys them:
he enlarges nations, and leads them away.
24 He takes away understanding from the chiefs of the people of the earth,
and makes them wander in a pathless waste.
25 They grope in the dark without light;
and he makes them stagger like a drunken man.

13 "Lo, my eye has seen all this,
my ear has heard and understood it.
2 What you know, I also know;
I am not inferior to you.
3 But I would speak to the Almighty,
and I desire to argue my case with God.
4 As for you, you whitewash with lies;
worthless physicians are you all.
5 Oh that you would keep silent,
and it would be your wisdom!
6 Hear now my reasoning,
and listen to the pleadings of my lips.
7 Will you speak falsely for God,
and speak deceitfully for him?
8 Will you show partiality toward him,
will you plead the case for God?
9 Will it be well with you when he searches you out?
Or can you deceive him, as one deceives a man?
10 He will surely rebuke you
if in secret you show partiality.
11 Will not his majesty terrify you,
and the dread of him fall upon you?
12 Your maxims are proverbs of ashes,
your defences are defences of clay.

13 "Let me have silence, and I will speak,
and let come on me what may.
14 I will take[i] my flesh in my teeth,
and put my life in my hand.
15 Behold, he will slay me; I have no hope;
yet I will defend my ways to his face.
16 This will be my salvation,
that a godless man shall not come before him.
17 Listen carefully to my words,
and let my declaration be in your ears.
18 Behold, I have prepared my case;
I know that I shall be vindicated.
19 Who is there that will contend with me?
For then I would be silent and die.
20 Only grant two things to me,
then I will not hide myself from thy face:
21 withdraw thy hand far from me,
and let not dread of thee terrify me.
22 Then call, and I will answer;
or let me speak, and do thou reply to me.
23 How many are my iniquities and my sins?
Make me know my transgression and my sin.
24 Why dost thou hide thy face,
and count me as thy enemy?
25 Wilt thou frighten a driven leaf
and pursue dry chaff?

[i] Gk: Heb *Why should I take?*

26 For thou writest bitter things against me,
and makest me inherit the iniquities of my youth.
27 Thou puttest my feet in the stocks,
and watchest all my paths;
thou settest a bound to the soles of my feet.
28 Man[j] wastes away like a rotten thing,
like a garment that is moth-eaten.

14 "Man that is born of a woman
is of few days, and full of trouble.
2 He comes forth like a flower, and withers;
he flees like a shadow, and continues not.
3 And dost thou open thy eyes upon such a one
and bring him[k] into judgment with thee?
4 Who can bring a clean thing out of an unclean?
There is not one.
5 Since his days are determined,
and the number of his months is with thee,
and thou hast appointed his bounds that he cannot pass,
6 look away from him, and desist,[l]
that he may enjoy, like a hireling, his day.

7 "For there is hope for a tree,
if it be cut down, that it will sprout again,
and that its shoots will not cease.
8 Though its root grow old in the earth,
and its stump die in the ground,
9 yet at the scent of water it will bud
and put forth branches like a young plant.
10 But man dies, and is laid low;
man breathes his last, and where is he?
11 As waters fail from a lake,
and a river wastes away and dries up,
12 So man lies down and rises not again;
till the heavens are no more he will not awake,
or be roused out of his sleep.
13 Oh that thou wouldest hide me in Sheol,
that thou wouldest conceal me until thy wrath be past,
that thou wouldest appoint me a set time, and remember me!
14 If a man die, shall he live again?
All the days of my service I would wait,
till my release should come.
15 Thou wouldest call, and I would answer thee;
thou wouldest long for the work of thy hands.
16 For then thou wouldest number my steps,
thou wouldest not keep watch over my sin;
17 my transgression would be sealed up in a bag,
and thou wouldest cover over my iniquity.

18 "But the mountain falls and crumbles away,
and the rock is removed from its place;
19 the waters wear away the stones;
the torrents wash away the soil of the earth;
so thou destroyest the hope of man.
20 Thou prevailest for ever against him, and he passes;
thou changest his countenance, and sendest him away.
21 His sons come to honor, and he does not know it;
they are brought low, and he perceives it not.
22 He feels only the pain of his own body,
and he mourns only for himself."

[j] Heb *He* [k] Gk Syr Vg: Heb *me* [l] Cn: Heb *that he may desist*

15 Then Eli'phaz the Te'manite
answered:
2 "Should a wise man answer with
windy knowledge,
and fill himself with the east
wind?
3 Should he argue in unprofitable
talk,
or in words with which he can
do no good?
4 But you are doing away with the
fear of God,
and hindering meditation before
God,
5 For your iniquity teaches your
mouth,
and you choose the tongue of the
crafty.
6 Your own mouth condemns you,
and not I;
your own lips testify against you.

7 "Are you the first man that was
born?
Or were you brought forth before
the hills?
8 Have you listened in the council of
God?
And do you limit wisdom to your-
self?
9 What do you know that we do not
know?
What do you understand that is
not clear to us?
10 Both the grayhaired and the aged
are among us,
older than your father.
11 Are the consolations of God too
small for you,
or the word that deals gently with
you?
12 Why does your heart carry you away,
and why do your eyes flash,
13 that you turn your spirit against
God,
and let such words go out of your
mouth?
14 What is man, that he can be clean?
Or he that is born of a woman,
that he can be righteous?
15 Behold, God puts no trust in his
holy ones,
and the heavens are not clean in
his sight;
16 how much less one who is abomi-
nable and corrupt,
a man who drinks iniquity like
water!

17 "I will show you, hear me;
and what I have seen I will de-
clare
18 (what wise men have told,
and their fathers have not hid-
den,
19 to whom alone the land was given,
and no stranger passed among
them).
20 The wicked man writhes in pain all
his days,
through all the years that are laid
up for the ruthless.
21 Terrifying sounds are in his ears;
in prosperity the destroyer will
come upon him.
22 He does not believe that he will re-
turn out of darkness,
and he is destined for the sword.
23 He wanders abroad for bread, say-
ing, 'Where is it?'
He knows that a day of darkness
is ready at his hand;
24 distress and anguish terrify him;
they prevail against him, like a
king prepared for battle.
25 Because he has stretched forth his
hand against God,
and bids defiance to the Al-
mighty,
26 running stubbornly against him
with a thick-bossed shield;
27 because he has covered his face with
his fat,
and gathered fat upon his loins,
28 and has lived in desolate cities,
in houses which no man should
inhabit,
which were destined to become
heaps of ruins;
29 he will not be rich, and his wealth
will not endure,
nor will he strike root in the
earth;[m]

[m] Vg: Heb obscure

30 he will not escape from darkness;
the flame will dry up his shoots,
and his blossom[n] will be swept away[o] by the wind.
31 Let him not trust in emptiness, deceiving himself;
for emptiness will be his recompense.
32 It will be paid in full before his time,
and his branch will not be green.
33 He will shake off his unripe grape, like the vine,
and cast off his blossom, like the olive tree.
34 For the company of the godless is barren,
and fire consumes the tents of bribery.
35 They conceive mischief and bring forth evil
and their heart prepares deceit."

16 Then Job answered:
2 "I have heard many such things;
miserable comforters are you all.
3 Shall windy words have an end?
Or what provokes you that you answer?
4 I also could speak as you do,
if you were in my place;
I could join words together against you,
and shake my head at you.
5 I could strengthen you with my mouth,
and the solace of my lips would assuage your pain.

6 "If I speak, my pain is not assuaged,
and if I forbear, how much of it leaves me?
7 Surely now God has worn me out;
he has[p] made desolate all my company.
8 And he has[p] shriveled me up,
which is a witness against me;
and my leanness has risen up against me,
it testifies to my face.
9 He has torn me in his wrath, and hated me;
he has gnashed his teeth at me;
my adversary sharpens his eyes against me.
10 Men have gaped at me with their mouth,
they have struck me insolently upon the cheek,
they mass themselves together against me.
11 God gives me up to the ungodly,
and casts me into the hands of the wicked.
12 I was at ease, and he broke me asunder;
he seized me by the neck and dashed me to pieces;
He set me up as his target,
13 his archers surround me.
He slashes open my kidneys, and does not spare;
he pours out my gall on the ground.
14 He breaks me with breach upon breach;
he runs upon me like a warrior.
15 I have sewed sackcloth upon my skin,
and have laid my strength in the dust.
16 My face is red with weeping,
and on my eyelids is deep darkness;
17 although there is no violence in my hands,
and my prayer is pure.

18 "O earth, cover not my blood,
and let my cry find no resting place.
19 Even now, behold, my witness is in heaven,
and he that vouches for me is on high.
20 My friends scorn me;
my eye pours out tears to God,
21 that he would maintain the right of a man with God,
like[q] that of a man with his neighbor.

[n] Gk: Heb *mouth* [o] Cn: Heb *will depart*
[p] Heb *thou hast* [q] Syr Vg Tg: Heb *and*

22 For when a few years have come
I shall go the way whence I shall
not return.

17 My spirit is broken, my days
are extinct,
the grave is ready for me.
2 Surely there are mockers about me,
and my eye dwells on their provocation.

3 "Lay down a pledge for me with
thyself;
who is there that will give surety
for me?
4 Since thou hast closed their minds
to understanding,
therefore thou wilt not let them
triumph.
5 He who informs against his friends
to get a share of their property,
the eyes of his children will fail.

6 "He has made me a byword of the
peoples,
and I am one before whom men
spit.
7 My eye has grown dim from grief,
and all my members are like a
shadow.
8 Upright men are appalled at this,
and the innocent stirs himself up
against the godless.
9 Yet the righteous holds to his way,
and he that has clean hands
grows stronger and stronger.
10 But you, come on again, all of you,
and I shall not find a wise man
among you.
11 My days are past, my plans are
broken off,
the desires of my heart.
12 They make night into day;
'The light,' they say, 'is near to
the darkness.'[r]
13 If I look for Sheol as my house,
if I spread my couch in darkness,
14 if I say to the pit, 'You are my
father,'
and to the worm, 'My mother,'
or 'My sister,'
15 where then is my hope?
Who will see my hope?
16 Will it go down to the bars of
Sheol?
Shall we descend together into
the dust?"

18 Then Bildad the Shuhite answered:
2 "How long will you hunt for words?
Consider, and then we will speak.
3 Why are we counted as cattle?
Why are we stupid in your sight?
4 You who tear yourself in your
anger,
shall the earth be forsaken for
you,
or the rock be removed out of its
place?

5 "Yea, the light of the wicked is put
out,
and the flame of his fire does not
shine.
6 The light is dark in his tent,
and his lamp above him is put
out.
7 His strong steps are shortened
and his own schemes throw him
down.
8 For he is cast into a net by his own
feet,
and he walks on a pitfall.
9 A trap seizes him by the heel,
a snare lays hold of him.
10 A rope is hid for him in the ground,
a trap for him in the path.
11 Terrors frighten him on every side,
and chase him at his heels.
12 His strength is hunger-bitten,
and calamity is ready for his
stumbling.
13 By disease his skin is consumed,[s]
the first-born of death consumes
his limbs.
14 He is torn from the tent in which
he trusted,
and is brought to the king of
terrors.
15 In his tent dwells that which is
none of his;
brimstone is scattered upon his
habitation.

[r] Heb obscure [s] Cn: Heb *it consumes the limbs of his skin*

16 His roots dry up beneath,
and his branches wither above.
17 His memory perishes from the earth,
and he has no name in the street.
18 He is thrust from light into darkness,
and driven out of the world.
19 He has no offspring or descendant among his people,
and no survivor where he used to live.
20 They of the west are appalled at his day,
and horror seizes them of the east.
21 Surely such are the dwellings of the ungodly,
such is the place of him who knows not God."

19 Then Job answered:
2 "How long will you torment me,
and break me in pieces with words?
3 These ten times you have cast reproach upon me;
are you not ashamed to wrong me?
4 And even if it be true that I have erred,
my error remains with myself.
5 If indeed you magnify yourselves against me,
and make my humiliation an argument against me,
6 know then that God has put me in the wrong,
and closed his net about me.
7 Behold, I cry out. 'Violence!' but I am not answered;
I call aloud, but there is no justice.
8 He has walled up my way, so that I cannot pass,
and he has set darkness upon my paths.
9 He has stripped from me my glory,
and taken the crown from my head.
10 He breaks me down on every side, and I am gone,
and my hope has he pulled up like a tree.
11 He has kindled his wrath against me,
and counts me as his adversary.
12 His troops come on together;
they have cast up siegeworks[t] against me,
and encamp round about my tent.

13 "He has put my brethren far from me,
and my acquaintances are wholly estranged from me.
14 My kinsfolk and my close friends have failed me;
15 the guests in my house have forgotten me;
my maidservants count me as a stranger;
I have become an alien in their eyes.
16 I call to my servant, but he gives me no answer;
I must beseech him with my mouth.
17 I am repulsive to my wife,
loathsome to the sons of my own mother.
18 Even young children despise me;
when I rise they talk against me.
19 All my intimate friends abhor me,
and those whom I loved have turned against me.
20 My bones cleave to my skin and to my flesh,
and I have escaped by the skin of my teeth.
21 Have pity on me, have pity on me,
O you my friends,
for the hand of God has touched me!
22 Why do you, like God, pursue me?
Why are you not satisfied with my flesh?

23 "Oh that my words were written!
Oh that they were inscribed in a book!

[t] Heb *their way*

24 Oh that with an iron pen and lead
they were graven in the rock for ever!
25 For I know that my Redeemer[u] lives,
and at last he will stand upon the earth;[v]
26 and after my skin has been thus destroyed,
then without[w] my flesh I shall see God,[x]
27 whom I shall see on my side,[y]
and my eyes shall behold, and not another.
My heart faints within me!
28 If you say, 'How we will pursue him!'
and, 'The root of the matter is found in him';
29 be afraid of the sword,
for wrath brings the punishment of the sword,
that you may know there is a judgment."

20 Then Zophar the Na'amathite answered:
2 "Therefore my thoughts answer me,
because of my haste within me.
3 I hear censure which insults me,
and out of my understanding a spirit answers me.
4 Do you not know this from of old,
since man was placed upon earth,
5 that the exulting of the wicked is short,
and the joy of the godless but for a moment?
6 Though his height mount up to the heavens,
and his head reach to the clouds,
7 he will perish for ever like his own dung;
those who have seen him will say, 'Where is he?'
8 He will fly away like a dream, and not be found;
he will be chased away like a vision of the night.
9 The eye which saw him will see him no more,
nor will his place any more behold him.
10 His children will seek the favor of the poor,
and his hands will give back his wealth.
11 His bones are full of youthful vigor,
but it will lie down with him in the dust.

12 "Though wickedness is sweet in his mouth,
though he hides it under his tongue,
13 though he is loath to let it go,
and holds it in his mouth,
14 yet his food is turned in his stomach;
it is the gall of asps within him.
15 He swallows down riches and vomits them up again;
God casts them out of his belly.
16 He will suck the poison of asps;
the tongue of a viper will kill him.
17 He will not look upon the rivers,
the streams flowing with honey and curds.
18 He will give back the fruit of his toil,
and will not swallow it down;
from the profit of his trading
he will get no enjoyment.
19 For he has crushed and abandoned the poor,
he has seized a house which he did not build.

20 "Because his greed knew no rest,
he will not save anything in which he delights.
21 There was nothing left after he had eaten;
therefore his prosperity will not endure.
22 In the fulness of his sufficiency he will be in straits;
all the force of misery will come upon him.

[u] Or *Vindicator* [v] Or *dust* [w] Or *from*
[x] The meaning of this verse is uncertain [y] Or *for myself*

23 To fill his belly to the full
God[z] will send his fierce anger into him,
and rain it upon him as his food.[a]
24 He will flee from an iron weapon;
a bronze arrow will strike him through.
25 It is drawn forth and comes out of his body,
the glittering point comes out of his gall;
terrors come upon him.
26 Utter darkness is laid up for his treasures;
a fire not blown upon will devour him;
what is left in his tent will be consumed.
27 The heavens will reveal his iniquity,
and the earth will rise up against him.
28 The possessions of his house will be carried away,
dragged off in the day of God's[b] wrath.
29 This is the wicked man's portion from God,
the heritage decreed for him by God."

21 Then Job answered:
2 "Listen carefully to my words,
and let this be your consolation.
3 Bear with me, and I will speak,
and after I have spoken, mock on.
4 As for me, is my complaint against man?
Why should I not be impatient?
5 Look at me, and be appalled,
and lay your hand upon your mouth.
6 When I think of it I am dismayed,
and shuddering seizes my flesh.
7 Why do the wicked live,
reach old age, and grow mighty in power?
8 Their children are established in their presence,
and their offspring before their eyes.
9 Their houses are safe from fear,
and no rod of God is upon them.
10 Their bull breeds without fail;
their cow calves, and does not cast her calf.
11 They send forth their little ones like a flock,
and their children dance.
12 They sing to the tambourine and the lyre,
and rejoice to the sound of the pipe.
13 They spend their days in prosperity,
and in peace they go down to Sheol.
14 They say to God, 'Depart from us!
We do not desire the knowledge of thy ways.
15 What is the Almighty, that we should serve him?
And what profit do we get if we pray to him?'
16 Behold, is not their prosperity in their hand?
The counsel of the wicked is far from me.

17 "How often is it that the lamp of the wicked is put out?
That their calamity comes upon them?
That God[c] distributes pains in his anger?
18 That they are like straw before the wind,
and like chaff that the storm carries away?
19 You say, 'God stores up their iniquity for their sons.'
Let him recompense it to themselves, that they may know it.
20 Let their own eyes see their destruction,
and let them drink of the wrath of the Almighty.
21 For what do they care for their houses after them,
when the number of their months is cut off?
22 Will any teach God knowledge,
seeing that he judges those that are on high?

[z] Heb *he* [a] Cn: Heb *in his flesh* [b] Heb *his* [c] Heb *he*

23 One dies in full prosperity,
being wholly at ease and secure,
24 his body[d] full of fat
and the marrow of his bones moist.
25 Another dies in bitterness of soul,
never having tasted of good.
26 They lie down alike in the dust,
and the worms cover them.

27 "Behold, I know your thoughts,
and your schemes to wrong me.
28 For you say, 'Where is the house of the prince?
Where is the tent in which the wicked dwelt?'
29 Have you not asked those who travel the roads,
and do you not accept their testimony
30 that the wicked man is spared in the day of calamity,
that he is rescued in the day of wrath?
31 Who declares his way to his face,
and who requites him for what he has done?
32 When he is borne to the grave,
watch is kept over his tomb.
33 The clods of the valley are sweet to him;
all men follow after him,
and those who go before him are innumerable.
34 How then will you comfort me with empty nothings?
There is nothing left of your answers but falsehood."

22 Then Eli'phaz the Te'manite answered:
2 "Can a man be profitable to God?
Surely he who is wise is profitable to himself.
3 Is it any pleasure to the Almighty if you are righteous,
or is it gain to him if you make your ways blameless?
4 Is it for your fear of him that he reproves you,
and enters into judgment with you?
5 Is not your wickedness great?
There is no end to your iniquities.
6 For you have exacted pledges of your brothers for nothing,
and stripped the naked of their clothing.
7 You have given no water to the weary to drink,
and you have withheld bread from the hungry.
8 The man with power possessed the land,
and the favored man dwelt in it.
9 You have sent widows away empty,
and the arms of the fatherless were crushed.
10 Therefore snares are round about you,
and sudden terror overwhelms you;
11 your light is darkened, so that[e] you cannot see,
and a flood of water covers you.

12 "Is not God high in the heavens?
See the highest stars, how lofty they are!
13 Therefore you say, 'What does God know?
Can he judge through the deep darkness?
14 Thick clouds enwrap him, so that he does not see,
and he walks on the vault of heaven.'
15 Will you keep to the old way
which wicked men have trod?
16 They were snatched away before their time;
their foundation was washed away.
17 They said to God, 'Depart from us,'
and 'What can the Almighty do to us?'[f]
18 Yet he filled their houses with good things—
but the counsel of the wicked is far from me.

[d] The meaning of the Hebrew word is uncertain
[e] Cn Compare Gk: Heb *or darkness* [f] Gk Syr: Heb *them*
22. 2, 3: 35. 6-8.

19 The righteous see it and are glad;
the innocent laugh them to scorn,
20 saying, 'Surely our adversaries are cut off,
and what they left the fire has consumed.'

21 "Agree with God, and be at peace;
thereby good will come to you.
22 Receive instruction from his mouth,
and lay up his words in your heart.
23 If you return to the Almighty and humble yourself,[g]
if you remove unrighteousness far from your tents,
24 if you lay gold in the dust,
and gold of Ophir among the stones of the torrent bed,
25 and if the Almighty is your gold,
and your precious silver;
26 then you will delight yourself in the Almighty,
and lift up your face to God.
27 You will make your prayer to him,
and he will hear you;
and you will pay your vows.
28 You will decide on a matter, and it will be established for you,
and light will shine on your ways.
29 For God abases the proud,[h]
but he saves the lowly.
30 He delivers the innocent man;[i]
you will be delivered through the cleanness of your hands."

23 Then Job answered:
2 "Today also my complaint is bitter,[j]
his[k] hand is heavy in spite of my groaning.
3 Oh, that I knew where I might find him,
that I might come even to his seat!
4 I would lay my case before him
and fill my mouth with arguments.
5 I would learn what he would answer me,
and understand what he would say to me.
6 Would he contend with me in the greatness of his power?
No; he would give heed to me.
7 There an upright man could reason with him,
and I should be acquitted for ever by my judge.

8 "Behold, I go forward, but he is not there;
and backward, but I cannot perceive him;
9 on the left hand I seek him,[l] but I cannot behold him;
I[m] turn to the right hand, but I cannot see him.
10 But he knows the way that I take;
when he has tried me, I shall come forth as gold.
11 My foot has held fast to his steps;
I have kept his way and have not turned aside.
12 I have not departed from the commandment of his lips;
I have treasured in[n] my bosom the words of his mouth.
13 But he is unchangeable and who can turn him?
What he desires, that he does.
14 For he will complete what he appoints for me;
and many such things are in his mind.
15 Therefore I am terrified at his presence;
when I consider, I am in dread of him.
16 God has made my heart faint;
the Almighty has terrified me;
17 for I am[o] hemmed in by darkness,
and thick darkness covers my face.[p]

[g] Gk: Heb *you will be built up* [h] Cn: Heb *when they abased you said, Proud*
[i] Gk Syr Vg: Heb *him that is not innocent* [j] Syr Vg Tg: Heb *rebellious* [k] Gk Syr: Heb *my*
[l] Compare Syr: Heb *on the left hand when he works* [m] Syr Vg: Heb *he* [n] Gk Vg: Heb *from*
[o] With one Ms: Heb *am not* [p] Vg: Heb *from my face*

24 "Why are not times of judgment kept by the Almighty,
and why do those who know him never see his days?
2 Men remove landmarks;
they seize flocks and pasture them.
3 They drive away the ass of the fatherless;
they take the widow's ox for a pledge.
4 They thrust the poor off the road;
the poor of the earth all hide themselves.
5 Behold, like wild asses in the desert
they go forth to their toil,
seeking prey in the wilderness
as food[q] for their children.
6 They gather their[r] fodder in the field
and they glean the vineyard of the wicked man.
7 They lie all night naked, without clothing,
and have no covering in the cold.
8 They are wet with the rain of the mountains,
and cling to the rock for want of shelter.
9 (There are those who snatch the fatherless child from the breast,
and take in pledge the infant of the poor.)
10 They go about naked, without clothing;
hungry, they carry the sheaves;
11 among the olive rows of the wicked[s]
they make oil;
they tread the wine presses, but suffer thirst.
12 From out of the city the dying groan,
and the soul of the wounded cries for help;
yet God pays no attention to their prayer.

13 "There are those who rebel against the light,
who are not acquainted with its ways,
and do not stay in its paths.
14 The murderer rises in the dark,[t]
that he may kill the poor and needy;
and in the night he is as a thief.
15 The eye of the adulterer also waits for the twilight,
saying, 'No eye will see me';
and he disguises his face.
16 In the dark they dig through houses;
by day they shut themselves up;
they do not know the light.
17 For deep darkness is morning to all of them;
for they are friends with the terrors of deep darkness.

18 "You say, 'They are swiftly carried away upon the face of the waters;
their portion is cursed in the land;
no treader turns toward their vineyards.
19 Drought and heat snatch away the snow waters;
so does Sheol those who have sinned.
20 The squares of the town[u] forget them;
their name[v] is no longer remembered;
so wickedness is broken like a tree.'

21 "They feed on the barren childless woman,
and do no good to the widow.
22 Yet God[w] prolongs the life of the mighty by his power;
they rise up when they despair of life.
23 He gives them security, and they are supported;
and his eyes are upon their ways.
24 They are exalted a little while, and then are gone;
they wither and fade like the mallow;[x]

[q] Heb *food to him* [r] Heb *his* [s] Heb *their olive rows* [t] Cn: Heb *at the light*
[u] Cn: Heb obscure [v] Cn: Heb *a worm* [w] Heb *he* [x] Gk: Heb *all*

they are cut off like the heads of
grain.
25 If it is not so, who will prove me a
liar,
and show that there is nothing
in what I say?"

25 Then Bildad the Shuhite
answered:
2 "Dominion and fear are with God;[y]
he makes peace in his high
heaven.
3 Is there any number to his armies?
Upon whom does his light not
arise?
4 How then can man be righteous before God?
How can he who is born of
woman be clean?
5 Behold, even the moon is not bright
and the stars are not clean in his
sight;
6 how much less man, who is a maggot,
and the son of man, who is a
worm!"

26 Then Job answered:
2 "How you have helped
him who has no power!
How you have saved the arm that
has no strength!
3 How you have counseled him who
has no wisdom,
and plentifully declared sound
knowledge!
4 With whose help have you uttered
words,
and whose spirit has come forth
from you?
5 The shades below tremble,
the waters and their inhabitants.
6 Sheol is naked before God,
and Abaddon has no covering.
7 He stretches out the north over the
void,
and hangs the earth upon nothing.
8 He binds up the waters in his thick
clouds,
and the cloud is not rent under
them.
9 He covers the face of the moon,[z]
and spreads over it his cloud.
10 He has described a circle upon the
face of the waters
at the boundary between light
and darkness.
11 The pillars of heaven tremble,
and are astounded at his rebuke.
12 By his power he stilled the sea;
by his understanding he smote
Rahab.
13 By his wind the heavens were made
fair;
his hand pierced the fleeing serpent.
14 Lo, these are but the outskirts of
his ways;
and how small a whisper do we
hear of him!
But the thunder of his power
who can understand?"

27 And Job again took up his
discourse, and said:
2 "As God lives, who has taken away
my right,
and the Almighty, who has made
my soul bitter;
3 as long as my breath is in me,
and the spirit of God is in my
nostrils;
4 my lips will not speak falsehood,
and my tongue will not utter
deceit.
5 Far be it from me to say that you
are right;
till I die I will not put away my
integrity from me.
6 I hold fast my righteousness, and
will not let it go;
my heart does not reproach me
for any of my days.

7 "Let my enemy be as the wicked,
and let him that rises up against
me be as the unrighteous.
8 For what is the hope of the godless when God cuts him off,
when God takes away his life?
9 Will God hear his cry,
when trouble comes upon him?

[y] Heb *him* [z] Or *his throne*

10 Will he take delight in the Almighty?
Will he call upon God at all times?
11 I will teach you concerning the hand of God;
what is with the Almighty I will not conceal.
12 Behold, all of you have seen it yourselves;
why then have you become altogether vain?

13 "This is the portion of a wicked man with God,
and the heritage which oppressors receive from the Almighty:
14 If his children are multiplied, it is for the sword;
and his offspring have not enough to eat.
15 Those who survive him the pestilence buries,
and their widows make no lamentation.
16 Though he heap up silver like dust,
and pile up clothing like clay;
17 he may pile it up, but the just will wear it,
and the innocent will divide the silver.
18 The house which he builds is like a spider's web,[a]
like a booth which a watchman makes.
19 He goes to bed rich, but will do so no more;[b]
he opens his eyes, and his wealth is gone.
20 Terrors overtake him like a flood;
in the night a whirlwind carries him off.
21 The east wind lifts him up and he is gone;
it sweeps him out of his place.
22 It[c] hurls at him without pity;
he flees from its[d] power in headlong flight.
23 It[c] claps its[d] hands at him,
and hisses at him from its[d] place.

28 "Surely there is a mine for silver,
and a place for gold which they refine.
2 Iron is taken out of the earth,
and copper is smelted from the ore.
3 Men put an end to darkness,
and search out to the farthest bound
the ore in gloom and deep darkness.
4 They open shafts in a valley away from where men live;
they are forgotten by travelers,
they hang afar from men, they swing to and fro.
5 As for the earth, out of it comes bread;
but underneath it is turned up as by fire.
6 Its stones are the place of sapphires,[e]
and it has dust of gold.

7 "That path no bird of prey knows,
and the falcon's eye has not seen it.
8 The proud beasts have not trodden it;
the lion has not passed over it.

9 "Man puts his hand to the flinty rock,
and overturns mountains by the roots.
10 He cuts out channels in the rocks,
and his eye sees every precious thing.
11 He binds up the streams so that they do not trickle,
and the thing that is hid he brings forth to light.

12 "But where shall wisdom be found?
And where is the place of understanding?

[a] Cn Compare Gk Syr: Heb *He builds his house like the moth*
[b] Gk Compare Syr: Heb *shall not be gathered*
[c] Or *he* (that is God) [d] Or *his* [e] Or *lapis lazuli*

13 Man does not know the way to it,[f]
and it is not found in the land of the living.
14 The deep says, 'It is not in me,'
and the sea says, 'It is not with me.'
15 It cannot be gotten for gold,
and silver cannot be weighed as its price.
16 It cannot be valued in the gold of Ophir,
in precious onyx or sapphire.[g]
17 Gold and glass cannot equal it,
nor can it be exchanged for jewels of fine gold.
18 No mention shall be made of coral or of crystal;
the price of wisdom is above pearls.
19 The topaz of Ethiopia cannot compare with it,
nor can it be valued in pure gold.

20 "Whence then comes wisdom?
And where is the place of understanding?
21 It is hid from the eyes of all living,
and concealed from the birds of the air.
22 Abaddon and Death say,
'We have heard a rumor of it with our ears.'

23 "God understands the way to it,
and he knows its place.
24 For he looks to the ends of the earth,
and sees everything under the heavens.
25 When he gave to the wind its weight,
and meted out the waters by measure;
26 when he made a decree for the rain,
and a way for the lightning of the thunder;
27 then he saw it and declared it;
he established it, and searched it out.
28 And he said to man,
'Behold, the fear of the Lord, that is wisdom;
and to depart from evil is understanding.' "

29 And Job again took up his discourse, and said:
2 "Oh, that I were as in the months of old,
as in the days when God watched over me;
3 when his lamp shone upon my head,
and by his light I walked through darkness;
4 as I was in my autumn days,
when the friendship of God was upon my tent;
5 when the Almighty was yet with me,
when my children were about me;
6 when my steps were washed with milk,
and the rock poured out for me streams of oil!
7 When I went out to the gate of the city,
when I prepared my seat in the square,
8 the young men saw me and withdrew,
and the aged rose and stood;
9 the princes refrained from talking,
and laid their hand on their mouth;
10 the voice of the nobles was hushed,
and their tongue cleaved to the roof of their mouth.
11 When the ear heard, it called me blessed,
and when the eye saw, it approved;
12 because I delivered the poor who cried,
and the fatherless who had none to help him.
13 The blessing of him who was about to perish came upon me,
and I caused the widow's heart to sing for joy.
14 I put on righteousness, and it clothed me;

[f] Gk.: Heb *its price* [g] Or *lapis lazuli*

my justice was like a robe and a
turban.
15 I was eyes to the blind,
and feet to the lame.
16 I was a father to the poor,
and I searched out the cause of
him whom I did not know.
17 I broke the fangs of the unrighteous,
and made him drop his prey from
his teeth.
18 Then I thought, 'I shall die in my
nest,
and I shall multiply my days as
the sand,
19 my roots spread out to the waters,
with the dew all night on my
branches,
20 my glory fresh with me,
and my bow ever new in my
hand.'

21 "Men listened to me, and waited,
and kept silence for my counsel.
22 After I spoke they did not speak
again,
and my word dropped upon
them.
23 They waited for me as for the rain;
and they opened their mouths
as for the spring rain.
24 I smiled on them when they had
no confidence;
and the light of my countenance
they did not cast down.
25 I chose their way, and sat as chief,
and I dwelt like a king among
his troops,
like one who comforts mourners.

30 "But now they make sport
of me,
men who are younger than I,
whose fathers I would have disdained
to set with the dogs of my flock.
2 What could I gain from the
strength of their hands,
men whose vigor is gone?
3 Through want and hard hunger
they gnaw the dry and desolate
ground;[h]
4 they pick mallow and the leaves of
bushes,
and to warm themselves the roots
of the broom.
5 They are driven out from among
men;
they shout after them as after a
thief.
6 In the gullies of the torrents they
must dwell,
in holes of the earth and of the
rocks.
7 Among the bushes they bray;
under the nettles they huddle together.
8 A senseless, a disreputable brood,
they have been whipped out of
the land.

9 "And now I have become their
song,
I am a byword to them.
10 They abhor me, they keep aloof
from me;
they do not hesitate to spit at
the sight of me.
11 Because God has loosed my cord
and humbled me,
they have cast off restraint in my
presence.
12 On my right hand the rabble rise,
they drive me[i] forth,
they cast up against me their
ways of destruction.
13 They break up my path,
they promote my calamity;
no one restrains[j] them.
14 As through[k] a wide breach they
come;
amid the crash they roll on.
15 Terrors are turned upon me;
my honor is pursued as by the
wind,
and my prosperity has passed
away like a cloud.

16 "And now my soul is poured out
within me;

[h] Heb *ground yesterday waste* [i] Heb *my feet* [j] Cn: Heb *helps* [k] Cn: Heb *like*

days of affliction have taken hold
of me.
17 The night racks my bones,
and the pain that gnaws me takes
no rest.
18 With violence it seizes my garment;[l]
it binds me about like the collar
of my tunic.
19 God has cast me into the mire,
and I have become like dust and
ashes.
20 I cry to thee and thou dost not
answer me;
I stand, and thou dost not[m] heed
me.
21 Thou hast turned cruel to me;
with the might of thy hand thou
dost persecute me.
22 Thou liftest me up on the wind,
thou makest me ride on it,
and thou tossest me about in
the roar of the storm.
23 Yea, I know that thou wilt bring
me to death,
and to the house appointed for
all living.

24 "Yet does not one in a heap of ruins
stretch out his hand,
and in his disaster cry for help?[n]
25 Did not I weep for him whose day
was hard?
Was not my soul grieved for the
poor?
26 But when I looked for good, evil
came;
and when I waited for light, darkness came.
27 My heart is in turmoil, and is never
still;
days of affliction come to meet
me.
28 I go about blackened, but not by
the sun;
I stand up in the assembly, and
cry for help.
29 I am a brother of jackals,
and a companion of ostriches.
30 My skin turns black and falls from
me,
and my bones burn with heat.
31 My lyre is turned to mourning,
and my pipe to the voice of those
who weep.

31 "I have made a covenant with
my eyes;
how then could I look upon a
virgin?
2 What would be my portion from
God above,
and my heritage from the Almighty on high?
3 Does not calamity befall the unrighteous,
and disaster the workers of iniquity?
4 Does not he see my ways,
and number all my steps?

5 "If I have walked with falsehood,
and my foot has hastened to deceit;
6 (Let me be weighed in a just balance,
and let God know my integrity!)
7 if my step has turned aside from
the way,
and my heart has gone after my
eyes,
and if any spot has cleaved to my
hands;
8 then let me sow, and another eat;
and let what grows for me be
rooted out.

9 "If my heart has been enticed to a
woman,
and I have lain in wait at my
neighbor's door;
10 then let my wife grind for another,
and let others bow down upon
her.
11 For that would be a heinous crime;
that would be an iniquity to be
punished by the judges;
12 for that would be a fire which consumes unto Abaddon,
and it would burn to the root all
my increase.

[l] Gk: Heb *my garment is disfigured*
[m] One Heb Ms and Vg: Heb lacks *not*
[n] Cn: Heb obscure

13 "If I have rejected the cause of my manservant or my maidservant,
when they brought a complaint against me;
14 what then shall I do when God rises up?
When he makes inquiry, what shall I answer him?
15 Did not he who made me in the womb make him?
And did not one fashion us in the womb?

16 "If I have withheld anything that the poor desired,
or have caused the eyes of the widow to fail,
17 or have eaten my morsel alone,
and the fatherless has not eaten of it
18 (for from his youth I reared him[o] as a father,
and from his mother's womb I guided him);
19 if I have seen anyone perish for lack of clothing,
or a poor man without covering;
20 if his loins have not blessed me,
and if he was not warmed with the fleece of my sheep;
21 if I have raised my hand against the fatherless,
because I saw help in the gate;
22 then let my shoulder blade fall from my shoulder,
and let my arm be broken from its socket.
23 For I was in terror of calamity from God,
and I could not have faced his majesty.

24 "If I have made gold my trust,
or called fine gold my confidence;
25 if I have rejoiced because my wealth was great,
or because my hand had gotten much;
26 if I have looked at the sun[p] when it shone,
or the moon moving in splendor,
27 and my heart has been secretly enticed,
and my mouth has kissed my hand;
28 this also would be an iniquity to be punished by the judges,
for I should have been false to God above.

29 "If I have rejoiced at the ruin of him that hated me,
or exulted when evil overtook him
30 (I have not let my mouth sin
by asking for his life with a curse);
31 if the men of my tent have not said,
'Who is there that has not been filled with his meat?'
32 (the sojourner has not lodged in the street;
I have opened my doors to the wayfarer);
33 if I have concealed my transgressions from men,[q]
by hiding my iniquity in my bosom,
34 because I stood in great fear of the multitude,
and the contempt of families terrified me,
so that I kept silence, and did not go out of doors—
35 Oh, that I had one to hear me!
(Here is my signature! let the Almighty answer me!)
Oh, that I had the indictment written by my adversary!
36 Surely I would carry it on my shoulder;
I would bind it on me as a crown;
37 I would give him an account of all my steps;
like a prince I would approach him.

38 "If my land has cried out against me,
and its furrows have wept together;

[o] Cn: Heb *for from my youth he grew up to me as a father, and from my mother's womb I guided her* [p] Heb *the light* [q] Cn: Heb *like men* or *like Adam*

39 if I have eaten its yield without payment,
and caused the death of its owners;
40 let thorns grow instead of wheat,
and foul weeds instead of barley."

The words of Job are ended.

32 So these three men ceased to
answer Job, because he was
righteous in his own eyes. 2 Then
Eli'hu the son of Bar'achel the Buzite,
of the family of Ram, became angry.
He was angry at Job because he justi-
fied himself rather than God; 3 he
was angry also at Job's three friends
because they had found no answer,
although they had declared Job to
be in the wrong. 4 Now Eli'hu had
waited to speak to Job because they
were older than he. 5 And when
Eli'hu saw that there was no answer
in the mouth of these three men, he
became angry.

6 And Eli'hu the son of Bar'achel the Buzite answered:
"I am young in years,
and you are aged;
therefore I was timid and afraid
to declare my opinion to you.
7 I said, 'Let days speak,
and many years teach wisdom.'
8 But it is the spirit in a man,
the breath of the Almighty,
that makes him understand.
9 It is not the old[r] that are wise,
nor the aged that understand what is right.
10 Therefore I say, 'Listen to me;
let me also declare my opinion.'

11 "Behold, I waited for your words,
I listened for your wise sayings,
while you searched out what to say.
12 I gave you my attention,
and, behold, there was none that confuted Job,
or that answered his words, among you.
13 Beware lest you say, 'We have found wisdom;
God may vanquish him, not man.'
14 He has not directed his words against me,
and I will not answer him with your speeches.

15 "They are discomfited, they answer no more;
they have not a word to say.
16 And shall I wait, because they do not speak,
because they stand there, and answer no more?
17 I also will give my answer;
I also will declare my opinion.
18 For I am full of words,
the spirit within me constrains me.
19 Behold, my heart is like wine that has no vent;
like new wineskins, it is ready to burst.
20 I must speak, that I may find relief;
I must open my lips and answer.
21 I will not show partiality to any person
or use flattery toward any man.
22 For I do not know how to flatter,
else would my Maker soon put an end to me.

33 "But now, hear my speech, O Job,
and listen to all my words.
2 Behold, I open my mouth;
the tongue in my mouth speaks.
3 My words declare the uprightness of my heart,
and what my lips know they speak sincerely.
4 The spirit of God has made me,
and the breath of the Almighty gives me life.
5 Answer me, if you can;
set your words in order before me; take your stand.
6 Behold, I am toward God as you are;

r Gk Syr Vg: Heb *many*

I too was formed from a piece of clay.
7 Behold, no fear of me need terrify you;
my pressure will not be heavy upon you.

8 "Surely, you have spoken in my hearing,
and I have heard the sound of your words.
9 You say, 'I am clean, without transgression;
I am pure, and there is no iniquity in me.
10 Behold, he finds occasions against me,
he counts me as his enemy;
11 he puts my feet in the stocks,
and watches all my paths.'

12 "Behold, in this you are not right.
I will answer you.
God is greater than man.
13 Why do you contend against him,
saying, 'He will answer none of my[s] words'?
14 For God speaks in one way,
and in two, though man does not perceive it.
15 In a dream, in a vision of the night,
when deep sleep falls upon men,
while they slumber on their beds,
16 then he opens the ears of men,
and terrifies them with warnings,
17 that he may turn man aside from his deed,
and cut off[t] pride from man;
18 he keeps back his soul from the Pit,
his life from perishing by the sword.

19 "Man is also chastened with pain upon his bed,
and with continual strife in his bones;
20 so that his life loathes bread,
and his appetite dainty food.
21 His flesh is so wasted away that it cannot be seen;
and his bones which were not seen stick out.
22 His soul draws near the Pit,
and his life to those who bring death.
23 If there be for him an angel,
a mediator, one of the thousand,
to declare to man what is right for him;
24 and he is gracious to him, and says,
'Deliver him from going down into the Pit,
I have found a ransom;
25 let his flesh become fresh with youth;
let him return to the days of his youthful vigor.'
26 Then man prays to God, and he accepts him,
he comes into his presence with joy.
He recounts[u] to men his salvation,
27 and he sings before men, and says:
'I sinned, and perverted what was right,
and it was not requited to me.
28 He has redeemed my soul from going down into the Pit,
and my life shall see the light.'

29 "Behold, God does all these things,
twice, three times, with a man,
30 to bring back his soul from the Pit,
that he may see the light of life.[v]
31 Give heed, O Job, listen to me;
be silent, and I will speak.
32 If you have anything to say, answer me;
speak, for I desire to justify you.
33 If not, listen to me;
be silent, and I will teach you wisdom."

34 Then Eli'hu said:
2 "Hear my words, you wise men,
and give ear to me, you who know;
3 for the ear tests words
as the palate tastes food.

[s] Compare Gk: Heb *his* [t] Cn: Heb *hide* [u] Cn: Heb *returns*
[v] Syr: Heb *to be lighted with the light of life*

[4] Let us choose what is right;
let us determine among ourselves
what is good.
[5] For Job has said, 'I am innocent,
and God has taken away my
right;
[6] in spite of my right I am counted
a liar;
my wound is incurable, though I
am without transgression.'
[7] What man is like Job,
who drinks up scoffing like water,
[8] who goes in company with evil-
doers
and walks with wicked men?
[9] For he has said, 'It profits a man
nothing
that he should take delight in
God.'

[10] "Therefore, hear me, you men of
understanding,
far be it from God that he
should do wickedness,
and from the Almighty that he
should do wrong.
[11] For according to the work of a man
he will requite him,
and according to his ways he will
make it befall him.
[12] Of a truth, God will not do
wickedly,
and the Almighty will not per-
vert justice.
[13] Who gave him charge over the
earth
and who laid on him[w] the whole
world?
[14] If he should take back his spirit[x]
to himself,
and gather to himself his breath,
[15] all flesh would perish together,
and man would return to dust.

[16] "If you have understanding, hear
this;
listen to what I say.
[17] Shall one who hates justice govern?
Will you condemn him who is
righteous and mighty,
[18] who says to a king, 'Worthless one,'
and to nobles, 'Wicked man';
[19] who shows no partiality to princes,
nor regards the rich more than
the poor,
for they are all the work of his
hands?
[20] In a moment they die;
at midnight the people are
shaken and pass away,
and the mighty are taken away
by no human hand.

[21] "For his eyes are upon the ways of
a man,
and he sees all his steps.
[22] There is no gloom or deep darkness
where evildoers may hide them-
selves.
[23] For he has not appointed a time[y]
for any man
to go before God in judgment.
[24] He shatters the mighty without in-
vestigation,
and sets others in their place.
[25] Thus, knowing their works,
he overturns them in the night,
and they are crushed.
[26] He strikes them for their wicked-
ness
in the sight of men,
[27] because they turned aside from fol-
lowing him,
and had no regard for any of his
ways,
[28] so that they caused the cry of the
poor to come to him,
and he heard the cry of the af-
flicted—
[29] When he is quiet, who can con-
demn?
When he hides his face, who can
behold him,
whether it be a nation or a
man?—
[30] that a godless man should not reign,
that he should not ensnare the
people.

[31] "For has any one said to God,
'I have borne chastisement; I will
not offend any more;
[32] teach me what I do not see;

[w] Heb lacks *on him* [x] Heb *his heart his spirit* [y] Cn: Heb *yet*

if I have done iniquity, I will do it no more'?
33 Will he then make requital to suit you,
because you reject it?
For you must choose, and not I;
therefore declare what you know.[z]
34 Men of understanding will say to me,
and the wise man who hears me will say:
35 'Job speaks without knowledge,
his words are without insight.'
36 Would that Job were tried to the end,
because he answers like wicked men.
37 For he adds rebellion to his sin;
he claps his hands among us,
and multiplies his words against God."

35 And Eli'hu said:
2 "Do you think this to be just?
Do you say, 'It is my right before God,'
3 that you ask, 'What advantage have I?
How am I better off than if I had sinned?'
4 I will answer you
and your friends with you.
5 Look at the heavens, and see;
and behold the clouds, which are higher than you.
6 If you have sinned, what do you accomplish against him?
And if your transgressions are multiplied, what do you do to him?
7 If you are righteous, what do you give to him;
or what does he receive from your hand?
8 Your wickedness concerns a man like yourself,
and your righteousness a son of man.

9 "Because of the multitude of oppressions people cry out;
they call for help because of the arm of the mighty.
10 But none says, 'Where is God my Maker,
who gives songs in the night,
11 who teaches us more than the beasts of the earth,
and makes us wiser than the birds of the air?'
12 There they cry out, but he does not answer,
because of the pride of evil men.
13 Surely God does not hear an empty cry,
nor does the Almighty regard it.
14 How much less when you say that you do not see him,
that the case is before him, and you are waiting for him!
15 And now, because his anger does not punish,
and he does not greatly heed transgression,[a]
16 Job opens his mouth in empty talk,
he multiplies words without knowledge."

36 And Eli'hu continued, and said:
2 "Bear with me a little, and I will show you,
for I have yet something to say on God's behalf.
3 I will fetch my knowledge from afar,
and ascribe righteousness to my Maker.
4 For truly my words are not false;
one who is perfect in knowledge is with you.

5 "Behold, God is mighty, and does not despise any;
he is mighty in strength of understanding.
6 He does not keep the wicked alive,
but gives the afflicted their right.

[z] The Hebrew of verses 29-33 is obscure
[a] Theodotion Symmachus Compare Vg: The meaning of the Hebrew word is uncertain
35. 6-8: 22. 2-3.

7 He does not withdraw his eyes from the righteous,
but with kings upon the throne
he sets them for ever, and they are exalted.
8 And if they are bound in fetters
and caught in the cords of affliction,
9 then he declares to them their work
and their transgressions, that they are behaving arrogantly.
10 He opens their ears to instruction,
and commands that they return from iniquity.
11 If they hearken and serve him,
they complete their days in prosperity,
and their years in pleasantness.
12 But if they do not hearken, they perish by the sword,
and die without knowledge.

13 "The godless in heart cherish anger;
they do not cry for help when he binds them.
14 They die in youth,
and their life ends in shame.[b]
15 He delivers the afflicted by their affliction,
and opens their ear by adversity.
16 He also allured you out of distress
into a broad place where there was no cramping,
and what was set on your table was full of fatness.

17 "But you are full of the judgment on the wicked;
judgment and justice seize you.
18 Beware lest wrath entice you into scoffing;
and let not the greatness of the ransom turn you aside.
19 Will your cry avail to keep you from distress,
or all the force of your strength?
20 Do not long for the night,
when peoples are cut off in their place.
21 Take heed, do not turn to iniquity,
for this you have chosen rather than affliction.
22 Behold, God is exalted in his power;
who is a teacher like him?
23 Who has prescribed for him his way,
or who can say, 'Thou hast done wrong'?

24 "Remember to extol his work,
of which men have sung.
25 All men have looked on it;
man beholds it from afar.
26 Behold, God is great, and we know him not;
the number of his years is unsearchable.
27 For he draws up the drops of water,
he[c] distils his mist in rain
28 which the skies pour down,
and drop upon man abundantly.
29 Can any one understand the spreading of the clouds,
the thunderings of his pavilion?
30 Behold, he scatters his lightning about him,
and covers the roots of the sea.
31 For by these he judges peoples;
he gives food in abundance.
32 He covers his hands with the lightning,
and commands it to strike the mark.
33 Its crashing declares concerning him,
who is jealous with anger against iniquity.

37 "At this also my heart trembles,
and leaps out of its place.
2 Hearken to the thunder of his voice
and the rumbling that comes from his mouth.
3 Under the whole heaven he lets it go,
and his lightning to the corners of the earth.
4 After it his voice roars;
he thunders with his majestic voice
and he does not restrain the lightnings[d] when his voice is heard.

[b] Heb *among the cult prostitutes* [c] Cn: Heb *they distill* [d] Heb *them*

5 God thunders wondrously with his
voice;
he does great things which we
cannot comprehend.
6 For to the snow he says, 'Fall on
the earth';
and to the shower and the rain,[e]
'Be strong.'
7 He seals up the hand of every man,
that all men may know his work.[f]
8 Then the beasts go into their lairs,
and remain in their dens.
9 From its chamber comes the whirlwind,
and cold from the scattering
winds.
10 By the breath of God ice is given,
and the broad waters are frozen
fast.
11 He loads the thick cloud with
moisture;
the clouds scatter his lightning.
12 They turn round and round by his
guidance,
to accomplish all that he commands
them
on the face of the habitable
world.
13 Whether for correction, or for his
land,
or for love, he causes it to happen.

14 "Hear this, O Job;
stop and consider the wondrous
works of God.
15 Do you know how God lays his
command upon them,
and causes the lightning of his
cloud to shine?
16 Do you know the balancings of the
clouds,
the wondrous works of him who
is perfect in knowledge,
17 you whose garments are hot
when the earth is still because of
the south wind?
18 Can you, like him, spread out the
skies,
hard as a molten mirror?
19 Teach us what we shall say to him;
we cannot draw up our case because
of darkness.
20 Shall it be told him that I would
speak?
Did a man ever wish that he
would be swallowed up?

21 "And now men cannot look on the
light
when it is bright in the skies,
when the wind has passed and
cleared them.
22 Out of the north comes golden
splendor;
God is clothed with terrible
majesty.
23 The Almighty—we cannot find
him;
he is great in power and justice,
and abundant righteousness he
will not violate.
24 Therefore men fear him;
he does not regard any who are
wise in their own conceit."

38 Then the LORD answered Job
out of the whirlwind:
2 "Who is this that darkens counsel
by words without knowledge?
3 Gird up your loins like a man,
I will question you, and you shall
declare to me.

4 "Where were you when I laid the
foundation of the earth?
Tell me, if you have understanding.
5 Who determined its measurements
—surely you know!
Or who stretched the line upon
it?
6 On what were its bases sunk,
or who laid its cornerstone,
7 when the morning stars sang together,
and all the sons of God shouted
for joy?

8 "Or who shut in the sea with doors,
when it burst forth from the
womb;

[e] Cn Compare Syr: Heb *shower of rain and shower of rains*
[f] Vg Compare Syr Tg: Heb *that all men whom he has made may know it*

[9] when I made clouds its garment,
and thick darkness its swaddling band,
[10] and prescribed bounds for it,
and set bars and doors,
[11] and said, 'Thus far shall you come, and no farther,
and here shall your proud waves be stayed'?

[12] "Have you commanded the morning since your days began,
and caused the dawn to know its place,
[13] that it might take hold of the skirts of the earth,
and the wicked be shaken out of it?
[14] It is changed like clay under the seal,
and it is dyed[g] like a garment.
[15] From the wicked their light is withheld,
and their uplifted arm is broken.

[16] "Have you entered into the springs of the sea,
or walked in the recesses of the deep?
[17] Have the gates of death been revealed to you,
or have you seen the gates of deep darkness?
[18] Have you comprehended the expanse of the earth?
Declare, if you know all this.

[19] "Where is the way to the dwelling of light,
and where is the place of darkness,
[20] that you may take it to its territory
and that you may discern the paths to its home?
[21] You know, for you were born then,
and the number of your days is great!

[22] "Have you entered the storehouses of the snow,
or have you seen the storehouses of the hail,
[23] which I have reserved for the time of trouble,
for the day of battle and war?
[24] What is the way to the place where the light is distributed,
or where the east wind is scattered upon the earth?

[25] "Who has cleft a channel for the torrents of rain,
and a way for the thunderbolt,
[26] to bring rain on a land where no man is,
on the desert in which there is no man;
[27] to satisfy the waste and desolate land,
and to make the ground put forth grass?

[28] "Has the rain a father,
or who has begotten the drops of dew?
[29] From whose womb did the ice come forth,
and who has given birth to the hoarfrost of heaven?
[30] The waters become hard like stone,
and the face of the deep is frozen.

[31] "Can you bind the chains of the Plei'ades,
or loose the cords of Orion?
[32] Can you lead forth the Maz'zaroth in their season,
or can you guide the Bear with its children?
[33] Do you know the ordinances of the heavens?
Can you establish their rule on the earth?

[34] "Can you lift up your voice to the clouds,
that a flood of waters may cover you?
[35] Can you send forth lightnings, that they may go
and say to you, 'Here we are'?
[36] Who has put wisdom in the clouds,[h]

[g] Cn: Heb *they stand forth* [h] The meaning of the Hebrew word is uncertain
38. 10: Jer. 5. 22.

or given understanding to the
mists?[h]
37 Who can number the clouds by
wisdom?
Or who can tilt the waterskins of
the heavens,
38 when the dust runs into a mass
and the clods cleave fast together?

39 "Can you hunt the prey for the
lion,
or satisfy the appetite of the
young lions,
40 when they crouch in their dens,
or lie in wait in their covert?
41 Who provides for the raven its prey,
when its young ones cry to God,
and wander about for lack of
food?

39 "Do you know when the
mountain goats bring forth?
Do you observe the calving of
the hinds?
2 Can you number the months that
they fulfil,
and do you know the time when
they bring forth,
3 when they crouch, bring forth their
offspring,
and are delivered of their young?
4 Their young ones become strong,
they grow up in the open;
they go forth, and do not return
to them.

5 "Who has let the wild ass go free?
Who has loosed the bonds of the
swift ass,
6 to whom I have given the steppe
for his home,
and the salt land for his dwelling
place?
7 He scorns the tumult of the city;
he hears not the shouts of the
driver.
8 He ranges the mountains as his
pasture,
and he searches after every green
thing.
9 "Is the wild ox willing to serve you?
Will he spend the night at your
crib?
10 Can you bind him in the furrow
with ropes,
or will he harrow the valleys after
you?
11 Will you depend on him because
his strength is great,
and will you leave to him your
labor?
12 Do you have faith in him that he
will return,
and bring your grain to your
threshing floor?[i]

13 "The wings of the ostrich wave
proudly;
but are they the pinions and
plumage of love?[j]
14 For she leaves her eggs to the earth,
and lets them be warmed on the
ground,
15 forgetting that a foot may crush
them,
and that the wild beast may
trample them.
16 She deals cruelly with her young,
as if they were not hers;
though her labor be in vain, yet
she has no fear;
17 because God has made her forget
wisdom,
and given her no share in understanding.
18 When she rouses herself to flee,[k]
she laughs at the horse and his
rider.

19 "Do you give the horse his might?
Do you clothe his neck with
strength?[l]
20 Do you make him leap like the
locust?
His majestic snorting is terrible.
21 He paws[m] in the valley, and exults
in his strength;
he goes out to meet the weapons.
22 He laughs at fear, and is not dismayed;

[i] Heb *your grain and your threshing floor* [j] Heb obscure [k] Heb obscure
[l] Tg: The meaning of the Hebrew word is obscure [m] Gk Syr Vg: Heb *they dig*

he does not turn back from the
sword.
23 Upon him rattle the quiver,
the flashing spear and the javelin.
24 With fierceness and rage he swallows the ground;
he cannot stand still at the sound
of the trumpet.
25 When the trumpet sounds, he says
'Aha!'
He smells the battle from afar,
the thunder of the captains, and
the shouting.

26 "Is it by your wisdom that the hawk
soars,
and spreads his wings toward the
south?
27 Is it at your command that the
eagle mounts up
and makes his nest on high?
28 On the rock he dwells and makes
his home
in the fastness of the rocky crag.
29 Thence he spies out the prey;
his eyes behold it afar off.
30 His young ones suck up blood;
and where the slain are, there is
he."

40 And the LORD said to Job:
2 "Shall a faultfinder contend
with the Almighty?
He who argues with God, let
him answer it."

3 Then Job answered the LORD:
4 "Behold, I am of small account;
what shall I answer thee?
I lay my hand on my mouth.
5 I have spoken once, and I will not
answer;
twice, but I will proceed no
further."

6 Then the LORD answered Job out
of the whirlwind:
7 "Gird up your loins like a man;
I will question you, and you declare to me.
8 Will you even put me in the wrong?
Will you condemn me that you
may be justified?
9 Have you an arm like God,
and can you thunder with a voice
like his?

10 "Deck yourself with majesty and
dignity;
clothe yourself with glory and
splendor.
11 Pour forth the overflowings of your
anger,
and look on every one that is
proud, and abase him.
12 Look on every one that is proud,
and bring him low;
and tread down the wicked
where they stand.
13 Hide them all in the dust together;
bind their faces in the world below.[n]
14 Then will I also acknowledge to
you,
that your own right hand can give
you victory.

15 "Behold, Be'hemoth,[o]
which I made as I made you;
he eats grass like an ox.
16 Behold, his strength in his loins,
and his power in the muscles of
his belly.
17 He makes his tail stiff like a cedar;
the sinews of his thighs are knit
together.
18 His bones are tubes of bronze,
his limbs like bars of iron.

19 "He is the first of the works[p] of
God;
let him who made him bring near
his sword!
20 For the mountains yield food for
him
where all the wild beasts play.
21 Under the lotus plants he lies,
in the covert of the reeds and in
the marsh.
22 For his shade the lotus trees cover
him;

[n] Heb *hidden place* [o] Or *the hippopotamus* [p] Heb *ways*

the willows of the brook surround him.
23 Behold, if the river is turbulent he is not frightened;
he is confident though Jordan rushes against his mouth.
24 Can one take him with hooks,[q]
or pierce his nose with a snare?

41 [r] "Can you draw out Levi'athan[s] with a fishhook,
or press down his tongue with a cord?
2 Can you put a rope in his nose,
or pierce his jaw with a hook?
3 Will he make many supplications to you?
Will he speak to you soft words?
4 Will he make a covenant with you
to take him for your servant for ever?
5 Will you play with him as with a bird,
or will you put him on leash for your maidens?
6 Will traders bargain over him?
Will they divide him up among the merchants?
7 Can you fill his skin with harpoons,
or his head with fishing spears?
8 Lay hands on him;
think of the battle; you will not do it again!
9 [t] Behold, the hope of a man is disappointed;
he is laid low even at the sight of him.
10 No one is so fierce that he dares to stir him up.
Who then is he that can stand before me?
11 Who has given to me,[u] that I should repay him?
Whatever is under the whole heaven is mine.

12 "I will not keep silence concerning his limbs,
or his mighty strength, or his goodly frame.
13 Who can strip off his outer garment?
Who can penetrate his double coat of mail?[v]
14 Who can open the doors of his face?
Round about his teeth is terror.
15 His back[w] is made of rows of shields,
shut up closely as with a seal.
16 One is so near to another
that no air can come between them.
17 They are joined one to another;
they clasp each other and cannot be separated.
18 His sneezings flash forth light,
and his eyes are like the eyelids of the dawn.
19 Out of his mouth go flaming torches;
sparks of fire leap forth.
20 Out of his nostrils comes forth smoke,
as from a boiling pot and burning rushes.
21 His breath kindles coals,
and a flame comes forth from his mouth.
22 In his neck abides strength,
and terror dances before him.
23 The folds of his flesh cleave together,
firmly cast upon him and immovable.
24 His heart is hard as a stone,
hard as the nether millstone.
25 When he raises himself up the mighty[x] are afraid;
at the crashing they are beside themselves.
26 Though the sword reaches him, it does not avail;
nor the spear, the dart, or the javelin.
27 He counts iron as straw,
and bronze as rotten wood.
28 The arrow cannot make him flee;
for him slingstones are turned to stubble.

[q] Cn: Heb *in his eyes*. [r] Ch 40. 25 in Heb [s] Or *the crocodile* [t] Ch 41. 1 in Heb
[u] The meaning of the Hebrew is uncertain [v] Gk: Heb *bridle*
[w] Cn Compare Gk Vg: Heb *pride* [x] Or *gods* 41. 11: Rom. 11. 35.

29 Clubs are counted as stubble;
he laughs at the rattle of javelins.
30 His underparts are like sharp potsherds;
he spreads himself like a threshing sledge on the mire.
31 He makes the deep boil like a pot;
he makes the sea like a pot of ointment.
32 Behind him he leaves a shining wake;
one would think the deep to be hoary.
33 Upon earth there is not his like,
a creature without fear.
34 He beholds everything that is high;
he is king over all the sons of pride."

42 Then Job answered the LORD:
2 "I know that thou canst do all things,
and that no purpose of thine can be thwarted.
3 'Who is this that hides counsel without knowledge?'
Therefore I have uttered what I did not understand,
things too wonderful for me, which I did not know.
4 'Hear, and I will speak;
I will question you, and you declare to me.'
5 I had heard of thee by the hearing of the ear,
but now my eye sees thee;
6 therefore I despise myself,
and repent in dust and ashes."

7 After the LORD had spoken these
words to Job, the LORD said to Eli'-
phaz the Te'manite: "My wrath is
kindled against you and against your
two friends; for you have not spoken
of me what is right, as my servant Job
has. 8 Now therefore take seven bulls
and seven rams, and go to my servant
Job, and offer up for yourselves a
burnt offering; and my servant Job
shall pray for you, for I will accept his
prayer not to deal with you according
to your folly; for you have not spoken
of me what is right, as my servant Job
has." 9 So Eli'phaz the Te'manite and
Bildad the Shuhite and Zophar the
Na'amathite went and did what the
LORD had told them; and the LORD
accepted Job's prayer.

10 And the LORD restored the fortunes of Job, when he had prayed for
his friends; and the LORD gave Job
twice as much as he had before.
11 Then came to him all his brothers
and sisters and all who had known
him before, and ate bread with him in
his house; and they showed him sympathy and comforted him for all the
evil that the LORD had brought upon
him; and each of them gave him a
piece of money[y] and a ring of gold.
12 And the LORD blessed the latter
days of Job more than his beginning;
and he had fourteen thousand sheep,
six thousand camels, a thousand yoke
of oxen, and a thousand she-asses.
13 He had also seven sons and three
daughters. 14 And he called the name
of the first Jemi'mah; and the name
of the second Kezi'ah; and the name
of the third Ker'en-hap'puch. 15 And
in all the land there were no women
so fair as Job's daughters; and their
father gave them inheritance among
their brothers. 16 And after this Job
lived a hundred and forty years, and
saw his sons, and his sons' sons, four
generations. 17 And Job died, an old
man, and full of days.

[y] Heb *kesitah*

"The Sermon on the Mount" from the Gospel according to Matthew is composed of various teachings of Jesus brought together by the writer into a single setting. These precepts form the heart of the Christian ethic.

# THE GOSPEL ACCORDING TO
# MATTHEW

## *The Sermon on the Mount*

5 WHEN HE SAW the crowds he went up the hill. There he took his seat,
2 and when his disciples had gathered round him he began to address
them. And this is the teaching he gave:

3 'How blest are those who know their need of God;
the kingdom of Heaven is theirs.
4 How blest are the sorrowful;
they shall find consolation.

[a] *Some witnesses omit* Repent; for. [b] *Greek* Decapolis.

How blest are those of a gentle spirit; 5
they shall have the earth for their possession.
How blest are those who hunger and thirst to see right prevail;[a] 6
they shall be satisfied.
How blest are those who show mercy; 7
mercy shall be shown to them.
How blest are those whose hearts are pure; 8
they shall see God.
How blest are the peacemakers; 9
God shall call them his sons.
How blest are those who have suffered persecution for the cause of right; 10
the kingdom of Heaven is theirs.

'How blest you are, when you suffer insults and persecution and every 11
kind of calumny for my sake. Accept it with gladness and exultation, for 12
you have a rich reward in heaven; in the same way they persecuted the
prophets before you.
'You are salt to the world. And if salt becomes tasteless, how is its salt- 13
ness to be restored? It is now good for nothing but to be thrown away and
trodden underfoot.
'You are light for all the world. A town that stands on a hill cannot be 14
hidden. When a lamp is lit, it is not put under the meal-tub, but on the 15
lamp-stand, where it gives light to everyone in the house. And you, like 16
the lamp, must shed light among your fellows, so that, when they see the
good you do, they may give praise to your Father in heaven.

'DO NOT SUPPOSE that I have come to abolish the Law and the prophets; 17
I did not come to abolish, but to complete. I tell you this: so long as heaven 18
and earth endure, not a letter, not a stroke, will disappear from the Law
until all that must happen has happened.[b] If any man therefore sets aside 19
even the least of the Law's demands, and teaches others to do the same, he
will have the lowest place in the kingdom of Heaven, whereas anyone who
keeps the Law, and teaches others so, will stand high in the kingdom of
Heaven. I tell you, unless you show yourselves far better men than the 20
Pharisees and the doctors of the law, you can never enter the kingdom of
Heaven.
'You have learned that our forefathers were told, "Do not commit 21
murder; anyone who commits murder must be brought to judgement."
But what I tell you is this: Anyone who nurses anger against his brother[c] 22
must be brought to judgement. If he abuses his brother he must answer
for it to the court; if he sneers at him he will have to answer for it in the
fires of hell.
'If, when you are bringing your gift to the altar, you suddenly remember 23
that your brother has a grievance against you, leave your gift where it is 24
before the altar. First go and make your peace with your brother, and only
then come back and offer your gift.

[a] *Or* to do what is right. [b] *Or* before all that it stands for is achieved. [c] *Some witnesses insert* without good cause.

25 'If someone sues you, come to terms with him promptly while you are
both on your way to court; otherwise he may hand you over to the judge,
26 and the judge to the constable, and you will be put in jail. I tell you, once
you are there you will not be let out till you have paid the last farthing.
27 'You have learned that they were told, "Do not commit adultery."
28 But what I tell you is this: If a man looks on a woman with a lustful eye,
he has already committed adultery with her in his heart.
29 'If your right eye is your undoing, tear it out and fling it away; it is better
for you to lose one part of your body than for the whole of it to be thrown
30 into hell. And if your right hand is your undoing, cut it off and fling it
away; it is better for you to lose one part of your body than for the whole
of it to go to hell.
31 'They were told, "A man who divorces his wife must give her a note of
32 dismissal." But what I tell you is this: If a man divorces his wife for any
cause other than unchastity he involves her in adultery; and anyone who
marries a divorced woman commits adultery.
33 'Again, you have learned that our forefathers were told, "Do not break
34 your oath", and, "Oaths sworn to the Lord must be kept." But what I tell
you is this: You are not to swear at all—not by heaven, for it is God's
35 throne, nor by earth, for it is his footstool, nor by Jerusalem, for it is the
36 city of the great King, nor by your own head, because you cannot turn
37 one hair of it white or black. Plain "Yes" or "No" is all you need to say;
anything beyond that comes from the devil.
38 'You have learned that they were told, "Eye for eye, tooth for tooth."
39 But what I tell you is this: Do not set yourself against the man who wrongs
you. If someone slaps you on the right cheek, turn and offer him your left.
40 If a man wants to sue you for your shirt, let him have your coat as well.
41 42 If a man in authority makes you go one mile, go with him two. Give when
you are asked to give; and do not turn your back on a man who wants to
borrow.
43 'You have learned that they were told, "Love your neighbour, hate your
44 enemy." But what I tell you is this: Love your enemies[a] and pray for your
45 persecutors;[b] only so can you be children of your heavenly Father, who
makes his sun rise on good and bad alike, and sends the rain on the honest
46 and the dishonest. If you love only those who love you, what reward can
47 you expect? Surely the tax-gatherers do as much as that. And if you greet
only your brothers, what is there extraordinary about that? Even the
48 heathen do as much. There must be no limit to your goodness, as your
heavenly Father's goodness knows no bounds.

6 'BE CAREFUL not to make a show of your religion before men; if you do,
no reward awaits you in your Father's house in heaven.
2 'Thus, when you do some act of charity, do not announce it with a flourish
of trumpets, as the hypocrites do in synagogue and in the streets to win
3 admiration from men. I tell you this: they have their reward already. No;
when you do some act of charity, do not let your left hand know what your

[a] *Some witnesses insert* bless those who curse you, do good to those who hate you.
[b] *Some witnesses insert* and those who treat you spitefully.

right is doing; your good deed must be secret, and your Father who sees 4
what is done in secret will reward you.[a]
'Again, when you pray, do not be like the hypocrites; they love to say 5
their prayers standing up in synagogue and at the street-corners, for
everyone to see them. I tell you this: they have their reward already. But 6
when you pray, go into a room by yourself, shut the door, and pray to your
Father who is there in the secret place; and your Father who sees what is
secret will reward you.[a]
'In your prayers do not go babbling on like the heathen, who imagine 7
that the more they say the more likely they are to be heard. Do not imitate 8
them. Your Father knows what your needs are before you ask him.
'This is how you should pray: 9

"Our Father in heaven,
thy name be hallowed;
thy kingdom come, 10
thy will be done,
on earth as in heaven.
Give us today our daily bread.[b] 11
Forgive us the wrong we have done, 12
as we have forgiven those who have wronged us.
And do not bring us to the test, 13
but save us from the evil one."[c] [d]

For if you forgive others the wrongs they have done, your heavenly Father 14
will also forgive you; but if you do not forgive others, then the wrongs you 15
have done will not be forgiven by your Father.
'So too when you fast, do not look gloomy like the hypocrites: they make 16
their faces unsightly so that other people may see that they are fasting.
I tell you this: they have their reward already. But when you fast, anoint 17
your head and wash your face, so that men may not see that you are fasting, 18
but only your Father who is in the secret place; and your Father who sees
what is secret will give you your reward.

'DO NOT STORE UP for yourselves treasure on earth, where it grows rusty 19
and moth-eaten, and thieves break in to steal it. Store up treasure in 20
heaven, where there is no moth and no rust to spoil it, no thieves to break
in and steal. For where your treasure is, there will your heart be also. 21
'The lamp of the body is the eye. If your eyes are sound, you will have 22
light for your whole body; if the eyes are bad, your whole body will be in 23
darkness. If then the only light you have is darkness, the darkness is
doubly dark.
'No servant can be the slave of two masters; for either he will hate the 24
first and love the second, or he will be devoted to the first and think
nothing of the second. You cannot serve God and Money.
'Therefore I bid you put away anxious thoughts about food and drink 25

[a] *Some witnesses add* openly. [b] *Or* our bread for the morrow. [c] *Or* from evil.
[d] *Some witnesses add* For thine is the kingdom and the power and the glory, for ever. Amen.

to keep you alive, and clothes to cover your body. Surely life is more than
26 food, the body more than clothes. Look at the birds of the air; they do not
sow and reap and store in barns, yet your heavenly Father feeds them. You
27 are worth more than the birds! Is there a man of you who by anxious
28 thought can add a foot to his height[a]? And why be anxious about clothes?
Consider how the lilies grow in the fields; they do not work, they do not
29 spin;[b] and yet, I tell you, even Solomon in all his splendour was not
30 attired like one of these. But if that is how God clothes the grass in the
fields, which is there today, and tomorrow is thrown on the stove, will he
31 not all the more clothe you? How little faith you have! No, do not ask
anxiously, "What are we to eat? What are we to drink? What shall we
32 wear?" All these are things for the heathen to run after, not for you,
33 because your heavenly Father knows that you need them all. Set your
mind on God's kingdom and his justice before everything else, and all the
34 rest will come to you as well. So do not be anxious about tomorrow;
tomorrow will look after itself. Each day has troubles enough of its own.

7 1 2 'PASS NO JUDGEMENT, and you will not be judged. For as you judge
others, so you will yourselves be judged, and whatever measure you deal
3 out to others will be dealt back to you. Why do you look at the speck of
sawdust in your brother's eye, with never a thought for the great plank in
4 your own? Or how can you say to your brother, "Let me take the speck out
5 of your eye", when all the time there is that plank in your own? You hypo-
crite! First take the plank out of your own eye, and then you will see clearly
to take the speck out of your brother's.

6 'Do not give dogs what is holy; do not throw your pearls to the pigs:
they will only trample on them, and turn and tear you to pieces.

7 'Ask, and you will receive; seek, and you will find; knock, and the door
8 will be opened. For everyone who asks receives, he who seeks finds, and
to him who knocks, the door will be opened.

9 'Is there a man among you who will offer his son a stone when he asks
10 11 for bread, or a snake when he asks for fish? If you, then, bad as you are,
know how to give your children what is good for them, how much more will
your heavenly Father give good things to those who ask him!

12 'Always treat others as you would like them to treat you: that is the Law
and the prophets.

13 'Enter by the narrow gate. The gate is wide that leads to perdition,
14 there is plenty of room on the road,[c] and many go that way; but the gate
that leads to life is small and the road is narrow,[d] and those who find it
are few.

15 'Beware of false prophets, men who come to you dressed up as sheep
16 while underneath they are savage wolves. You will recognize them by the
fruits they bear. Can grapes be picked from briars, or figs from thistles?
17 In the same way, a good tree always yields good fruit, and a poor tree bad

[a] *Or* a day to his life.
[b] *One witness reads* Consider the lilies: they neither card nor spin, nor labour.
[c] *Some witnesses read* The road that leads to perdition is wide with plenty of room.
[d] *Some witnesses read* but the road that leads to life is small and narrow.

fruit. A good tree cannot bear bad fruit, or a poor tree good fruit. And when 18 19
a tree does not yield good fruit it is cut down and burnt. That is why I say 20
you will recognize them by their fruits.

'Not everyone who calls me "Lord, Lord" will enter the kingdom of 21
Heaven, but only those who do the will of my heavenly Father. When that 22
day comes, many will say to me, "Lord, Lord, did we not prophesy in your
name, cast out devils in your name, and in your name perform many
miracles?" Then I will tell them to their face, "I never knew you; out of my 23
sight, you and your wicked ways!"

'What then of the man who hears these words of mine and acts upon 24
them? He is like a man who had the sense to build his house on rock. The 25
rain came down, the floods rose, the wind blew, and beat upon that house;
but it did not fall, because its foundations were on rock. But what of the 26
man who hears these words of mine and does not act upon them? He is
like a man who was foolish enough to build his house on sand. The rain 27
came down, the floods rose, the wind blew, and beat upon that house;
down it fell with a great crash.'

When Jesus had finished this discourse the people were astounded at 28
his teaching; unlike their own teachers he taught with a note of authority. 29

# 5

Dostoyevsky, THE BROTHERS KARAMAZOV

(Trans. by Constance Garnett)

1. Why does the Grand Inquisitor accuse Christ of interfering with the work of the Roman Catholic Church?

2. What are the three temptations of Christ mentioned in the chapter and why does the Grand Inquisitor believe Christ's rejection of Satan's offer was a mistake?

3. What does the Grand Inquisitor believe is the essence of Christ's gift to mankind and how has mankind reacted to that gift?

4. How does the Grand Inquisitor account for the power and influence of the Roman Catholic Church?

5. Is Alyosha right when he says to Ivan, "Your inquisitor does not believe in God, that's his secret!"?

6. What is the mission of the church according to the Grand Inquisitor, Dostoyevsky, and you? Should the church serve only the spiritual needs of man?

*The Brothers Karamazov,* the last of Dostoyevsky's novels, was first published in serial form during 1879-1880. The following excerpt, "The Grand Inquisitor," is a chapter from the novel in which the author raises some fundamental questions about the nature of man, the Roman Catholic Church, and Christianity.

# THE BROTHERS KARAMAZOV

## *The Grand Inquisitor*

"EVEN this must have a preface—that is, a literary preface," laughed Ivan, "and I am a poor hand at making one. You see, my action takes place in the sixteenth century, and at that time, as you probably learnt at school, it was customary in poetry to bring down heavenly powers on earth.

Not to speak of Dante, in France, clerks, as well as the monks in the monasteries, used to give regular performances in which the Madonna, the saints, the angels, Christ, and God Himself were brought on the stage. In those days it was done in all simplicity. In Victor Hugo's 'Notre Dame de Paris' an edifying and gratuitous spectacle was provided for the people in the Hotel de Ville of Paris in the reign of Louis XI. in honour of the birth of the dauphin. It was called *Le bon jugement de la très sainte et gracieuse Vierge Marie*, and she appears herself on the stage and pronounces her *bon jugement*. Similar plays, chiefly from the Old Testament, were occasionally performed in Moscow too, up to the times of Peter the Great. But besides plays there were all sorts of legends and ballads scattered about the world, in which the saints and angels and all the powers of Heaven took part when required. In our monasteries the monks busied themselves in translating, copying, and even composing such poems—and even under the Tatars. There is, for instance, one such poem (of course, from the Greek), 'The Wanderings of Our Lady through Hell,' with descriptions as bold as Dante's. Our Lady visits Hell, and the Archangel Michael leads her through the torments. She sees the sinners and their punishment. There she sees among others one noteworthy set of sinners in a burning lake; some of them sink to the bottom of the lake so that they can't swim out, and 'these God forgets'—an expression of extraordinary depth and force. And so Our Lady, shocked and weeping, falls before the throne of God and begs for mercy for all in Hell—for all she has seen there, indiscriminately. Her conversation with God is immensely interesting. She beseeches Him, she will not desist, and when God points to the hands and feet of her Son, nailed to the Cross, and asks, 'How can I forgive His tormentors?' she bids all the saints, all the martyrs, all the angels and archangels to fall down with her and pray for mercy on all without distinction. It ends by her winning from God a respite of suffering every year from Good Friday till Trinity day, and the sinners at once raise a cry of thankfulness from Hell, chanting, 'Thou art just, O Lord, in this judgment.' Well, my poem would have been of that kind if it had appeared at that time. He comes on the scene in my poem, but He says nothing, only appears and passes on. Fifteen centuries have passed since He promised to come in His glory, fifteen centuries since His prophet wrote, 'Behold, I come quickly'; 'Of that day and that hour knoweth no man, neither the Son, but the Father,' as He Himself predicted on earth. But humanity awaits him with the same faith and with the same love. Oh, with greater faith, for it is fifteen centuries since man has ceased to see signs from Heaven.

*No signs from Heaven come to-day*
*To add to what the heart doth say.*

There was nothing left but faith in what the heart doth say. It is true there were many miracles in those days. There were saints who performed miraculous cures; some holy people, according to their biographies, were visited by the Queen of Heaven herself. But the devil did not slumber, and doubts were already arising among men of the truth of these miracles. And just then there appeared in the north of Germany a terrible new heresy. 'A huge star like to a torch' (that is, to a church) 'fell on the sources of the waters and they became bitter.' These heretics began blasphemously denying miracles. But those who remained faithful were all the more ardent in their faith. The tears of humanity rose up to Him as before, awaited His coming, loved Him, hoped for Him, yearned to suffer and die for Him as before. And so many ages mankind had prayed with faith and fervour, 'O Lord our God, hasten Thy coming,' so many ages called upon Him, that in His infinite mercy He deigned to come down to His servants. Before that day He had come down, He had visited some holy men, martyrs and hermits, as is written in their 'Lives.' Among us, Tyutchev, with absolute faith in the truth of his words, bore witness that

*Bearing the Cross, in slavish dress,*
*Weary and worn, the Heavenly King*
*Our mother, Russia, came to bless,*
*And through our land went wandering.*

And that certainly was so, I assure you.

"And behold, He deigned to appear for a moment to the people, to the tortured, suffering people, sunk in iniquity, but loving Him like children. My story is laid in Spain, in Seville, in the most terrible time of the Inquisition, when fires were lighted every day to the glory of God, and 'in the splendid *auto da fé* the wicked heretics were burnt.' Oh, of course, this was not the coming in which He will appear according to His promise at the end of time in all His heavenly glory, and which will be sudden 'as lightning flashing from east to west.' No, He visited His children only for a moment, and there where the flames were crackling round the heretics. In His infinite mercy He came once more among men in that human shape in which He walked among men for three years fifteen centuries ago. He came down to the 'hot pavement' of the southern town in which on the day before almost a hundred heretics had, *ad majorem gloriam Dei*, been burnt by the cardinal, the Grand Inquisitor, in a magnificent *auto da fé*, in the presence of the king, the court, the knights, the cardinals, the most charming ladies of the court, and the whole population of Seville.

"He came softly, unobserved, and yet, strange to say, every one recognised Him. That might be one of the best passages in the poem. I mean, why they recognised Him. The people are irresistibly drawn to Him, they surround Him, they flock about Him, follow Him. He moves silently in their midst with a gentle smile of infinite compassion. The sun of love burns in His heart, light and power shine from His eyes, and their radiance, shed on the people, stirs their hearts with responsive love. He holds out His hands to them, blesses them, and a healing virtue comes from contact with Him, even with His garments. An old man in the crowd, blind from childhood, cries out, 'O Lord, heal me and I shall see Thee!' and, as it were, scales fall from his eyes and the blind man sees Him. The crowd weeps and kisses the earth under His feet. Children throw flowers before Him, sing, and cry hosannah. 'It is He—it is He!' all repeat. 'It must be He, it can be no one but Him!' He stops at the steps of the Seville cathedral at the moment when the weeping mourners are bringing in a little open white coffin. In it lies a child of seven, the only daughter of a prominent citizen. The dead child lies hidden in flowers. 'He will raise your child,' the crowd shouts to the weeping mother. The priest, coming to meet the coffin, looks perplexed, and frowns, but the mother of the dead child throws herself at His feet with a wail. 'If it is Thou, raise my child!' she cries, holding out her hands to Him. The procession halts, the coffin is laid on the steps at His feet. He looks with compassion, and His lips once more softly pronounce, 'Maiden, arise!' and the maiden arises. The little girl sits up in the coffin and looks round, smiling with wide-open wondering eyes, holding a bunch of white roses they had put in her hand.

"There are cries, sobs, confusion among the people, and at that moment the cardinal himself, the Grand Inquisitor, passes by the cathedral. He is an old man, almost ninety, tall and erect, with a withered face and sunken eyes, in which there is still a gleam of light. He is not dressed in his gorgeous cardinal's robes, as he was the day before, when he was burning the enemies of the Roman Church—at that moment he was wearing his coarse, old, monk's cassock. At a distance behind him come his gloomy assistants and slaves and the 'holy guard.' He stops at the sight of the crowd and watches it from a distance. He sees everything; he sees them set the coffin down at His feet, sees the child rise up, and his face darkens. He knits his thick grey brows and his eyes gleam with a sinister fire. He holds out his finger and bids the guards take Him. And such is his power, so completely are the people cowed into submission and trembling obedience to him, that the crowd immediately make way for the guards, and in the midst of deathlike silence they lay hands on Him and lead Him away. The crowd instantly bows down to the earth, like one man, before the old inquisitor. He blesses the people in silence and passes on. The guards lead their prisoner to the close, gloomy vaulted prison in the ancient palace of the Holy Inquisition and shut Him in it. The day passes and is followed by the dark, burning 'breathless' night of Seville. The air is 'fragrant with laurel and lemon.' In the pitch darkness the iron door of the prison is suddenly opened and the Grand Inquisitor himself comes in with a light in his hand. He is alone; the door is closed at once behind him. He stands in the doorway and for a minute or two gazes into His face. At last he goes up slowly, sets the light on the table and speaks.

" 'Is it Thou? Thou?' but receiving no answer, he adds at once, 'Don't answer, be silent. What canst Thou say, indeed? I know too well what Thou wouldst say. And Thou hast no right to add anything to what Thou hadst said of old. Why, then, art Thou come to hinder us? For Thou hast come to hinder us, and Thou knowest that. But dost Thou know what will be to-morrow? I know not who Thou art and care not to know whether it is Thou or only a semblance of Him, but to-morrow I shall condemn Thee and burn Thee at the stake as the worst of heretics. And the very people who have to-day kissed Thy feet, to-morrow at the faintest sign from me will rush to heap up the embers of Thy fire. Knowest Thou that? Yes, maybe Thou knowest it,' he added with thoughtful penetration, never for a moment taking his eyes off the Prisoner."

"I don't quite understand, Ivan. What does it mean?" Alyosha, who had been listening in silence, said with a smile. "Is it simply a wild fantasy, or a mistake on the part of the old man—some impossible *quiproquo?*"

"Take it as the last," said Ivan, laughing, "if you are so corrupted by modern realism and can't stand anything fantastic. If you like it to be a case of mistaken identity, let it be so. It is true," he went on, laughing, "the old man was ninety, and he might well be crazy over his set idea. He might have been struck by the appearance of the Prisoner. It might, in fact, be simply his ravings, the delusion of an old man of ninety, over-excited by the *auto da fé* of a hundred heretics the day before. But does it matter to us after all whether it was a mistake of identity or a wild fantasy? All that matters is that the old man should speak out, should speak openly of what he has thought in silence for ninety years."

"And the Prisoner too is silent? Does He look at him and not say a word?"

"That's inevitable in any case," Ivan laughed again. "The old man has told Him He hasn't the right to add anything to what He has said of old. One may say it is the most fundamental feature of Roman Catholicism, in my opinion at least. 'All has been given by Thee to the Pope,' they say, 'and all, therefore, is still in the Pope's hands, and there is no need for Thee to come now at all. Thou must not meddle for the time, at least.' That's how they speak and write too—the Jesuits, at any rate. I have read it myself in the works of their theologians. 'Hast Thou the right to reveal to us one of the mysteries of that world from which Thou hast come?' my old man asks Him, and answers the question for Him. 'No, Thou hast not; that Thou mayest not add to what has been said of old, and mayest not take from men the freedom which Thou didst exalt when Thou wast on earth. Whatsoever Thou revealest anew will encroach on men's freedom of faith; for it will be manifest as a miracle, and the freedom of their faith was dearer to Thee than anything in those days fifteen hundred years ago. Didst Thou not often say then, "I will make you free"? But now Thou hast seen these "free" men,' the old man adds suddenly, with a pensive smile. 'Yes, we've paid dearly for it,' he goes on, looking sternly at Him, 'but at last we have completed that work in Thy name. For fifteen centuries we have been wrestling with Thy freedom, but now it is ended and over for good. Dost Thou not believe that it's over for good? Thou lookest meekly at me and deignest not even to be wroth with me. But let me tell Thee that now, to-day, people are more persuaded than ever that they have perfect freedom, yet they have brought their freedom to us and laid it humbly at our feet. But that has been our doing. Was this what Thou didst? Was this Thy freedom?' "

"I don't understand again," Alyosha broke in. "Is he ironical, is he jesting?"

"Not a bit of it! He claims it as a merit for himself and his Church that at last they have vanquished freedom and have done so to make men happy. 'For now' (he is speaking of the Inquisition, of course) 'for the first time it has become possible to think of the happiness of men. Man was created a rebel; and how can rebels be happy? Thou wast warned,' he says to Him. 'Thou hast had no lack of admonitions and warnings, but Thou didst not listen to those warnings; Thou didst reject the only way by which men might be made happy. But, fortunately, departing Thou didst hand on the work to us. Thou hast promised, Thou hast established by Thy word, Thou hast given to us the right to bind and to unbind, and now, of course, Thou canst not think of taking it away. Why, then, hast Thou come to hinder us?' "

"And what's the meaning of 'no lack of admonitions and warnings'?" asked Alyosha.

"Why, that's the chief part of what the old man must say."

" 'The wise and dread spirit, the spirit of self-destruction and non-existence,' the old man goes on, 'the great spirit talked with Thee in the wilderness, and we are told in the books that he "tempted" Thee. Is that so? And could anything truer be said than what he revealed to Thee in three questions and what Thou didst reject, and what in the books is called "the temptation"? And yet if there has ever been on earth a real stupendous miracle, it took place on that day, on the day of the three temptations. The statement of those three questions was itself the miracle. If it were possible to imagine simply for the sake of argument that those three questions of the dread spirit had perished utterly from the books, and that we had to restore them and to invent them anew, and to do so had gathered together all the wise men of the earth—rulers, chief priests, learned men, philosophers, poets—and had set them the task to invent three questions, such as would not only fit the occasion, but express in three words, three human phrases, the whole future history of the world and of humanity—dost Thou believe that all the wisdom of the earth united could have invented anything in depth and force equal to the three questions which were actually put to Thee then by the wise and mighty spirit in the wilderness? From those questions alone, from the miracle of their statement, we can see that we have here to do not with the fleeting human intelligence, but with the absolute and eternal. For in those three questions the whole subsequent history of mankind is, as it were, brought together into one whole, and foretold, and in them are united all the unsolved historical contradictions of human nature. At the time it could not be so clear, since the future was unknown; but now that fifteen hundred years have passed, we see that everything in those three questions was so justly divined and foretold, and has been so truly fulfilled, that nothing can be added to them or taken from them.

"'Judge Thyself who was right—Thou or he who questioned Thee then? Remember the first question; its meaning, in other words, was this: "Thou wouldst go into the world, and art going with empty hands, with some promise of freedom which men in their simplicity and their natural unruliness cannot even understand, which they fear and dread—for nothing has ever been more insupportable for a man and a human society than freedom. But seest Thou these stones in this parched and barren wilderness? Turn them into bread, and mankind will run after Thee like a flock of sheep, grateful and obedient, though for ever trembling, lest Thou withdraw Thy hand and deny them Thy bread." But Thou wouldst not deprive man of freedom and didst reject the offer, thinking, what is that freedom worth, if obedience is bought with bread? Thou didst reply that man lives not by bread alone. But dost Thou know that for the sake of that earthly bread the spirit of the earth will rise up against Thee and will strive with Thee and overcome Thee, and all will follow him, crying, "Who can compare with this beast? He has given us fire from heaven!" Dost Thou know that the ages will pass, and humanity will proclaim by the lips of their sages that there is no crime, and therefore no sin; there is only hunger? "Feed men, and then ask of them virtue!" that's what they'll write on the banner, which they will raise against Thee, and with which they will destroy Thy temple. Where Thy temple stood will rise a new building; the terrible tower of Babel will be built again, and though, like the one of old, it will not be finished, yet Thou mightest have prevented that new tower and have cut short the sufferings of men for a thousand years; for they will come back to us after a thousand years of agony with their tower. They will seek us again, hidden underground in the catacombs, for we shall be again persecuted and tortured. They will find us and cry to us, "Feed us, for those who have promised us fire from heaven haven't given it!" And then we shall finish building their tower, for he finishes the building who feeds them. And we alone shall feed them in Thy name, declaring falsely that it is in Thy name. Oh, never, never can they feed themselves without us! No science will give them bread so long as they remain free. In the end they will lay their freedom at our feet, and say to us, "Make us your slaves, but feed us." They will understand themselves, at last, that freedom and bread enough for all are inconceivable together, for never, never will they be able to share between them! They will be convinced, too, that they can never be free, for they are weak, vicious, worthless and rebellious. Thou didst promise them the bread of Heaven, but, I repeat again, can it compare with earthly bread in the eyes of the weak, ever sinful and ignoble race of man? And if for the sake of the bread of Heaven thousands and tens of thousands shall follow Thee, what is to become of the millions and tens of thousands of millions of creatures who will not have the strength to forego the earthly bread for the sake of the heavenly? Or dost Thou care only for the tens of thousands of the great and strong, while the millions, numerous as the sands of the sea, who are weak but love Thee, must exist only for the sake of the great and strong? No, we care for the weak too. They are sinful and rebellious, but in the end they too will become obedient. They will marvel at us and look on us as gods, because we are ready to endure the freedom which they have found so dreadful and to rule over them—so awful it will seem to them to be free. But we shall tell them that we are Thy servants and rule them in Thy name. We shall deceive them again, for we will not let Thee come to us again. That deception will be our suffering, for we shall be forced to lie.

" 'This is the significance of the first question in the wilderness, and this is what Thou hast rejected for the sake of that freedom which Thou hast exalted above everything. Yet in this question lies hid the great secret of this world. Choosing "bread," Thou wouldst have satisfied the universal and everlasting craving of humanity—to find some one to worship. So long as man remains free he strives for nothing so incessantly and so painfully as to find some one to worship. But man seeks to worship what is established beyond dispute, so that all men would agree at once to worship it. For these pitiful creatures are concerned not only to find what one or the other can worship, but to find something that all would believe in and worship; what is essential is that all may be *together* in it. This craving for *community* of worship is the chief misery of every man individually and of all humanity from the beginning of time. For the sake of common worship they've slain each other with the sword. They have set up gods and challenged one another, "Put away your gods and come and worship ours, or we will kill you and your gods!" And so it will be to the end of the world, even when gods disappear from the earth; they will fall down before idols just the same. Thou didst know, Thou couldst not but have known, this fundamental secret of human nature, but Thou didst reject the one infallible banner which was offered Thee to make all men bow down to Thee alone—the banner of earthly bread; and Thou hast rejected it for the sake of freedom and the bread of Heaven. Behold what Thou didst further. And all again in the name of freedom! I tell Thee that man is tormented by no greater anxiety than to find some one quickly to whom he can hand over that gift of freedom with which the ill-fated creature is born. But only one who can appease their conscience can take over their freedom. In bread there was offered Thee an invincible banner; give bread, and man will worship Thee, for nothing is more certain than bread. But if some one else gains possession of his conscience—oh! then he will cast away Thy bread and follow after him who has ensnared his conscience. In that Thou wast right. For the secret of man's being is not only to live but to have something to live for. Without a stable conception of the object of life, man would not consent to go on living, and would rather destroy himself than remain on earth, though he had bread in abundance. That is true. But what happened? Instead of taking men's freedom from them, Thou didst make it greater than ever! Didst Thou forget that man prefers peace, and even death, to freedom of choice in the knowledge of good and evil? Nothing is more seductive for man than his freedom of conscience, but nothing is a greater cause of suffering. And behold, instead of giving a firm foundation for setting the conscience of man at rest for ever, Thou didst choose all that is exceptional, vague and enigmatic; Thou didst choose what was utterly beyond the strength of men, acting as though Thou didst not love them at all—Thou who didst come to give Thy life for them! Instead of taking possession of men's freedom, Thou didst increase it, and burdened the spiritual kingdom of mankind with its sufferings for ever. Thou didst desire man's free love, that he should follow Thee freely, enticed and taken captive by Thee. In place of the rigid ancient law, man must hereafter with free heart decide for himself what is good and what is evil, having only Thy image before him as his guide. But didst Thou not know he would at last reject even Thy image and Thy truth, if he is weighed down with the fearful burden of free choice? They will cry aloud at last that the truth is not in Thee, for they could not have been left in greater confusion and suffering than Thou hast caused, laying upon them so many cares and unanswerable problems.

" 'So that, in truth, Thou didst Thyself lay the foundation for the destruction of Thy kingdom, and no one is more to blame for it. Yet what was offered Thee? There are three powers, three powers alone, able to conquer and to hold captive for ever the conscience of these impotent rebels for their happiness—those forces are miracle, mystery and authority. Thou hast rejected all three and hast set the example for doing so. When the wise and dread spirit set Thee on the pinnacle of the temple and said to Thee, "If Thou wouldst know whether Thou art the Son of God then cast Thyself down, for it is written: the angels shall hold him up lest he fall and bruise himself, and Thou shalt know then whether Thou art the Son of God and shalt prove then how great is Thy faith in Thy Father." But Thou didst refuse and wouldst not cast Thyself down. Oh! of course, Thou didst proudly and well, like God; but the weak, unruly race of men, are they gods? Oh, Thou didst know then that in taking one step, in making one movement to cast Thyself down, Thou wouldst be tempting God and have lost all Thy faith in Him, and wouldst have been dashed to pieces against that earth which Thou didst come to save. And the wise spirit that tempted Thee would have rejoiced. But I ask again, are there many like Thee? And couldst Thou believe for one moment that men, too, could face such a temptation? Is the nature of men such, that they can reject miracle, and at the great moments of their life, the moments of their deepest, most agonising spiritual difficulties, cling only to the free verdict of the heart? Oh, Thou didst know that Thy deed would be recorded in books, would be handed down to remote times and the utmost ends of the earth, and Thou didst hope that man, following Thee, would cling to God and not ask for a miracle. But Thou didst not know that when man rejects miracle he rejects God too; for man seeks not so much God as the miraculous. And as man cannot bear to be without the miraculous, he will create new miracles of his own for himself, and will worship deeds of sorcery and witchcraft, though he might be a hundred times over a rebel, heretic and infidel. Thou didst not come down from the Cross when they shouted to Thee, mocking and reviling Thee, "Come down from the cross and we will believe that Thou art He." Thou didst not come down, for again Thou wouldst not enslave man by a miracle, and didst crave faith given freely, not based on miracle. Thou didst crave for free love and not the base raptures of the slave before the might that has overawed him for ever. But Thou didst think too highly of men therein, for they are slaves, of course, though rebellious by nature. Look round and judge; fifteen centuries have passed, look upon them. Whom hast Thou raised up to Thyself? I swear, man is weaker and baser by nature than Thou hast believed him! Can he, can he do what Thou didst? By showing him so much respect, Thou didst, as it were, cease to feel for him, for Thou didst ask far too much from him—Thou who hast loved him more than Thyself! Respecting him less, Thou wouldst have asked less of him. That would have been more like love, for his burden would have been lighter. He is weak and vile. What though he is everywhere now rebelling against our power, and proud of his rebellion? It is the pride of a child and a schoolboy. They are little children rioting and barring out the teacher at school. But their childish delight will end; it will cost them dear. They will cast down temples and drench the earth with blood. But they will see at last, the foolish children, that, though they are rebels, they are impotent rebels, unable to keep up their own rebellion. Bathed in their foolish tears, they will recognise at last that He who created them rebels must have meant to mock at them. They will say this in despair, and their utterance will be a blasphemy which will make them more unhappy still, for man's nature cannot bear blasphemy, and in the end always avenges it on itself. And so unrest, confusion and unhappiness—that is the present lot of man after Thou didst bear so much for their freedom! Thy great prophet tells in vision and in image, that he saw all those who took part in the first resurrection and that there were of each tribe twelve thousand. But if there were so many of them, they must have been not men but gods. They had borne Thy cross, they had endured scores of years in the barren, hungry wilderness, living upon locusts and roots—and Thou mayest indeed point with pride at those children of freedom, of free love, of free and splendid sacrifice for Thy name. But remember that they were only some thousands; and what of the rest?

And how are the other weak ones to blame, because they could not endure what the strong have endured? How is the weak soul to blame that it is unable to receive such terrible gifts? Canst Thou have simply come to the elect and for the elect? But if so, it is a mystery and we cannot understand it. And if it is a mystery, we too have a right to preach a mystery, and to teach them that it's not the free judgment of their hearts, not love that matters, but a mystery which they must follow blindly, even against their conscience. So we have done. We have corrected Thy work and have founded it upon *miracle, mystery* and *authority*. And men rejoiced that they were again led like sheep, and that the terrible gift that had brought them such suffering, was, at last, lifted from their hearts. Were we right teaching them this? Speak! Did we not love mankind, so meekly acknowledging their feebleness, lovingly lightening their burden, and permitting their weak nature even sin with our sanction? Why hast Thou come now to hinder us? And why dost Thou look silently and searchingly at me with Thy mild eyes? Be angry. I don't want Thy love, for I love Thee not. And what use is it for me to hide anything from Thee? Don't I know to Whom I am speaking? All that I can say is known to Thee already. And is it for me to conceal from Thee our mystery? Perhaps it is Thy will to hear it from my lips. Listen, then. We are not working with Thee, but with *him*—that is our mystery. It's long—eight centuries—since we have been on *his* side and not on Thine. Just eight centuries ago, we took from him what Thou didst reject with scorn, that last gift he offered Thee, showing Thee all the kingdoms of the earth. We took from him Rome and the sword of Cæsar, and proclaimed ourselves sole rulers of the earth, though hitherto we have not been able to complete our work. But whose fault is that? Oh, the work is only beginning, but it has begun. It has long to await completion and the earth has yet much to suffer, but we shall triumph and shall be Cæsars, and then we shall plan the universal happiness of man. But Thou mightest have taken even then the sword of Cæsar. Why didst Thou reject that last gift? Hadst Thou accepted that last counsel of the mighty spirit, Thou wouldst have accomplished all that man seeks on earth—that is, some one to worship, some one to keep his conscience, and some means of uniting all in one unanimous and harmonious ant-heap, for the craving for universal unity is the third and last anguish of men. Mankind as a whole has always striven to organise a universal state. There have been many great nations with great histories, but the more highly they were developed the more unhappy they were, for they felt more acutely than other people the craving for worldwide union. The great conquerors, Timours and Ghenghis-Khans, whirled like hurricanes over the face of the earth striving to subdue its people, and they too were but the unconscious expression of the same craving for universal unity. Hadst Thou taken the world and Cæsar's purple, Thou wouldst have founded the universal state and have given universal peace. For who can rule men if not he who holds their conscience and their bread in his hands? We have taken the sword of Cæsar, and in taking it, of course, have rejected Thee and followed *him*. Oh, ages are yet to come of the confusion of free thought, of their science and cannibalism. For having begun to build their tower of Babel without us, they will end, of course, with cannibalism. But then the beast will crawl to us and lick our feet and spatter them with tears of blood. And we shall sit upon the beast and raise the cup, and on it will be written, "Mystery." But then, and only then, the reign of peace and happiness will come for men. Thou art proud of Thine elect, but Thou hast only the elect, while we give rest to all. And besides, how many of those elect, those mighty ones who could become elect, have grown weary waiting for Thee, and have transferred and will transfer the powers of their spirit and the warmth of their heart to the other camp, and end by raising their *free* banner against Thee. Thou didst Thyself lift up that banner. But with us all will be happy and will no more rebel nor destroy one another as under Thy freedom. Oh, we shall persuade them that they will only become free when they renounce their freedom to us and submit to us. And shall we be right or shall we be lying? They will be convinced that we are right, for they will remember the horrors of slavery and confusion to which Thy freedom brought them. Freedom, free thought and science, will lead them into such straits and will bring them face to face with such marvels and insoluble mysteries, that some of them, the fierce and rebellious, will destroy themselves, others, rebellious but weak, will destroy one another, while the rest, weak and unhappy, will crawl fawning to our feet and whine to us: "Yes, you were right, you alone possess His mystery, and we come back to you, save us from ourselves!"

" 'Receiving bread from us, they will see clearly that we take the bread made by their hands from them, to give it to them, without any miracle. They will see that we do not change the stones to bread, but in truth they will be more thankful for taking it from our hands than for the bread itself! For they will remember only too well that in old days, without our help, even the bread they made turned to stones in their hands, while since they have come back to us, the very stones have turned to bread in their hands. Too, too well they know the value of complete submission! And until men know that, they will be unhappy. Who is most to blame for their not knowing it, speak? Who scattered the flock and sent it astray on unknown paths? But the flock will come together again and will submit once more, and then it will be once for all. Then we shall give them the quiet humble happiness of weak creatures such as they are by nature. Oh, we shall persuade them at last not to be proud, for Thou didst lift them up and thereby taught them to be proud. We shall show them that they are weak, that they are only pitiful children, but that childlike happiness is the sweetest of all. They will become timid and will look to us and huddle close to us in fear, as chicks to the hen. They will marvel at us and will be awe-stricken before us, and will be proud at our being so powerful and clever, that we have been able to subdue such a turbulent flock of thousands of millions. They will tremble impotently before our wrath, their minds will grow fearful, they will be quick to shed tears like women and children, but they will be just as ready at a sign from us to pass to laughter and rejoicing, to happy mirth and childish song. Yes, we shall set them to work, but in their leisure hours we shall make their life like a child's game, with children's songs and innocent dance. Oh, we shall allow them even sin, they are weak and helpless, and they will love us like children because we allow them to sin. We shall tell them that every sin will be expiated, if it is done with our permission, that we allow them to sin because we love them, and the punishment for these sins we take upon ourselves. And we shall take it upon ourselves, and they will adore us as their saviours who have taken on themselves their sins before God. And they will have no secrets from us. We shall allow or forbid them to live with their wives and mistresses, to have or not to have children—according to whether they have been obedient or disobedient—and they will submit to us gladly and cheerfully. The most painful secrets of their conscience, all, all they will bring to us, and we shall have an answer for all. And they will be glad to believe our answer, for it will save them from the great anxiety and terrible agony they endure at present in making a free decision for themselves. And all will be happy, all the millions of creatures except the hundred thousand who rule over them. For only we, we who guard the mystery, shall be unhappy. There will be thousands of millions of happy babes, and a hundred thousand sufferers who have taken upon themselves the curse of the knowledge of good and evil. Peacefully they will die, peacefully they will expire in Thy name, and beyond the grave they will find nothing but death. But we shall keep the secret, and for their happiness we shall allure them with the reward of heaven and eternity. Though if there were anything in the other world, it certainly would not be for such as they. It is prophesied that Thou wilt come again in victory, Thou wilt come with Thy chosen, the proud and strong, but we will say that they have only saved themselves, but we have saved all. We are told that the harlot who sits upon the beast, and holds in her hands the *mystery,* shall be put to shame, that the weak will rise up again, and will rend her royal purple and will strip naked her loathsome body. But then I will stand up and point out to Thee the thousand millions of happy children who have known no sin. And we who have taken their sins upon us for their happiness will stand up before Thee and say: "Judge us if Thou canst and darest." Know that I fear Thee not. Know that I too have been in the wilderness, I too have lived on roots and locusts, I too prized the freedom with which Thou hast blessed men, and I too was striving to stand among Thy elect, among the strong and powerful, thirsting "to make up the number." But I awakened and would not serve madness. I turned back and joined the ranks of those *who have corrected Thy work.* I left the proud and went back to the humble, for the happiness of the humble. What I say to Thee will come to pass, and our dominion will be built up. I repeat, to-morrow Thou shalt see that obedient flock who at a sign from me will hasten to heap up the hot cinders about the pile on which I shall burn Thee for coming to hinder us. For if any one has ever deserved our fires, it is Thou. To-morrow I shall burn Thee. Dixi.' "

Ivan stopped. He was carried away as he talked and spoke with excitement; when he had finished, he suddenly smiled.

Alyosha had listened in silence; towards the end he was greatly moved and seemed several times on the point of interrupting, but restrained himself. Now his words came with a rush.

"But . . . that's absurd!" he cried, flushing. "Your poem is in praise of Jesus, not in blame of Him—as you meant it to be. And who will believe you about freedom? Is that the way to understand it? That's not the idea of it in the Orthodox Church . . . That's Rome, and not even the whole of Rome, it's false—those are the worst of the Catholics, the Inquisitors, the Jesuits! . . . And there could not be such a fantastic creature as your Inquisitor. What are these sins of mankind they take on themselves? Who are these keepers of the mystery who have taken some curse upon themselves for the happiness of mankind? When have they been seen? We know the Jesuits, they are spoken ill of, but surely they are not what you describe? They are not that at all, not at all. . . . They are simply the Romish army for the earthly sovereignty of the world in the future, with the Pontiff of Rome for Emperor . . . that's their ideal, but there's no sort of mystery or lofty melancholy about it. . . . It's simple lust of power, of filthy earthly gain, of domination—something like a universal serfdom with them as masters—that's all they stand for. They don't even believe in God perhaps. Your suffering inquisitor is a mere fantasy."

"Stay, stay," laughed Ivan, "how hot you are! A fantasy you say, let it be so! Of course it's a fantasy. But allow me to say: do you really think that the Roman Catholic movement of the last centuries is actually nothing but the lust of power, of filthy earthly gain? Is that Father Païssy's teaching?"

"No, no, on the contrary, Father Païssy did once say something rather the same as you . . . but of course it's not the same, not a bit the same," Alyosha hastily corrected himself.

"A precious admission, in spite of your 'not a bit the same.' I ask you why your Jesuits and Inquisitors have united simply for vile material gain? Why can there not be among them one martyr oppressed by great sorrow and loving humanity? You see, only suppose that there was one such man among all those who desire nothing but filthy material gain—if there's only one like my old inquisitor, who had himself eaten roots in the desert and made frenzied efforts to subdue his flesh to make himself free and perfect. But yet all his life he loved humanity, and suddenly his eyes were opened, and he saw that it is no great moral blessedness to attain perfection and freedom, if at the same time one gains the conviction that millions of God's creatures have been created as a mockery, that they will never be capable of using their freedom, that these poor rebels can never turn into giants to complete the tower, that it was not for such geese that the great idealist dreamt his dream of harmony. Seeing all that he turned back and joined—the clever people. Surely that could have happened?"

"Joined whom, what clever people?" cried Alyosha, completely carried away. "They have no such great cleverness and no mysteries and secrets. . . . Perhaps nothing but Atheism, that's all their secret. Your inquisitor does not believe in God, that's his secret!"

"What if it is so! At last you have guessed it. It's perfectly true that that's the whole secret, but isn't that suffering, at least for a man like that, who has wasted his whole life in the desert and yet could not shake off his incurable love of humanity? In his old age he reached the clear conviction that nothing but the advice of the great dread spirit could build up any tolerable sort of life for the feeble, unruly, 'incomplete, empirical creatures created in jest.' And so, convinced of this, he sees that he must follow the counsel of the wise spirit, the dread spirit of death and destruction, and therefore accept lying and deception, and lead men consciously to death and destruction, and yet deceive them all the way so that they may not notice where they are being led, that the poor blind creatures may at least on the way think themselves happy. And note, the deception is in the name of Him in Whose ideal the old man had so fervently believed all his life long. Is not that tragic? And if only one such stood at the head of the whole army 'filled with the lust of power only for the sake of filthy gain'—would not one such be enough to make a tragedy? More than that, one such standing at the head is enough to create the actual leading idea of the Roman Church with all its armies and Jesuits, its highest idea. I tell you frankly that I firmly believe that there has always been such a man among those who stood at the head of the movement. Who knows, there may have been some such even among the Roman Popes. Who knows, perhaps the spirit of that accursed old man who loves mankind so obstinately in his own way, is to be found even now in a whole multitude of such old men, existing not by chance but by agreement, as a secret league formed long ago for the guarding of the mystery, to guard it from the weak and the unhappy, so as to make them happy. No doubt it is so, and so it must be indeed. I fancy that even among the Masons there's something of the same mystery at the bottom, and that that's why the Catholics so detest the Masons as their rivals breaking up the unity of the idea, while it is so essential that there should be one flock and one shepherd. . . . But from the way I defend my idea I might be an author impatient of your criticism. Enough of it."

"You are perhaps a Mason yourself!" broke suddenly from Alyosha. "You don't believe in God," he added, speaking this time very sorrowfully. He fancied besides that his brother was looking at him ironically. "How does your poem end?" he asked, suddenly looking down. "Or was it the end?"

"I meant to end it like this. When the Inquisitor ceased speaking he waited some time for his Prisoner to answer him. His silence weighed down upon him. He saw that the Prisoner had listened intently all the time, looking gently in his face and evidently not wishing to reply. The old man longed for Him to say something, however bitter and terrible. But He suddenly approached the old man in silence and softly kissed him on his bloodless aged lips. That was all his answer. The old man shuddered. His lips moved. He went to the door, opened it, and said to Him: 'Go, and come no more. . . . come not at all, never, never!' And he let Him out into the dark alleys of the town. The Prisoner went away."

"And the old man?"

"The kiss glows in his heart, but the old man adheres to his idea."

"And you with him, you too?" cried Alyosha, mournfully.

Ivan laughed.

"Why, it's all nonsense, Alyosha. It's only a senseless poem of a senseless student, who could never write two lines of verse. Why do you take it so seriously? Surely you don't suppose I am going straight off to the Jesuits, to join the men who are correcting His work? Good Lord, it's no business of mine. I told you, all I want is to live on to thirty, and then . . . dash the cup to the ground!"

"But the little sticky leaves, and the precious tombs, and the blue sky, and the woman you love! How will you live, how will you love them?" Alyosha cried sorrowfully. "With such a hell in your heart and your head, how can you? No, that's just what you are going away for, to join them . . . if not, you will kill yourself, you can't endure it!"

"There is a strength to endure everything," Ivan said with a cold smile.

"What strength?"

"The strength of the Karamazov—the strength of the Karamazov baseness."

"To sink into debauchery, to stifle your soul with corruption, yes?"

"Possibly even that . . . only perhaps till I am thirty I shall escape it, and then."

"How will you escape it? By what will you escape it? That's impossible with your ideas."

"In the Karamazov way, again."

" 'Everything is lawful,' you mean? Everything is lawful, is that it?"

Ivan scowled, and all at once turned strangely pale.

"Ah, you've caught up yesterday's phrase, which so offended Miüsov—and which Dmitri pounced upon so naïvely and paraphrased!" he smiled queerly. "Yes, if you like, 'everything is lawful' since the word has been said. I won't deny it. And Mitya's version isn't bad."

Alyosha looked at him in silence.

"I thought that going away from here I have you at least,"

Ivan said suddenly, with unexpected feeling; "but now I see that there is no place for me even in your heart, my dear hermit. The formula, 'all is lawful,' I won't renounce—will you renounce me for that, yes?"

Alyosha got up, went to him and softly kissed him on the lips.

"That's plagiarism," cried Ivan, highly delighted. "You stole that from my poem. Thank you though. Get up, Alyosha, it's time we were going, both of us."

They went out, but stopped when they reached the entrance of the restaurant.

"Listen, Alyosha," Ivan began in a resolute voice, "if I am really able to care for the sticky little leaves I shall only love them, remembering you. It's enough for me that you are somewhere here, and I shan't lose my desire for life yet. Is that enough for you? Take it as a declaration of love if you like. And now you go to the right and I to the left. And it's enough, do you hear, enough. I mean even if I don't go away to-morrow (I think I certainly shall go) and we meet again, don't say a word more on these subjects. I beg that particularly. And about Dmitri too, I ask you specially never speak to me again," he added, with sudden irritation; "it's all exhausted, it has all been said over and over again, hasn't it? And I'll make you one promise in return for it. When at thirty, I want to 'dash the cup to the ground,' wherever I may be I'll come to have one more talk with you, even though it were from America, you may be sure of that. I'll come on purpose. It will be very interesting to have a look at you, to see what you'll be by that time. It's rather a solemn promise, you see. And we really may be parting for seven years or ten. Come, go now to your Pater Seraphicus, he is dying. If he dies without you, you will be angry with me for having kept you. Good-bye, kiss me once more; that's right, now go."

Ivan turned suddenly and went his way without looking back. It was just as Dmitri had left Alyosha the day before, though the parting had been very different. The strange resemblance flashed like an arrow through Alyosha's mind in the distress and dejection of that moment. He waited a little, looking after his brother. He suddenly noticed that Ivan swayed as he walked and that his right shoulder looked lower than his left. He had never noticed it before. But all at once he turned too, and almost ran to the monastery. It was nearly dark, and he felt almost frightened; something new was growing up in him for which he could not account. The wind had risen again as on the previous evening, and the ancient pines murmured gloomily about him when he entered the hermitage copse. He almost ran. "Pater Seraphicus—he got that name from somewhere—where from?" Alyosha wondered. "Ivan, poor Ivan, and when shall I see you again? . . . Here is the hermitage. Yes, yes, that he is, Pater Seraphicus, he will save me—from him and for ever!"

Several times afterwards he wondered how he could on leaving Ivan so completely forget his brother Dmitri, though he had that morning, only a few hours before, so firmly resolved to find him and not to give up doing so, even should he be unable to return to the monastery that night.

Thomas Merton, THE SEVEN STOREY MOUNTAIN

Gerard Manley Hopkins, "GOD'S GRANDEUR"
"WINDHOVER"

1. Compare and contrast Merton's view of the Jesuit Order with the Views of Dostoyevsky.

2. Merton knew well and loved the poetry of Gerard Manley Hopkins and believed that "the artistic experience, at its highest, was actually a natural analogue of mystical experience." Study carefully the two poems of Hopkins included in this unit and explain what Merton meant.

3. What emotional, intellectual, and spiritual needs are fulfilled for Merton when he finally becomes a Catholic? What causes him to make this decision?

4. Do Merton's experiences and conflicts as an adolescent seem typical or extraordinary?

5. Does Merton's account of his variety of religious experience seem credible and interesting? Why or why not?

Thomas Merton's intense, vivid, and highly descriptive account of his life in *The Seven Storey Mountain* was written in the Trappist monastery at Gethsemane, Kentucky, and published in 1948. In this autobiography, which takes its title from Dante's image of Purgatory, Merton describes his sometimes painful but often exultant journey up the seven story mountain from what he considered an idle, boring, and sinful life to a spiritually rewarding life of worship and contemplation as a monk.

V

In three months, the summer of 1931, I suddenly matured like a weed.

I cannot tell which is the more humiliating: the memory of the half-baked adolescent I was in June or the glib and hard-boiled specimen I was in October when I came back to Oakham full of a thorough and deep-rooted sophistication of which I was both conscious and proud.

The beginning was like this: Pop wrote to me to come to America. I got a brand-new suit made. I said to myself, "On the boat I am going to meet a beautiful girl, and I am going to fall in love."

So I got on the boat. The first day I sat in a deck chair and read the correspondence of Goethe and Schiller which had been imposed on me as a duty, in preparation for the scholarship examinations at the university. What is worse, I not only tolerated this imposition but actually convinced myself that it was interesting.

The second day I had more or less found out who was on the boat. The third day I was no longer interested in Goethe and Schiller. The fourth day I was up to my neck in the trouble that I was looking for.

It was a ten-day boat.

I would rather spend two years in a hospital than go through that anguish again! That devouring, emotional, passionate love of adolescence that sinks its claws into you and consumes you day and night and eats into the vitals of your soul! All the self-tortures of doubt and anxiety and imagination and hope and despair that you go through when you are a child, trying to break out of your shell, only to find yourself in the middle of a legion of full-armed emotions against which you have no defense! It is like being flayed alive. No one can go through it twice. This kind of a love affair can really happen only once in a man's life. After that he is calloused. He is no longer capable of so many torments. He can suffer, but not from so many matters of no account. After one such crisis he has experience and the possibility of a second time no longer exists, because the secret of the anguish was his own utter guilelessness. He is no longer capable of such complete and absurd surprises. No matter how simple a man may be, the obvious cannot go on astonishing him for ever.

I was introduced to this particular girl by a Catholic priest who came from Cleveland and played shuffleboard in his shirt sleeves without a Roman collar on. He knew everybody on the boat in the first day, and as for me, two days had gone by before I even realized that she was on board. She was travelling with a couple of aunts and the three of them did not mix in with the other passengers very much. They kept to themselves in their three deck chairs and had nothing to do with the gentlemen in tweed caps and glasses who went breezing around and around the promenade deck.

When I first met her I got the impression she was no older than I was. As a matter of fact she was about twice my age: but you could be twice sixteen without being old, as I now realize, sixteen years after the event. She was small and delicate and looked as if she were made out of porcelain. But she had big wide-open California eyes and was not afraid to talk in a voice that was at once ingenuous and independent and had some suggestion of weariness about it as if she habitually stayed up too late at night.

To my dazzled eyes she immediately became the heroine of every novel and I all but flung myself face down on the deck at her feet. She could have put a collar on my neck and led me around from that time forth on the end of a chain. Instead of that I spent my days telling her and her aunts all about my ideals and my ambitions and she in her turn attempted to teach me how to play bridge. And that is the surest proof of her conquest, for I never allowed anyone else to try such a thing as that on me, never! But even she could not succeed in such an enterprise.

We talked. The insatiable wound inside me bled and grew, and I was doing everything I could to make it bleed more. Her perfume and the peculiar smell of the denicotinized cigarettes she smoked followed me everywhere and tortured me in my cabin.

She told me how once she was in a famous night club in a famous city when a famous person, a prince of the royal blood, had stared very intently at her for a long time and had finally got up and started to lurch in the direction of her table when his friends had made him sit down and behave himself.

I could see that all the counts and dukes who liked to marry people like Constance Bennett would want also to marry her. But the counts and dukes were not here on board this glorified cargo boat that was carrying us all peacefully across the mild dark waves of the North Atlantic. The thing that crushed me was that I had never learned to dance.

We made Nantucket Light on Sunday afternoon and had to anchor in quarantine that night. So the ship rode in the Narrows on the silent waters, and the lights of Brooklyn glittered in the harbor like jewels. The boat was astir with music and with a warm glowing life that pulsated within the dark hull and poured out into the July night through every porthole. There were parties in all the cabins. Everywhere you went, especially on deck where it was quiet, you were placed in the middle of movie scenery—the setting for the last reel of the picture.

I made a declaration of my undying love. I would not, could not, ever love anyone else but her. It was impossible, unthinkable. If she went to the ends of the earth, destiny would bring us together again. The stars in their courses from the beginning of the world had plotted this meeting which was the central fact in the whole history of the universe. Love like this was immortal. It conquered time and outlasted the futility of human history. And so forth.

She talked to me, in her turn, gently and sweetly. What it sounded like was: "You do not know what you are saying. This can never be. We shall never meet again." What it meant was: "You are a nice kid. But for heaven's sake grow up before someone makes a fool of you." I went to my cabin and sobbed over my diary for a while and then, against all the laws of romance, went peacefully to sleep.

However, I could not sleep for long. At five o'clock I was up again, and walking restlessly around the deck. It was hot. A grey mist lay on the Narrows. But when it became light, other anchored ships began to appear as shapes in the mist. One of them was a Red Star liner on which, as I learned from the papers when I got on shore, a passenger was at that precise moment engaged in hanging himself.

At the last minute before landing I took a snapshot of her which, to my intense sorrow, came out blurred. I was so avid for a picture of her that I got too close with the camera and it was out of focus. It was a piece of poetic justice that filled me with woe for months.

Of course the whole family was there on the dock. But the change was devastating. With my heart ready to explode with immature emotions I suddenly found myself surrounded by all the cheerful and peaceful and comfortable solicitudes of home. Everybody wanted to talk. Their voices were full of questions and information. They took me for a drive on Long Island and showed me where Mrs. Hearst lived and everything. But I only hung my head out of the window of the car and watched the green trees go swirling by, and wished that I were dead.

I would not tell anybody what was the matter with me, and this reticence was the beginning of a kind of estrangement between us. From that time on no one could be sure what I was doing or thinking. I would go to New York and I would not come home for meals and I would not tell anyone where I had been.

Most of the time I had not been anywhere special; I would go to the movies, and then wander around the streets and look at the crowds of people and eat hot dogs and drink orange juice at Nedicks. Once with great excitement I got inside a speak-easy. And when I found out that the place was raided a few days later I grew so much in my own estimation that I began to act as if I had shot my way out of the wildest joints in town.

Bonnemaman was the one who suffered most from my reticence. For years she had been sitting at home wondering what Pop was doing in the city all day, and now that I was developing the same wandering habits it was quite natural for her to imagine strange things about me, too.

But the only wickedness I was up to was that I roamed around the city smoking cigarettes and hugging my own sweet sense of independence.

I found out that Grosset and Dunlap published more than the Rover Boys. They brought out reprints of writers like Hemingway and Aldous Huxley and D. H. Lawrence and I devoured them all, on the cool sleeping porch of the house at Douglaston, while the moths of the summer darkness came batting and throbbing against the screens, attracted by my light that burned until all hours.

Most of the time I was running into my uncle's room to borrow his dictionary, and when he found out what words I was looking up he arched his eyebrows and said: "What are you reading, anyway?"

At the end of the summer I started back for England on the same boat on which I had come. This time the passenger list included some girls from Bryn Mawr and some from Vassar and some from somewhere else, all of whom were going to a finishing school in France. It seems as if all the rest of the people on board were detectives. Some of them were professional detectives. Others were amateurs; all of them made me and the Bryn Mawr girls the object of their untiring investigations. But in any case the ship was divided into these two groups: on the one hand the young people, on the other the elders. We sat in the smoking room all the rainy days playing Duke Ellington records on the portable vic that belonged to one of the girls. When we got tired of that we wandered all over the ship looking for funny things to do. The hold was full of cattle, and there was also a pack of fox-hounds down there. We used to go down and play with the dogs. At Le Havre, when the cattle were unloaded, one of the cows broke loose and ran all over the dock in a frenzy. One night three of us got up in the crow's nest on the foremast, where we certainly did not belong. Another time we had a party with the radio operators and I got into a big argument about Communism.

That was another thing that had happened that summer: I had begun to get the idea that I was a Communist, although I wasn't quite sure what Communism was. There are a lot of people like that. They do no little harm by virtue of their sheer, stupid inertia, lost in between all camps, in the no-man's-land of their own confusion. They are fair game for anybody. They can be turned into fascists just as quickly as they can be pulled into line with those who are really Reds.

The other group was made up of the middle-aged people. At their core were the red-faced, hard-boiled cops who spent their time drinking and gambling and fighting among themselves and spreading scandal all over the boat about the young ones who were so disreputable and wild.

The truth is that we did have quite a big bar bill, the Bryn Mawr girls and myself, but we were never drunk, because we drank slowly and spent the whole time stuffing ourselves with sardines on toast and all the other dainties which are the stock in trade of English liners.

In any case, I set foot once more on the soil of England dressed up in a gangster suit which Pop had bought me at Wallach's, complete with padded shoulders. And I had a new, pale grey hat over my eye and walked into England pleased with the consciousness that I had easily acquired a very lurid reputation for myself with scarcely any trouble at all.

The separation of the two generations on board the ship had pleased me. It had flattered me right down to the soles of my feet. It was just what I wanted. It completed my self-confidence, guaranteed my self-assertion. Anyone older than myself symbolized authority. And the vulgarity of the detectives and the stupidity of the other middle-aged people who had believed all their stories about us fed me with a pleasantly justifiable sense of contempt for their whole generation. Therefore I concluded that I was now free of all authority, and that nobody could give me any advice that I had to listen to. Because advice was only the cloak of hypocrisy or weakness or vulgarity or fear. Authority was constituted by the old and weak, and had its roots in their envy for the joys and pleasures of the young and strong. . . .

Finally, when I arrived at Oakham several days after the beginning of the term I was convinced that I was the only one in the whole place who knew anything about life, from the Headmaster on down.

I was now a house prefect in Hodge Wing with a great big study and a lot of slightly lop-sided wicker armchairs full of cushions. On the walls I hung Medici prints of Manet and some other impressionists and photographs of various Greco-Roman Venuses from museums in Rome. And my bookshelf was full of a wide variety of strange bright-colored novels and pamphlets, all of which were so inflammatory that there would never be any special need for the Church to put them on the *Index*, for they would all be damned *ipso jure*—most of them by the natural law itself. I will not name the ones I remember, because some fool might immediately go and read them all: but I might mention that one of the pamphlets was Marx's Communist Manifesto—not because I was seriously exercised about the injustices done to the working class, which were and are very real, but were too serious for my empty-headed vanity—but simply because I thought it fitted in nicely with the décor in which I now moved in all my imaginings.

For it had become evident to me that I was a great rebel. I fancied that I had suddenly risen above all the errors and stupidities and mistakes of modern society—there are enough of them to rise above, I admit—and that I had taken my place in the ranks of those who held up their heads and squared their shoulders and marched into the future. In the modern world, people are always holding up their heads and marching into the future, although they haven't the slightest idea what they think the "future" is or could possibly mean. The only future we seem to walk into, in actual fact, is full of bigger and more terrible wars, wars well calculated to knock our upraised heads off those squared shoulders.

Here in this study I edited the school magazine which had fallen into my hands that autumn, and read T. S. Eliot, and even tried to write a poem myself about Elpenor, in Homer, getting drunk and falling off the roof of a palace. And his soul fled into the shades of hell. And the rest of the time I played Duke Ellington's records or got into arguments about politics and religion.

All those vain and absurd arguments! My advice to an ordinary religious man, supposing anyone were to desire my advice on this point, would be to avoid all arguments about religion, and especially about the existence of God. However, to those who know some philosophy I would recommend the study of Duns Scotus' proofs for the actual existence of an Infinite Being, which are given in the Second Distinction of the First Book of the *Opus Oxoniense*—in Latin that is hard enough to give you many headaches. It is getting to be rather generally admitted that, for accuracy and depth and scope, this is the most perfect and complete and thorough proof for the existence of God that has ever been worked out by any man.

I doubt if it would have done much good to bring these considerations before me in those days, when I was just turning seventeen, and thought I knew all about philosophy without ever having learned any. However, I did have a desire to learn. I was attracted to philosophy. It was an attraction the Headmaster had worked hard to implant in our souls: but there was, and could be, no course in philosophy at Oakham. I was left to my own devices.

I remember once mentioning all this to Tom, my guardian. We were walking out of his front door, into Harley Street, and I told him of my desire to study philosophy, and to know the philosophers.

He, being a doctor, told me to leave philosophy alone: there were few things, he told me, that were a greater waste of time.

Fortunately, this was one of the matters in which I decided to ignore his advice. Anyway, I went ahead and tried to read some philosophy. I never got very far with it. It was too difficult for me to master all by myself. People who are immersed in sensual appetites and desires are not very well prepared to handle abstract ideas. Even in the purely natural order, a certain amount of purity of heart is required before an intellect can get sufficiently detached and clear to work out the problems of metaphysics. I say a certain amount, however, because I am sure that no one needs to be a saint to be a clever metaphysician. I dare say there are plenty of metaphysicians in hell.

However, the philosophers to whom I was attracted were not the best. For the most part, I used to take their books out of libraries, and return them without ever having opened them. It was just as well. Nevertheless during the Easter vacation, when I was seventeen, I earnestly and zealously set about trying to figure out Spinoza.

I had gone to Germany, by myself as usual, for the vacation. In Cologne I had bought a big rucksack and slung it over my shoulders and started up the Rhine valley on foot, in a blue jersey and an old pair of flannel bags, so that people in the inns along the road asked me if I was a Dutch sailor off one of the river barges. In the rucksack, which was already heavy enough, I had a couple of immoral novels and the Everyman Library edition of Spinoza. Spinoza and the Rhine valley! I certainly had a fine sense of appropriateness. The two go very well together. However I was about eighty years too late. And the only thing that was lacking was that I was not an English or American student at Heidelberg: then the mixture would have been perfect in all its mid-nineteenth-century ingredients.

I picked up more, on this journey, than a few intellectual errors, half understood. Before I got to Koblenz, I had trouble in one foot. Some kind of an infection seemed to be developing under one of the toenails. But it was not especially painful, and I ignored it. However, it made walking unpleasant, and so, after going on as far as St. Goar, I gave up in disgust. Besides, the weather had turned bad, and I had got lost in the forest, trying to follow the imaginary hiker's trail called the Rheinhöhenweg.

I went back to Koblenz, and sat in a room over a big beer hall called the Neuer Franziskaner and continued my desultory study of Spinoza and my modern novelists. Since I understood the latter much better than the philosopher, I soon gave him up and concentrated on the novels.

After a few days, I returned to England, passing through Paris, where Pop and Bonnemaman were. There I picked up some more and even worse books, and went back to school.

I had not been back for more than a few days when I began to feel ill. At first, I thought I was only out of sorts because of the sore foot and a bad toothache, which had suddenly begun to afflict me.

They sent me down to the school dentist, Dr. McTaggart, who lived in a big brick building like a barracks, on the way to the station. Dr. McTaggart was a lively little fellow. He knew me well, for I was always having trouble with my teeth. He had a theory that you should kill the nerves of teeth, and he had already done so to half a dozen of mine. For the rest, he would trot gaily around and around the big chair in which I sat, mute and half frozen with terror. And he would sing, as he quickly switched his drills: "It won't be a stylish marriage— We can't afford a carriage— But you'll look sweet— Upon the seat— Of a bicycle built for two."

Then he would start wrecking my teeth once again, with renewed gusto.

This time he tapped at the tooth, and looked serious.

"It will have to come out," he said.

I was not sorry. The thing was hurting me, and I wanted to get rid of it as soon as possible.

But Dr. McTaggart said: "I can't give you anything to deaden the pain, you know."

"Why not?"

"There is a great deal of infection, and the matter has spread far beyond the roots of the tooth."

I accepted his reasoning on trust and said: "Well, go ahead."

And I sat back in the chair, mute with misgivings, while he happily trotted over to his tool-box singing "It won't be a stylish marriage" and pulled out an ugly-looking forceps.

"All ready?" he said, jacking back the chair, and brandishing the instrument of torture. I nodded, feeling as if I had gone pale to the roots of my hair.

But the tooth came out fast, in one big, vivid flash of pain and left me spitting a lot of green and red business into the little blue whispering whirlpool by the side of the dentist's chair.

"Oh, goodness," said Dr. McTaggart, "I don't like that very much, I must say."

I walked wearily back to school, reflecting that it was not really so terrible after all to have a tooth pulled out without novocain. However, instead of getting better, I got worse. By evening, I was really ill, and that night—that sleepless night—was spent in a fog of sick confusedness and general pain. The next morning they took my temperature and put me to bed in the sick-room, where I eventually got to sleep.

That did not make me any better. And I soon gathered in a vague way that our matron, Miss Harrison, was worried about me, and communicated her worries to the Headmaster, in whose own house this particular sick-room was.

Then the school doctor came around. And he went away again, returning with Dr. McTaggart who, this time, did not sing.

And I heard them agreeing that I was getting to be too full of gangrene for my own good. They decided to lance a big hole in my gum, and see if they could not drain the pocket of infection there and so, having given me a little ether, they went ahead. I awoke with my mouth full of filth, both doctors urging me to hurry up and get rid of it.

When they had gone, I lay back in bed and closed my eyes and thought: "I have blood-poisoning."

And then my mind went back to the sore foot I had developed in Germany. Well, I would tell them about it when they came back the next time.

Sick, weary, half asleep, I felt the throbbing of the wound in my mouth. Blood-poisoning.

The room was very quiet. It was rather dark, too. And as I lay in bed, in my weariness and pain and disgust, I felt for a moment the shadow of another visitor pass into the room.

It was death, that came to stand by my bed.

I kept my eyes closed, more out of apathy than anything else. But anyway, there was no need to open one's eyes to see the visitor, to see death. Death is someone you see very clearly with eyes in the center of your heart: eyes that see not by reacting to light, but by reacting to a kind of a chill from within the marrow of your own life.

And, with those eyes, those interior eyes, open upon that coldness, I lay half asleep and looked at the visitor, death.

What did I think? All I remember was that I was filled with a deep and tremendous apathy. I felt so sick and disgusted that I did not very much care whether I died or lived. Perhaps death did not come very close to me, or give me a good look at the nearness of his coldness and darkness, or I would have been more afraid.

But at any rate, I lay there in a kind of torpor and said: "Come on, I don't care." And then I fell asleep.

What a tremendous mercy it was that death did not take me at my word, that day, when I was still only seventeen years old. What a thing it would have been if the trapdoors that were prepared for me had yawned and opened their blackness and swallowed me down in the middle of that sleep! Oh, I tell you, it is a blessing beyond calculation that I woke up again, that day, or the following night, or in the week or two that came after.

And I lay there with nothing in my heart but apathy—there was a kind of pride and spite in it: as if it was life's fault that I had to suffer a little discomfort, and for that I would show my scorn and hatred of life, and die, as if that were a revenge of some sort. Revenge upon what? What was life? Something existing apart from me, and separate from myself? Don't worry, I did not enter into any speculations. I only thought: "If I have to die—what of it. What do I care? Let me die, then, and I'm finished."

Religious people, those who have faith and love God and realize what life is and what death means, and know what it is to have an immortal soul, do not understand how it is with the ones who have no faith, and who have already thrown away their souls. They find it hard to conceive that anyone could enter into the presence of death without some kind of compunction. But they should realize that millions of men die the way I was then prepared to die, the way I then might have died.

They might say to me: "Surely you thought of God, and you wanted to pray to Him for mercy."

No. As far as I remember, the thought of God, the thought of prayer did not even enter my mind, either that day, or all the rest of the time that I was ill, or that whole year, for that matter. Or if the thought did come to me, it was only as an occasion for its denial and rejection. I remember that in that year, when we stood in the chapel and recited the Apostles' Creed, I used to keep my lips tight shut, with full deliberation and of set purpose, by way of declaring my own creed which was: "I believe in nothing." Or at least I thought I believed in nothing. Actually, I had only exchanged a certain faith, faith in God, Who is Truth, for a vague uncertain faith in the opinions and authority of men and pamphlets and newspapers—wavering and varying and contradictory opinions which I did not even clearly understand.

I wish I could give those who believe in God some kind of an idea of the state of a soul like mine was in then. But it is impossible to do it in sober, straight, measured, prose terms. And, in a sense, image and analogy would be even more misleading, by the very fact that they would have life in them, and convey the notion of some real entity, some kind of energy, some sort of activity. But my soul was simply dead. It was a blank, a nothingness. It was empty, it was a kind of a spiritual vacuum, as far as the supernatural order was concerned. Even its natural faculties were shrivelled husks of what they ought to have been.

A soul is an immaterial thing. It is a principle of activity, it is an "act," a "form," an energizing principle. It is the life of the body, and it must also have a life of its own. But the life of the soul does not inhere in any physical, material subject. So to compare a soul without grace to a corpse without life is only a metaphor. But it is very true.

St. Theresa had a vision of hell. She saw herself confined in a narrow hole in a burning wall. The vision terrified her above all with the sense of the appalling stress of this confinement and heat. All this is symbolic, of course. But a poetic grasp of the meaning of the symbol should convey something of the experience of a soul which is reduced to an almost infinite limit of helplessness and frustration by the fact of dying in sin, and thus being eternally separated from the principle of all vital activity which, for the soul in its own proper order, means intellection and love.

But I now lay on this bed, full of gangrene, and my soul was rotten with the corruption of my sins. And I did not even care whether I died or lived.

The worst thing that can happen to anyone in this life is to lose all sense of these realities. The worst thing that had ever happened to me was this consummation of my sins in abominable coldness and indifference, even in the presence of death.

What is more, there was nothing I could do for myself. There was absolutely no means, no natural means within reach, for getting out of that state. Only God could help me. Who prayed for me? One day I shall know. But in the economy of God's love, it is through the prayers of other men that these graces are given. It was through the prayers of someone who loved God that I was, one day, to be delivered out of that hell where I was already confined without knowing it.

The big gift God gave me was that I got well. They bundled me up and put me on a stretcher with blankets all up around my face and nothing sticking out but my nose, and carried me across the stone quadrangle where my friends were playing "quad-cricket" with a sawed-off bat and a grey tennis ball. They stood aside in awe as I passed on the way to the school sanatorium.

I had explained to the doctor about my foot, and they came and cut off the toenail and found the toe full of gangrene. But they gave me some anti-toxin and did not have to cut off the toe. Dr. McTaggart came around every day or two to treat the infected place in my mouth, and gradually I began to get better, and to eat, and sit up, and read my filthy novels again. Nobody thought of prohibiting them, because nobody else had heard of the authors.

It was while I was in the sanatorium that I wrote a long essay on the modern novel—Gide, Hemingway, Dos Passos, Jules Romains, Dreiser, and so on, for the Bailey English Prize, and won a lot of books bound in tree-calf for my efforts.

Two attempts were made to convert me to less shocking tastes. The music master lent me a set of records of Bach's B Minor Mass, which I liked, and sometimes played on my portable gramophone, which I had with me in the big airy room looking out on the Headmaster's garden. But most of the time I played the hottest and loudest records, turning the vic towards the classroom building, eighty yards away across the flowerbeds, hoping that my companions, grinding out the syntax of Virgil's *Georgics,* would be very envious of me.

The other loan was that of a book. The Headmaster came along, one day, and gave me a little blue book of poems. I looked at the name on the back. "Gerard Manley Hopkins." I had never heard of him. But I opened the book, and read the "Starlight Night" and the Harvest poem and the most lavish and elaborate early poems. I noticed that the man was a Catholic and a priest and, what is more, a Jesuit.

I could not make up my mind whether I liked his verse or not. It was elaborate and tricky and in places it was a little lush and overdone, I thought. Yet it was original and had a lot of vitality and music and depth. In fact the later poems were all far too deep for me, and I could not make anything out of them at all.

Nevertheless, I accepted the poet, with reservations. I gave the book back to the Head, and thanked him, and never altogether forgot Hopkins, though I was not to read him again for several years.

I got out of the sanatorium in a month or six weeks. With the end of June, came our big examination—the higher certificate, which I took in French and German and Latin. Then we went away for the vacation, and I settled down to wait until September for the results of the exam. Pop and Bonnemaman and John Paul were once again in Europe for the summer, and we all spent a couple of months in a big, dreary hotel in Bournemouth, standing on top of a cliff and facing the sea with a battery of white iron balconies, painted silver, so that they gleamed in the pale, English summer sun and in the morning mists. I will not go into the emotions of that summer, in which I and a girl I met there kept going through storms of sentiment alternating with adolescent quarrels, during which I used to escape from Bournemouth into the Dorset downs and wander around for the whole day in the country trying to recover my equilibrium.

But at the end of the summer, when she went back to London, and my family also took the boat at Southampton and went home, I packed up my rucksack and went into the New Forest, with a pup tent, and sat down under some pine trees at the edge of a common a couple of miles from Brockenhurst. Oh, the tremendous loneliness of that first night in the forest! The frogs sang in the brackish stream, and the fireflies played in the gorse, and occasionally a lone car would pass along the distant road, exaggerating the silence by the sound that died in the wake of its passing. And I sat in the door of my tent, uneasily trying to digest the eggs and bacon I had fried and the bottle of cider I had brought out from the village.

She had said she would write me a letter, addressed to the Post-office at Brockenhurst, as soon as she got home, but I thought this camp site at the edge of the common was too dreary. Besides, the water of the stream tasted funny and I thought maybe I might get poisoned, so I moved on down toward Beaulieu, where I did not have to eat my own cooking, but ate in an inn. And I spent the afternoon lying in the grass in front of the old Cistercian abbey, copiously pitying myself for my boredom and for the loneliness of immature love. At the same time, however, I was debating in my mind whether to go to a "Gymkhana," that is a sort of a polite amateur horse-show, and mingle with all the gentry of the county, perhaps meeting someone even more beautiful than the girl for whom I thought I was, at the moment, pining away even unto death. However, I wisely decided to avoid the tents of such a dull affair.

As for the Cistercian abbey, which was the scene of these meditations, I did not think much about it at all. I had wandered through the ruins of the old buildings, and had stood in the parish church that had taken over the old refectory of the monks, and I had tasted a little of the silence and peacefulness of the greensward under the trees, where the cloister used to be. But it was all in the usual picnic spirit with which the average modern Englishman visits one of his old abbeys. If he does happen to wonder what kind of men once lived in such places, or why they ever did so, he does not ask himself if people still try to do the same thing today. That would seem to him a kind of impertinence. But by this time I had practically lost all interest in such speculations. What did I care about monks and monasteries? The world was going to open out before me, with all its entertainments, and everything would be mine and with my intelligence and my five sharp senses I would rob all its treasures and rifle its coffers and empty them all. And I would take what pleased me, and the rest I would throw away. And if I merely felt like spoiling the luxuries I did not want to use, I would spoil them and misuse them, to suit myself, because I was master of everything. It did not matter that I would not have much money: I would have enough, and my wits would do the rest. And I was aware that the best pleasures can be had without very much money—or with none at all.

I was at the house of one of my friends from school when the results of the higher certificate came out in September, and I could not decently indulge all my vanity at my success, because he had failed. However, he and I were to go up to Cambridge together for the scholarship examinations that December.

Andrew was the son of a country parson in the Isle of Wight and he had been cricket captain at Oakham. He wore horn-rimmed spectacles and had a great chin that he held up in the air, and a lock of black hair fell down over his forehead, and he was one of the school intellectuals. He and I used to work, or rather sit, in the library at Oakham, with many books open before us, but talking about impertinent matters and drinking a foul purple concoction called Vimto out of bottles which we concealed under the table or behind the volumes of the Dictionary of National Biography.

He had discovered a black book called, as I think, *The Outline of Modern Knowledge,* which was something that had just come to the library and was full of information about psychoanalysis. Indeed, it went into some details of psychoanalytical fortune-telling by the inspection of faeces which I never ran into anywhere else, and which I still preserved enough sense to laugh at, at that time. But later, at Cambridge, psychoanalysis was to provide me with a kind of philosophy of life and even a sort of pseudo-religion which was nearly the end of me altogether. By that time, Andrew himself had lost interest in it.

When we went up to the university, to sit for the scholarship exam, in the dank heavy-hanging mists of December, I spent most of the time between papers devouring D. H. Lawrence's *Fantasia of the Unconscious* which, even as psychoanalysis, is completely irresponsible and, just as it says, a fantasia. Lawrence picked up a lot of terms like "lumbar ganglion" and threw them all together and stewed them up with his own worship of the sex-instinct to produce the weird mixture which I read as reverently as if it were some kind of sacred revelation, sitting in the rooms of an undergraduate who liked Picasso, but who had gone down for the Christmas vacation. Andrew, for his part, was at St. Catherine's, terrified of a tutor who had a reputation for being a very ferocious person. All that week I sat under the high, silent rafters of the Hall, at Trinity College, and covered long sheets of foolscap with my opinions concerning Molière and Racine and Balzac and Victor Hugo and Goethe and Schiller and all the rest, and a few days after it was all over, we looked in the *Times* and this time both Andrew and I had succeeded. We were exhibitioners, he at St. Catherine's and I at Clare, while his study-mate, Dickens, who was the only other person at Oakham besides myself who liked hot records, had another exhibition at St. John's.

My satisfaction was very great. I was finished with Oakham—not that I disliked the school, but I was glad of my liberty. Now, at last, I imagined that I really was grown up and independent, and I could stretch out my hands and take all the things I wanted.

So during the Christmas holidays I ate and drank so much and went to so many parties that I made myself sick.

But I picked myself up, and dusted myself off, and on January 31st of the New Year, my eighteenth birthday, Tom took me to the Café Anglais and treated me to champagne and the next day I was off on the way to Italy.

vi

Already at Avignon I foresaw that I was going to run out of money before I got to Genoa. I had a letter of credit on a bank there. So from Avignon I wrote back to Tom asking for money. From Marseilles I started out on foot along the coast, walking on the white mountain road, overlooking the bright blue water, having on my hip a flask of rum and in the rucksack some more of the same novels. At Cassis all the restaurants were crammed with people who had come out from Marseilles for the day, since it was Sunday, and I had to wait long for my *bouillabaisse*. It was dark by the time I arrived at the grim little port of La Ciotat, under its sugarloaf rock. Tired, I sat on the jetty and contemplated the moon.

At Hyères I had to wait a couple of days before the money arrived, and when it did, the letter that went with it was filled with sharp reproofs. Tom, my guardian, took occasion of my impracticality to call attention to most of my other faults as well, and I was very humiliated. So after a month of my precious liberty, I received my first indication that my desires could never be absolute: they must necessarily be conditioned and modified by contacts and conflicts with the desires and interests of others. This was something that it would take me a long time to find out, and indeed in the natural order alone I would never really get to understand it. I believed in the beautiful myth about having a good time so long as it does not hurt anybody else. You cannot live for your own pleasure and your own convenience without inevitably hurting and injuring the feelings and the interests of practically everybody you meet. But, as a matter of fact, in the natural order no matter what ideals may be theoretically possible, most people more or less live for themselves and for their own interests and pleasures or for those of their own family or group, and therefore they are constantly interfering with one another's aims, and hurting one another and injuring one another, whether they mean it or not.

I started out from Hyères again, this time more weary and depressed, walking among the pines, under the hot sun, looking at the rocks and the yellow mimosas and the little pink villas and the light blazing on the sea. That night I came down a long hill in the dusk to a hamlet called Cavalaire, and slept in a boarding house full of sombre retired accountants who drank vin-rosé with their wives under the dim light of weak electric bulbs, and I went to bed and dreamt that I was in jail.

At Saint Tropez I had a letter of introduction to a friend of Tom's, a man with t.b., living in a sunny house on top of a hill, and there I met a couple of Americans who had rented a villa in the hills behind Cannes and they invited me there, when I came that way.

On the way to Cannes, I got caught by a storm, towards evening, in the mountains of the Esterel, and was picked up by a chauffeur driving a big fancy Delage. I slung my rucksack off my shoulder and threw it in the back seat and settled down, with the warmth of the motor seeping up through the boards and into my wet, tired feet. The chauffeur was an Englishman who had an auto-hiring business in Nice and said he had just picked up the Lindbergh family off the liner at Villefranche and had taken them somewhere down the road here. At Cannes he took me to a very dull place, a club for English chauffeurs and sailors off the yachts of the rich people who were wintering on the Riviera. There I ate ham and eggs and watched the chauffeurs politely playing billiards, and grew depressed at the smell of London that lingered in the room—the smell of English cigarettes and English beer. It reminded me of the fogs I thought I had escaped.

Then I found the villa of the people I had met at Saint Tropez, and stayed there a couple of days, and finally, fed up with walking, and seeing that I would probably be bored with the rest of the road along the coast, I got on the train and went to Genoa.

Perhaps the boredom that I felt had its roots in some physical cause, because the first morning I woke up in Genoa, with a bunch of Italian housepainters working on the roof outside my window,

I was out of sorts and had a great boil on my elbow, which I clumsily tried to heal by my own private treatments, which did not work.

So I cashed my letter of credit and got on another train and went to Florence, where I had another letter of introduction to a man who was a sculptor. Florence was freezing. I took a trolley out across the Arno, and found the steep road up the hill where my man lived, and climbed it in the icy silence of a Tuscan winter evening. At first I thought nobody was going to answer my knock on the big hollow-sounding door, but presently an old Italian cook came out, and led me in to the studio where I made myself known and explained that I had a boil on my elbow. So the cook got some hot water and I sat in the dry dust of plaster and among the stone chips around the base of some half-finished work, and talked to the sculptor while his cook fixed up a poultice for my boil.

The artist was the brother of the former Headmaster of Oakham, the one who had preceded Doherty. I had seen some of his bas-reliefs which decorated the front of the school chapel. He was not as old as his brother, the ex-head. But he was a kind, stoop-shouldered person with greying hair, and had most of the old head's geniality. He said to me: "I was thinking of going down and seeing the Greta Garbo film in town this evening. Do you like Greta Garbo?"

I admitted that I did. "Very well, then," he said, "we will go."

But Florence was too cold, and I thought the boil was getting better. So the next day I left, on the way to Rome. I was tired of passing through places. I wanted to get to the term of my journey, where there was some psychological possibility that I would stop in one place and remain.

The train ambled slowly through the mountains of Umbria. The blue sky glared down upon the rocks. The compartment was empty save for myself, and nobody got in until one of the last stations before Rome. All day I stared out at the bare hills, at the wild, ascetic landscape. Somewhere out there, on one of those mountains, St. Francis had been praying and the seraph with the fiery, blood-red wings had appeared before him with the Christ in the midst of those wings: and from the wounds, other wounds had been nailed in Francis's hands and feet and side. If I had thought of that, that day, it would have been all I needed to complete the discouragement of my pagan soul, for it turned out that the boil was no better after all, and that I had another toothache. For that matter, my head felt as if I had a fever as well, and I wondered if the old business of blood-poisoning was starting once again.

So there I was, with all the liberty that I had been promising myself for so long. The world was mine. How did I like it? I was doing just what I pleased, and instead of being filled with happiness and well-being, I was miserable. The love of pleasure is destined by its very nature to defeat itself and end in frustration. But I was one of the last men in the world who would have been convinced by the wisdom of a St. John of the Cross in those strange days.

But now I was entering a city which bears living testimony to these truths, to those who can see it, to those who know where to look for it—to those who know how to compare the Rome of the Caesars with the Rome of the martyrs.

I was entering the city that had been thus transformed by the Cross. Square white apartment houses were beginning to appear in thick clusters at the foot of the bare, grey-green hills, with clumps of cypress here and there, and presently over the roofs of the buildings, I saw, rising up in the dusk, the mighty substance of St. Peter's dome. The realization that it was not a photograph filled me with great awe.

My first preoccupation in Rome was to find a dentist. The people in the hotel sent me to one nearby. There were a couple of nuns in the waiting room. After they left, I entered. The dentist had a brown beard. I did not trust my Italian for so important a matter as a toothache. I spoke to him in French. He knew a little French. And he looked at the tooth.

He knew what he thought was wrong with it, but he did not know the technical word in French.

"Ah," he said, "vous avez un *colpo d'aria*."

I figured it out easily enough to mean that I had caught a chill in my tooth—according to this man with the brown beard. But still, cowardice closed my mouth, and I was content not to argue that I thought it was by no means a chill, but an abscess.

"I shall treat it with ultra-violet rays," said the dentist. With a mixture of relief and scepticism, I underwent this painless and futile process. It did nothing whatever to relieve the toothache. But I left with warm assurances from the dentist that it would all disappear during the night.

Far from disappearing during the night, the toothache did what all toothaches do during the night: kept me awake, in great misery, cursing my fate.

The next morning I got up and staggered back to my friend *colpo d'aria* next door. I met him coming down the stairs with his beard all brushed and a black hat on his head, with gloves and spats and everything. Only then did I realize that it was Sunday. However, he consented to give a look at the chilled tooth.

In a mixture of French and Italian he asked me if I could stand ether. I said yes, I could. He draped a clean handkerchief over my nose and mouth and dropped a couple of drops of ether on it. I breathed deeply, and the sweet sick knives of the smell reached in to my consciousness and the drumming of the heavy dynamos began. I hoped that he wasn't breathing too deeply himself, or that his hand wouldn't slip, and spill the whole bottle of it in my face.

However, a minute or two later I woke up again and he was waving the red, abscessed roots of the tooth in my face and exclaiming: "*C'est fini!*"

I moved out of my hotel and found a *pensione* with windows that looked down on the sunny Triton fountain in the middle of the Piazza Barberini and the Bristol Hotel and the Barberini Cinema and the Barberini Palace, and the maid brought me some hot water to treat the boil on my arm. I went to bed and tried to read a novel by Maxim Gorki which very quickly put me to sleep.

I had been in Rome before, on an Easter vacation from school, for about a week. I had seen the Forum and the Colosseum and the Vatican museum and St. Peter's. But I had not really seen Rome.

This time, I started out again, with the misconception common to Anglo-Saxons, that the real Rome is the Rome of the ugly ruins, the Rome of all those grey cariated temples wedged in between the hills and the slums of the city. I tried to reconstruct the ancient city, in my mind—a dream which did not work very well, because of the insistent shouting of the sellers of postcards who beset me on every side. After a few days of trying the same thing, it suddenly struck me that it was not worth the trouble. It was so evident, merely from the masses of stone and brick that still represented the palaces and temples and baths, that imperial Rome must have been one of the most revolting and ugly and depressing cities the world has ever seen. In fact, the ruins with cedars and cypresses and umbrella pines scattered about among them were far more pleasant than the reality must have been.

However, I still roamed about the museums, especially the one in the Baths of Diocletian, which had also been, at one time, a Carthusian monastery—probably not a very successful one—and I studied Rome in a big learned book that I had bought, together with an old second-hand Baedeker in French.

And after spending the day in museums and libraries and bookstores and among the ruins, I would come home again and read my novels. In fact, I was also beginning to write one of my own, although I did not get very far with it as long as I was at Rome.

I had a lot of books with me—a strange mixture: Dryden, the poems of D. H. Lawrence, some Tauchnitz novels, and James Joyce's *Ulysses* in a fancy India-paper edition, slick and expensive, which I lent to someone, later on, and never got back.

Things were going on as they usually did with me. But after about a week—I don't know how it began—I found myself looking into churches rather than into ruined temples. Perhaps it was the frescoes on the wall of an old chapel—ruined too—at the foot of the Palatine, at the edge of the Forum, that first aroused my interest in another and a far different Rome. From there it was an easy step to Sts. Cosmas and Damian, across the Forum, with a great mosaic, in the apse, of Christ coming in judgement in a dark blue sky, with a suggestion of fire in the small clouds beneath His feet. The effect of this discovery was tremendous. After all the vapid, boring, semi-pornographic statuary of the Empire, what a thing it was to come upon the genius of an art full of spiritual vitality and earnestness and power—an art that was tremendously serious and alive and eloquent and urgent in all that it had to say. And it was without pretentiousness, without fakery, and had nothing theatrical about it. Its solemnity was made all the more astounding by its simplicity—and by the obscurity of the places where it lay hid, and by its subservience to higher ends, architectural, liturgical and spiritual ends which I could not even begin to understand, but which I could not avoid guessing, since the nature of the mosaics themselves and their position and everything about them proclaimed it aloud.

I was fascinated by these Byzantine mosaics. I began to haunt the churches where they were to be found, and, as an indirect consequence, all the other churches that were more or less of the same period. And thus without knowing anything about it I became a pilgrim. I was unconsciously and unintentionally visiting all the great shrines of Rome, and seeking out their sanctuaries with some of the eagerness and avidity and desire of a true pilgrim, though not quite for the right reason. And yet it was not for a wrong reason either. For these mosaics and frescoes and all the ancient altars and thrones and sanctuaries were designed and built for the instruction of people who were not capable of immediately understanding anything higher.

I never knew what relics and what wonderful and holy things were hidden in the churches whose doors and aisles and arches had become the refuge of my mind. Christ's cradle and the pillar of the Flagellation and the True Cross and St. Peter's chains, and the tombs of the great martyrs, the tomb of the child St. Agnes and the martyr St. Cecilia and of Pope St. Clement and of the great deacon St. Lawrence who was burned on a gridiron. . . . These things did not speak to me, or at least I did not know they spoke to me. But the churches that enshrined them did, and so did the art on their walls.

And now for the first time in my life I began to find out something of Who this Person was that men called Christ. It was obscure, but it was a true knowledge of Him, in some sense, truer than I knew and truer than I would admit. But it was in Rome that my conception of Christ was formed. It was there I first saw Him, Whom I now serve as my God and my King, and Who owns and rules my life.

It is the Christ of the Apocalypse, the Christ of the Martyrs, the Christ of the Fathers. It is the Christ of St. John, and of St. Paul, and of St. Augustine and St. Jerome and all the Fathers—and of the Desert Fathers. It is Christ God, Christ King, "*for in Him dwelleth the fulness of the Godhead corporeally, and you are filled in Him, Who is the Head of all principality and power . . . For in Him were all things created in heaven and on earth, visible and invisible, whether thrones or dominations or principalities or powers, all things were created by Him and in Him. And He is before all, and by Him all things consist . . . because in Him it hath well pleased the Father that all fulness should dwell . . . Who is the image of the invisible God, the first-born of every creature . . .*[1]" "*The first-begotten of the dead, and the prince of the kings of the earth, Who hath loved us, and washed us from our sins in His own Blood, and hath made us a kingdom and priests to God His Father.*"[2]

The saints of those forgotten days had left upon the walls of their churches words which by the peculiar grace of God I was able in some measure to apprehend, although I could not decode them all. But above all, the realest and most immediate source of this grace was Christ Himself, present in those churches, in all His power, and in His Humanity, in His Human Flesh and His material, physical, corporeal Presence. How often I was left en-

[1] Col. I and II. [2] Apoc. I.

tirely alone in these churches with the tremendous God, and knew nothing of it—except I had to know something of it, as I say, obscurely. And it was He Who was teaching me Who He was, more directly than I was capable of realising.

These mosaics told me more than I had ever known of the doctrine of a God of infinite power, wisdom and love Who had yet become Man, and revealed in His Manhood the infinity of power, wisdom and love that was His Godhead. Of course I could not grasp and believe these things explicitly. But since they were implicit in every line of the pictures I contemplated with such admiration and love, surely I grasped them implicitly—I had to, in so far as the mind of the artist reached my own mind, and spoke to it his conception and his thought. And so I could not help but catch something of the ancient craftsman's love of Christ, the Redeemer and Judge of the World.

It was more or less natural that I should want to discover something of the meaning of the mosaics I saw—of the Lamb standing as though slain, and of the four-and-twenty elders casting down their crowns. And I had bought a Vulgate text, and was reading the New Testament. I had forgotten all about the poems of D. H. Lawrence except for the fact that he had four poems about the Four Evangelists, based on the traditional symbols from Ezechiel and the Apocalypse of the four mystical creatures. One evening, when I was reading these poems, I became so disgusted with their falseness and futility that I threw down the book and began to ask myself why I was wasting my time with a man of such unimportance as this. For it was evident that he had more or less completely failed to grasp the true meaning of the New Testament, which he had perverted in the interests of a personal and home-made religion of his own which was not only fanciful, but full of unearthly seeds, all ready to break forth into hideous plants like those that were germinating in Germany's unweeded garden, in the dank weather of Nazism.

So for once I put my favorite aside. And I read more and more of the Gospels, and my love for the old churches and their mosaics grew from day to day. Soon I was no longer visiting them merely for the art. There was something else that attracted me: a kind of interior peace. I loved to be in these holy places. I had a kind of deep and strong conviction that I belonged there: that my rational nature was filled with profound desires and needs that could only find satisfaction in churches of God. I remember that one of my favorite shrines was that of St. Peter in Chains, and I did not love it for any work of art that was there, since the big attraction, the big "number," the big "feature" in that place is Michelangelo's Moses. But I had always been extremely bored by that horned and pop-eyed frown and by the crack in the knee. I'm glad the thing couldn't speak, for it would probably have given out some very heavy statements.

Perhaps what was attracting me to that Church was the Apostle himself to whom it is dedicated. And I do not doubt that he was praying earnestly to get me out of my own chains: chains far heavier and more terrible than ever were his.

Where else did I like to go? St. Pudenziana, St. Praxed's, above all St. Mary Major and the Lateran, although as soon as the atmosphere got heavy with baroque melodrama I would get frightened, and the peace and the obscure, tenuous sense of devotion I had acquired would leave me.

So far, however, there had been no deep movement of my will, nothing that amounted to a conversion, nothing to shake the iron tyranny of moral corruption that held my whole nature in fetters. But that also was to come. It came in a strange way, suddenly, a way that I will not attempt to explain.

I was in my room. It was night. The light was on. Suddenly it seemed to me that Father, who had now been dead more than a year, was there with me. The sense of his presence was as vivid and as real and as startling as if he had touched my arm or spoken to me. The whole thing passed in a flash, but in that flash, instantly, I was overwhelmed with a sudden and profound insight into the misery and corruption of my own soul, and I was pierced deeply with a light that made me realize something of the condition I was in, and I was filled with horror at what I saw, and my whole being rose up in revolt against what was within me, and my soul desired escape and liberation and freedom from all this with an intensity and an urgency unlike anything I had ever known before. And now I think for the first time in my whole life I really began to pray—praying not with my lips and with my intellect and my imagination, but praying out of the very roots of my life and of my being, and praying to the God I had never known, to reach down towards me out of His darkness and to help me to get free of the thousand terrible things that held my will in their slavery.

There were a lot of tears connected with this, and they did me good, and all the while, although I had lost that first vivid, agonizing sense of the presence of my father in the room, I had him in my mind, and I was talking to him as well as to God, as though he were a sort of intermediary. I do not mean this in any way that might be interpreted that I thought he was among the saints. I did not really know what that might mean then, and now that I do know I would hesitate to say that I thought he was in Heaven. Judging by my memory of the experience I should say it was "as if" he had been sent to me out of Purgatory. For after all, there is no reason why the souls in Purgatory should not help those on earth by their prayers and influence, just like those in Heaven: although usually they need our help more than we need theirs. But in this case, assuming my guess has some truth in it, things were the other way 'round.

However, this is not a thing on which I would place any great stress. And I do not offer any definite explanation of it. How do I know it was not merely my own imagination, or something that could be traced to a purely natural, psychological cause—I mean the part about my father? It is impossible to say. I do not offer any explanation. And I have always had a great antipathy for everything that smells of necromancy—table-turning and communications with the dead, and I would never deliberately try to enter in to any such thing. But whether it was imagination or nerves or whatever else it may have been, I can say truly that I did feel, most vividly, as if my father were present there, and the consequences that I have described followed from this, as though he had communicated to me without words an interior light from God, about the condition of my own soul—although I wasn't even sure I had a soul.

The one thing that seems to me morally certain is that this was really a grace, and a great grace. If I had only followed it through, my life might have been very different and much less miserable for the years that were to come.

Before now I had never prayed in the churches I had visited. But I remember the morning that followed this experience. I remember how I climbed the deserted Aventine, in the spring sun, with my soul broken up with contrition, but broken and clean, painful but sanitary like a lanced abscess, like a bone broken and re-set. And it was true contrition, too, for I don't think I was capable of mere attrition, since I did not believe in hell. I went to the Dominicans' Church, Santa Sabina. And it was a very definite experience, something that amounted to a capitulation, a surrender, a conversion, not without struggle, even now, to walk deliberately into the church with no other purpose than to kneel down and pray to God. Ordinarily, I never knelt in these churches, and never paid any formal or official attention to Whose house it was. But now I took holy water at the door and went straight up to the altar rail and knelt down and said, slowly, with all the belief I had in me, the Our Father.

It seems almost unbelievable to me that I did no more than this, for the memory remains in me as that of such an experience that it would seem to have implied at least a half hour of impassioned prayer and tears. The thing to remember is that I had not prayed at all for some years.

Another thing which Catholics do not realize about converts is the tremendous, agonizing embarrassment and self-consciousness which they feel about praying publicly in a Catholic Church. The effort it takes to overcome all the strange imaginary fears that everyone is looking at you, and that they all think you are crazy or ridiculous, is something that costs a tremendous effort. And that day in Santa Sabina, although the church was almost entirely empty, I walked across the stone floor mortally afraid that a poor devout old Italian woman was following me with suspicious eyes. As I knelt to pray, I wondered if she would run out and accuse me at once to the priests, with scandalous horror, for coming and praying in their church—as if Catholics were perfectly content to have a lot of heretic tourists walking about their churches with complete indifference and irreverence, and would get angry if one of them so far acknowledged God's presence there as to go on his knees for a few seconds and say a prayer!

However, I prayed, then I looked about the church, and went into a room where there was a picture by Sassoferrato, and stuck my face out a door into a tiny, simple cloister, where the sun shone down on an orange tree. After that I walked out into the open feeling as if I had been reborn, and crossed the street, and strolled through the suburban fields to another deserted church where I did not pray, being scared by some carpenters and scaffolding. I sat outside, in the sun, on a wall and tasted the joy of my own inner peace, and turned over in my mind how my life was now going to change, and how I would become better.

## vii

It was a wan hope, however. But the last week or ten days that I was in Rome were very happy and full of joy, and on one of those afternoons I took the trolley out to San Paolo, and after that got on a small rickety bus which went up a country road into a shallow saucer of a valley in the low hills south of the Tiber, to the Trappist monastery of Tre Fontane. I went in to the dark, austere old church, and liked it. But I was scared to visit the monastery. I thought the monks were too busy sitting in their graves beating themselves with disciplines. So I walked up and down in the silent afternoon, under the eucalyptus trees, and the thought grew on me: "I should like to become a Trappist monk."

There was very little danger of my doing so, then. The thought was only a daydream—and I suppose it is a dream that comes to many men, even men who don't believe in anything. Is there any man who has ever gone through a whole lifetime without dressing himself up, in his fancy, in the habit of a monk and enclosing himself in a cell where he sits magnificent in heroic austerity and solitude, while all the young ladies who hitherto were cool to his affections in the world come and beat on the gates of the monastery crying, "Come out, come out!"

Ultimately, I suppose, that is what my dream that day amounted to. I had no idea what Trappist monks were, or what they did, except that they kept silence. In fact, I also thought they lived in cells like the Carthusians, all alone.

In the bus, going back to San Paolo, I ran into a student from the American Academy whom I knew. He was riding with his mother, and introduced me to her, and we talked about the monastery, and I said I wished I were a monk. The student's mother looked at me with a horror and astonishment so extreme that I was really a little shocked by it.

The days went by. Letters came from America, telling me to take the boat and come there. Finally I bade farewell to the Italian typewriter salesman and the other inhabitants of the *pensione*, including the lady who ran the place and whose mother had been overwhelmed with thoughts of death when I played *St. Louis Blues* on the piano, sending in the maid to ask me to desist.

With sorrow in my heart I saw the last of the Piazza Barberini and the big curved boulevard that ran into it; and the last of the Pincio gardens, and St. Peter's dome in the distance and the Piazza di Spagna; but above all, I had sorrow and emptiness in my heart at leaving my beloved churches—San Pietro in Vincoli, Santa Maria Maggiore, San Giovanni in Laterano, Santa Pudenziana, Santa Prassede, Santa Sabina, Santa Maria sopra Minerva, Santa Maria in Cosmedin, Santa Maria in Trastevere, Santa Agnese, San Clemente, Santa Cecilia . . .

The train crossed the Tiber. The little pyramid and the cypresses of the English cemetery where Keats was buried disappeared. I remembered some allusion in Plautus to a big hill of rubbish and potsherds that had once stood in this part of the city. Then we came out into the bare plain between Rome and the sea. In this distance were San Paolo, and the low hills that concealed the Trappist monastery of Tre Fontane. "O Rome," I said in my heart, "will I ever see you again?"

The first two months after I landed in New York, and went to the house in Douglaston, I continued to read the Bible surreptitiously—I was afraid someone might make fun of me. And since I slept on the sleeping porch, which opened on the upstairs hall through glass doors and which, in any case, I shared with my uncle, I no longer dared to pray on my knees before going to sleep, though I am sure everybody would have been pleased and edified. The real reason for this was that I did not have the humility to care nothing about what people thought or said. I was afraid of their remarks, even kind ones, even approving ones. Indeed, it is a kind of quintessence of pride to hate and fear even the kind and legitimate approval of those who love us! I mean, to resent it as a humiliating patronage.

There is no point in telling all the details of how this real but temporary religious fervor of mine cooled down and disappeared. At Easter we went to the church where my father had once been organist, Zion Church, with the white spire standing among the locust trees on the hill between us and the station. And there I was very irritated by the services, and my own pride increased the irritation and complicated it. And I used to walk about the house or sit at the dinner table telling everybody what a terrible place Zion Church was, and condemning everything that it stood for.

One Sunday I went to the Quaker meeting house in Flushing, where Mother had once sat and meditated with the Friends. I sat down there too, in a deep pew in the back, near a window. The place was about half full. The people were mostly middle-aged or old, and there was nothing that distinguished them in any evident way from the congregation in a Methodist or a Baptist or an Episcopalian or any other Protestant church, except that they sat silent, waiting for the inspiration of the Holy Ghost. I liked that. I liked the silence. It was peaceful. In it, my shyness began to die down, and I ceased to look about and criticize the people, and entered, somewhat superficially, into my own soul, and some nebulous good resolutions began to take shape there.

But it did not get very far, for presently one of the middle-aged ladies thought the Holy Ghost was after her to get up and talk.

I secretly suspected that she had come to the meeting all prepared to make a speech anyway, for she reached into her handbag, as she stood up, and cried out in a loud earnest voice:

"When I was in Switzerland I took this snapshot of the famous Lion of Lucerne. . . ." With that she pulled out a picture. Sure enough, it was the famous Lion of Lucerne. She held it up and tried to show it around to the Friends, at the same time explaining that she thought it was a splendid exemplification of Swiss courage and manliness and patience and all the other virtues of the watch-making Swiss which she mentioned and which I have now forgotten.

The Friends accepted it in patience, without enthusiasm or resentment. But I went out of the meeting house saying to myself: "They are like all the rest. In other churches it is the minister who hands out the commonplaces, and here it is liable to be just anybody."

Still, I think I had enough sense to know that it would be madness to look for a group of people, a society, a religion, a church from which all mediocrity would absolutely be excluded. But when I read the works of William Penn and found them to be about as supernatural as a Montgomery Ward catalogue I lost interest in the Quakers. If I had run across something by Evelyn Underhill it might have been different.

I think that one could find much earnest and pure and humble worship of God and much sincere charity among the Quakers. Indeed, you are bound to find a little of this in every religion. But I have never seen any evidence of its rising above the natural order. They are full of natural virtues and some of them are contemplatives in a natural sense of the word. Nor are they excluded from God's graces if He wills. For He loves them, and He will not withhold His light from good people anywhere. Yet I cannot see that they will ever be anything more than what they claim to be—a "Society of Friends."

That summer, when I went on a slow and dirty train in a roundabout way to Chicago to see the World's Fair, I picked up two pamphlets on the Mormons in the Hall of Religion, but the story of the holy books discovered through revelation on a hill in upper New York State did not convince me and I was not converted. The thin red and yellow walls of the palaces of the Fair, scattered between the lake and the slums and freight-yards, amused me with their noise, and for the first time I walked in the wide-open air of the flat and endless Middle West.

Out of sheer bravado I got myself a job for a few days as a barker in front of a side-show in a part of the Fair called the Streets of Paris, the nature of which is sufficiently evident from that name. The ease with which I got the job astounded and flattered me, and it gave me a sense of power and importance to be so suddenly transported from the order of those who were fleeced of their money to the level of those who did the fleecing. However, in a couple of days I also discovered that perhaps I had not risen above the ranks of the "suckers" after all, since the boss of the side-show was more ready to pay me in promises and fancy words than in dollars, for my services. Besides, it was very tiring to stand in the heat and just from noon to midnight shouting at the sea of straw-hatted heads and shoulders dressed in duck and seersucker or in open-necked shirts and dresses soaked with healthy Middle-Western sweat. The absolutely open and undisguised and non-committal frankness of the paganism of Chicago and of this Fair and of this particular part of the Fair and, apparently, of the whole country which it represented, amazed me after the complicated reticences of England and the ornate pornography of France.

When I got back to New York I had lost most of my temporary interest in religion. My friends in that city had a religion of their own: a cult of New York itself, and of the peculiar manner in which Manhattan expressed the bigness and gaudiness and noisiness and frank animality and vulgarity of this American paganism.

I used to go to the Burlesque and hang around Fourteenth Street with Reg Marsh, who was an old friend of my father's, and who is famous for painting all these things in his pictures. Reginald Marsh was (and I suppose still is) a thick-set man of short stature who gave the impression that he was a retired light-weight prize-fighter. He had a way of talking out of the corner of his mouth, and yet at the same time his face had something babyish and cherubic about it, as he looked out at the world through the simple and disinterested and uncritical eyes of the artist, taking everything as he found it, and considering everything as possible subject matter for one of his Hogarthian compositions, provided only it was alive.

We got along very well together, because of the harmony of our views, I worshipping life as such, and he worshipping it especially in the loud, wild bedlam of the crowded, crazy city that he loved. His favorite places of devotion were Union Square and the Irving Place Burlesque, stinking of sweat and cheap cigars and ready to burn down or collapse at any minute. But I guess his cathedral was Coney Island. Everybody who has ever seen his pictures, knows that much about Reg Marsh.

All that summer I hung around his Fourteenth Street studio, and went with him to many of the parties to which he was invited, and got to know my way around New York.

But when September came I sailed for England once more. This time I made the crossing on the *Manhattan*, a garish and turbulent cabin class steamer full of Nazi spies working as stewards and detesting the Jewish passengers. The voyage was a violent one. One night I looked down one of the deep stair-wells and saw six or seven half-drunk passengers having a general fight on the swaying linoleum floor of E deck. And one afternoon in the middle of one of those paralyzing synthetic amusements that are fixed up for the passengers on Atlantic liners—I think it must have been the "horse race"—an American dentist stood up with a loud roar and challenged a French tailor to come out and fight him on the promenade deck The challenge was not taken up, but all the business men and tourists savored the delicious scandal, for there was no one on board who was not aware that behind it all stood the six-foot daughter of someone prominent in Washington, D. C.

At Plymouth they put those of us who were bound for London on to a fat launch in the middle of the harbor, and once again I looked upon the pale green downs of England. I landed with one of the worst colds I ever had in my life.

And so on the tide of all these circumstances of confusion I swept into the dark, sinister atmosphere of Cambridge and began my university career.

## iv

The last week of that school year at Columbia had been rather chaotic. Lax and Freedgood had been making futile efforts to get their belongings together and go home. Bramachari was living in their room, perched on top of a pile of books. Lax was trying to finish a novèl for Professor Nobbe's course in novel-writing, and all his friends had volunteered to take a section of the book and write it, simultaneously: but in the end the book turned out to be more or less a three-cornered affair—by Lax and me and Dona Eaton. When Nobbe got the thing in his hands he could not figure it out at all, but he gave us a B-minus, with which we were more than satisfied.

Then Lax's mother had come to town to live near him in the last furious weeks before graduation and catch him if he collapsed. He had to take most of his meals in the apartment she had rented in Butler Hall. I sometimes went along and helped him nibble the various health-foods.

At the same time, we were planning to get a ride on an oil barge up the Hudson and the Erie Canal to Buffalo—because Lax's brother-in-law was in the oil business. After that we would go to the town where Lax lived, which was Olean, up in that corner of New York state.

On "Class Day" we leaned out the window of Lax's room and drank a bottle of champagne, looking at the sun on South Field, and watching the people beginning to gather under the trees in front of Hamilton, where we would all presently hear some speeches and shake hands with Nicholas Murray Butler.

It was not my business to graduate that June at all. My graduation was all over when I picked up my degree in the registrar's office last February. However, I borrowed the cap and gown with which Dona Eaton had graduated from Barnard a year before, and went and sat with all the rest, mocking the speeches, with the edge of my sobriety slightly dulled by the celebration that had just taken place with the champagne in Furnald.

Finally we all got up and filed slowly up the rickety wooden steps to the temporary platform to shake hands with all the officials. President Butler was a much smaller man than I had expected. He looked intensely miserable, and murmured something or other to each student, as he shook hands. It was inaudible. I was given to understand that for the past six or seven years people had been in the habit of insulting him, on these occasions, as a kind of a farewell.

I didn't say anything. I just shook his hand, and passed on. The next one I came to was Dean Hawkes who looked up with surprise, from under his bushy white eyebrows, and growled:

"What are *you* doing here, anyway?"

I smiled and passed on.

We did not get the ride on the oil barge, after all, but went to Olean on a train, and for the first time I saw a part of the world in which I was one day going to learn how to be very happy—and that day was not now very far away.

It is the association of that happiness which makes upper New York state seem, in my memory, to be so beautiful. But it is objectively so, there is no doubt of that. Those deep valleys and miles and miles of high, rolling wooded hills: the broad fields, the big red barns, the white farm houses and the peaceful towns: all this looked more and more impressive and fine in the long slanting rays of the sinking sun after we had passed Elmira.

And you began to get some of the feeling of the bigness of America, and to develop a continental sense of the scope of the country and of the vast, clear sky, as the train went on for mile after mile, and hour after hour. And the color, and freshness, and bigness, and richness of the land! The cleanness of it. The wholesomeness. This was new and yet it was old country. It was mellow country. It had been cleared and settled for much more than a hundred years.

When we got out at Olean, we breathed its health and listened to its silence.

I did not stay there for more than a week, being impatient to get back to New York on account of being, as usual, in love.

But one of the things we happened to do was to turn off the main road, one afternoon on the way to the Indian reservation, to look at the plain brick buildings of a college that was run by the Franciscans.

It was called St. Bonaventure's. Lax had a good feeling about the place. And his mother was always taking courses there, in the evenings—courses in literature from the Friars. He was a good friend of the Father Librarian and liked the library. We drove in to the grounds and stopped by one of the buildings.

But when Lax tried to make me get out of the car, I would not

"Let's get out of here," I said.

"Why? It's a nice place."

"It's O.K., but let's get out of here. Let's go to the Indian reservation."

"Don't you want to see the library?"

"I can see enough of it from here. Let's get going."

I don't know what was the matter. Perhaps I was scared of the thought of nuns and priests being all around me—the elemental fear of the citizen of hell, in the presence of anything that savors of the religious life, religious vows, official dedication to God through Christ. Too many crosses. Too many holy statues. Too much quiet and cheerfulness. Too much pious optimism. It made me very uncomfortable. I had to flee.

When I got back to New York, one of the first things I did was to break away, at last, from the household in Douglaston. The family had really practically dissolved with the death of my grandparents, and I could get a lot more work done if I did not have to spend so much time on subways and the Long Island train.

One rainy day in June, then, I made a bargain with Herb, the colored taximan at Douglaston, and he drove me and all my bags and books and my portable vic and all my hot records and pictures to put on the wall and even a tennis racquet which I never used, uptown to a rooming-house on 114th Street, just behind the Columbia library.

All the way up we discussed the possible reasons for the mysterious death of Rudolph Valentino, once a famous movie star: but it was certainly not what you would call a live issue. Valentino had died at least ten years before.

"This is a nice spot you got here," said Herb, approving of the room I was renting for seven-fifty a week. It was shiny and clean and filled with new furniture and had a big view of a pile of coal, in a yard by the campus tennis courts, with South Field and the steps of the old domed library beyond. The panorama even took in a couple of trees.

"I guess you're going to have a pretty hot time, now you got away from your folks," Herb remarked, as he took his leave.

Whatever else may have happened in that room, it was also there that I started to pray again more or less regularly, and it was there that I added, as Bramachari had suggested, *The Imitation of Christ* to my books, and it was from there that I was eventually to be driven out by an almost physical push, to go and look for a priest.

July came, with its great, misty heats, and Columbia filled with all the thousands of plump, spectacled ladies in pink dresses, from the Middle-West, and all the grey gents in seersucker suits, all the dried-up high-school principals from Indiana and Kansas and Iowa and Tennessee, with their veins shrivelled up with positivism and all the reactions of the behaviorist flickering behind their spectacles as they meditated on the truths they learned in those sweltering halls.

The books piled higher and higher on my desk in the Graduate reading room and in my own lodgings. I was in the thick of my thesis, making hundreds of mistakes that I would not be able to detect for several years to come, because I was far out of my depth. Fortunately, nobody else detected them either. But for my own part, I was fairly happy, and learning many things. The discipline of the work itself was good for me, and helped to cure me, more than anything else did, of the illusion that my health was poor.

And it was in the middle of all this that I discovered Scholastic philosophy.

The subject I had finally chosen was "Nature and Art in William Blake." I did not realize how providential a subject it actually was! What it amounted to, was a study of Blake's reaction against every kind of literalism and naturalism and narrow, classical realism in art, because of his own ideal which was essentially mystical and supernatural. In other words, the topic, if I treated it at all sensibly, could not help but cure me of all the naturalism and materialism in my own philosophy, besides resolving all the inconsistencies and self-contradictions that had persisted in my mind for years, without my being able to explain them.

After all, from my very childhood, I had understood that the artistic experience, at its highest, was actually a natural analogue of mystical experience. It produced a kind of intuitive perception of reality through a sort of affective identification with the object contemplated—the kind of perception that the Thomists call "connatural." This means simply a knowledge that comes about as it were by the identification of natures: in the way that a chaste man understands the nature of chastity because of the very fact that his soul is full of it—it is a part of his own nature, since habit is second nature. Non-connatural knowledge of chastity would be that of a philosopher who, to borrow the language of the *Imitation*, would be able to define it, but would not possess it.

I had learned from my own father that it was almost blasphemy to regard the function of art as merely to reproduce some kind of a sensible pleasure or, at best, to stir up the emotions to a transitory thrill. I had always understood that art was contemplation, and that it involved the action of the highest faculties of man.

When I was once able to discover the key to Blake, in his rebellion against literalism and naturalism in art, I saw that his Prophetic Books and the rest of his verse at large represented a rebellion against naturalism in the moral order as well.

What a revelation that was! For at sixteen I had imagined that Blake, like the other romantics, was glorifying passion, natural energy, for their own sake. Far from it! What he was glorifying was the transfiguration of man's natural love, his natural powers, in the refining fires of mystical experience: and that, in itself, implied an arduous and total purification, by faith and love and desire, from all the petty materialistic and commonplace and earthly ideals of his rationalistic friends.

Blake, in his sweeping consistency, had developed a moral insight that cut through all the false distinctions of a worldly and interested morality. That was why he saw that, in the legislation of men, some evils had been set up as standards of right by which other evils were to be condemned: and the norms of pride or greed had been established in the judgement seat, to pronounce a crushing and inhuman indictment against all the normal healthy strivings of human nature. Love was outlawed, and became lust, pity was swallowed up in cruelty, and so Blake knew how:

> The harlot's cry from street to street
> Shall weave old England's winding-sheet.

I had heard that cry and that echo. I had seen that winding sheet. But I had understood nothing of all that. I had tried to resolve it into a matter of sociological laws, of economic forces. If I had been able to listen to Blake in those old days, he would have told me that sociology and economics, divorced from faith and charity, become nothing but the chains of his aged, icy demon Urizen! But now, reading Maritain, in connection with Blake, I saw all these difficulties and contradictions disappear.

I, who had always been anti-naturalistic in art, had been a pure naturalist in the moral order. No wonder my soul was sick and torn apart: but now the bleeding wound was drawn together by the notion of Christian virtue, ordered to the union of the soul with God.

The word virtue: what a fate it has had in the last three hundred years! The fact that it is nowhere near so despised and ridiculed in Latin countries is a testimony to the fact that it suffered mostly from the mangling it underwent at the hands of Calvinists and Puritans. In our own days the word leaves on the lips of cynical high-school children a kind of flippant smear, and it is exploited in theaters for the possibilities it offers for lewd and cheesy sarcasm. Everybody makes fun of virtue, which now has, as its primary meaning, an affectation of prudery practiced by hypocrites and the impotent.

When Maritain—who is by no means bothered by such trivialities—in all simplicity went ahead to use the term in its Scholastic sense, and was able to apply it to art, a "virtue of the practical intellect," the very newness of the context was enough to disinfect my mind of all the miasmas left in it by the ordinary prejudice against "virtue" which, if it was ever strong in anybody, was strong in me. I was never a lover of Puritanism. Now at last I came around to the sane conception of virtue—without which there can be no happiness, because virtues are precisely the powers by which we can come to acquire happiness: without them, there can be no joy, because they are the habits which coordinate and canalize our natural energies and direct them to the harmony and perfection and balance, the unity of our nature with itself and with God, which must, in the end, constitute our everlasting peace.

By the time I was ready to begin the actual writing of my thesis, that is, around the beginning of September 1938, the groundwork of conversion was more or less complete. And how easily and sweetly it had all been done, with all the external graces that had been arranged, along my path, by the kind Providence of God! It had taken little more than a year and a half, counting from the time I read Gilson's *The Spirit of Medieval Philosophy* to bring me up from an "atheist"—as I considered myself—to one who accepted all the full range and possibilities of religious experience right up to the highest degree of glory.

I not only accepted all this, intellectually, but now I began to desire it. And not only did I begin to desire it, but I began to do so efficaciously: I began to want to take the necessary means to achieve this union, this peace. I began to desire to dedicate my life to God, to His service. The notion was still vague and obscure, and it was ludicrously impractical in the sense that I was already dreaming of mystical union when I did not even keep the simplest rudiments of the moral law. But nevertheless I was convinced of the reality of the goal, and confident that it could be achieved: and whatever element of presumption was in this confidence I am sure God excused, in His mercy, because of my stupidity and helplessness, and because I was really beginning to be ready to do whatever I thought He wanted me to do to bring me to Him.

But, oh, how blind and weak and sick I was, although I thought I saw where I was going, and half understood the way! How deluded we sometimes are by the clear notions we get out of books. They make us think that we really understand things of which we have no practical knowledge at all. I remember how learnedly and enthusiastically I could talk for hours about mysticism and the experimental knowledge of God, and all the while I was stoking the fires of the argument with Scotch and soda.

That was the way it turned out that Labor Day, for instance. I went to Philadelphia with Joe Roberts, who had a room in the same house as I, and who had been through all the battles on the Fourth Floor of John Jay for the past four years. He had graduated and was working on some trade magazine about women's hats. All one night we sat, with a friend of his, in a big dark roadhouse outside of Philadelphia, arguing and arguing about mysticism, and smoking more and more cigarettes and gradually getting drunk. Eventually, filled with enthusiasm for the purity of heart which begets the vision of God, I went on with them into the city, after the closing of the bars, to a big speak-easy where we completed the work of getting plastered.

My internal contradictions were resolving themselves out, indeed, but still only on the plane of theory, not of practice: not for lack of good-will, but because I was still so completely chained and fettered by my sins and my attachments.

I think that if there is one truth that people need to learn, in the world, especially today, it is this: the intellect is only theoretically independent of desire and appetite in ordinary, actual practice. It is constantly being blinded and perverted by the ends and aims of passion, and the evidence it presents to us with such a show of impartiality and objectivity is fraught with interest and propaganda. We have become marvelous at self-delusion; all the more so, because we have gone to such trouble to convince ourselves of our own absolute infallibility. The desires of the flesh—and by that I mean not only sinful desires, but even the ordinary, normal appetites for comfort and ease and human respect, are fruitful sources of every kind of error and misjudgement, and because we have these yearnings in us, our intellects (which, if they operated all alone in a vacuum, would indeed register with pure impartiality what they saw) present to us everything distorted and accommodated to the norms of our desire.

And therefore, even when we are acting with the best of intentions, and imagine that we are doing great good, we may be actually doing tremendous material harm and contradicting all our good intentions. There are ways that seem to men to be good, the end whereof is in the depths of hell.

The only answer to the problem is grace, grace, docility to grace. I was still in the precarious position of being my own guide and my own interpreter of grace. It is a wonder I ever got to the harbor at all!

Sometime in August, I finally answered an impulsion that had been working on me for a long time. Every Sunday, I had been going out on Long Island to spend the day with the same girl who had brought me back in such a hurry from Lax's town Olean. But every week, as Sunday came around, I was filled with a growing desire to stay in the city and go to some kind of a church.

At first, I had vaguely thought I might try to find some Quakers, and go and sit with them. There still remained in me something of the favorable notion about Quakers that I had picked up as a child, and which the reading of William Penn had not been able to overcome.

But, naturally enough, with the work I was doing in the library, a stronger drive began to assert itself, and I was drawn much more imperatively to the Catholic Church. Finally the urge became so strong that I could not resist it. I called up my girl and told her that I was not coming out that week-end, and made up my mind to go to Mass for the first time in my life.

The first time in my life! That was true. I had lived for several years on the continent, I had been to Rome, I had been in and out of a thousand Catholic cathedrals and churches, and yet I had never heard Mass. If anything had ever been going on in the churches I visited, I had always fled, in wild Protestant panic.

I will not easily forget how I felt that day. First, there was this sweet, strong, gentle, clean urge in me which said: "Go to Mass! Go to Mass!" It was something quite new and strange, this voice that seemed to prompt me, this firm, growing interior conviction of what I needed to do. It had a suavity, a simplicity about it that I could not easily account for. And when I gave in to it, it did not exult over me, and trample me down in its raging haste to land on its prey, but it carried me forward serenely and with purposeful direction.

That does not mean that my emotions yielded to it altogether quietly. I was really still a little afraid to go to a Catholic church, of set purpose, with all the other people, and dispose myself in a pew, and lay myself open to the mysterious perils of that strange and powerful thing they called their "Mass."

God made it a very beautiful Sunday. And since it was the first time I had ever really spent a sober Sunday in New York, I was surprised at the clean, quiet atmosphere of the empty streets uptown. The sun was blazing bright. At the end of the street, as I came out the front door, I could see a burst of green, and the blue river and the hills of Jersey on the other side.

Broadway was empty. A solitary trolley came speeding down in front of Barnard College and past the School of Journalism. Then, from the high, grey, expensive tower of the Rockefeller Church, huge bells began to boom. It served very well for the eleven o'clock Mass at the little brick Church of Corpus Christi, hidden behind Teachers College on 121st Street.

How bright the little building seemed. Indeed, it was quite new. The sun shone on the clean bricks. People were going in the wide open door, into the cool darkness and, all at once, all the churches of Italy and France came back to me. The richness and fulness of the atmosphere of Catholicism that I had not been able to avoid apprehending and loving as a child, came back to me with a rush: but now I was to enter into it fully for the first time. So far, I had known nothing but the outward surface.

It was a gay, clean church, with big plain windows and white columns and pilasters and a well-lighted, simple sanctuary. Its style was a trifle eclectic, but much less perverted with incongruities than the average Catholic church in America. It had a kind of a seventeenth-century, oratorian character about it, though with a sort of American colonial tinge of simplicity. The blend was effective and original: but although all this affected me, without my thinking about it, the thing that impressed me most was that the place was full, absolutely full. It was full not only of old ladies and broken-down gentlemen with one foot in the grave, but of men and women and children young and old—especially young: people of all classes, and all ranks on a solid foundation of workingmen and -women and their families.

I found a place that I hoped would be obscure, over on one side, in the back, and went to it without genuflecting, and knelt down. As I knelt, the first thing I noticed was a young girl, very pretty too, perhaps fifteen or sixteen, kneeling straight up and praying quite seriously. I was very much impressed to see that someone who was young and beautiful could with such simplicity make prayer the real and serious and principal reason for going to church. She was clearly kneeling that way because she meant it, not in order to show off, and she was praying with an absorption which, though not the deep recollection of a saint, was serious enough to show that she was not thinking at all about the other people who were there.

What a revelation it was, to discover so many ordinary people in a place together, more conscious of God than of one another: not there to show off their hats or their clothes, but to pray, or at least to fulfil a religious obligation, not a human one. For even those who might have been there for no better motive than that they were obliged to be, were at least free from any of the self-conscious and human constraint which is never absent from a Protestant church where people are definitely gathered together as people, as neighbors, and always have at least half an eye for one another, if not all of both eyes.

Since it was summer time, the eleven o'clock Mass was a Low Mass: but I had not come expecting to hear music. Before I knew it, the priest was in the sanctuary with the two altar boys, and was busy at the altar with something or other which I could not see very well, but the people were praying by themselves, and I was engrossed and absorbed in the thing as a whole: the business at the altar and the presence of the people. And still I had not got rid of my fear. Seeing the late-comers hastily genuflecting before entering the pew, I realised my omission, and got the idea that people had spotted me for a pagan and were just waiting for me to miss a few more genuflections before throwing me out or, at least, giving me looks of reproof.

Soon we all stood up. I did not know what it was for. The priest was at the other end of the altar, and, as I afterwards learned, he was reading the Gospel. And then the next thing I knew there was someone in the pulpit.

It was a young priest, perhaps not much over thirty-three or -four years old. His face was rather ascetic and thin, and its asceticism was heightened with a note of intellectuality by his horn-rimmed glasses, although he was only one of the assistants, and he did not consider himself an intellectual, nor did anyone else apparently consider him so. But anyway, that was the impression he made on me: and his sermon, which was simple enough, did not belie it.

It was not long: but to me it was very interesting to hear this young man quietly telling the people in language that was plain, yet tinged with scholastic terminology, about a point in Catholic Doctrine. How clear and solid the doctrine was: for behind those words you felt the full force not only of Scripture but of centuries of a unified and continuous and consistent tradition. And above all, it was a vital tradition: there was nothing studied or antique about it. These words, this terminology, this doctrine, and these convictions fell from the lips of the young priest as something that were most intimately part of his own life. What was more, I sensed that the people were familiar with it all, and that it was also, in due proportion, part of their life also: it was just as much integrated into their spiritual organism as the air they breathed or the food they ate worked in to their blood and flesh.

What was he saying? That Christ was the Son of God. That, in Him, the Second Person of the Holy Trinity, God, had assumed a Human Nature, a Human Body and Soul, and had taken Flesh and dwelt amongst us, full of grace and truth: and that this Man, Whom men called the Christ, was God. He was both Man and God: two Natures hypostatically united in one Person or suppositum, one individual Who was a Divine Person, having assumed to Himself a Human Nature. And His works were the works of God: His acts were the acts of God. He loved us: God, and walked among us: God, and died for us on the Cross, God of God, Light of Light, True God of True God.

Jesus Christ was not simply a man, a good man, a great man, the greatest prophet, a wonderful healer, a saint: He was something that made all such trivial words pale into irrelevance. He was God. But nevertheless He was not merely a spirit without a true body, God hiding under a visionary body: He was also truly a Man, born of the Flesh of the Most Pure Virgin, formed of her Flesh by the Holy Spirit. And what He did, in that Flesh, on earth, He did not only as Man but as God. He loved us as God, He suffered and died for us, God.

And how did we know? Because it was revealed to us in the Scriptures and confirmed by the teaching of the Church and of the powerful unanimity of Catholic Tradition from the First Apostles, from the first Popes and the early Fathers, on down through the Doctors of the Church and the great scholastics, to our own day. *De Fide Divina*. If you believed it, you would receive light to grasp it, to understand it in some measure. If you did not believe it, you would never understand: it would never be anything but scandal or folly.

And no one can believe these things merely by wanting to, of his own volition. Unless he receive grace, an actual light and impulsion of the mind and will from God, he cannot even make an act of living faith. It is God Who gives us faith, and no one cometh to Christ unless the Father draweth him.

I wonder what would have happened in my life if I had been given this grace in the days when I had almost discovered the Divinity of Christ in the ancient mosaics of the churches of Rome. What scores of self-murdering and Christ-murdering sins would have been avoided—all the filth I had plastered upon His image in my soul during those last five years that I had been scourging and crucifying God within me?

It is easy to say, after it all, that God had probably foreseen my infidelities and had never given me the grace in those days because He saw how I would waste and despise it: and perhaps that rejection would have been my ruin. For there is no doubt that one of the reasons why grace is not given to souls is because they have so hardened their wills in greed and cruelty and selfishness that their refusal of it would only harden them more. . . . But now I had been beaten into the semblance of some kind of humility by misery and confusion and perplexity and secret, interior fear, and my ploughed soul was better ground for the reception of good seed.

The sermon was what I most needed to hear that day. When the Mass of the Catechumens was over, I, who was not even a catechumen, but only a blind and deaf and dumb pagan as weak and dirty as anything that ever came out of the darkness of Imperial Rome or Corinth or Ephesus, was not able to understand anything else.

It all became completely mysterious when the attention was refocussed on the altar. When the silence grew more and more profound, and little bells began to ring, I got scared again and, finally, genuflecting hastily on my left knee, I hurried out of the church in the middle of the most important part of the Mass. But it was just as well. In a way, I suppose I was responding to a kind of liturgical instinct that told me I did not belong there for the celebration of the Mysteries as such. I had no idea what took place in them: but the fact was that Christ, God, would be visibly present on the altar in the Sacred Species. And although He was there, yes, for love of me: yet He was there in His power and His might, and what was I? What was on my soul? What was I in His sight?

It was liturgically fitting that I should kick myself out at the end of the Mass of the Catechumens, when the ordained *ostiarii* should have been there to do it. Anyway, it was done.

Now I walked leisurely down Broadway in the sun, and my eyes looked about me at a new world. I could not understand what it was that had happened to make me so happy, why I was so much at peace, so content with life for I was not yet used to the clean savor that comes with an actual grace—indeed, there was no impossibility in a person's hearing and believing such a sermon and being justified, that is, receiving sanctifying grace in his soul as a habit, and beginning, from that moment, to live the divine and supernatural life for good and all. But that is something I will not speculate about.

All I know is that I walked in a new world. Even the ugly buildings of Columbia were transfigured in it, and everywhere was peace in these streets designed for violence and noise. Sitting outside the gloomy little Childs restaurant at 111th Street, behind the dirty, boxed bushes, and eating breakfast, was like sitting in the Elysian Fields.

## V

My reading became more and more Catholic. I became absorbed in the poetry of Hopkins and in his notebooks—that poetry which had only impressed me a little six years before. Now, too, I was deeply interested in Hopkins' life as a Jesuit. What was that life? What did the Jesuits do? What did a priest do? How did he live? I scarcely knew where to begin to find out about all such things: but they had started to exercise a mysterious attraction over me.

And here is a strange thing. I had by now read James Joyce's *Ulysses* twice or three times. Six years before—on one of those winter vacations in Strasbourg—I had tried to read *Portrait of the Artist* and had bogged down in the part about his spiritual crisis. Something about it had discouraged, bored and depressed me. I did not want to read about such a thing: and I finally dropped it in the middle of the "Mission." Strange to say, sometime during this summer—I think it was before the first time I went to Corpus Christi—I reread *Portrait of the Artist* and was fascinated precisely by that part of the book, by the "Mission," by the priest's sermon on hell. What impressed me was not the fear of hell, but the expertness of the sermon. Now, instead of being repelled by the thought of such preaching—which was perhaps the author's intention—I was stimulated and edified by it. The style in which the priest in the book talked, pleased me by its efficiency and solidity and drive: and once again there was something eminently satisfying in the thought that these Catholics knew what they believed, and knew what to teach, and all taught the same thing, and taught it with coordination and purpose and great effect. It was this that struck me first of all, rather than the actual subject matter of their doctrine—until, that is, I heard the sermon at Corpus Christi.

So then I continued to read Joyce, more and more fascinated by the pictures of priests and Catholic life that came up here and there in his books. That, I am sure, will strike many people as a strange thing indeed. I think Joyce himself was only interested in rebuilding the Dublin he had known as objectively and vitally as he could. He was certainly very alive to all the faults in Irish Catholic society, and he had practically no sympathy left for the Church he had abandoned: but in his intense loyalty to the vocation of artist for which he had abandoned it (and the two vocations are not *per se* irreconcilable: they only became so because of peculiar subjective circumstances in Joyce's own case) he meant to be as accurate as he could in rebuilding his world as it truly was.

Therefore, reading Joyce, I was moving in his Dublin, and breathing the air of its physical and spiritual slums: and it was not the most Catholic side of Dublin that he always painted. But in the background was the Church, and its priests, and its devotions, and the Catholic life in all its gradations, from the Jesuits down to those who barely clung to the hem of the Church's garments. And it was this background that fascinated me now, along with the temper of Thomism that had once been in Joyce himself. If he had abandoned St. Thomas, he had not stepped much further down than Aristotle.

Then, of course, I was reading the metaphysical poets once again—especially Crashaw—and studying his life, too, and his conversion. That meant another avenue which led more or less directly to the Jesuits. So in the late August of 1938, and September of that year, my life began to be surrounded, interiorly, by Jesuits. They were the symbols of my new respect for the vitality and coordination of the Catholic Apostolate. Perhaps, in the back of my mind, was my greatest Jesuit hero: the glorious Father Rothschild of Evelyn Waugh's *Vile Bodies*, who plotted with all the diplomats, and rode away into the night on a motorcycle when everybody else was exhausted.

Yet with all this, I was not yet ready to stand beside the font. There was not even any interior debate as to whether I ought to become a Catholic. I was content to stand by and admire. For the rest, I remember one afternoon, when my girl had come in to town to see me, and we were walking around the streets uptown, I subjected her to the rather disappointing entertainment of going to Union Theological Seminary, and asking for a catalogue of their courses which I proceeded to read while we were walking around on

Riverside Drive. She was not openly irritated by it: she was a very good and patient girl anyway. But still you could see she was a little bored, walking around with a man who was not sure whether he ought to enter a theological seminary.

There was nothing very attractive in that catalogue. I was to get much more excited by the article on the Jesuits in the *Catholic Encyclopaedia*—breathless with the thought of so many novitiates and tertianships and what not—so much scrutiny, so much training. What monsters of efficiency they must be, these Jesuits, I kept thinking to myself, as I read and reread the article. And perhaps, from time to time, I tried to picture myself with my face sharpened by asceticism, its pallor intensified by contrast with a black cassock, and every line of it proclaiming a Jesuit saint, a Jesuit master-mind. And I think the master-mind element was one of the strongest features of this obscure attraction.

Apart from this foolishness, I came no nearer to the Church, in practice, than adding a "Hail Mary" to my night prayers. I did not even go to Mass again, at once. The following week-end I went to see my girl once again; it was probably after that that I went on the expedition to Philadelphia. It took something that belongs to history to form and vitalize these resolutions that were still only vague and floating entities in my mind and will.

One of those hot evenings at the end of summer the atmosphere of the city suddenly became terribly tense with some news that came out of the radios. Before I knew what the news was, I began to feel the tension. For I was suddenly aware that the quiet, disparate murmurs of different radios in different houses had imperceptibly merged into one big, ominous unified voice, that moved at you from different directions and followed you down the street, and came to you from another angle as soon as you began to recede from any one of its particular sources.

I heard "Germany—Hitler—at six o'clock this morning the German Army . . . the Nazis . . ." What had they done?

Then Joe Roberts came in and said there was about to be a war. The Germans had occupied Czechoslovakia, and there was bound to be a war.

The city felt as if one of the doors of hell had been half opened, and a blast of its breath had flared out to wither up the spirits of men. And people were loitering around the newsstands in misery.

Joe Roberts and I sat in my room, where there was no radio, until long after midnight, drinking canned beer and smoking cigarettes, and making silly and excited jokes but, within a couple of days, the

English Prime Minister had flown in a big hurry to see Hitler and had made a nice new alliance at Munich that cancelled everything that might have caused a war, and returned to England. He alighted at Croydon and came stumbling out of the plane saying "Peace in our time!"

I was very depressed. I was beyond thinking about the intricate and filthy political tangle that underlay the mess. I had given up politics as more or less hopeless, by this time. I was no longer interested in having any opinion about the movement and interplay of forces which were all more or less iniquitous and corrupt, and it was far too laborious and uncertain a business to try and find out some degree of truth and justice in all the loud, artificial claims that were put forward by the various sides.

All I could see was a world in which everybody said they hated war, and in which we were all being rushed into a war with a momentum that was at last getting dizzy enough to affect my stomach. All the internal contradictions of the society in which I lived were at last beginning to converge upon its heart. There could not be much more of a delay in its dismembering. Where would it end? In those days, the future was obscured, blanked out by war as by a dead-end wall. Nobody knew if anyone at all would come out of it alive. Who would be worse off, the civilians or the soldiers? The distinction between their fates was to be abolished, in most countries, by aerial warfare, by all the new planes, by all the marvelous new bombs. What would the end of it be?

I knew that I myself hated war, and all the motives that led to war and were behind wars. But I could see that now my likes or dislikes, beliefs or disbeliefs meant absolutely nothing in the external, political order. I was just an individual, and the individual had ceased to count. I meant nothing, in this world, except that I would probably soon become a number on the list of those to be drafted. I would get a piece of metal with my number on it, to hang around my neck, so as to help out the circulation of red-tape that would necessarily follow the disposal of my remains, and that would be the last eddy of mental activity that would close over my lost identity.

The whole business was so completely unthinkable that my mind, like almost all the other minds that were in the same situation, simply stopped trying to cope with it, and refixed its focus on the ordinary routine of life.

I had my thesis to type out, and a lot of books to read, and I was thinking of preparing an article on Crashaw which perhaps I would send to T. S. Eliot for his *Criterion.* I did not know that *Criterion* had printed its last issue, and that Eliot's reaction to the situation that so depressed me was to fold up his magazine.

The days went on and the radios returned to their separate and individual murmuring, not to be regimented back into their appalling shout for yet another year. September, as I think, must have been more than half gone.

I borrowed Father Leahy's life of Hopkins from the library. It was a rainy day. I had been working in the library in the morning. I had gone to buy a thirty-five-cent lunch at one of those little pious kitchens on Broadway—the one where Professor Gerig, of the graduate school of French, sat daily in silence over a very small table, eating his Brussels sprouts. Later in the afternoon, perhaps about four, I would have to go down to Central Park West and give a Latin lesson to a youth who was sick in bed, and who ordinarily came to the tutoring school run by my landlord, on the ground floor of the house where I lived.

I walked back to my room. The rain was falling gently on the empty tennis courts across the street, and the huge old domed library stood entrenched in its own dreary greyness, arching a cyclops eyebrow at South Field.

I took up the book about Gerard Manley Hopkins. The chapter told of Hopkins at Balliol, at Oxford. He was thinking of becoming a Catholic. He was writing letters to Cardinal Newman (not yet a cardinal) about becoming a Catholic.

All of a sudden, something began to stir within me, something began to push me, to prompt me. It was a movement that spoke like a voice.

"What are you waiting for?" it said. "Why are you sitting here? Why do you still hesitate? You know what you ought to do? Why don't you do it?"

I stirred in the chair, I lit a cigarette, looked out the window at the rain, tried to shut the voice up. "Don't act on impulses," I thought. "This is crazy. This is not rational. Read your book."

Hopkins was writing to Newman, at Birmingham, about his indecision.

"What are you waiting for?" said the voice within me again. "Why are you sitting there? It is useless to hesitate any longer. Why don't you get up and go?"

I got up and walked restlessly around the room. "It's absurd," I thought. "Anyway, Father Ford would not be there at this time of day. I would only be wasting time."

Hopkins had written to Newman, and Newman had replied to him, telling him to come and see him at Birmingham.

Suddenly, I could bear it no longer. I put down the book, and got into my raincoat, and started down the stairs. I went out into the street. I crossed over, and walked along by the grey wooden fence, towards Broadway, in the light rain.

And then everything inside me began to sing—to sing with peace, to sing with strength and to sing with conviction.

I had nine blocks to walk. Then I turned the corner of 121st Street, and the brick church and presbytery were before me. I stood in the doorway and rang the bell and waited.

When the maid opened the door, I said:

"May I see Father Ford, please?"

"But Father Ford is out."

I thought: well, it is not a waste of time, anyway. And I asked when she expected him back. I would come back later, I thought.

The maid closed the door. I stepped back into the street. And then I saw Father Ford coming around the corner from Broadway. He approached, with his head down, in a rapid, thoughtful walk. I went to meet him and said:

"Father, may I speak to you about something?"

"Yes," he said, looking up, surprised. "Yes, sure, come into the house."

We sat in the little parlor by the door. And I said: "Father, I want to become a Catholic."

## vi

I came out of the presbytery with three books under my arm. I had hoped that I could begin taking instructions at once, but the pastor had told me to read these books, and pray and think and see how I felt about it in a week or ten days' time. I did not argue with him: but the hesitation that had been in my mind only an hour or so before seemed to have vanished so completely that I was astonished and a little abashed at this delay. So it was arranged that I should come in the evenings, twice a week.

"Father Moore will be your instructor," said the Pastor.

There were four assistants at Corpus Christi, but I guessed that Father Moore was going to be the one whom I had heard preaching the sermon on the divinity of Christ and, as a matter of fact, he was the one who, in the designs of Providence, had been appointed for this work of my salvation.

If people had more appreciation of what it means to be converted from rank, savage paganism, from the spiritual level of a cannibal or of an ancient Roman, to the living faith and to the Church, they would not think of catechism as something trivial or unimportant. Usually the word suggests the matter-of-course instructions that children have to go through before First Communion and Confirmation. Even where it is a matter-of-course, it is one of the most tremendous things in the world, this planting of the word of God in a soul. It takes a conversion to really bring this home.

I was never bored. I never missed an instruction, even when it cost me the sacrifice of some of my old amusements and attractions, which had such a strong hold over me and, while I had been impatient of delay from the moment I had come to that first sudden decision, I now began to burn with desire for Baptism, and to throw out hints and try to determine when I would be received into the Church.

My desire became much greater still, by the end of October, for I made the Mission with the men of the parish, listening twice a day to sermons by two Paulist Fathers and hearing Mass and kneeling at Benediction before the Christ Who was gradually revealing Himself to me.

When the sermon on hell began, I was naturally making mental comparisons with the one in Joyce's *Portrait of the Artist* and reflecting on it in a kind of detached manner, as if I were a third and separate person watching myself hearing this sermon and seeing how it affected me. As a matter of fact this was the sermon which should have done me the most good and did, in fact, do so.

My opinion is that it is a very extraordinary thing for anyone to be upset by such a topic. Why should anyone be shattered by the thought of hell? It is not compulsory for anyone to go there. Those who do, do so by their own choice, and against the will of God, and they can only get into hell by defying and resisting all the work of Providence and grace. It is their own will that takes them there, not God's. In damning them He is only ratifying their own decision—a decision which He has left entirely to their own choice. Nor will He ever hold our weakness alone responsible for our damnation. Our weakness should not terrify us: it is the source of our strength. *Libenter gloriabor in infirmitatibus meis ut inhabitet in me virtus Christi*. Power is made perfect in infirmity, and our very helplessness is all the more potent a claim on that Divine Mercy Who calls to Himself the poor, the little ones, the heavily burdened.

My reaction to the sermon on hell was, indeed, what spiritual writers call "confusion"—but it was not the hectic, emotional confusion that comes from passion and from self-love. It was a sense of quiet sorrow and patient grief at the thought of these tremendous and terrible sufferings which I deserved and into which I stood a very good chance of entering, in my present condition: but at the same time, the magnitude of the punishment gave me a special and particular understanding of the greatness of the evil of sin. But the final result was a great deepening and awakening of my soul, a real increase in spiritual profundity and an advance in faith and love and confidence in God, to Whom alone I could look for salvation from these things. And therefore I all the more earnestly desired Baptism.

I went to Father Moore after the sermon on hell and said that I hoped he was going to baptize me really soon. He laughed, and said that it would not be much longer. By now, it was the beginning of November.

Meanwhile, there had been another thought, half forming itself in the back of my mind—an obscure desire to become a priest. This was something which I tended to hold separate from the thought of my conversion, and I was doing my best to keep it in the background. I did not mention it either to Father Ford or Father Moore, for the chief reason that in my mind it constituted a kind of admission that I was taking the thought more seriously than I wanted to—it almost amounted to a first step towards application for admission to a seminary.

However, it is a strange thing: there was also in my mind a kind of half-formed conviction that there was one other person I should consult about becoming a priest before I took the matter to the rectory. This man was a layman, and someone I had never yet seen, and it was altogether strange that I should be inclined so spontaneously to put the matter up to him, as if he were the only logical one to give me advice. In the end, he was the one I first consulted—I mean, the one from whom I first seriously asked advice, for I had long been talking about it to my friends, before I came around to him.

This man was Daniel Walsh, about whom I had heard a great deal from Lax and Gerdy. Gerdy had taken his course on St. Thomas Aquinas in the graduate school of Philosophy: and now as the new school year began, my attention centered upon this one course. It had nothing directly to do with my preparation for the exams for the M.A. degree in January. By now degrees and everything else to do with a university career had become very unimportant in comparison with the one big thing that occupied my mind and all my desires.

I registered for the course, and Dan Walsh turned out to be another one of those destined in a providential way to shape and direct my vocation. For it was he who pointed out my way to the place where I now am.

When I was writing about Columbia and its professors, I was not thinking of Dan Walsh: and he really did not belong to Columbia at all. He was on the faculty of the Sacred Heart College at Manhattanville, and came to Columbia twice a week to lecture on St. Thomas and Duns Scotus. His class was a small one and was, as far as Columbia was concerned, pretty much of an academic bypath. And that was in a sense an additional recommendation—it was off that broad and noisy highway of pragmatism which leads between its banks of artificial flowers to the gates of despair.

Walsh himself had nothing of the supercilious self-assurance of the ordinary professor: he did not need this frail and artificial armor for his own insufficiency. He did not need to hide behind tricks and vanities any more than Mark Van Doren did; he never even needed to be brilliant. In his smiling simplicity he used to efface himself entirely in the solid and powerful mind of St. Thomas. Whatever brilliance he allowed himself to show forth in his lectures was all thrown back upon its source, the Angel of the Schools.

Dan Walsh had been a student and collaborator of Gilson's and knew Gilson and Maritain well. In fact, later on he introduced me to Maritain at the Catholic Book Club, where this most saintly philosopher had been giving a talk on Catholic Action. I only spoke a few conventional words to Maritain, but the impression you got from this gentle, stooping Frenchman with much grey hair, was one of tremendous kindness and simplicity and godliness. And that was enough: you did not need to talk to him. I came away feeling very comforted that there was such a person in the world, and confident that he would include me in some way in his prayers.

But Dan himself had caught a tremendous amount of this simplicity and gentleness and godliness too: and perhaps the impression that he made was all the more forceful because his square jaw had a kind of potential toughness about it. Yet no: there he sat, this little, stocky man, who had something of the appearance of a good-natured prize fighter, smiling and talking with the most childlike delight and cherubic simplicity about the *Summa Theologica*.

His voice was low and, as he spoke, he half apologetically searched the faces of his hearers for signs of understanding and, when he found it, he seemed surprised and delighted.

I very quickly made friends with him, and told him all about my thesis and the ideas I was trying to work with, and he was very pleased. And one of the things he sensed at once was something that I was far from being able to realize: but it was that the bent of my mind was essentially "Augustinian." I had not yet followed Bramachari's advice to read St. Augustine and I did not take Dan's evaluation of my ideas as having all the directive force that was potentially in it—for it did not even come clothed in suggestion or advice.

Of course, to be called "Augustinian" by a Thomist might not in every case be a compliment. But coming from Dan Walsh, who was a true Catholic philosopher, it was a compliment indeed.

For he, like Gilson, had the most rare and admirable virtue of being able to rise above the petty differences of schools and systems, and seeing Catholic philosophy in its wholeness, in its variegated unity, and in its true Catholicity. In other words, he was able to study St. Thomas and St. Bonaventure and Duns Scotus side by side, and to see them as complementing and reinforcing one another, as throwing diverse and individual light on the same truths from different points of view, and thus he avoided the evil of narrowing and restricting Catholic philosophy and theology to a single school, to a single attitude, a single system.

I pray to God that there may be raised up more like him in the Church and in our universities, because there is something stifling and intellectually deadening about textbooks that confine themselves to giving a superficial survey of the field of philosophy according to Thomist principles and then discard all the rest in a few controversial objections. Indeed, I think it a great shame and a danger of no small proportions, that Catholic philosophers should be trained in division against one another, and brought up to the bitterness and smallness of controversy: because this is bound to narrow their views and dry up the unction that should vivify all philosophy in their souls.

Therefore, to be called an "Augustinian" by Dan Walsh was a compliment, in spite of the traditional opposition between the Thomist and Augustinian schools, Augustinian being taken not as confined to the philosophers of that religious order, but as embracing all the intellectual descendants of St. Augustine. It is a great compliment to find oneself numbered as part of the same spiritual heritage as St. Anselm, St. Bernard, St. Bonaventure, Hugh and Richard of St. Victor, and Duns Scotus also. And from the tenor of his course, I realized that he meant that my bent was not so much towards the intellectual, dialectical, speculative character of Thomism, as towards the spiritual, mystical, voluntaristic and practical way of St. Augustine and his followers.

His course and his friendship were most valuable in preparing me for the step I was about to take. But as time went on, I decided to leave the notion of becoming a priest out of the way for the time being. So I never even mentioned it to Dan in those days.

As November began, my mind was taken up with this one thought: of getting baptized and entering at last into the supernatural life of the Church. In spite of all my studying and all my reading and all my talking, I was still infinitely poor and wretched in my appreciation of what was about to take place within me. I was about to set foot on the shore at the foot of the high, seven-circled mountain of a Purgatory steeper and more arduous than I was able to imagine, and I was not at all aware of the climbing I was about to have to do.

The essential thing was to begin the climb. Baptism was that beginning, and a most generous one, on the part of God. For, although I was baptized conditionally, I hope that His mercy swallowed up all the guilt and temporal punishment of my twenty-three black years of sin in the waters of the font, and allowed me a new start. But my human nature, my weakness, and the cast of my evil habits still remained to be fought and overcome.

Towards the end of the first week in November, Father Moore told me I would be baptized on the sixteenth. I walked out of the rectory that evening happier and more contented than I had ever been in my life. I looked at a calendar to see what saint had that day for a feast, and it was marked for St. Gertrude.

It was only in the last days before being liberated from my slavery to death, that I had the grace to feel something of my own weakness and helplessness. It was not a very vivid light that was given to me on the subject: but I was really aware, at last, of what a poor and miserable thing I was. On the night of the fifteenth of November, the eve of my Baptism and First Communion, I lay in my bed awake and timorous for fear that something might go wrong the next day. And to humiliate me still further, as I lay there, fear came over me that I might not be able to keep the eucharistic fast. It only meant going from midnight to ten o'clock without drinking any water or taking any food, yet all of a sudden this little act of self-denial which amounts to no more, in reality, than a sort of an abstract token, a gesture of good-will, grew in my imagination until it seemed to be utterly beyond my strength—as if I were about to go without food and drink for ten days, instead of ten hours. I had enough sense left to realize that this was one of those curious psychological reactions with which our nature, not without help from the devil, tries to confuse us and avoid what reason and our will demand of it, and so I forgot about it all and went to sleep.

In the morning, when I got up, having forgotten to ask Father Moore if washing your teeth was against the eucharistic fast or not, I did not wash them, and, facing a similar problem about cigarettes, I resisted the temptation to smoke.

I went downstairs and out into the street to go to my happy execution and rebirth.

The sky was bright and cold. The river glittered like steel. There was a clean wind in the street. It was one of those fall days full of life and triumph, made for great beginnings, and yet I was not altogether exalted: for there were still in my mind these vague, half animal apprehensions about the externals of what was to happen in the church—would my mouth be so dry that I could not swallow the Host? If that happened, what would I do? I did not know.

Gerdy joined me as I was turning in to Broadway. I do not remember whether Ed Rice caught up with us on Broadway or not. Lax and Seymour came after we were in church.

Ed Rice was my godfather. He was the only Catholic among us—the only Catholic among all my close friends. Lax, Seymour, and Gerdy were Jews. They were very quiet, and so was I. Rice was the only one who was not cowed or embarrassed or shy.

The whole thing was very simple. First of all, I knelt at the altar of Our Lady where Father Moore received my abjuration of heresy and schism. Then we went to the baptistery, in a little dark corner by the main door.

I stood at the threshold.

"*Quid Petis ab ecclesia Dei?*" asked Father Moore.

"*Fidem!*"

"*Fides quid tibi praestat?*"

"*Vitam aeternam.*"

Then the young priest began to pray in Latin, looking earnestly and calmly at the page of the *Rituale* through the lenses of his glasses. And I, who was asking for eternal life, stood and watched him, catching a word of the Latin here and there.

He turned to me:

"*Abrenuntias Satanae?*"

In a triple vow I renounced Satan and his pomps and his works.

"Dost thou believe in God the Father almighty, Creator of heaven and earth?"

*"Credo!"*

"Dost thou believe in Jesus Christ His only Son, Who was born, and suffered?"

*"Credo!"*

"Dost thou believe in the Holy Spirit, in the Holy Catholic Church, the Communion of saints, the remission of sins, the resurrection of the body and eternal life?"

*"Credo!"*

What mountains were falling from my shoulders! What scales of dark night were peeling off my intellect, to let in the inward vision of God and His truth! But I was absorbed in the liturgy, and waiting for the next ceremony. It had been one of the things that had rather frightened me—or rather, which frightened the legion that had been living in me for twenty-three years.

Now the priest blew into my face. He said: *"Exi ab eo, spiritus immunde:* Depart from him, thou impure spirit, and give place to the Holy Spirit, the Paraclete."

It was the exorcism. I did not see them leaving, but there must have been more than seven of them. I had never been able to count them. Would they ever come back? Would that terrible threat of Christ be fulfilled, that threat about the man whose house was clean and garnished, only to be reoccupied by the first devil and many others worse than himself?

The priest, and Christ in him—for it was Christ that was doing these things through his visible ministry, in the Sacrament of my purification—breathed again into my face.

"Thomas, receive the good Spirit through this breathing, and receive the Blessing of God. Peace be with thee."

Then he began again to pray, and sign me with Crosses, and presently came the salt which he put on my tongue—the salt of wisdom, that I might have the savor of divine things, and finally he poured the water on my head, and named me Thomas, "if thou be not already baptized."

After that, I went into the confessional, where one of the other assistants was waiting for me. I knelt in the shadows. Through the dark, close-meshed wire of the grille between us, I saw Father McGough, his head bowed, and resting on his hand, inclining his ear towards me. "Poor man," I thought. He seemed very young and he had always looked so innocent to me that I wondered how he was going to identify and understand the things I was about to tell him.

But one by one, that is, species by species, as best I could, I tore out all those sins by their roots, like teeth. Some of them were hard, but I did it quickly, doing the best I could to approximate the number of times all these things had happened—there was no counting them, only guessing.

I did not have any time to feel how relieved I was when I came stumbling out, as I had to go down to the front of the church where Father Moore would see me and come out to begin his—and my—Mass. But ever since that day, I have loved confessionals.

Now he was at the altar, in his white vestments, opening the book. I was kneeling right at the altar rail. The bright sanctuary was all mine. I could hear the murmur of the priest's voice, and the responses of the server, and it did not matter that I had no one to look at, so that I could tell when to stand up and kneel down again, for I was still not very sure of these ordinary ceremonies. But when the little bells were rung I knew what was happening. And I saw the raised Host—the silence and simplicity with which Christ once again triumphed, raised up, drawing all things to Himself—drawing me to Himself.

Presently the priest's voice was louder, saying the *Pater Noster*. Then, soon, the server was running through the *Confiteor* in a rapid murmur. That was for me. Father Moore turned around and made a big cross in absolution, and held up the little Host.

"Behold the Lamb of God: behold Him Who taketh away the sins of the world."

And my First Communion began to come towards me, down the steps. I was the only one at the altar rail. Heaven was entirely mine—that Heaven in which sharing makes no division or diminution. But this solitariness was a kind of reminder of the singleness with which this Christ, hidden in the small Host, was giving Himself for me, and to me, and, with Himself, the entire Godhead and Trinity—a great new increase of the power and grasp of their indwelling that had begun only a few minutes before at the font.

I left the altar rail and went back to the pew where the others were kneeling like four shadows, four unrealities, and I hid my face in my hands.

In the Temple of God that I had just become, the One Eternal and Pure Sacrifice was offered up to the God dwelling in me: the sacrifice of God to God, and me sacrificed together with God, incorporated in His Incarnation. Christ born in me, a new Bethlehem, and sacrificed in me, His new Calvary, and risen in me: offering me to the Father, in Himself, asking the Father, my Father and His, to receive me into His infinite and special love—not the love He has for all things that exist—for mere existence is a token of God's love, but the love of those creatures who are drawn to Him in and with the power of His own love for Himself.

For now I had entered into the everlasting movement of that gravitation which is the very life and spirit of God: God's own gravitation towards the depths of His own infinite nature, His goodness without end. And God, that center Who is everywhere, and whose circumference is nowhere, finding me, through incorporation with Christ, incorporated into this immense and tremendous gravitational movement which is love, which is the Holy Spirit, loved me.

And He called out to me from His own immense depths.

Gerard Manley Hopkins was a Victorian aesthetician and Jesuit priest. He has been described as a man who struggled to find words to match his vision. (1884-1889)

## *God's Grandeur*

THE world is charged with the grandeur of God.
It will flame out, like shining from shook foil;
It gathers to a greatness, like the ooze of oil
Crushed. Why do men then now not reck his rod?
Generations have trod, have trod, have trod;
And all is seared with trade; bleared, smeared with toil;
And wears man's smudge and shares man's smell: the soil
Is bare now, nor can foot feel, being shod.

And for all this, nature is never spent;
There lives the dearest freshness deep down things;
And though the last lights off the black West went
Oh, morning, at the brown brink eastward, springs—
Because the Holy Ghost over the bent
World broods with warm breast and with ah! bright wings.

## *The Windhover:*

*To Christ our Lord*

I CAUGHT this morning morning's minion, king-
dom of daylight's dauphin, dapple-dawn-drawn Falcon, in his riding
Of the rolling level underneath him steady air, and striding
High there, how he rung upon the rein of a wimpling wing
In his ecstasy! then off, off forth on swing,
As a skate's heel sweeps smooth on a bow-bend: the hurl and gliding
Rebuffed the big wind. My heart in hiding
Stirred for a bird,—the achieve of, the mastery of the thing!

Brute beauty and valour and act, oh, air, pride, plume, here
Buckle! AND the fire that breaks from thee then, a billion
Times told lovelier, more dangerous, O my chevalier!

No wonder of it: shéer plód makes plough down sillion
Shine, and blue-bleak embers, ah my dear,
Fall, gall themselves, and gash gold-vermilion.

# 7

Reinhold Niebuhr, MORAL MAN AND IMMORAL SOCIETY

Robert N. Bellah, BEYOND BELIEF
"BIBLICAL RELIGION AND SOCIAL SCIENCE IN THE MODERN WORLD"

1. In what way does the behavior of an individual differ from that of a group?

2. What does Niebuhr think of the likelihood of putting an end to injustice which results from collective egoism by using rationality, religious goodwill, or power?

3. Is Niebuhr optimistic or pessimistic about the eventual elimination of social conflict? What is his reason?

4. Niebuhr states that political opinions are rooted in economic interests, and that this fact leads inevitably to injustice which groups rationalize. Discuss a current situation which illustrates his statement.

5. Niebuhr writes that a man sublimates his individual will-to-power into pride in his nation and its power. Describe some situation in today's world which illustrates this view.

6. Do you think Bellah is correct in his assessment of the formative role religion played in the thought of the early American Statesmen? Explain.

7. Is his application of Rousseau's concept of civil religion to the American experience credible?

   How did the Civil War affect the development of American civil religion?

8. Could the acceptance of the legitimacy of American civil religion lend support to zealous nationalism? If so, what danger does this pose regarding our role in the modern world?

9. Who is the "god" of civil religion?

10. What are the characteristics of mainstream social science as Bellah traces its development? Do you agree? Why or why not?

11. How do these characteristics contrast with Bellah's understanding of biblical religion?

12. Have the modern social sciences severed themselves from spiritual and aesthetic goals in the pursuit of material comfort?

13. Do you see any signs today in America of groups who are revolting against modernity as Bellah discusses this revolt?

14. What does Bellah mean when he asserts that biblical religion must undertake a deeper criticism of society than the traditional function of providing a moral ecology?

Reinhold Niebuhr (1892-1971), American theologian, social thinker, and activist, was professor of Christian Ethics at Union Theological Seminary in New York from 1930 to 1960. In *Moral Man and Immoral Society*, published in 1932, and in other works written before the end of World War II, he urged the clergy to take part in social reforms, and advanced the belief that society is ruled by self-interest.

# MORAL MAN AND IMMORAL SOCIETY

THE thesis to be elaborated in these pages is that a sharp distinction must be drawn between the moral and social behavior of individuals and of social groups, national, racial, and economic; and that this distinction justifies and necessitates political policies which a purely individualistic ethic must always find embarrassing. The title "Moral Man and Immoral Society" suggests the intended distinction too unqualifiedly, but it is nevertheless a fair indication of the argument to which the following pages are devoted. Individual men may be moral in the sense that they are able to consider interests other than their own in determining problems of conduct, and are capable, on occasion, of preferring the advantages of others to their own. They are endowed by nature with a measure of sympathy and consideration for their kind, the breadth of which may be extended by an astute social pedagogy. Their rational faculty prompts them to a sense of justice which educational discipline may refine and purge of egoistic elements until they are able to view a social situation, in which their own interests are involved, with a fair measure of objectivity. But all these achievements are more difficult, if not impossible, for human societies and social groups. In every human group there is less reason to guide and to check impulse, less capacity for self-transcendence, less ability to comprehend the needs of others and therefore more unrestrained egoism

Reinhold Niebuhr, *Moral Man and Immoral Society*. Charles Scribner's Sons, c.1932. Reproduced by permission of Charles Scribner's Sons.

than the individuals, who compose the group, reveal in their personal relationships.

The inferiority of the morality of groups to that of individuals is due in part to the difficulty of establishing a rational social force which is powerful enough to cope with the natural impulses by which society achieves its cohesion; but in part it is merely the revelation of a collective egoism, compounded of the egoistic impulses of individuals, which achieve a more vivid expression and a more cumulative effect when they are united in a common impulse than when they express themselves separately and discreetly.

Inasfar as this treatise has a polemic interest it is directed against the moralists, both religious and secular, who imagine that the egoism of individuals is being progressively checked by the development of rationality or the growth of a religiously inspired goodwill and that nothing but the continuance of this process is necessary to establish social harmony between all the human societies and collectives. Social analyses and prophecies made by moralists, sociologists and educators upon the basis of these assumptions lead to a very considerable moral and political confusion in our day. They completely disregard the political necessities in the struggle for justice in human society by failing to recognise those elements in man's collective behavior which belong to the order of nature and can never be brought completely under the dominion of reason or conscience. They do not recognise that when collective power, whether in the form of imperialism or class domination, exploits weakness, it can never be dislodged unless power is raised against it.

If conscience and reason can be insinuated into the resulting struggle they can only qualify but not abolish it.

The most persistent error of modern educators and moralists is the assumption that our social difficulties are due to the failure of the social sciences to keep pace with the physical sciences which have created our technological civilisation. The invariable implication of this assumption is that, with a little more time, a little more adequate moral and social pedagogy and a generally higher development of human intelligence, our social problems will approach solution. "It is," declares Professor John Dewey, "our human intelligence and our human courage which is on trial; it is incredible that men who have brought the technique of physical discovery, invention and use to such a pitch of perfection will abdicate in the face of the infinitely more important human problem. What stands in the way (of a planned economy) is a lot of outworn traditions, moth-eaten slogans and catchwords that do substitute duty for thought, as well as our entrenched predatory self-interest. We shall only make a real beginning in intelligent thought when we cease mouthing platitudes. . . . Just as soon as we begin to use the knowledge and skills we have, to control social consequences in the interest of a shared, abundant and secured life, we shall cease to complain of the backwardness of our social knowledge. . . . We shall then take the road which leads to the assured building up of social science just as men built up physicial science when they actively used techniques and tools and numbers in physical experimentation."[1] In spite of Professor Dewey's great interest in

[1] John Dewey, *Philosophy and Civilization* (New York: Minton, Balch), p. 329.

and understanding of the modern social problem there is very little clarity in this statement. The real cause of social inertia, "our predatory self-interest," is mentioned only in passing without influencing his reasoning, and with no indication that he understands how much social conservatism is due to the economic interests of the owning classes. On the whole, social conservatism is ascribed to ignorance, a viewpoint which states only part of the truth and reveals the natural bias of the educator. The suggestion that we will only make a beginning in intelligent thought when we "cease mouthing platitudes," is itself so platitudinous that it rather betrays the confusion of an analyst who has no clear counsels about the way to overcome social inertia. The idea that we cannot be socially intelligent until we begin experimentation in social problems in the way that the physical scientists experimented fails to take account of an important difference between the physical and the social sciences. The physical sciences gained their freedom when they overcame the traditionalism based on ignorance, but the traditionalism which the social sciences face is based upon the economic interest of the dominant social classes who are trying to maintain their special privileges in society. Nor can the difference between the very character of social and physical sciences be overlooked. Complete rational objectivity in a social situation is impossible. The very social scientists who are so anxious to offer our generation counsels of salvation and are disappointed that an ignorant and slothful people are so slow to accept their wisdom, betray middle-class prejudices in almost everything they write. Since reason is always, to some degree, the servant of interest in a social situation, social injustice cannot be resolved by moral and rational suasion alone, as the educator and social scientist usually believes. Conflict is inevitable, and in this conflict power must be challenged by power. That fact is not recognized by most of the educators, and only very grudgingly admitted by most of the social scientists.

If social conflict be a part of the process of gaining social justice, the idea of most of Professor Dewey's disciples that our salvation depends upon the development of "experimental procedures"[2] in social life, commensurate with the experimentalism of the physical sciences, does not have quite the plausibility which they attribute to it. Contending factions in a social struggle require morale; and morale is created by the right dogmas, symbols and emotionally potent oversimplifications. These are at least as necessary as the scientific spirit of tentativity. No class of industrial workers will ever win freedom from the dominant classes if they give themselves completely to the "experimental techniques" of the modern educators. They will have to believe rather more firmly in the justice and in the probable triumph of their cause, than any impartial science would give them the right to believe, if they are to have enough energy to contest the power of the strong. They may be very scientific in projecting their social goal and in choosing the most effective instruments for its attainment, but a motive force will be required to nerve them for their task which is not easily derived from the cool objectivity of science. Modern educators

[2] *Cf. inter alia*, John Childs, *Education and the Philosophy of Experimentalism*, p. 37.

are, like rationalists of all the ages, too enamored of the function of reason in life. The world of history, particularly in man's collective behavior, will never be conquered by reason, unless reason uses tools, and is itself driven by forces which are not rational.

The sociologists, as a class, understand the modern social problem even less than the educators. They usually interpret social conflict as the result of a clash between different kinds of "behavior patterns," which can be eliminated if the contending parties will only allow the social scientist to furnish them with a new and more perfect pattern which will do justice to the needs of both parties. With the educators they regard ignorance rather than self-interest as the cause of conflict. "Apparently," declares Kimball Young, "the only way in which collective conflicts, as well as individual conflicts, can be successfully and hygienically solved is by securing a redirection of behavior toward a more feasible environmental objective. This can be accomplished most successfully by the rational reconditioning of attitudes on a higher neuro-psychic or intellectual symbolic plane to the facts of science, preferably through a free discussion with a minimum of propaganda. This is not an easy road to mental and social sanity but it appears to be the only one which arrives at the goal."[3] Here a technique which works very well in individual relations, and in certain types of social conflict due to differences in culture, is made a general panacea. How is it to solve the problem between England and India? Through the Round-Table Conference? But how much would England have

[3] Kimball Young, *Social Attitudes*, p. 72.

granted India at the conference if a non-co-operation campaign, a type of conflict, had not forced the issue?

A favorite counsel of the social scientists is that of accommodation. If two parties are in a conflict, let them, by conferring together, moderate their demands and arrive at a *modus vivendi*. This is, among others, the advice of Professor Hornell Hart.[4] Undoubtedly there are innumerable conflicts which must be resolved in this fashion. But will a disinherited group, such as the Negroes for instance, ever win full justice in society in this fashion? Will not even its most minimum demands seem exorbitant to the dominant whites, among whom only a very small minority will regard the inter-racial problem from the perspective of objective justice? Or how are the industrial workers to follow Professor Hart's advice in dealing with industrial owners, when the owners possess so much power that they can win the debate with the workers, no matter how unconvincing their arguments? Only a very few sociologists seem to have learned that an adjustment of a social conflict, caused by the disproportion of power in society, will hardly result in justice as long as the disproportion of power remains. Sometimes the sociologists are so completely oblivious to the real facts of an industrial civilisation that, as Floyd Allport for instance, they can suggest that the unrest of industrial workers is due not to economic injustice but to a sense of inferiority which will be overcome just as soon as benevolent social psychologists are able to teach the workers that "no one is charging them with inferiority except themselves."[5] These omniscient social scientists will

[4] Hornell Hart, *The Science of Social Relations.*

[5] Floyd Allport, *Social Psychology*, pp. 14–27.

also teach the owners that "interests and profits must be tempered by regard for the worker." Thus "the socialisation of individual control" in industry will obviate the necessity of "socialistic control." Most of the social scientists are such unqualified rationalists that they seem to imagine that men of power will immediately check their exactions and pretensions in society, as soon as they have been apprised by the social scientists that their actions and attitudes are anti-social. Professor Clarence Marsh Case, in an excellent analysis of the social problem, places his confidence in a "reorganisation of values" in which, among other things, industrial leaders must be made to see "that despotically controlled industry in a society that professes democracy as an article of faith is an anachronism that cannot endure."[6] It may be that despotism cannot endure but it will not abdicate merely because the despots have discovered it to be anachronistic. Sir Arthur Salter, to name a brilliant economist among the social scientists, finishes his penetrating analysis of the distempers of our civilisation by expressing the usual hope that a higher intelligence or a sincerer morality will prevent the governments of the future from perpetrating the mistakes of the past. His own analysis proves conclusively that the failure of governments is due to the pressure of economic interest upon them rather than to the "limited capacities of human wisdom." In his own words "government is failing above all because it has become enmeshed in the task of giving discretionary, particularly preferential, privileges to competitive industry."[7] In spite

[6] Clarence Marsh Case, *Social Process and Human Progress*, p. 233.
[7] Sir Arthur Salter, *Recovery*, p. 341.

of this analysis Sir Arthur expects the governments to redeem our civilisation by becoming more socially minded and he thinks that one method which will help them to do so is to "draw into the service of the public the great private institutions which represent the organised activities of the country, chambers of commerce, banking institutions, industrial and labor organisations." His entire hope for recovery rests upon the possibility of developing a degree of economic disinterestedness among men of power which the entire history of mankind proves them incapable of acquiring. It is rather discouraging to find such naïve confidence in the moral capacities of collective man, among men who make it their business to study collective human behavior. Even when, as Professor Howard Odum, they are prepared to admit that "conflict will be necessary" as long as "unfairness in the distribution of the rewards of labor exists," they put their hope in the future. They regard social conflict as only an expedient of the moment "until broader principles of education and cooperation can be established."[8] Anarchism, with an uncoerced and voluntary justice, seems to be either an explicit or implicit social goal of every second social scientist.

Modern religious idealists usually follow in the wake of social scientists in advocating compromise and accommodation as the way to social justice. Many leaders of the church like to insist that it is not their business to champion the cause of either labor or capital, but only to admonish both sides to a spirit of fairness and accommodation. "Between the far-visioned capitalism of Owen

[8] Howard W. Odum, *Man's Quest for Social Guidance*, p. 477.

Young and the hard-headed socialism of Ramsay MacDonald," declares Doctor Justin Wroe Nixon, "there is probably no impassable gulf. The progress of mankind . . . depends upon following the MacDonalds and Youngs into those areas."[9] Unfortunately, since those lines were written the socialism of MacDonald has been revealed as not particularly hard-headed, and the depression has shown how little difference there really is between Mr. Young's "new capitalism" and the older and less suave types of capitalism.

What is lacking among all these moralists, whether religious or rational, is an understanding of the brutal character of the behavior of all human collectives, and the power of self-interest and collective egoism in all inter-group relations. Failure to recognise the stubborn resistance of group egoism to all moral and inclusive social objectives inevitably involves them in unrealistic and confused political thought. They regard social conflict either as an impossible method of achieving morally approved ends or as a momentary expedient which a more perfect education or a purer religion will make unnecessary. They do not see that the limitations of the human imagination, the easy subservience of reason to prejudice and passion, and the consequent persistence of irrational egoism, particularly in group behavior, make social conflict an inevitability in human history, probably to its very end.

[9] Justin Wroe Nixon, *An Emerging Christian Faith*, p. 294.

Robert N. Bellah is a sociologist on the faculty of the University of California at Berkeley. He has described "Civil Religion in America," written in 1967, as an essay he has never been allowed to forget. The second essay was published in 1981.

BEYOND BELIEF

# 9 Civil Religion in America

While some have argued that Christianity is the national faith, and others that church and synagogue celebrate only the generalized religion of "the American Way of Life," few have realized that there actually exists alongside of and rather clearly differentiated from the churches an elaborate and well-institutionaliezed civil religion in America. This article argues not only that there is such a thing, but also that this religion—or perhaps better, this religious dimension—has its own seriousness and integrity and requires the same care in understanding that any other religion does.[1]

## The Kennedy Inaugural

John F. Kennedy's inaugural address of January 20, 1961, serves as an example and a clue with which to introduce this complex subject. That address began:

> We observe today not a victory of party but a celebration of freedom—symbolizing an end as well as a beginning—signifying renewal as well as change. For I have sworn before you and Almighty God the same solemn oath our forebears prescribed nearly a century and three quarters ago.

*This chapter was written for a* Daedalus *conference on American Religion in May 1966. It was reprinted with comments and a rejoinder in* The Religious Situation: 1968, *where I defend myself against the accusation of supporting an idolatrous worship of the American nation. I think it should be clear from the text that I conceive of the central tradition of the American civil religion not as a form of national self-worship but as the subordination of the nation to ethical principles that transcend it and in terms of which it should be judged. I am convinced that every nation and every people come to some form of religious self-understanding whether the critics like it or not. Rather than simply denounce what seems in any case inevitable, it seems more responsible to seek within the civil religious tradition for those critical principles which undercut the everpresent danger of national self-idolization.*

The world is very different now. For man holds in his mortal hands the power to abolish all forms of human poverty and to abolish all forms of human life. And yet the same revolutionary beliefs for which our forebears fought are still at issue around the globe—the belief that the rights of man come not from the generosity of the state but from the hand of God.

And it concluded:

Finally, whether you are citizens of America or of the world, ask of us the same high standards of strength and sacrifice that we shall ask of you. With a good conscience our only sure reward, with history the final judge of our deeds, let us go forth to lead the land we love, asking His blessing and His help, but knowing that here on earth God's work must truly be our own.

These are the three places in this brief address in which Kennedy mentioned the name of God. If we could understand why he mentioned God, the way in which he did it, and what he meant to say in those three references, we would understand much about American civil religion. But this is not a simple or obvious task, and American students of religion would probably differ widely in their interpretation of these passages.

Let us consider first the placing of the three references. They occur in the two opening paragraphs and in the closing paragraph, thus providing a sort of frame for the more concrete remarks that form the middle part of the speech. Looking beyond this particular speech, we would find that similar references to God are almost invariably to be found in the pronouncements of American presidents on solemn occasions, though usually not in the working messages that the President sends to Congress on various concrete issues. How, then, are we to interpret this placing of references to God?

It might be argued that the passages quoted reveal the essentially irrelevant role of religion in the very secular society that is America. The placing of the references in this speech as well as in public life generally indicates that religion has "only a ceremonial significance"; it gets only a sentimental nod that serves largely to placate the more unenlightened members of the community before a discussion of the really serious business with which religion has nothing whatever to do. A cynical observer might even say that an American President has to mention God or risk losing votes. A semblance of piety is merely one of the unwritten qualifications for the office, a bit more traditional than but not essentially different from the present-day requirement of a pleasing television personality.

But we know enough about the function of ceremonial and ritual in various societies to make us suspicious of dismissing something as unimportant because it is "only a ritual." What people say on solemn occasions need not be taken at face value, but it is often indicative of deep-seated values and commitments that are not made explicit in the course of everyday life. Following this line of argument, it is worth considering whether the very special placing of the references to God in Kennedy's address may not reveal something rather important and serious about religion in American life.

It might be countered that the very way in which Kennedy made his references reveals the essentially vestigial place of religion today. He did not refer to any religion in particular. He did not refer to Jesus Christ, or to Moses, or to the Christian church; certainly he did not refer to the Catholic church. In fact, his only reference was to the concept of God, a word that almost all Americans can accept but that means so many different things to so many different people that it is almost an empty sign. Is this not just another indication that in America religion is considered vaguely to be a good thing, but that people care so little about it that it has lost any content whatever? Isn't Dwight Eisenhower reported to have said "Our government makes no sense unless it is founded in a deeply felt religious faith—and I don't care what it is,"[2] and isn't that a complete negation of any real religion?

These questions are worth pursuing because they raise the issue of how civil religion relates to the political society on the one hand and to private religious organization on the other. President Kennedy was a Christian, more specifically a Catholic Christian. Thus his general references to God do not mean that he lacked a specific religious commitment. But why, then, did he not include some remark to the effect that Christ is the Lord of the world or some indication of respect for the Catholic church? He did not because these are matters of his own private religious belief and of his relation to his own particular church; they are not matters relevant in any direct way to the conduct of his public office. Others with different religious views and commitments to different churches or denominations are equally qualified participants in the political process. The principle of separation of church and state guarantees the freedom of religious belief and association, but at the same time clearly segregates the religious sphere, which is considered to be essentially private, from the political one.

Considering the separation of church and state, how is a president justified in using the word "God" at all? The answer is that the separation of church and state has not denied the political realm a religious dimension. Although matters of personal religious belief, worship, and association are considered to be strictly private affairs, there are, at the same time, certain common elements of religious orientation that the great majority of Americans share. These have played a crucial role in the development of American institutions and still provide a religious dimension for the whole fabric of American life, including the political sphere. This public religious dimension is expressed in a set of beliefs, symbols, and rituals that I am calling the American civil religion. The inauguration of a president is an important ceremonial event in this religion. It reaffirms, among other things, the religious legitimation of the highest political authority.

Let us look more closely at what Kennedy actually said. First he said, "I have sworn before you and Almighty God the same solemn oath our forebears prescribed nearly a century and three quarters ago." The oath is the oath of office, including the acceptance of the obligation to uphold the Constitution. He swears it before the people (you) and God. Beyond the Constitution, then, the president's obligation extends not only to the people but to God. In American political theory, sovereignty rests, of course, with the people, but implicitly, and often explicitly, the ultimate sovereignty has been attributed to God. This is the meaning of the motto, "In God we trust," as well as the inclusion of the phrase "under God" in the pledge to the flag. What difference does it make that sovereignty belongs to God? Though the will of the people as expressed in majority vote is carefully institutionalized as the operative source of political authority, it is deprived of an ultimate significance. The will of the people is not itself the criterion of right and wrong. There is a higher criterion in terms of which this will can be judged; it is possible that the people may be wrong. The president's obligation extends to the higher criterion.

When Kennedy says that "the rights of man come not from the generosity of the state but from the hand of God," he is stressing this point again. It does not matter whether the state is the expression of the will of an autocratic monarch or of the "people"; the rights of man are more basic than any political structure and provide a point of revolutionary leverage from which any state structure may be radically altered. That is the basis for his reassertion of the revolutionary significance of America.

But the religious dimension in political life as recognized by Kennedy not only provides a grounding for the rights of man that makes any form of political absolutism illegitimate, it also provides a transcendent goal for the political process. This is implied in his final words that "here on earth God's work must truly be our own." What he means here is, I think, more clearly spelled out in a previous paragraph, the wording of which, incidentally, has a distinctly biblical ring:

> Now the trumpet summons us again—not as a call to bear arms, though arms we need—not as a call to battle, though embattled we are—but a call to bear the burden of a long twilight struggle, year in and year out, "rejoicing in hope, patient in tribulation"—a struggle against the common enemies of man: tyranny, poverty, disease and war itself.

The whole address can be understood as only the most recent statement of a theme that lies very deep in the American tradition, namely the obligation, both collective and individual, to carry out God's will on earth. This was the motivating spirit of those who founded America, and it has been present in every generation since. Just below the surface throughout Kennedy's inaugural address, it becomes explicit in the closing statement that God's work must be our own. That this very activist and noncontemplative conception of the fundamental religious obligation, which has been historically associated with the Protestant position, should be enunciated so clearly in the first major statement of the first Catholic president seems to underline how deeply established it is in the American outlook. Let us now consider the form and history of the civil religious tradition in which Kennedy was speaking.

## The Idea of a Civil Religion

The phrase "civil religion" is, of course, Rousseau's. In chapter 8, book 4 of *The Social Contract,* he outlines the simple dogmas of the civil religion: the existence of God, the life to come, the reward of virtue and the punishment of vice, and the exclusion of religious intolerance. All other religious opinions are outside the cognizance of the state and may be freely held by citizens. While the phrase "civil religion" was not used, to the best of my knowledge, by the founding fathers, and I am certainly not arguing for the particular influence of Rousseau, it is clear that similar ideas, as part of the cultural climate of the late eighteenth century, were to be found among the Americans. For example, Benjamin Franklin writes in his autobiography,

I never was without some religious principles. I never doubted, for instance, the existence of the Deity; that he made the world and govern'd it by his Providence; that the most acceptable service of God was the doing of good to men; that our souls are immortal; and that all crime will be punished, and virtue rewarded either here or hereafter. These I esteemed the essentials of every religion; and, being to be found in all the religions we had in our country, I respected them all, tho' with different degrees of respect, as I found them more or less mix'd with other articles, which, without any tendency to inspire, promote or confirm morality, serv'd principally to divide us, and make us unfriendly to one another.

It is easy to dispose of this sort of position as essentially utilitarian in relation to religion. In Washington's Farewell Address (though the words may be Hamilton's) the utilitarian aspect is quite explicit:

Of all the dispositions and habits which lead to political prosperity, Religion and Morality are indispensable supports. In vain would that man claim the tribute of Patriotism, who should labour to subvert these great Pillars of human happiness, these firmest props of the duties of men and citizens. The mere politician, equally with the pious man ought to respect and cherish them. A volume could not trace all their connections with private and public felicity. Let it simply be asked where is the security for property, for reputation, for life, if the sense of religious obligation *desert* the oaths, which are the instruments of investigation in Courts of Justice? And let us with caution indulge the supposition, that morality can be maintained without religion. Whatever may be conceded to the influence of refined education on minds of peculiar structure, reason and experience both forbid us to expect that National morality can prevail in exclusion of religious principle.

But there is every reason to believe that religion, particularly the idea of God, played a constitutive role in the thought of the early American statesmen.

Kennedy's inaugural pointed to the religious aspect of the Declaration of Independence, and it might be well to look at that document a bit more closely. There are four references to God. The first speaks of the "Laws of Nature and of Nature's God" that entitle any people to be independent. The second is the famous statement that all men "are endowed by their Creator with certain inalienable Rights." Here Jefferson is locating the fundamental legitimacy of the new nation in a conception of "higher law" that is itself based on both classical natural law and biblical religion. The third is an appeal to "the Supreme Judge of the world for the rectitude of our intentions," and the last indicates "a firm reliance on the protection of divine Providence." In these last two references, a biblical God of history who stands in judgment over the world is indicated.

The intimate relation of these religious notions with the self-conception of the new republic is indicated by the frequency of their appearance in early official documents. For example, we find in Washington's first inaugural address of April 30, 1789:

> It would be peculiarly improper to omit in this first official act my fervent supplications to that Almighty Being who rules over the universe, who presides in the councils of nations, and whose providential aids can supply every defect, that His benediction may consecrate to the liberties and happiness of the people of the United States a Government instituted by themselves for these essential purposes, and may enable every instrument employed in its administration to execute with success the functions allotted to his charge.
>
> No people can be bound to acknowledge and adore the Invisible Hand which conducts the affairs of man more than those of the United States. Every step by which we have advanced to the character of an independent nation seems to have been distinguished by some token of providential agency. . . .
>
> The propitious smiles of Heaven can never be expected on a nation that disregards the eternal rules of order and right which Heaven itself has ordained. . . . The preservation of the sacred fire of liberty and the destiny of the republican model of government are justly considered, perhaps, as *deeply,* as *finally,* staked on the experiment intrusted to the hands of the American people.

Nor did these religious sentiments remain merely the personal expression of the President. At the request of both Houses of Congress, Washington proclaimed on October 3 of that same first year as President that November 26 should be "a day of public thanksgiving and prayer," the first Thanksgiving Day under the Constitution.

The words and acts of the founding fathers, especially the first few presidents, shaped the form and tone of the civil religion as it has been maintained ever since. Though much is selectively derived from Christianity, this religion is clearly not itself Christianity. For one thing, neither Washington nor Adams nor Jefferson mentions Christ in his inaugural address; nor do any of the subsequent presidents, although not one of them fails to mention God.[3] The God of the civil religion is not only rather "unitarian," he is also on the austere side, much more related to order, law, and right than to salvation and love. Even though he is somewhat deist in cast, he is by no means simply a watchmaker God. He is actively interested and involved in history, with a special concern for America. Here the analogy has much less to do with natural law than with ancient Israel; the equation of America with Israel in the idea of the "American Israel" is not infrequent.[4] What was implicit in the words of Washington already quoted becomes explicit in Jefferson's second inaugural when he said: "I shall need, too, the favor of that Being in whose hands we are, who led our fathers, as Israel of old, from their native land and planted them in a country flowing with all the necessaries and comforts of life." Europe is Egypt; America, the promised land. God has led his people to establish a new sort of social order that shall be a light unto all the nations.[5]

This theme, too, has been a continuous one in the civil religion. We have already alluded to it in the case of the Kennedy inaugural. We find it again in President Johnson's inaugural address:

> They came here—the exile and the stranger, brave but frightened—to find a place where a man could be his own man. They made a covenant with this land. Conceived in justice, written in liberty, bound in union, it was meant one day to inspire the hopes of all mankind; and it binds us still. If we keep its terms, we shall flourish.

What we have, then, from the earliest years of the republic is a collection of beliefs, symbols, and rituals with respect to sacred things and institutionalized in a collectivity. This religion—there seems no other word for it—while not antithetical to and indeed sharing much in common with Christianity, was neither sectarian nor in any specific sense Christian. At a time when the society was overwhelmingly Christian, it seems unlikely that this lack of Christian reference was meant to spare the feelings of the tiny non-Christian minority. Rather, the civil religion expressed what those who set the precedents felt was appropriate under the circumstances. It reflected their private as well as public views. Nor was the civil religion simply "religion in general." While generality was undoubtedly seen as a virtue by some, as in the quotation from Franklin above, the civil religion was specific enough when it came to the topic of America. Precisely because of this specificity, the civil religion was saved from empty formalism and several as a genuine vehicle of national religious self-understanding.

But the civil religion was not, in the minds of Franklin, Washington, Jefferson, or other leaders, with the exception of a few radicals like Tom Paine, ever felt to be a substitute for Christianity. There was an implicit but quite clear division of function between the civil religion and Christianity. Under the doctrine of religious liberty, an exceptionally wide sphere of personal piety and voluntary social action was left to the churches. But the churches were neither to control the state nor to be controlled by it. The national magistrate, whatever his private religious views, operates under the rubrics of the civil religion as long as he is in his official capacity, as we have already seen in the case of Kennedy. This accommodation was undoubtedly the product of a particular historical moment and of a cultural background dominated by Protestantism of several varieties and by the Enlightenment, but it has survived despite subsequent changes in the cultural and religious climate.

## Civil War and Civil Religion

Until the Civil War, the American civil religion focused above all on the event of the Revolution, which was seen as the final act of the Exodus from the old lands across the waters. The Declaration of Independence and the Constitution were the sacred scriptures and Washington the divinely appointed Moses who led his people out of the hands of tyranny. The Civil War, which Sidney Mead calls "the center of American history,"[6] was the second great event that involved the national self-understanding so deeply as to require expression in the civil religion. In 1835, Alexis de Tocqueville wrote that the American republic had never really been tried and that victory in the Revolutionary War was more the result of British preoccupation elsewhere and the presence of a powerful ally than of any great military success of the Americans. But in 1861 the time of testing had indeed come. Not only did the Civil War have the tragic intensity of fratricidal strife, but it was one of the bloodiest wars of the nineteenth century; the loss of life was far greater than any previously suffered by Americans.

The Civil War raised the deepest questions of national meaning. The man who not only formulated but in his own person embodied its meaning for Americans was Abraham Lincoln. For him the issue was not in the first instance slavery but "whether that nation, or any nation so conceived, and so dedicated, can long endure." He had said in Independence Hall in Philadelphia on February 22, 1861:

> All the political sentiments I entertain have been drawn, so far as I have been able to draw them, from the sentiments which originated in and were given to the world from this Hall. I have never had a feeling, politically, that did not spring from the sentiments embodied in the Declaration of Independence.[7]

The phrases of Jefferson constantly echo in Lincoln's speeches. His task was, first of all, to save the Union—not for America alone but for the meaning of America to the whole world so unforgettably etched in the last phrase of the Gettysburg Address.

But inevitably the issue of slavery as the deeper cause of the conflict had to be faced. In his second inaugural, Lincoln related slavery and the war in an ultimate perspective:

> If we shall suppose that American slavery is one of those offenses which, in the providence of God, must needs come, but which, having continued through His appointed time, He now wills to remove, and that He gives to both North and South this terrible war as the woe due to those by whom the offense came, shall we discern therein any departure from those divine attributes which the believers in a living God always ascribe to Him? Fondly do we hope, fervently do we pray, that this mighty scourge of war may speedily pass away. Yet, if God wills that it continue until all the wealth piled by the bondsman's two hundred and fifty years of unrequited toil shall be sunk, and until every drop of blood drawn with the lash shall be paid by another drawn with the sword, as was said three thousand years ago, so still it must be said "the judgements of the Lord are true and righteous altogether."

But he closes on a note if not of redemption then of reconciliation—"With malice toward none, with charity for all."

With the Civil War, a new theme of death, sacrifice, and rebirth enters the civil religion. It is symbolized in the life and death of Lincoln. Nowhere is it stated more vividly than in the Gettysburg Address, itself part of the Lincolnian "New Testament" among the civil scriptures. Robert Lowell has recently pointed out the "insistent use of birth images" in this speech explicitly devoted to "these honored dead": "brought forth," "conceived," "created," "a new birth of freedom." He goes on to say:

The Gettysburg Address is a symbolic and sacramental act. Its verbal quality is resonance combined with a logical, matter of fact, prosaic brevity. . . . In his words, Lincoln symbolically died, just as the Union soldiers really died—and as he himself was soon really to die. By his words, he gave the field of battle a symbolic significance that it had lacked. For us and our country, he left Jefferson's ideals of freedom and equality joined to the Christian sacrificial act of death and rebirth. I believe this is a meaning that goes beyond sect or religion and beyond peace and war, and is now part of our lives as a challenge, obstacle and hope.[8]

Lowell is certainly right in pointing out the Christian quality of the symbolism here, but he is also right in quickly disavowing any sectarian implication. The earlier symbolism of the civil religion had been Hebraic without in any specific sense being Jewish. The Gettysburg symbolism (". . . those who here gave their lives, that that nation might live") is Christian without having anything to do with the Christian church.

The symbolic equation of Lincoln with Jesus was made relatively early. W. H. Herndon, who had been Lincoln's law partner, wrote:

For fifty years God rolled Abraham Lincoln through his fiery furnace. He did it to try Abraham and to purify him for his purposes. This made Mr. Lincoln humble, tender, forbearing, sympathetic to suffering, kind, sensitive, tolerant; broadening, deepening and widening his whole nature; making him the noblest and loveliest character since Jesus Christ. . . . I believe that Lincoln was God's chosen one.[9]

With the Christian archetype in the background, Lincoln, "our martyred president," was linked to the war dead, those who "gave the last full measure of devotion." The theme of sacrifice was indelibly written into the civil religion.

The new symbolism soon found both physical and ritualistic expression. The great number of the war dead required the establishment of a number of national cemeteries. Of these, the Gettysburg National Cemetery, which Lincoln's famous address served to dedicate, has been overshadowed only by the Arlington National Cemetery. Begun somewhat vindictively on the Lee estate across the river from Washington, partly with the end that the Lee family could never reclaim it,[10] it has subsequently become the most hallowed monument of the civil religion. Not only was a section set aside for the Confederate dead, but it has received the dead of each succeeding American war. It is the site of the one important new symbol to come out of World War I, the Tomb of the Unknown Soldier; more recently it has become the site of the tomb of another martyred President and its symbolic eternal flame.

Memorial Day, which grew out of the Civil War, gave ritual expression to the themes we have been discussing. As Lloyd Warner has so brilliantly analyzed it, the Memorial Day observance, especially in the towns and smaller cities of America, is a major event for the whole community involving a rededication to the martyred dead, to the spirit of sacrifice, and to the American vision.[11] Just as Thanksgiving Day, which incidentally was securely institutionalized as an annual national holiday only under the presidency of Lincoln, serves to integrate the family into the civil religion, so Memorial Day has acted to integrate the local community into the national cult. Together with the less overtly religious Fourth of July and the more minor celebrations of Veterans Day and the birthdays of Washington and Lincoln, these two holidays provide an annual ritual calendar for the civil religion. The public school system serves as a particularly important context for the cultic celebration of the civil rituals.

## The Civil Religion Today

In reifying and giving a name to something that, though pervasive enough when you look at it, has gone on only semiconsciously, there is risk of severely distorting the data. But the reification and the naming have already begun. The religious critics of "religion in general," or of the "religion of the 'American Way of Life,' " or of "American Shinto" have really been talking about the civil religion. As usual in religious polemic, they take as criteria the best in their own religious tradition and as typical the worst in the tradition of the civil religion. Against these critics, I would argue that the civil religion at its best is a genuine apprehension of universal and transcendent religious reality as seen in or, one could almost say, as revealed through the experience of the American people. Like all religions, it has suffered various deformations and demonic distortions. At its best, it has neither been so general that it has lacked incisive relevance to the American scene nor so particular that it has placed American society above universal human values. I am not at all convinced that the leaders of the churches have consistently represented a higher level of religious insight than the spokesmen of the civil religion. Reinhold Niebuhr has this to say of Lincoln, who never joined a church and who certainly represents civil religion at its best:

> An analysis of the religion of Abraham Lincoln in the context of the traditional religion of his time and place and of its polemical use on the slavery issue, which corrupted religious life in the days before and during the Civil War, must lead to the conclusion that Lincoln's religious convictions were superior in depth and purity to those, not only of the political leaders of his day, but of the religious leaders of the era.[12]

Perhaps the real animus of the religious critics has been not so much against the civil religion in itself but against its pervasive and dominating influence within the sphere of church religion. As S. M. Lipset has recently shown, American religion at least since the early nineteenth century has been predominantly activist, moralistic, and social rather than contemplative, theological, or innerly spiritual.[13] De Tocqueville spoke of American church religion as "a political institution which powerfully contributes to the maintenance of a democratic republic among the Americans"[14] by supplying a strong moral consensus amidst continuous political change. Henry Bargy in 1902 spoke of American church religion as "la poésie du civisme."[15]

It is certainly true that the relation between religion and politics in America has been singularly smooth. This is in large part due to the dominant tradition. As de Tocqueville wrote:

> The greatest part of British America was peopled by men who, after having shaken off the authority of the Pope, acknowledged no other religious supremacy: they brought with them into the New World a form of Christianity which I cannot better describe than by styling it a democratic and republican religion.[16]

The churches opposed neither the Revolution nor the establishment of democratic institutions. Even when some of them opposed the full institutionalization of religious liberty, they accepted the final outcome with good grace and without nostalgia for an *ancien régime*. The American civil religion was never anticlerical or militantly secular. On the contrary, it borrowed selectively from the religious tradition in such a way that the average American saw no conflict between the two. In this way, the civil religion was able to build up without any bitter struggle with the church powerful symbols of national solidarity and to mobilize deep levels of personal motivation for the attainment of national goals.

Such an achievement is by no means to be taken for granted. It would seem that the problem of a civil religion is quite general in modern societies and that the way it is solved or not solved will have repercussions in many spheres. One need only to think of France to see how differently things can go. The French Revolution was anticlerical to the core and attempted to set up an anti-Christian civil religion. Throughout modern French history, the chasm between traditional Catholic symbols and the symbolism of 1789 has been immense.

American civil religion is still very much alive. Just three years ago we participated in a vivid reenactment of the sacrifice theme in connection with the funeral of our assassinated President. The American Israel theme is clearly behind both Kennedy's New Frontier and Johnson's Great Society. Let me give just one recent illustration of how the civil religion serves to mobilize support for the attainment of national goals. On March 15, 1965, President Johnson went before Congress to ask for a strong voting-rights bill. Early in the speech he said:

> Rarely are we met with the challenge, not to our growth or abundance, or our welfare or our security—but rather to the values and the purposes and the meaning of our beloved nation.
>
> The issue of equal rights for American Negroes is such an issue. And should we defeat every enemy, and should we double our wealth and conquer the stars and still be unequal to this issue, then we will have failed as a people and as a nation.
>
> For with a country as with a person, "What is a man profited, if he shall gain the whole world, and lose his own soul?"

And in conclusion he said:

> Above the pyramid on the great seal of the United States it says in Latin, "God has favored our undertaking."
>
> God will not favor everything that we do. It is rather our duty to divine his will. I cannot help but believe that He truly understands and that He really favors the undertaking that we begin here tonight.[17]

The civil religion has not always been invoked in favor of worthy causes. On the domestic scene, an American-Legion type of ideology that fuses God, country, and flag has been used to attack nonconformist and liberal ideas and groups of all kinds. Still, it has been difficult to use the words of Jefferson and Lincoln to support special interests and undermine personal freedom. The defenders of slavery before the Civil War came to reject the thinking of the Declaration of Independence. Some of the most consistent of them turned against not only Jeffersonian democracy but Reformation religion; they dreamed of a South dominated by medieval chivalry and divine-right monarchy.[18] For all the overt religiosity of the radical right today, their relation to the civil religious consensus is tenuous, as when the John Birch Society attacks the central American symbol of Democracy itself.

With respect to America's role in the world, the dangers of distortion are greater and the built-in safeguards of the tradition weaker. The theme of the American Israel was used, almost from the beginning, as a justification for the shameful treatment of the Indians so characteristic of our history. It can be overtly or implicitly linked to the idea of manifest destiny that has been used to legitimate several adventures in imperialism since the early nineteenth century. Never has the danger been greater than today. The issue is not so much one of imperial expansion, of which we are accused, as of the tendency to assimilate all governments or parties in the world that support our immediate policies or call upon our help by invoking the notion of free institutions and democratic values. Those nations that are for the moment "on our side" become "the free world." A repressive and unstable military dictatorship in South Vietnam becomes "the free people of South Vietnam and their government." It is then part of the role of America as the New Jerusalem and "the last best hope of earth" to defend such governments with treasure and eventually with blood. When our soldiers are actually dying, it becomes possible to consecrate the struggle further by invoking the great theme of sacrifice. For the majority of the American people who are unable to judge whether the people in South Vietnam (or wherever) are "free like us," such arguments are convincing. Fortunately President Johnson has been less ready to assert that "God has favored our undertaking" in the case of Vietnam than with respect to civil rights. But others are not so hesitant. The civil religion has exercised long-term pressure for the humane solution of our greatest domestic problem, the treatment of the Negro American.

It remains to be seen how relevant it can become for our role in the world at large, and whether we can effectually stand for "the revolutionary beliefs for which our forebears fought," in John F. Kennedy's words.

The civil religion is obviously involved in the most pressing moral and political issues of the day. But it is also caught in another kind of crisis, theoretical and theological, of which it is at the moment largely unaware. "God" has clearly been a central symbol in the civil religion from the beginning and remains so today. This symbol is just as central to the civil religion as it is to Judaism or Christianity. In the late eighteenth century this posed no problem; even Tom Paine, contrary to his detractors, was not an atheist. From left to right and regardless of church or sect, all could accept the idea of God. But today, as even *Time* has recognized, the meaning of "God" is by no means so clear or so obvious. There is no formal creed in the civil religion. We have had a Catholic president; it is conceivable that we could have a Jewish one. But could we have an agnostic president? Could a man with conscientious scruples about using the word "God" the way Kennedy and Johnson have used it be elected chief magistrate of our country? If the whole God symbolism requires reformulation, there will be obvious consequences for the civil religion, consequences perhaps of liberal alienation and of fundamentalist ossification that have not so far been prominent in this realm. The civil religion has been a point of articulation between the profoundest commitments of the Western religious and philosophical tradition and the common beliefs of ordinary Americans. It is not too soon to consider how the deepening theological crisis may affect the future of this articulation.

## The Third Time of Trial

In conclusion it may be worthwhile to relate the civil religion to the most serious situation that we as Americans now face, what I call the third time of trial. The first time of trial had to do with the question of independence, whether we should or could run our own affairs in our own way. The second time of trial was over the issue of slavery, which in turn was only the most salient aspect of the more general problem of the full institutionalization of democracy within our country. This second problem we are still far from solving though we have some notable successes to our credit. But we have been overtaken by a third great problem that has led to a third great crisis, in the midst of which we stand. This is the problem of responsible action in a revolutionary world, a world seeking to attain many of the things, material and spiritual, that we have already attained. Americans have, from the beginning, been aware of the responsibility and the significance our republican experiment has for the whole world. The first internal political polarization in the new nation had to do with our attitude toward the French Revolution. But we were small and weak then, and "foreign entanglements" seemed to threaten our very survival. During the last century, our relevance for the world was not forgotten, but our role was seen as purely exemplary. Our democratic republic rebuked tyranny by merely existing. Just after World War I we were on the brink of taking a different role in the world, but once again we turned our backs.

Since World War II the old pattern has become impossible. Every president since Franklin Roosevelt has been groping toward a new pattern of action in the world, one that would be consonant with our power and our responsibilities. For Truman and for the period dominated by John Foster Dulles that pattern was seen to be the great Manichaean confrontation of East and West, the confrontation of democracy and "the false philosophy of Communism" that provided the structure of Truman's inaugural address. But with the last years of Eisenhower and with the successive two presidents, the pattern began to shift. The great problems came to be seen as caused not solely by the evil intent of any one group of men, but as stemming from much more complex and multiple sources. For Kennedy it was not so much a struggle against particular men as against "the common enemies of man: tyranny, poverty, disease and war itself."

But in the midst of this trend toward a less primitive conception of ourselves and our world, we have somehow, without anyone really intending it, stumbled into a military confrontation where we have come to feel that our honor is at stake. We have in a moment of uncertainty been tempted to rely on our overwhelming physical power rather than on our intelligence, and we have, in part, succumbed to this temptation. Bewildered and unnerved when our terrible power fails to bring immediate success, we are at the edge of a chasm the depth of which no man knows.

I cannot help but think of Robinson Jeffers, whose poetry seems more apt now that when it was written, when he said:

> Unhappy country, what wings you have! . . .
> Weep (it is frequent in human affairs), weep for
> the terrible magnificence of the means,
> The ridiculous incompetence of the reasons, the
> bloody and shabby
> Pathos of the result.

But as so often before in similar times, we have a man of prophetic stature, without the bitterness or misanthropy of Jeffers, who, as Lincoln before him, calls this nation to its judgment:

> When a nation is very powerful but lacking in self-confidence, it is likely to behave in a manner that is dangerous both to itself and to others.
>
> Gradually but unmistakably, America is succumbing to that arrogance of power which has afflicted, weakened and in some cases destroyed great nations in the past.
>
> If the war goes on and expands, if that fatal process continues to accelerate until America becomes what it is not now and never has been, a seeker after unlimited power and empire, then Vietnam will have had a mighty and tragic fallout indeed.
>
> I do not believe that will happen. I am very apprehensive but I still remain hopeful, and even confident, that America, with its humane and democratic traditions, will find the wisdom to match its power.[19]

Without an awareness that our nation stands under higher judgment, the tradition of the civil religion would be dangerous indeed. Fortunately, the prophetic voices have never been lacking. Our present situation brings to mind the Mexican-American war that Lincoln, among so many others, opposed. The spirit of civil disobedience that is alive today in the civil rights movement and the opposition to the Vietnam War was already clearly outlined by Henry David Thoreau when he wrote, "If the law is of such a nature that it requires you to be an agent of injustice to another, then I say, break the law." Thoreau's words, "I would remind my countrymen that they are men first, and Americans at a late and convenient hour,"[20] provide an essential standard for any adequate thought and action in our third time of trial. As Americans, we have been well favored in the world, but it is as men that we will be judged.

Out of the first and second times of trial have come, as we have seen, the major symbols of the American civil religion. There seems little doubt that a successful negotiation of this third time of trial—the attainment of some kind of viable and coherent world order—would precipitate a major new set of symbolic forms. So far the flickering flame of the United Nations burns too low to be the focus of a cult, but the emergence of a genuine transnational sovereignty would certainly change this. It would necessitate the incorporation of vital international symbolism into our civil religion, or, perhaps a better way of putting it, it would result in American civil religion becoming simply one part of a new civil religion of the world. It is useless to speculate on the form such a civil religion might take, though it obviously would draw on religious traditions beyond the sphere of biblical religion alone. Fortunately, since the American civil religion is not the worship of the American nation but an understanding of the American experience in the light of ultimate and universal reality, the reorganization entailed by such a new situation need not disrupt the American civil religion's continuity. A world civil religion could be accepted as a fulfillment and not as a denial of American civil religion. Indeed, such an outcome has been the eschatological hope of American civil religion from the beginning. To deny such an outcome would be to deny the meaning of America itself.

Behind the civil religion at every point lie biblical archetypes: Exodus, Chosen People, Promised Land, New Jerusalem, and Sacrificial Death and Rebirth. But it is also genuinely American and genuinely new. It has its own prophets and its own martyrs, its own sacred events and sacred places, its own solemn rituals and symbols. It is concerned that America be a society as perfectly in accord with the will of God as men can make it, and a light to all the nations.

It has often been used and is being used today as a cloak for petty interests and ugly passions. It is in need—as is any living faith—of continual reformation, of being measured by universal standards. But it is not evident that it is incapable of growth and new insight.

It does not make any decision for us. It does not remove us from moral ambiguity, from being, in Lincoln's fine phrase, an "almost chosen people." But it is a heritage of moral and religious experience from which we still have much to learn as we formulate the decisions that lie ahead.

BEYOND BELIEF

# NOTES

1 Why something so obvious should have escaped serious analytical attention is in itself an interesting problem. Part of the reason is probably the controversial nature of the subject. From the earliest years of the nineteenth century, conservative religious and political groups have argued that Christianity is, in fact, the national religion. Some of them have from time to time and as recently as the 1950s proposed constitutional amendments that would explicitly recognize the sovereignty of Christ. In defending the doctrine of separation of church and state, opponents of such groups have denied that the national polity has, intrinsically, anything to do with religion at all. The moderates on this issue have insisted that the American state has taken a permissive and indeed supportive attitude toward religious groups (tax exemption, et cetera), thus favoring religion but still missing the positive institutionalization with which I am concerned. But part of the reason this issue has been left in obscurity is certainly due to the peculiarly Western concept of "religion" as denoting a single type of collectivity of which an individual can be a member of one and only one at a time. The Durkheimian notion that every group has a religious dimension, which would be seen as obvious in southern or eastern Asia, is foreign to us. This obscures the recognition of such dimensions in our society.

2 Dwight D. Eisenhower, in Will Herberg, *Protestant-Catholic-Jew* (Garden City, N.Y.: Doubleday & Co., 1955), p. 97.

3 God is mentioned or referred to in all inaugural addresses but Washington's second, which is a very brief (two paragraphs) and perfunctory acknowledgment. It is not without interest that the actual word "God" does not appear until Monroe's second inaugural, March 5, 1821. In his first inaugural, Washington refers to God as "that Almighty Being who rules the universe," "Great Author of every public and private good," "Invisible Hand," and "benign Parent of the Human Race." John Adams refers to God as "Providence," "Being who is supreme over all," "Patron of Order," "Fountain of Justice," and "Protector in all ages of the world of virtuous liberty." Jefferson speaks of "that Infinite Power which rules the destinies of the universe," and "that Being in whose

hands we are." Madison speaks of "that Almighty Being whose power regulates the destiny of nations," and "Heaven." Monroe uses "Providence" and "the Almighty" in his first inaugural and finally "Almighty God" in his second. See *Inaugural Addresses of the Presidents of the United States from George Washington 1789 to Harry S. Truman 1949,* 82d Congress, 2d Session, House Document No. 540, 1952.

4 For example, Abiel Abbot, pastor of the First Church in Haverhill, Massachusetts, delivered a Thanksgiving sermon in 1799, *Traits of Resemblance in the People of the United States of America to Ancient Israel,* in which he said, "It has been often remarked that the people of the United States come nearer to a parallel with Ancient Israel, than any other nation upon the globe. Hence 'Our American Israel' is a term frequently used; and common consent allows it apt and proper." In Hans Kohn, *The Idea of Nationalism* (New York: Macmillan Co., 1961), p. 665.

5 That the Mosaic analogy was present in the minds of leaders at the very moment of the birth of the republic is indicated in the designs proposed by Franklin and Jefferson for a seal of the United States of America. Together with Adams, they formed a committee of three delegated by the Continental Congress on July 4, 1776, to draw up the new device. "Franklin proposed as the device Moses lifting up his wand and dividing the Red Sea while Pharaoh was overwhelmed by its waters, with the motto 'Rebellion to tyrants is obedience to God.' Jefferson proposed the children of Israel in the wilderness 'led by a cloud by day and a pillar of fire at night.' " Anson Phelps Stokes, *Church and State in the United States,* vol. 1 (New York: Harper & Co., 1950), pp. 467–68.

6 Sidney E. Mead, *The Lively Experiment* (New York: Harper & Row, 1963), p. 12.

7 Abraham Lincoln, in Allan Nevins, ed., *Lincoln and the Gettysburg Address* (Urbana, Ill.: Univ. of Ill. Press, 1964), p. 39.

8 Robert Lowell, in *ibid.,* "On the Gettysburg Address," pp. 88–89.

9 William Henry Herndon, in Sherwood Eddy, *The Kingdom of God and the American Dream* (New York: Harper & Row, 1941), p. 162.

10 Karl Decker and Angus McSween, *Historic Arlington* (Washington, D.C., 1892), pp. 60–67.

11 How extensive the activity associated with Memorial Day can be is indicated by Warner: "The sacred symbolic behavior of Memorial Day, in which scores of the town's organizations are involved, is ordinarily divided into four periods. During the year separate rituals are held by many of the associations for their dead, and many of these activities are connected with later Memorial Day events. In the second phase, preparations are made during the last three or four weeks for the ceremony itself, and some of the associations perform public rituals. The

third phase consists of scores of rituals held in all the cemeteries, churches, and halls of the associations. These rituals consist of speeches and highly ritualized behavior. They last for two days and are climaxed by the fourth and last phase, in which all the separate celebrants gather in the center of the business district on the afternoon of Memorial Day. The separate organizations, with their members in uniform or with fitting insignia, march through the town, visit the shrines and monuments of the hero dead, and, finally, enter the cemetery. Here dozens of ceremonies are held, most of them highly symbolic and formalized." During these various ceremonies Lincoln is continually referred to and the Gettysburg Address recited many times. W. Lloyd Warner, *American Life* (Chicago: Univ. of Chicago Press, 1962), pp. 8–9.

12 Reinhold Niebuhr, "The Religion of Abraham Lincoln," in Nevins, ed., *op. cit.*, p. 72. William J. Wolfe of the Episcopal Theological School in Cambridge, Massachusetts, has written: "Lincoln is one of the greatest theologians of America—not in the technical meaning of producing a system of doctrine, certainly not as the defender of some one denomination, but in the sense of seeing the hand of God intimately in the affairs of nations. Just so the prophets of Israel criticized the events of their day from the perspective of the God who is concerned for history and who reveals His will within it. Lincoln now stands among God's latter-day prophets." *The Religion of Abraham Lincoln* (New York, 1963), p. 24.

13 Seymour Martin Lipset, "Religion and American Values" in *The First New Nation* (New York: Basic Books, 1964), chap. 4.

14 Alexis de Tocqueville, *Democracy in America,* vol. 1 (Garden City, N.Y.: Doubleday & Co., Anchor Books, 1954), p. 310.

15 Henry Bargy, *La Religion dans la Société aux États-Unis* (Paris, 1902), p. 31.

16 De Tocqueville, *op. cit.,* p. 311. Later he says, "In the United States even the religion of most of the citizens is republican, since it submits the truths of the other world to private judgment, as in politics the care of their temporal interests is abandoned to the good sense of the people. Thus every man is allowed freely to take that road which he thinks will lead him to heaven, just as the law permits every citizen to have the right of choosing his own government" (p. 436).

17 Lyndon B. Johnson, in U.S., *Congressional Record,* House, March 15, 1965, pp. 4924, 4926.

18 See Louis Hartz, "The Feudal Dream of the South," pt. 4, *The Liberal Tradition in America* (New York: Harcourt, Brace & Co., 1955).

19 Senator J. William Fulbright, speech of April 28, 1966, as reported in *The New York Times,* April 29, 1966.

20 Henry David Thoreau, In Yehoshua Arieli, *Individualism and Nationalism in American Ideology* (Cambridge, Mass.: Harvard Univ. Press, 1964), p. 274.

# BIBLICAL RELIGION AND SOCIAL SCIENCE IN THE MODERN WORLD

**Robert N. Bellah**

I have frequently experienced the uncomfortable disparity between the acceptance of an intellectual obligation and its fulfillment, but never more acutely than on the present occasion. Myron Bloy asked me "to compare/contrast the assumptions of the biblical worldview with those implicit in the social sciences today." Since the relation of social science and religion is something I have long been interested in, this seemed a natural and an exciting challenge. Only on further reflection did the terms of the charge seem staggering. Do I have anything like the scholarly competence to characterize the biblical worldview? Who among us could begin to catalogue the variety of disparate assumptions that can be found in the cacophony of the contemporary social sciences? I must therefore make more than a perfunctory bow in the direction of scholarly modesty. What follows can only be a few preliminary considerations toward dealing with the topic that Myron Bloy posed for me.

I would like to begin with the assertion that the assumptions of social science are the assumptions of the modern world. They came into existence together and are indissolubly interlinked. A critique of social science cannot but be simultaneously a critique of modern society and vice versa. Biblical religion has not been extruded from the modern world, though many of the prophets of modernity predicted that it would be. But biblical religion has certainly been pushed to the periphery, especially in the intellectual world where modernity has enjoyed its greatest triumphs. In some respects we can even say that in contemporary society social science has usurped the traditional position of theology. It is now social science that tells us what kind of creatures we are and what we are about on this planet. It is social science that provides us images of personal behavior and legitimations of the structures that govern us. It is to social science that the task is entrusted, so far as it is entrusted at all, of, in whatever the contemporary terms for it would be, "justifying the ways of God to man."

Of course this is not entirely the case. Our language, both public and private, is saturated with terminology that is biblical in origin. But there are very few law schools which spend much time in showing how "the laws of nature and of Nature's God" have much to do with our legal system. The latter is much more apt to be explained in terms of legal realism or legal positivism. Every president since Washington has invoked the name of God in his inaugural address, but there are very few political scientists who think that has anything to do with the American political system. The latter is much more apt to be interpreted in terms of conflicting interest groups, the dynamics of bureaucracy, or considerations having to do with political economy.

In some research on public and private commitments of middle class Americans in which I am currently involved we are finding that the language of psychology has penetrated deeply into popular usage, whether derived from Sigmund Freud or Fritz Perls.[1] Politically concerned citizens with whom we have talked depend implicitly on social science to construct their arguments whether they are free enterprise enthusiasts or are working for "economic democracy." It is true that biblical language is not absent. We have come across those among whom biblical words like faith and love still inform personal existence. And we have talked to some whose political commitments seem to derive more from biblical prophecy than from Milton Friedman or Karl Marx. But often the biblical and the contemporary sociological or psychological terminologies are hopelessly confused, and it does not always seem that the biblical discourse carries the determining weight. Nevertheless the presence of communities and practices still oriented to biblical religion in our society is a fact of great importance to which I will return.

There is a mainstream in social science just as there is a mainstream in modern liberal capitalist society. There have been rebellions and critiques of the mainstream, in philosophy, art and politics, that have had their social scientific counterparts. Indeed the greatest figures in modern social science are ambivalent toward the mainstream and are among its most somber critics. I am thinking not only of Marx but of Freud, Durkheim and Weber. Yet the mainstream has carried the day and informs the presuppositions and the practices of most working social scientists. Intellectually, mainstream social science is derived from seventeenth century English social thought and the French Enlightenment. Charles Taylor characterized the Enlightenment version as "a view of man as the subject of egoistic desires, for which nature and society

---

1. The project is entitled "The Moral Basis of Social Commitment in America" and is funded by the National Endowment for the Humanities and the Ford and Rockefeller Foundations. The field researchers are Richard Madsen, William Sullivan, Ann Swidler and Steven Tipton. Also see Steven Tipton, *Getting Saved from the Sixties*, University of California Press, forthcoming.

provided merely the means to fulfillment. It was a philosophy which was utilitarian in its ethical outlook, atomistic in its social philosophy, analytic in its science of man, and which looked to a scientific social engineering to reorganize man and society and bring men happiness through perfect mutual adjustment."[2] While "perfect mutual adjustment" seems a bit beyond our grasp just now, this characterization would be remarkably apt for most members not only of American faculties of social science but of professional schools as well.

The assumptions underlying mainstream social science can be briefly listed: positivism, reductionism, relativism and determinism.[3] I am not saying that working social scientists could give a good philosophical defense of these assumptions, or even that they are fully conscious of holding them. I mean to refer only to, in a descriptive sense, their prejudices, their pre-judgments about the nature of reality. By positivism I mean no more than the assumption that the methods of natural science are the only approach to valid knowledge, and the corollary that social science differs from natural science only in maturity and that the two will become ever more alike. By reductionism I mean the tendency to explain the complex in terms of the simple and to find behind complex cultural forms biological, psychological or sociological drives, needs and interests. By relativism I mean the assumption that matters of morality and religion, being explicable by particular constellations of psychological and sociological conditions, cannot be judged true or false, valid or invalid, but simply vary with persons, cultures and societies. By determinism I do not mean any sophisticated philosophical view, but only the tendency to think that human actions are explained in terms of "variables" that will account for them.

Most social scientists do not think of these assumptions as conflicting with the assumptions of biblical religion. The assumptions are so self-evidently true that they are beyond contradiction. Biblical religion, being "unscientific," could have no reality claim in any case, though as a private belief or practice it may by some be admitted to have a "psychological" truth. Yet these assumptions conflict, and conflict sharply, not only with biblical religion but with every one of the great traditional religions and philosophies of mankind. For social science, in these regards embodying the very ethos of modernity, there is no cosmos,

---

2. Charles Taylor, *Hegel and Modern Society*, Cambridge University Press, 1979. This book is drawn largely from Taylor's much more comprehensive *Hegel*, Cambridge University Press, 1979, but is a remarkably powerful treatment of certain aspects of modernity in itself.
3. This list is drawn in part from E. F. Schumacher, *Small is Beautiful: Economics as if People Mattered*, Harper and Row, 1973, and is somewhat differently developed in my essay "Faith Communities Challenge – and are Challenged by – the Changing World Order," in Joseph Gremillion and William Ryan, eds., *World Faiths and the New World Order*, Interreligious Peace Colloquium, 1978.

that is, no whole relative to which human action makes sense. There is, of course, no God, or any other "ultimate" reality, but there is no nature either in the traditional sense of a creation or expression of transcendent reality. Similarly no social relationship can have any sacramental quality. No social form can reflect or be infused with a divine or cosmological significance. Rather every social relationship can be explained in terms of its social or psychological utility. Finally, though the social scientist says a lot about the "self," he has nothing to say about the soul. The very notion of soul entails a divine or cosmological context that is missing in modern thought. To put the contrast in another way, the traditionally religious view found the world intrinsically meaningful. The drama of personal and social existence was lived out in the context of continual cosmic and spiritual meaning. The modern view finds the world intrinsically meaningless, endowed with meaning only by individual actors, and the societies they construct, for their own ends.

Most social scientists would politely refuse to discuss the contrasts just mentioned. They would profess no ill will toward biblical or any other kind of religion. They are largely unaware of the degree to which what they teach and write undermines all traditional thought and belief. Unlike an earlier generation of iconoclasts they feel no mission to undermine "superstition." They would consider the questions raised above to be, simply, "outside my field," and would refer one to philosophers, humanists or students of religion to discuss them. So fragmented is our intellectual life, even in the best universities, that such questions are apt never to be raised. That does not mean that they are not implicitly answered.

Christians have not always been clear about the contrast between their faith and modern ideology, either. Some have accepted without quite realizing it the assumptions of empiricism and positivism and tried to prove biblical faith on scientific grounds, as in the current creationist controversy. We call them fundamentalists. Others, liberal Christians, have tried to believe there is perfect harmony between biblical religion and modern thought and have even gratefully accepted the idea that their religion has only psychological or sociological truth. Yet from the very beginning of the modern era there have been those, like Pascal, who have seen the enormity of the problem.

It is interesting how clearly John Winthrop, writing before *Leviathan* was published in 1651, saw the contrast between Christianity and what will be fundamental tenets of modern social thought. Let us consider the contrasts he draws between two conceptions of love and freedom, basic issues for both Christianity and social science. In 1630 he wrote that Christians are members of one body in Christ and that the "ligamentes of this body which knitt together are love." This love gives Christians a "sensiblenes and Sympathy of each others Condicions," to the extent that they not only bear each other's burdens but are willing to lay down their lives for one another. But then Winthrop adds:

> The next consideracion is how this love comes to be wrought; Adam in his first estate was a perfect modell of mankinde in all their generacions, and in him this love was perfected in regard of the habit, but Adam Rent in himselfe from his Creator, rent all his posterity alsoe one from another, whence it comes that every man is borne with this principle in him, to love and seeke himselfe only and thus a man continueth till Christ comes and takes possession of the soule, and infuseth another principle love to God and our brother.[4]

With respect to liberty Winthrop makes a comparable contrast, writing this time in 1745:

> There is a liberty of corrupt nature, which is affected both by men and beasts, to do what they list; and this liberty is inconsistent with authority, impatient of all restraint; by this liberty *sumus omnes deteriores;* 'tis the grand enemy of truth and peace, and all the ordinances of God are bent against it. But there is a civil, a moral, a federal liberty, which is the proper end and object of authority; it is a liberty for that only which is just and good; for this liberty you are to stand with the hazard of your very lives; and whatsoever crosses it is not authority but a distemper thereof.[5]

Winthrop thus contrasts love of brother to love of oneself alone and freedom to do what one lists with freedom to do only that which is just and good.

But Hobbes in *Leviathan,* the basic if often unrecognized textbook of contemporary social science, portrays precisely an atomistic man rent from God and from all other men, who loves and seeks himself only. His freedom certainly is to do what he lists, for "just" and "good" are only names that men give to what they desire. Winthrop knew what was coming, so to speak, because Hobbes' portrait of man is so similar to Augustine's picture of natural man in his *City of God.* What was new in Hobbes, and would be true in modern thought ever after, is the idea that such fallen, corrupt men (in the traditional view) could construct a good, indeed an excellent society, relying neither on divine reason or guidance, but on their own devices (and social science) alone.

---

4. From "A Model of Christian Charity" in Edmund S. Morgan, ed., *Puritan Political Ideas 1558-1794,* Bobbs-Merrill, 1965, pp. 84-86.
5. From a speech by Winthrop in 1745 in the General Court following his acquittal from impeachment in the office of Deputy Governor as contained in Cotton Mather's "*Nehemias Americanus.* The Life of John Winthrop, Esq., Governor of the Massachusetts Colony," reprinted in Sacvan Bercovitch, *The Puritan Origins of the American Self,* Yale University Press, 1975, p. 200. It is interesting that Tocqueville, in quoting the same passage from the Mather biography, omits the phrase "and whatsoever crosses it is not authority but a distemper thereof." Alexis de Tocqueville, *Democracy in America,* tr. by George Lawrence, Anchor Books, 1969, p. 46.

We should not forget, of course, that Hobbes had good reason to be suspicious of just such men as John Winthrop. Christians have often in history been arrogant and willing to inflict their views on others at great cost to those with whom they differed, as Winthrop on occasion was and as Augustine was. Hobbes understood very well freedom to do what one lists and how to manage it but he was acutely anxious about the subversive potentialities of a freedom which men assert is to do the just and good and for which they are willing to lay down their lives. Sectarian fanaticism seemed to him one of the most potent sources of the English civil wars. Relative to Christian arrogance he offered his own lower view of man as more realistic and practical. It had, however, its own potentiality for arrogance and distortion.

It was Hobbes who indelibly introduced the natural science model into social thought. But to the extent that traditional practical reason now became social science, the moral bond between the theorist and those he studies was broken. The social scientist is rent, morally, because of the purely cognitive natural science model, from those he studies. The results can be destructive indeed, as in what Edward Shils calls technological sociology:

> The manipulative conception of man and society entails the perception of the object of manipulation of a discrete entity having no social relationship with the manipulator except with regard to the manipulative actions themselves. It denies the object's capacities for and claims for moral regard by the manipulating person . . .
>
> The technological self-interpretation of man and society accepts either a mechanistic, conventionally behavioristic conception of man as incapable of valid reasoning and as unable to make choices guided by moral standards. Or it sees them as capable of rational decisions based on scientific knowledge and obdurately resistant to considerations of moral obligation.
>
> A sociology which conforms entirely to either of the divergent postulates of the technology of control is one which sees the relationship between controller and controlled as wholly devoid of any moral and cultural content . . .[6]

Freedom, in the sense of freedom to do what one lists, essentially following one's desires and interests, has been linked to manipulative control throughout the history of modern thought, from Hobbes to B. F. Skinner by way of Mandeville, Adam Smith, *The Federalist Papers*, and many others. Personal passions, even quite base ones, can be channeled, by way of proper social engineering (even the free market requires its structures) so as to produce a good society. Private vice, as Mandeville

6. Edward Shils, *The Calling of Sociology and Other Essays on the Pursuit of Learning*, University of Chicago Press, 1980, p. 36.

put it, can render public benefit. Both capitalist economics and liberal politics were based on that view.

It is perhaps less interesting to contrast the theoretical premises of this modern view of man and society with those of traditional religion than it is to look at their consequences in practice. What kind of human beings are these atomized individuals each pursuing his or her own utility that the new society, embodying what Louis Dumont calls "the triumph of economic ideology,"[7] produces? They have been anxiously described by many of the greatest thinkers since the eighteenth century: Rousseau, Hegel, Tocqueville, Marx, Nietzsche. Perhaps no one has given us a more careful or a more sober portrait than Tocqueville in *Democracy in America*. Tocqueville was greatly concerned that Americans, archetypal representatives of the new society, were abandoning all heroic, spiritual or aesthetic goals for the sheer pursuit of material comfort. In a description that applies, if anything, more to us today than 150 years ago, he says that in America there are:

> . . . more and more people who though neither rich nor powerful enough to have much hold over others, have gained or kept enough wealth and enough understanding to look after their own needs. Such folk owe no man anything and hardly expect anything from anybody. They form the habit of thinking of themselves in isolation and imagine that their whole destiny is in their own hands.

Forgetting ancestors, unable to think of descendents and isolated from contemporaries, "each man is forever thrown back on himself alone, and there is danger that he may be shut up in the solitude of his own heart."[8] Tocqueville feared that a society of such isolated self-regarding individuals would be unable to sustain free institutions and would fall victim to despotism, a form of manipulation which from Hobbes on was always in the background. In the TV series "Dallas" this ethos of self-regarding individualism reaches a kind of culmination, and the overtones of despotism are quite explicit.

But Tocqueville does not believe that atomistic utilitarianism is the whole story in America. He explicitly points to John Winthrop and the tradition descending from him as mitigating the destructive implications of America's economic passion. It is precisely through religiously based *mores*, "habits of the heart,"[9] that self-interest could be mitigated and socialized. Tocqueville argued that it was only the presence of a vital religious life based on very different premises, supporting, for example, public cooperation for the common good, that gave him any hope for

7. Louis Dumont, *From Mandeville to Marx: the Genesis and Triumph of Economic Ideology*, University of Chicago Press, 1977.
8. Tocqueville, p. 508.
9. Tocqueville, p. 287.

America. Hegel too felt that bourgeois "civil society" would be self-destructive without the presence of *Sittlichkeit*, concrete ethical obligations quite comparable to Tocqueville's *mores*.[10] We can ask whether biblical religion today still can provide what William Sullivan calls the "moral ecology" to control our self-destructive tendencies.[11] But first we must consider a more radical alternative.

From relatively early on the emergence of modern society and its social scientific ideology has aroused profound antipathies and revulsions. Rousseau was convinced that bourgeois man could never be a citizen and proposed instead the ancient *polis* revived in modern form and based on a general will that would unite the whole. The French Revolution, that may in some of its expressions have been more inspired by Rousseau than historians have recently thought, was both the triumph of the bourgeoisie and a strange critique of it, with its almost inhuman attempt at a reign of virtue. Romanticism, partly inspired by Rousseau, spawned a wide array of artistic, spiritual, intellectual and ultimately political assaults on modernity.[12]

One tendency which appeared in the Romantic era was a desire to cancel the whole project of modernity and return to the hierarchical organic unity of the Middle Ages. This appealed not only to artists and poets but to a variety of Christians, some of whom were militantly reactionary, but others of whom were genuinely searching for a life of simple dignity, close to the soil, and characterized by the pleasure of artistic and craft creations.

Another tendency was to assert primordial loyalties of blood, language and culture, that seemed about to be swept away by the free market and the culture of universal scientific utility. Some of those reacting in this way were defending the legitimate claims of particular cultural loyalties in the face of modern economic and scientific abstractness. But some would follow this tendency into an ardent nationalism that would consume all other values and eventually lead to the twentieth century phenomenon of fascism.

A more complex reaction developed from the thought of Hegel. Following the dialectical logic of Hegel, Marx, the greatest exemplar of this tendency, sought not to deny the modern project and return to some earlier epoch or some particularistic loyalty. Rather he wanted to accept the chief features of modernity, including industrial production, technology and science, but move to a new form of society that would

---

10. Taylor in *Hegel and Modern Society*, p. 118, makes the comparison between Tocqueville and Hegel but does not make explicit the equation of *mores* and *Sittlichkeit*.
11. Sullivan develops his notion of moral ecology in his *Reconstructing Public Philosophy*, University of California Press, forthcoming.
12. Taylor's discussion of Romanticism in *Hegel and Modern Society*, *passim*, is especially helpful.

replace atomistic individualism with a new free form of social unity. Marx developed an elaborate analysis that I cannot reproduce here. Greatly simplifying, it involves the transition from the subjective dependency of pre-capitalist (feudal) society to the subjective independence but objective dependence (on the structures of capitalist production) of bourgeois society to the subjectively social and universal individuality of socialism.[13] Instead of the alienated pursuit of wealth, socialism will bring a multiplex self-realization. As Marx says,

> [W]hen the limited bourgeois form is stripped away, what is wealth other than the universality of individual needs, capacities, pleasures, productive forces, etc., created through universal exchange? The full development of human mastery over the forces of nature, those of so-called nature as well as humanity's own nature? The absolute working out of his creative potentialities, with no presupposition other than the previous historic development which makes this totality of development, i.e., the development of all human powers as such the end in itself, not as measured on a *predetermined* yardstick?[14]

That sounds more like Marin County in California than the Soviet Union. Unfortunately the manipulative potentialities of modern society that slipped into socialism along with industrialization, technology and science, have reached a degree of intensity in Soviet society only rivaled by that other revolt against modernity, Nazi Germany.

Certainly the effort to "overcome the modern" (*kindai o chōkoku suru*), as the Japanese ideologists of the early 1940's put it, has produced some of the greatest pathological disturbances of the twentieth century.[15] The Chinese cultural revolution, in its effort to oppose "taking the capitalist road," instituted a reign of virtue that was also a reign of terror whose final destructiveness for Chinese society we are only now beginning to see.[16]

And yet the problem persists. Sheer defense of the modern project may be a hopeless enterprise. Mainstream modern society expressed in liberal capitalism and interest-group politics, and rationalized by the individualistic utilitarianism of modern economics and much of the rest of social science, seems bent on the destruction of the conditions of its existence, the context or moral ecology that Tocqueville and Hegel thought were necessary for its survival. Daniel Bell has well described the failure

---

13. This discussion is indebted to Carol C. Gould, *Marx's Social Ontology: Individuality and Community in Marx's Theory of Social Reality*, MIT Press, 1978, Chapter 1.
14. Karl Marx, *Grundrisse: Foundation of the Critique of Political Economy*, tr. by M. Nicolaus, Vintage Books, 1973, p. 488; cited by Gould, p. 25.
15. See my essay, "Japan's Cultural Identity: Some Reflections on the Work of Watsuji Tetsuro," *The Journal of Asian Studies*, Vol. 24, No. 4, 1965, pp. 573-594.
16. See Richard Madsen, *The Moral Basis of Political Activism in Rural China*, University of California Press, forthcoming.

of commitment that today characterizes all the advanced industrial societies as

> the loss of *civitas*, that spontaneous willingness to obey the law, to respect the rights of others, to forgo the temptations of private enrichment at the expense of the public weal — in short, to honor the "city" of which one is a member. Instead, each man goes his own way, pursuing his private vices, which can be indulged only at the expense of public benefits.[17]

Bell's inversion of Mandeville suggests how the whole modern project comes apart when its moral ecology is destroyed.

And it is hard to see how a culture that systematically deprives the cosmos, nature, society and the person of any intrinsic meaning or sacrality, which declares that the only truth of the human condition is the desires and fears of individuals, and that the only formula for social harmony is the systematic manipulation of those desires and fears, could do anything but destroy moral ecology and provoke periodic revolts and outbursts of ferocity and destructiveness. Under these circumstances what do adherents of traditional religions who have never wholly accepted the terms of modern ideology, or to speak more directly, what do Christians do under these circumstances?

One approach is to continue the search for a third way that will overcome the defects of modernity, reassert some of the virtues of traditional society but neither reject the achievements of modern reason nor reassert the oppressive features of traditional society.[18] Since the efforts to find a radically new solution to the impasse of modernity are themselves in part secular expressions of Christian apocalypticism it is natural that such alternatives would continue to have a Christian appeal, as in the liberation theologies of Latin America and elsewhere. The catastrophic failure of most of these efforts so far to do anything but exacerbate the worst features of modernity should give us pause. We might also ask about the fact that if few of the architects of modern utilitarian individualism have been believers, so very few of the critics of modernity have been. Most of them have been profoundly doubtful of the value or relevance of traditional religion in the modern world, even the most sympathetic of them, such as Hegel and Tocqueville.[19] Does this mean that Christians should exclude themselves from the search for a viable alter-

17. Daniel Bell, *The Cultural Contradictions of Capitalism*, Basic Books, 1976, p. 245. Chapter 6 of this book, "The Public Household," is particularly germane to the themes of this essay.
18. Roberto Mangabeira Unger in his *Knowledge and Politics*, Free Press, 1975, gives a helpful recent interpretation of the problem, trying to give some descriptive depth to a possible form of society that would move beyond and incorporate the positive features of traditional and modern societies.
19. Hegel was suspicious mainly of Catholicism. Tocqueville wondered at the frequent appearance of a contrast "between Christian virtue and what I call public virtue." From a letter of July 20, 1856, quoted by Marvin Zetterbaum, *Tocqueville and the Problem of Democracy*, Stanford University Press, 1975, p.50.

native to the self-destructiveness that seems endemic in modern society? Not at all, but it probably does mean that Christians should devote themselves to that search with caution and detachment, not forgetting that in even the best of societies we will be as strangers and wayfarers. Such an attitude may provide just the reservation against total commitment that could help future efforts to find a third way from becoming as idolatrous and destructive as past ones.

But for Americans in particular we might ask whether the more modest traditional role of biblical religion in providing a moral ecology that would mitigate the worst features of modern society is still viable. To the extent possible I think that Christians should continue to try to provide that moral context. But we should be clear about the increasing difficulties, and even while we continue our traditional functions in American society we need to undertake a much deeper and more searching criticism of our society than we have ever made before, one that does not ignore what social sciences has to say but one that will be ethically and theologically informed. The first thing to be aware of is how much the traditional role of Christianity in America is already undermined. There has been a long tradition of ethically and spiritually narrow criticism of certain aspects of modern American society that today is particularly widespread among self-styled Christians such as the Moral Majority. What is sad about them is not only that their anti-intellectualism deprives them of the tools to understand the society in which they live, but that while they oppose vehemently certain symptoms of our corruption, they may contribute fundamentally to its worsening. This they do by a politics that strengthens our amoral majority that is bent on the elimination of the last vestiges of our life as a covenant people genuinely concerned with all its members.

For the liberal churches which have always had far more cultural and social influence than their fundamentalist brethren there are other dangers. For one thing the ideology of secular modernism has won away large portions of the youth of these churches in the last 30 years, in part because of the influence of college education, the missionary outpost of modern culture, which has become available to a much higher percentage of our middle class than ever before.[20] Even more insidious is the invasion of that culture into our lives even when we explicitly deny its central tenets. We cannot avoid radical secular individualism simply by ideological critique. It is much more than an ideology; it is a way of life. It resonates with our economy, our political system, even with the way

20. On this point see particularly Dean R. Hoge and David A. Roozen, eds., *Understanding Church Growth and Decline 1950-1978*, Pilgrim Press, 1979. Hoge argues in Chapter 8 that the mainline liberal churches have not lost membership but have failed to gain the commitment of many of the children of their now aging membership.

we organize our private lives. It is rooted in wholly unconscious preconceptions and practices that pervade us even when we wish ardently that this were not the case. Therefore not only a profound intellectual criticism but an alternative lifestyle may be necessary for us to withstand the pressures to be absorbed into a system that we cannot accept and remain faithful to our religious calling.

We live in a social system that tells us, not just verbally but in the daily practice of life, that we are alone, that we are here to pursue our own interests, that neither anyone nor anything can save us except ourselves. It tells us that we must mistrust every noble impulse we feel because it must be only a form of our own self-seeking. We live in a society where a book entitled *Looking Out for Number One* was a best seller for many weeks and has spawned a whole series of successful imitations. Intellectuals seldom read or mention works of such vulgarity, though they may be telling us something of great importance about our society. But even a distinguished philosophical work like John Rawls' *Theory of Justice* premises the radically self-interested individual as the necessary starting point. Though Rawls' argument far transcends that framework, he believes that to be convincing that is where he must start. That fact is as culturally telling as is Robert Ringer's book.

What I am describing is not simply an ideology but a whole set of social practices and institutions that breed, support and reinforce it. The belief in the isolated self is reinforced by what happens to us in our daily experience. Together with the full stomach has come the empty soul. For many our freedom is contentless and our daily life barren of meaning. The research project referred to above has found that for many Americans occupation causes psychic isolation. Work lacks the articulation with a larger organic society that it often has in other cultures and civilizations. Instead work creates a boredom from which one seeks to escape if one is on the lower rungs or if one is on the higher rungs it often requires a degree of anxious self-manipulation from which one desperately seeks relief whenever possible. Above all work does not provide a way to tie one into larger structures of meaning and participation. Public life outside of work is often equally if not more barren, consisting of encounters either with the market, where virtually everything from the most private to the most material needs can be met by the payment of money, or with large impersonal bureaucracies that one learns at best to manipulate. We are studying that still sizeable minority of Americans who resist the tendency to locate real life in one's own living room in front of the TV screen. There are millions still struggling in one way or another to make a public life in America possible, but the cost is high and "burnout" a constant theme among those who are publicly active.

What life in this extraordinarily rich society lacks above all is what traditional cultures have: that round of meaningful action that ties them into society, nature and the cosmos. For us it is not only nature that has become cold, lifeless and abstract. Society too is cold, lifeless and abstract. Even intimate relations grow more and more calculating. One of the things my research group did not expect is that the word *love* is viewed with suspicion among many of the people we are studying. Love is seen as dangerous because it threatens the autonomy and independence of the individual.

Cumulatively the pressures and tensions of our way of life are very great and require certain reactions in order for us to stay alive and functioning at all. One increasingly important reaction is to alleviate the greyness and deadness of one's daily life by a stress on purely private inner experience.

Owen Barfield points to the eighteenth century as a time when subjective experience was beginning to be emphasized as expressed in the appearance of such words as *interesting, entertaining* and *exhilarating.*[21] These words, he tells us, point to inner states with no necessary correlate with anything in the external world. Our research is finding an advanced stage of the same tendency. The words that come up again and again in our interviews are *feeling, creative* and *creativity, aliveness, excitement,* and *energy.* Increasingly we come across rather cryptic phrases like *to get it* or onomatopoetic expressions like *zing.* What is striking is that we are discovering a private world of great intensity and no content whatever. There is a vehement insistence on selfhood but it is an absolutely empty self; except for the sheer quantity of excitation there is nothing there at all. Symbolic, ethical or religious content terms get swallowed up in the language or psychic process. *Creative* for example would certainly be used more circumspectly in a society that deeply believed in God as the real creator. Among us *creative* tends to be a contentless quality pointing to the intensity of inner experience.

The extreme individualism of our culture entails a functional, though not always an ethical, egalitarianism. Individuals are both absolutely unique and absolutely interchangeable. There are no organic connections between them that would allow for an ethically meaningful hierarchy. Functions are different and some may supervise others but there is no sense of a whole of which all are parts. There are also no standards from which an ethical hierarchy could be deduced. No unique individual can be judged by any other. There can be no notion of noble and base. My sensations are as good as your sensations and who is to say

21. Owen, Barfield, "Language, Evolution of Consciousness, and the Recovery of Human Meaning," *Teacher's College Record,* Vol. 82, No. 3, Spring 1981, pp.-427-433.

anything about better or worse. We maximize individual choice beyond what any traditional society has ever done and then we deny all objective standards of choice. Choice is finally completely private. We stress human rights as our most sacred belief but we define rights as the absence of external limits on individual decision. The ultimate right becomes the right to commit suicide. Who is to tell me I shouldn't?

While this whole system obviously works and a complete collapse is not in sight, the level of dissatisfaction is clearly on the rise. It isn't working very well and all the signs are that it is going to be working less well in the years ahead. If, then, we are not moving into a utopia of human happiness and fulfillment, if indeed our society is less and less capable of giving people a sense of meaning about who they are in relation to the world in which they live, how can religious communities make any difference? To the extent that the religious communities are themselves pervaded by the ethos of utilitarian individualism and the desacralized world view that supports it, and it is hard not to be when one's daily life is based on those premises, then there is little they can do. To the extent, however, that religious communities can retain or recover a sense of being in but not of this world, can live, at least to some extent, in patterns of voluntary simplicity and mutual concern, then they may act as genuine alternatives to the prevailing current.

I am not suggesting that Christians or followers of other traditional religions abandon the larger society and try to save only themselves, as some sectarians of various faiths are indeed doing. Christians have contributed centrally to every great movement for social reform in American history. It is still possible, as our situation worsens, that drastic reforms in our economic and political life may occur, probably as a result of a large scale social movement and a spiritual awakening, as has been the case before in America.[22] Certainly all our intelligence as well as all our faith deserve to be committed to that end.

It is also possible, however, that modern society is not going to solve its problems, that it will sink into a time of protracted troubles with regression along many dimensions. Such periods have not been few in human history. Some of our ablest observers, such as Robert Heilbroner,[23] are close to predicting such an outcome. In that event too there is much to be done by the faithful. As corruption widens it is more than ever necessary that there be demonstration communities where elementary decencies can be maintained and handed down, humanizing a

22. See William G. McLoughlin's valuable essay *Revivals, Awakenings and Reform*, Chicago University Press, 1978.
23. Robert L. Heilbroner, *An Inquiry into the Human Prospect*, Norton, 1974.

bad situation as long as it exists, and providing seedbeds for larger efforts at social amelioration when that becomes possible.

As our society fails to realize the promises upon which it was launched several centuries ago it may be possible to question, even in the central citadels of intellectual life, the basic assumptions of the modern project. As a first step it might be possible to reclaim the idea of practical reason as the true calling of social science. Somewhere further on, a practical reason rejoined to the ecstatic reason of religious insight might even appear.

## TIDBALL: Response to Bellah

Professor Bellah has expressed certainly clearly and, I think, rather poignantly, a point of view which I suspect all of us hold or have held, more or less, at one time or another: namely, that modernity has rendered us isolated from a biblical perspective, from a congruence between our religious beliefs and our work, and from each other. He is in mourning, so to speak, and that arouses in me a desire to comfort. I hear Job not only running out of patience but also running out of hope. I would that my words might provide more assistance than those of Elihu as I attempt to speak to our common concerns!

Professor Bellah's presentation called to my mind the work of such social scientists as Freud, Piaget, Erikson, Kohlberg and, more recently, Levinson. Each in his own way has told the story of human development which may be summarized, albeit sketchily, by saying that, except for the first year of life, the process is one of continual individuation in the name of developing autonomous thinking, clear decision making, and responsible action as the hallmarks of adulthood. Psychosocial and moral maturity thus come to be defined in terms of an autonomous life of work in which moral dilemmas are resolved through the universal ethical principle of justice.

Professor Bellah suggests that there has been steady progress toward maturity in these terms: he states that our society has become one which is atomistic, in which people feel isolated from one another, and in which it is every man for himself. There is, indeed, a lack of context, for the great minds of these most influential researchers and practitioners have been telling us for many years that our goal should be, and is in fact becoming, a maturity characterized by the firm ego boundaries of separateness. We may feel bereft, but we should not be startled at our current condition.

But I believe there is still promise for us all, that there is hope available in our midst without having to look to the establishment of separate communities which will preserve and carry forward alternative goals for living and working with each other. In its broadest sense, that third way, that alternative community, already exists and has existed for a very long time. It is now a matter of recognizing, affirming and incorporating into our collective life many of the insights and modalities long known within this alternative lifestyle.

I refer to the area of experience, now "legitimized" by the research of such thoughtful and articulate scholars as Block, Gilligan and Chodorow, the experience of women. Women's development has proceeded along a rather different path. This different path has been both a curse and a blessing: a curse because "different" in our world has tended to connote inferior, incomplete or maladapted; a "blessing" because it has not only provided strength and courage to women but also because it holds promise for both men and women in the days to come. My optimism springs from the fact that the story of women's development is the story of a thriving moral ecology, that critical world view which Professor Bellah longs for but finds missing in our collective modern life.

The latter researchers I have mentioned have been dedicated not merely to documenting women's life experience; additionally they have been laboring to gain an understanding of women's place in the prevailing view of the human life cycle. Briefly stated, they have found that women's development proceeds from early dependence (as is true for men), not so much toward separation and autonomy but rather toward the mutuality of interdependence. Attachment, rather than separateness, is the central theme and the organizing focus. The importance of context more than abstraction leads women toward the universal ethical principle of nonviolence as evidenced by care, rather than to that of perfect justice. Responsibility for self and others regularly informs women's moral judgments as contrasted with men's concerns for individual's rights. Indeed, again and again, we find maturity for men described in terms that consider the individual as primary, while, for women, it is the relationship that is so.

The chief element, then, that characterizes women's experience and distinguishes it from men's is that of context: women's mode of thinking and doing is contextual and inductive rather than formal and abstract. Embedded as women are in the fabric of relationships, they thus have much to teach us about life's meaning, about success, work and love, and about spiritual development.

If we are in need of a moral ecology, and I agree with Professor Bellah that we are, then let us encourage and listen to a different voice, a complementary voice, a voice that speaks from a long history of living an alternative lifestyle, the voice of woman that knows it is possible, even in the modern world, to establish meaningful relationships with others, with nature and with the cosmos.

## HANDLIN: Response to Bellah

My comments will be brief not only because of the hour but also because Professor Bellah's statement leaves me puzzled, with more questions than answers. He isolates the problem of modernity in individualism (atomistic and utilitarian), and relates many of the least lovely manifestations of our society to that series of traits associated with individuals.

What puzzles me is this: He is quite right when he points to Toqueville as the critic who attached this label, "modernity," to American society. But when Toqueville's book appeared in English translation, Americans did not know what he was talking about, lacking an American or English equivalent for "individualism," and simply adopted the French word. Yet the United States was the prototypical society, moving in the direction of individualism, although its people could not even name the concept.

The other problem I have is this: Professor Bellah contrasts atomistic individualism with more traditional societies in which there is a fixed round of life and a known set of meanings. I suppose John Winthrop's Bible Commonwealth was an illustration of that kind of traditionally oriented society. Yet, a kind of individualism prevailed even in that society, indeed in many Christian societies, and we ought not to overlook it. Among the reasons why Winthrop and the other Puritans objected to and finally expelled Anne Hutchinson was that they believed her guilty of the heresy of mortalism, and that is the belief that the soul expired at death and would cease to exist until the final resurrection. To people like Winthrop, this was a horrible heresy because it detached the individual who was responsible for his acts in this life from the soul in an afterlife where rewards and punishments would come. Denial of the identity of the individual and of his immortal soul, detached the consequences of present actions from the standards of the community. However integrated communities were in the Christian past, they always consisted of individuals, brothers who lived side by side, but with some destined for perdition and others for salvation. Now that's a kind of individualism, too, I believe, associated in the 19th century and later with many strands in Western thought that have a significance not quite of that utilitarian form of which Professor Bellah spoke.

So I'm left with a lot of questions. Certainly the unlovely aspects of our society to which Professor Bellah refers are repulsive, but are they really aspects of individualism or that isolated self? Are they aspects of a particular manifestation of individualism, that kind of utilitarian weighing of actions in terms of interest and advantage, or are they not really relevant to individualism at all, but relevant to the dominance in our society of materialistic, sensate impulses which could operate in a communal fashion as negatively as they could operate in isolated individualism?

## BROWN: Response to Bellah

Five minutes does not allow time to do much by way of thanking the author for a stimulating paper, but I want to express personal gratitude for much stretching in ways that are exhilarating as well as uncomfortable.

I will raise three points in ascending order of importance, which I have been able to identify by the alliterative sequence of a quibble, a query and a quandary.

1. The quibble. Professor Bellah proposes that one resolution for Christians is the search for a way that will "reassert some of the virtues of traditional society but neither reject the achievements of modern reason nor reassert the oppressive features of traditional society." He says most such efforts have resulted in "catastrophic failure" (which may be true), and cites Latin American liberation theology as an example of such failure (which may be false). My own reaction is that these third world attempts at a politically and economically responsible theology are among the few signs of hope for the churches on the contemporary scene, and if the point seems worth pursuing I would appreciate an indication of reasons for the charge.

Footnote to the quibble: Professor Bellah suggests that if Christians pursue such paths, they had best do so "with caution and detachment," and maintain "a reservation against total commitment." I appreciate those strictures as important safeguards against the idolatry of new structures – something against which new movements always need to be alerted – but I would suggest that in relation to ecclesiastical structures those virtues soon become vices. While Professor Bellah's own life is anything but one of timidity, I am a little worried that people in the churches might hear him as apparently counseling timidity, and using his advice as ways to avoid the more reckless engagement that is surely needed by our churches today.

2. The query. In his helpful delineation of the underlying assumptions of mainstream social science, Professor Bellah cites "relativism" as one of these, defining it as the view that "matters of morality and religion . . . cannot be judged true or false, valid or invalid, but simply vary with persons, cultures and societies." I am sure this is widespread in *academe*. My query is this: is there not a possibility that such views are going to unravel simply because of their own inner inconsistences, as they are *forced* to confront a world "out there" that will not allow the luxury of such aloof speculation? I am reminded of a comment years ago by Bertrand Aussel, no friend of objective absolute values, who nevertheless said, "I confess that I am bothered by a conclusion that torture is wrong only because I happen to have a personal dislike of it." Does not the nature of our modern world, where such things as torture, let alone starvation and war, are of incomparable magnitude, mean that those who stand in the mainstream of social scientific detachment, can no longer occupy that citadel, and will be increasingly on the defensive, rather than representing a worldview on the ascendancy? If the response continues to be, "Such matters are outside my field," then finally the only appropriate response will be, "So much the worse for your field."

3. A quandary. Here I want not so much to direct a question at Professor Bellah as to struggle with him, for I am much attracted by what seems to me a major thrust of the paper, namely his proposal that an appropriate Christian response to the dilemmas he describes may be the creation of alternate community structures, or at least alternative life styles. These would provide, as he initially states it, "ways to avoid being absorbed into a system we cannot accept," a theme made more explicit a few pages later as the adoption of patterns of "voluntary simplicity and mutual concern," and becoming still more explicit later on as the task of becoming "demonstration communities where elementary decencies can be maintained and handed down, humanizing a bad situation as long as it exists, and providing seedbeds for larger efforts at social amelioration when that becomes possible."

I find this alternative an attractive one. The idea of impacting society from within – during the era of David Stockman, Alexander Haig and Caspar Weinberger – seems to me an increasingly vain hope, and the notion of the creation of alternative models is at least one way to plan for the future. So my quandary is: what are the next extrapolations of this proposal? Each reference within the paper is more explicit than the preceding one; what would the details of alternative life styles begin to look like on p. 24 or p. 32, if we had been privileged to have that much further input from Professor Bellah?

## RICOEUR: Response to Bellah

I would like to limit my remarks to the epistemological side of Professor Bellah's paper since my colleagues have focused on the themes of personal and social commitment. More specifically, I want to address myself to this paper as a contribution to the theory of the social sciences in relation to the assumptions of the Christian point of view.

I see three interesting points along this line of thought. First, a critique of the social sciences as an extension of the natural sciences – and I think that for this purpose the paper is very strong – in order to show that it is a wrong assumption in the social sciences to think that they can be value-free (to use an expression of Max Weber's) as natural science can be; that is, a critique of the presupposition that the social scientist can be related to the social world as the natural scientist is related to the physical world. Whereas physicists are not a part of the set of objects they are studying, social scientists are a part of the world they are studying. For example, historians are a part of the history they describe or explain. Yet because of this, the social sciences do have an autonomy of their own, because they themselves belong to the social system that they describe and analyze. Accordingly, the most important statement of this paper is that modern social science is a part of modernity. It is this connection between modernity and social science that has to be discussed, as Professor Bellah recognizes. But I was struck by the fact that you did not quote from a contemporary scientist, but rather returned to Marx as the one who broke the boundary between the natural sciences and social sciences. I would like to know more about current thought concerning this issue.

My second suggestion concerns the last part of your paper. At that point, you connect the presuppositions of the social sciences to what we may call "practical reason," "mores," "*wirklichkeit*," "moral ecology." I am interested in this connection because I think that understanding the biblical message belongs to the same level of intelligibility. The modes of discourse at work in the Bible – narratives, prophecies, laws, hymns, and so on – require from us a kind of understanding that intersects the kind of intelligibility proper to the human sciences, when they are ascribed to their proper place in the realm of intelligibility. I don't think that this question concerns only the personal or the public commitment of the scholar; it also concerns the epistemology of the social sciences as disciplined forms of inquiry. Hence I should like to ask, do you think that your plea for "practical reason," for "moral ecology," has epistemological implications for your own science? If so, what are they?

These questions bring me to my third point. What I found missing in your paper was any assessment of the trends in the social sciences that seem to comply with these epistemological implications. I have in mind such examples as the critical sciences as developed by the post-Marxist Frankfurt school, from Horkheimer to Habermas, the phenomenological approach to the social world such as it has been developed by Alfred Schutz, and the kind of hermeneutical sociology generated by Max Weber's comprehensive sociology and exemplified today in the work of Victor Turner, Clifford Geertz, and even you yourself. I would have liked to hear more discussion of your own contributions to sociology.

William James, THE VARIETIES OF RELIGIOUS EXPERIENCE

1. On what grounds does James argue that our faith cannot be secured by the logical reason of man?

2. How does James apply the principle of pragmatism to God's metaphysical and moral attributes?

3. What is the relationship between thought and feeling in religion as James sees it?

4. In James' opinion, what can philosophy do for religion?

5. How does James stand on the existence of numerous religious types and sects?

6. According to James, what is common to all religious creeds? How does he treat this "common nucleus"?

7. What does James mean when he says, "Religion, in short, is a monumental chapter in the history of human egotism"?

8. What does James mean by "over-beliefs" and how does he describe his own "over-belief"?

9. What are James' conclusions regarding the "survival theory" of religion?

10. What are the characteristics of the religious life as James summarizes them?

11. How does James attempt to reconcile differences in religious creeds with the conclusions of physical science.

12. Outline James' pragmatic view of religion.

William James (1842-1910) was educated in chemistry and then medicine at Harvard. Later he served as an assistant on an expedition to the Amazon with naturalist, Louis Agassiz. After further studies in medicine and psychology in Germany, James returned to Harvard first to teach anatomy and physiology, and then psychology. A pioneer in psychology, he established the first laboratory in experimental psychology in America in 1874. But the last twenty years of his life, he devoted almost entirely to philosophy in which he became the leader of American pragmatism.

To make his great contributions to psychology and philosophy, James had to overcome long periods of ill health and a reading disability which is suspected to have been dyslexia.

*The Varieties of Religious Experience* was first presented as the Gifford Lectures at the University of Edinburgh in 1901-1902.

THE

# VARIETIES OF RELIGIOUS EXPERIENCE

## Lecture XVIII

## PHILOSOPHY

THE subject of Saintliness left us face to face with the question, Is the sense of divine presence a sense of anything objectively true? We turned first to mysticism for an answer, and found that although mysticism is entirely willing to corroborate religion, it is too private (and also too various) in its utterances to be able to claim a universal authority. But philosophy publishes results which claim to be universally valid if they are valid at all, so we now turn with our question to philosophy. Can philosophy stamp a warrant of veracity upon the religious man's sense of the divine?

I imagine that many of you at this point begin to indulge in guesses at the goal to which I am tending. I have undermined the authority of mysticism, you say, and the next thing I shall probably do is to seek to discredit that of philosophy. Religion, you expect to hear me conclude, is nothing but an affair of faith, based either on vague sentiment, or on that vivid sense of the reality of things unseen of which in my second lecture and in the lecture on Mysticism I gave so many examples. It is essentially private and individualistic; it always exceeds our powers of formulation; and although attempts to pour its contents into a philosophic mould will probably always go on, men being what they are, yet these attempts are always secondary processes which in no way add to the authority, or warrant the veracity, of the sentiments from which they derive their own stimulus and borrow whatever glow of conviction they may themselves possess. In short, you suspect that I am planning to defend feeling at the expense of reason, to rehabilitate the primitive and unreflective, and to dissuade you from the hope of any Theology worthy of the name.

To a certain extent I have to admit that you guess rightly. I do believe that feeling is the deeper source of religion, and that philosophic and theological formulas are secondary products, like translations of a text into another tongue. But all such statements are misleading from their brevity, and it will take the whole hour for me to explain to you exactly what I mean.

When I call theological formulas secondary products, I mean that in a world in which no religious feeling had ever existed, I doubt whether any philosophic theology could ever have been framed. I doubt if dispassionate intellectual contemplation of the universe, apart from inner unhappiness and need of deliverance on the one hand and mystical emotion on the other, would ever have resulted in religious philosophies such as we now possess. Men would have begun with animistic explanations of natural fact, and criticised these away into scientific ones, as they actually have done. In the science they would have left a certain amount of "psychical research," even as they now will probably have to re-admit a certain amount. But high-flying speculations like those of either dogmatic or idealistic theology, these they would have had no motive to venture on, feeling no need of commerce with such deities. These speculations must, it seems to me, be classed as over-beliefs, buildings-out performed by the intellect into directions of which feeling originally supplied the hint.

But even if religious philosophy had to have its first hint supplied by feeling, may it not have dealt in a superior way with the matter which feeling suggested? Feeling is private and dumb, and unable to give an account of itself. It allows that its results are mysteries and enigmas, declines to justify them rationally, and on occasion is willing that they should even pass for paradoxical and absurd. Philosophy takes just the opposite attitude. Her aspiration is to reclaim from mystery and paradox whatever territory she touches. To find an escape from obscure and wayward personal persuasion to truth objectively valid for all thinking men has ever been the intellect's most cherished ideal. To redeem religion from unwholesome privacy, and to give public status and universal right of way to its deliverances, has been reason's task.

I believe that philosophy will always have opportunity to labor at this task.[1] We are thinking beings, and we cannot exclude the intellect from participating in any of our functions. Even in soliloquizing with ourselves, we construe our feelings intellectually. Both our personal ideals and our religious and mystical experiences must be interpreted congruously with the kind of scenery which our thinking mind inhabits. The philosophic climate of our time inevitably forces its own clothing on us. Moreover, we must exchange our feelings with one another, and in doing so we have to speak, and to use general and abstract verbal formulas. Conceptions and constructions are thus a necessary part of our religion; and as moderator amid the clash of hypotheses, and mediator among the criticisms of one man's constructions by another, philosophy will always have much to do. It would be strange if I disputed this, when these very lectures which I am giving are (as you will see more clearly from now onwards) a laborious attempt to extract from the privacies of religious experience some general facts which can be defined in formulas upon which everybody may agree.

Religious experience, in other words, spontaneously and inevitably engenders myths, superstitions, dogmas, creeds, and metaphysical theologies, and criticisms of one set of

[1] Compare Professor W. Wallace's Gifford Lectures, in Lectures and Essays, Oxford, 1898, pp. 17 ff.

these by the adherents of another. Of late, impartial classifications and comparisons have become possible, alongside of the denunciations and anathemas by which the commerce between creeds used exclusively to be carried on. We have the beginnings of a "Science of Religions," so-called; and if these lectures could ever be accounted a crumb-like contribution to such a science, I should be made very happy.

But all these intellectual operations, whether they be constructive or comparative and critical, presuppose immediate experiences as their subject-matter. They are interpretative and inductive operations, operations after the fact, consequent upon religious feeling, not coördinate with it, not independent of what it ascertains.

The intellectualism in religion which I wish to discredit pretends to be something altogether different from this. It assumes to construct religious objects out of the resources of logical reason alone, or of logical reason drawing rigorous inference from non-subjective facts. It calls its conclusions dogmatic theology, or philosophy of the absolute, as the case may be; it does not call them science of religions. It reaches them in an *a priori* way, and warrants their veracity.

Warranted systems have ever been the idols of aspiring souls. All-inclusive, yet simple; noble, clean, luminous, stable, rigorous, true;—what more ideal refuge could there be than such a system would offer to spirits vexed by the muddiness and accidentality of the world of sensible things? Accordingly, we find inculcated in the theological schools of to-day, almost as much as in those of the fore-time, a disdain for merely possible or probable truth, and of results that only private assurance can grasp. Scholastics and idealists both express this disdain. Principal John Caird, for example, writes as follows in his Introduction to the Philosophy of Religion:—

"Religion must indeed be a thing of the heart; but in order to elevate it from the region of subjective caprice and waywardness, and to distinguish between that which is true and false in religion, we must appeal to an objective standard. That which enters the heart must first be discerned by the intelligence to be *true*. It must be seen as having in its own nature a *right* to dominate feeling, and as constituting the principle by which feeling must be judged.[1] In estimating the religious character of individuals, nations, or races, the first question is, not how they feel, but what they think and believe—not whether their religion is one which manifests itself in emotions, more or less vehement and enthusiastic, but what are the *conceptions* of God and divine things by which these emotions are called forth. Feeling is necessary in religion, but it is by the *content* or intelligent basis of a religion, and not by feeling, that its character and worth are to be determined."[2]

Cardinal Newman, in his work, The Idea of a University, gives more emphatic expression still to this disdain for sentiment.[3] Theology, he says, is a science in the strictest sense of the word. I will tell you, he says, what it is not—not "physical evidences" for God, not "natural religion," for these are but vague subjective interpretations:—

"If," he continues, "the Supreme Being is powerful or skillful, just so far as the telescope shows power, or the microscope shows skill, if his moral law is to be ascertained simply by the physical processes of the animal frame, or his will gathered from the immediate issues of human affairs, if his Essence is just as high and deep and broad as the universe and no more; if this be the fact, then will I confess that there is no specific science about God, that theology is but a name, and a protest in its behalf an hypocrisy. Then, pious as it is to think of Him, while the pageant of experiment or abstract reasoning passes by,

[1] Op. cit., p. 174, abridged.
[2] Ibid., p. 186, abridged and italicized.
[3] Discourse II. § 7.

still such piety is nothing more than a poetry of thought, or an ornament of language, a certain view taken of Nature which one man has and another has not, which gifted minds strike out, which others see to be admirable and ingenious, and which all would be the better for adopting. It is but the theology of Nature, just as we talk of the *philosophy* or the *romance* of history, or the *poetry* of childhood, or the picturesque or the sentimental or the humorous, or any other abstract quality which the genius or the caprice of the individual, or the fashion of the day, or the consent of the world, recognizes in any set of objects which are subjected to its contemplation. I do not see much difference between avowing that there is no God, and implying that nothing definite can be known for certain about Him."

What I mean by Theology, continues Newman, is none of these things: "I simply mean the *Science of God,* or the truths we know about God, put into a system, just as we have a science of the stars and call it astronomy, or of the crust of the earth and call it geology."

In both these extracts we have the issue clearly set before us: Feeling valid only for the individual is pitted against reason valid universally. The test is a perfectly plain one of fact. Theology based on pure reason must in point of fact convince men universally. If it did not, wherein would its superiority consist? If it only formed sects and schools, even as sentiment and mysticism form them, how would it fulfill its programme of freeing us from personal caprice and waywardness? This perfectly definite practical test of the pretensions of philosophy to found religion on universal reason simplifies my procedure to-day. I need not discredit philosophy by laborious criticism of its arguments. It will suffice if I show that as a matter of history it fails to prove its pretension to be "objectively" convincing. In fact, philosophy does so fail. It does not banish differences; it founds schools and sects just as feeling does. I believe, in fact, that the logical reason of man operates in this field of divinity exactly as it has always operated in love, or in patriotism, or in politics, or in any other of the wider affairs of life, in which our passions or our mystical intuitions fix our beliefs beforehand. It finds arguments for our conviction, for indeed it *has* to find them. It amplifies and defines our faith, and dignifies it and lends it words and plausibility. It hardly ever engenders it; it cannot now secure it.[1]

Lend me your attention while I run through some of the points of the older systematic theology. You find them in both Protestant and Catholic manuals, best of all in the innumerable text-books published since Pope Leo's Encyclical recommending the study of Saint Thomas. I glance first at the arguments by which dogmatic theology establishes God's existence, after that at those by which it establishes his nature.[2]

The arguments for God's existence have stood for hundreds of years with the waves of unbelieving criticism breaking against them, never totally discrediting them in the ears of the faithful, but on the whole slowly and surely washing out the mortar from between their joints. If you have a God

[1] As regards the secondary character of intellectual constructions, and the primacy of feeling and instinct in founding religious beliefs, see the striking work of H. Fielding, The Hearts of Men, London, 1902, which came into my hands after my text was written. "Creeds," says the author, "are the grammar of religion, they are to religion what grammar is to speech. Words are the expression of our wants; grammar is the theory formed afterwards. Speech never proceeded from grammar, but the reverse. As speech progresses and changes from unknown causes, grammar must follow" (p. 313). The whole book, which keeps unusually close to concrete facts, is little more than an amplification of this text.

[2] For convenience' sake, I follow the order of A. Stöckl's Lehrbuch der Philosophie, 5te Auflage, Mainz, 1881, Band ii. B. Boedder's Natural Theology, London, 1891, is a handy English Catholic Manual; but an almost identical doctrine is given by such Protestant theologians as C. Hodge: Systematic Theology, New York, 1873, or A H. Strong: Systematic Theology, 5th edition, New York, 1896.

already whom you believe in, these arguments confirm you. If you are atheistic, they fail to set you right. The proofs are various. The "cosmological" one, so-called, reasons from the contingence of the world to a First Cause which must contain whatever perfections the world itself contains. The "argument from design" reasons, from the fact that Nature's laws are mathematical, and her parts benevolently adapted to each other, that this cause is both intellectual and benevolent. The "moral argument" is that the moral law presupposes a lawgiver. The "argument *ex consensu gentium*" is that the belief in God is so widespread as to be grounded in the rational nature of man, and should therefore carry authority with it.

As I just said, I will not discuss these arguments technically. The bare fact that all idealists since Kant have felt entitled either to scout or to neglect them shows that they are not solid enough to serve as religion's all-sufficient foundation. Absolutely impersonal reasons would be in duty bound to show more general convincingness. Causation is indeed too obscure a principle to bear the weight of the whole structure of theology. As for the argument from design, see how Darwinian ideas have revolutionized it. Conceived as we now conceive them, as so many fortunate escapes from almost limitless processes of destruction, the benevolent adaptations which we find in Nature suggest a deity very different from the one who figured in the earlier versions of the argument.[1] The fact is that these arguments

[1] It must not be forgotten that any form of *dis*order in the world might, by the design argument, suggest a God for just that kind of disorder. The truth is that any state of things whatever that can be named is logically susceptible of teleological interpretation. The ruins of the earthquake at Lisbon, for example: the whole of past history had to be planned exactly as it was to bring about in the fullness of time just that particular arrangement of debris of masonry, furniture, and once living bodies. No other train of causes would have been sufficient. And so of any other arrangement, bad or good, which might

do but follow the combined suggestions of the facts and of our feeling. They prove nothing rigorously. They only corroborate our preëxistent partialities.

as a matter of fact be found resulting anywhere from previous conditions. To avoid such pessimistic consequences and save its beneficent designer, the design argument accordingly invokes two other principles, restrictive in their operation. The first is physical: Nature's forces tend of their own accord only to disorder and destruction, to heaps of ruins, not to architecture. This principle, though plausible at first sight, seems, in the light of recent biology, to be more and more improbable. The second principle is one of anthropomorphic interpretation. No arrangement that for *us* is "disorderly" can possibly have been an object of design at all. This principle is of course a mere assumption in the interests of anthropomorphic Theism.

When one views the world with no definite theological bias one way or the other, one sees that order and disorder, as we now recognize them, are purely human inventions. We are interested in certain types of arrangement, useful, æsthetic, or moral—so interested that whenever we find them realized, the fact emphatically rivets our attention. The result is that we work over the contents of the world selectively. It is overflowing with disorderly arrangements from our point of view, but order is the only thing we care for and look at, and by choosing, one can always find some sort of orderly arrangement in the midst of any chaos. If I should throw down a thousand beans at random upon a table, I could doubtless, by eliminating a sufficient number of them, leave the rest in almost any geometrical pattern you might propose to me, and you might then say that that pattern was the thing prefigured beforehand, and that the other beans were mere irrelevance and packing material. Our dealings with Nature are just like this. She is a vast *plenum* in which our attention draws capricious lines in innumerable directions. We count and name whatever lies upon the special lines we trace, whilst the other things and the untraced lines are neither named nor counted. There are in reality infinitely more things "unadapted" to each other in this world than there are things "adapted"; infinitely more things with irregular relations than with regular relations between them. But we look for the regular kind of thing exclusively, and ingeniously discover and preserve it in our memory. It accumulates with other regular kinds, until the collection of them fills our encyclopædias. Yet all the while between and around them lies an

If philosophy can do so little to establish God's existence, how stands it with her efforts to define his attributes? It is worth while to look at the attempts of systematic theology in this direction.

Since God is First Cause, this science of sciences says, he differs from all his creatures in possessing existence *a se*. From this "a-se-ity" on God's part, theology deduces by mere logic most of his other perfections. For instance, he must be both *necessary* and *absolute*, cannot not be, and cannot in any way be determined by anything else. This makes Him absolutely unlimited from without, and unlimited also from within; for limitation is non-being; and God is being itself. This unlimitedness makes God infinitely perfect. Moreover, God is *One*, and *Only*, for the infinitely perfect can admit no peer. He is *Spiritual*, for were He composed of physical parts, some other power would have to combine them into the total, and his aseity would thus be contradicted. He is therefore both simple and non-physical in nature. He is *simple metaphysically* also, that is to say, his nature and his existence cannot be distinct, as they are in finite substances which share their formal natures with one another, and are individual only in their material aspect. Since God is one and only, his *essentia* and his *esse* must be given at one stroke. This excludes from his being all those distinctions, so familiar in the world of finite things, between potentiality and actuality, substance and accidents, being and activity, existence and attributes. We can talk, it is true, of God's powers, acts, and attributes, but these discriminations are only "virtual," and made from the human point of view. In God all these points of view fall into an absolute identity of being.

infinite anonymous chaos of objects that no one ever thought of together, of relations that never yet attracted our attention.

The facts of order from which the physico-theological argument starts are thus easily susceptible of interpretation as arbitrary human products. So long as this is the case, although of course no argument against God follows, it follows that the argument for him will fail to constitute a knockdown proof of his existence. It will be convincing only to those who on other grounds believe in him already.

This absence of all potentiality in God obliges Him to be *immutable*. He is actuality, through and through. Were there anything potential about Him, He would either lose or gain by its actualization, and either loss or gain would contradict his perfection. He cannot, therefore, change. Furthermore, He is *immense, boundless;* for could He be outlined in space, He would be composite, and this would contradict his indivisibility. He is therefore *omnipresent*, indivisibly there, at every point of space. He is similarly wholly present at every point of time—in other words *eternal*. For if He began in time, He would need a prior cause, and that would contradict his aseity. If He ended, it would contradict his necessity. If He went through any succession, it would contradict his immutability.

He has *intelligence* and *will* and every other creature-perfection, for *we* have them, and *effectus nequit superare causam*. In Him, however, they are absolutely and eternally in act, and their *object*, since God can be bounded by naught that is external, can primarily be nothing else than God himself. He knows himself, then, in one eternal indivisible act, and wills himself with an infinite self-pleasure.[1] Since He must of logical necessity thus love and will himself, He cannot be called "free" *ad intra*, with the freedom of contrarieties that characterizes finite creatures. *Ad extra*, however, or with respect to his creation, God is free. He cannot *need* to create, being perfect in being and in happiness already. He *wills* to create, then, by an absolute freedom.

Being thus a substance endowed with intellect and will and freedom, God is a *person;* and a *living* person also, for He is both object and subject of his own activity, and to be this distinguishes the living from the lifeless. He is thus absolutely *self-sufficient:* his *self-knowledge* and *self-love* are both of them infinite and adequate, and need no extraneous conditions to perfect them.

He is *omniscient*, for in knowing himself as Cause He knows all creature things and events by implication. His knowledge is *previsive*, for He is present to all time. Even our free acts are

[1] For the scholastics the *facultas appetendi* embraces feeling, desire, and will.

known beforehand to Him, for otherwise his wisdom would admit of successive moments of enrichment, and this would contradict his immutability. He is *omnipotent* for everything that does not involve logical contradiction. He can make *being* —in other words his power includes *creation*. If what He creates were made of his own substance, it would have to be infinite in essence, as that substance is; but it is finite; so it must be non-divine in substance. If it were made of a substance, an eternally existing matter, for example, which God found there to his hand, and to which He simply gave its form, that would contradict God's definition as First Cause, and make Him a mere mover of something caused already. The things he creates, then, He creates *ex nihilo,* and gives them absolute being as so many finite substances additional to himself. The forms which he imprints upon them have their prototypes in his ideas. But as in God there is no such thing as multiplicity, and as these ideas for us are manifold, we must distinguish the ideas as they are in God and the way in which our minds externally imitate them. We must attribute them to Him only in a *terminative* sense, as differing aspects, from the finite point of view, of his unique essence.

God of course is holy, good, and just. He can do no evil, for He is positive being's fullness, and evil is negation. It is true that He has created physical evil in places, but only as a means of wider good, for *bonum totius præeminet bonum partis.* Moral evil He cannot will, either as end or means, for that would contradict his holiness. By creating free beings He *permits* it only, neither his justice nor his goodness obliging Him to prevent the recipients of freedom from misusing the gift.

As regards God's purpose in creating, primarily it can only have been to exercise his absolute freedom by the manifestation to others of his glory. From this it follows that the others must be rational beings, capable in the first place of knowledge, love, and honor, and in the second place of happiness, for the knowledge and love of God is the mainspring of felicity. In so far forth one may say that God's secondary purpose in creating is *love.*

I will not weary you by pursuing these metaphysical determinations farther, into the mysteries of God's Trinity, for example. What I have given will serve as a specimen of the orthodox philosophical theology of both Catholics and Protestants. Newman, filled with enthusiasm at God's list of perfections, continues the passage which I began to quote to you by a couple of pages of a rhetoric so magnificent that I can hardly refrain from adding them, in spite of the inroad they would make upon our time.[1] He first enumerates God's attributes sonorously, then celebrates his ownership of everything in earth and Heaven, and the dependence of all that happens upon his permissive will. He gives us scholastic philosophy "touched with emotion," and every philosophy should be touched with emotion to be rightly understood. Emotionally, then, dogmatic theology is worth something to minds of the type of Newman's. It will aid us to estimate what it is worth intellectually, if at this point I make a short digression.

What God hath joined together, let no man put asunder. The Continental schools of philosophy have too often overlooked the fact that man's thinking is organically connected with his conduct. It seems to me to be the chief glory of English and Scottish thinkers to have kept the organic connection in view. The guiding principle of British philosophy has in fact been that every difference must *make* a difference, every theoretical difference somewhere issue in a practical difference, and that the best method of discussing points of theory is to begin by ascertaining what practical difference would result from one alternative or the other being true. What is the particular truth in question *known as?* In what facts does it result? What is its cash-value in

[1] Op. cit., Discourse III. § 7.

terms of particular experience? This is the characteristic English way of taking up a question. In this way, you remember, Locke takes up the question of personal identity. What you mean by it is just your chain of particular memories, says he. That is the only concretely verifiable part of its significance. All further ideas about it, such as the oneness or manyness of the spiritual substance on which it is based, are therefore void of intelligible meaning; and propositions touching such ideas may be indifferently affirmed or denied. So Berkeley with his "matter." The cash-value of matter is our physical sensations. That is what it is known as, all that we concretely verify of its conception. That, therefore, is the whole meaning of the term "matter"—any other pretended meaning is mere wind of words. Hume does the same thing with causation. It is known as habitual antecedence, and as tendency on our part to look for something definite to come. Apart from this practical meaning it has no significance whatever, and books about it may be committed to the flames, says Hume. Dugald Stewart and Thomas Brown, James Mill, John Mill, and Professor Bain, have followed more or less consistently the same method; and Shadworth Hodgson has used the principle with full explicitness. When all is said and done, it was English and Scotch writers, and not Kant, who introduced "the critical method" into philosophy, the one method fitted to make philosophy a study worthy of serious men. For what seriousness can possibly remain in debating philosophic propositions that will never make an appreciable difference to us in action? And what could it matter, if all propositions were practically indifferent, which of them we should agree to call true or which false?

An American philosopher of eminent originality, Mr. Charles Sanders Peirce, has rendered thought a service by disentangling from the particulars of its application the principle by which these men were instinctively guided, and by singling it out as fundamental and giving to it a Greek name. He calls it the principle of *pragmatism*, and he defends it somewhat as follows:[1] —

Thought in movement has for its only conceivable motive the attainment of belief, or thought at rest. Only when our thought about a subject has found its rest in belief can our action on the subject firmly and safely begin. Beliefs, in short, are rules for action; and the whole function of thinking is but one step in the production of active habits. If there were any part of a thought that made no difference in the thought's practical consequences, then that part would be no proper element of the thought's significance. To develop a thought's meaning we need therefore only determine what conduct it is fitted to produce; that conduct is for us its sole significance; and the tangible fact at the root of all our thought-distinctions is that there is no one of them so fine as to consist in anything but a possible difference of practice. To attain perfect clearness in our thoughts of an object, we need then only consider what sensations, immediate or remote, we are conceivably to expect from it, and what conduct we must prepare in case the object should be true. Our conception of these practical consequences is for us the whole of our conception of the object, so far as that conception has positive significance at all.

This is the principle of Peirce, the principle of pragmatism. Such a principle will help us on this occasion to decide, among the various attributes set down in the scholastic inventory of God's perfections, whether some be not far less significant than others.

If, namely, we apply the principle of pragmatism to God's metaphysical attributes, strictly so called, as distinguished from his moral attributes, I think that, even were we forced by a coercive logic to believe them, we still should have to

In an article, How to make our Ideas Clear, in the Popular Science Monthly for January, 1878, vol. xii. p. 286.

confess them to be destitute of all intelligible significance. Take God's aseity, for example; or his necessariness; his immateriality; his "simplicity" or superiority to the kind of inner variety and succession which we find in finite beings, his indivisibility, and lack of the inner distinctions of being and activity, substance and accident, potentiality and actuality, and the rest; his repudiation of inclusion in a genus; his actualized infinity; his "personality," apart from the moral qualities which it may comport; his relations to evil being permissive and not positive; his self-sufficiency, self-love, and absolute felicity in himself:—candidly speaking, how do such qualities as these make any definite connection with our life? And if they severally call for no distinctive adaptations of our conduct, what vital difference can it possibly make to a man's religion whether they be true or false?

For my own part, although I dislike to say aught that may grate upon tender associations, I must frankly confess that even though these attributes were faultlessly deduced, I cannot conceive of its being of the smallest consequence to us religiously that any one of them should be true. Pray, what specific act can I perform in order to adapt myself the better to God's simplicity? Or how does it assist me to plan my behavior, to know that his happiness is anyhow absolutely complete? In the middle of the century just past, Mayne Reid was the great writer of books of out-of-door adventure. He was forever extolling the hunters and field-observers of living animals' habits, and keeping up a fire of invective against the "closet-naturalists," as he called them, the collectors and classifiers, and handlers of skeletons and skins. When I was a boy, I used to think that a closet-naturalist must be the vilest type of wretch under the sun. But surely the systematic theologians are the closet-naturalists of the deity, even in Captain Mayne Reid's sense. What is their deduction of metaphysical attributes but a shuffling and matching of pedantic dictionary-adjectives, aloof from morals, aloof from human needs, something that might be worked out from the mere word "God" by one of those logical machines of wood and brass which recent ingenuity has contrived as well as by a man of flesh and blood. They have the trail of the serpent over them. One feels that in the theologians' hands, they are only a set of titles obtained by a mechanical manipulation of synonyms; verbality has stepped into the place of vision, professionalism into that of life. Instead of bread we have a stone; instead of a fish, a serpent. Did such a conglomeration of abstract terms give really the gist of our knowledge of the deity, schools of theology might indeed continue to flourish, but religion, vital religion, would have taken its flight from this world. What keeps religion going is something else than abstract definitions and systems of concatenated adjectives, and something different from faculties of theology and their professors. All these things are after-effects, secondary accretions upon those phenomena of vital conversation with the unseen divine, of which I have shown you so many instances, renewing themselves *in sæcula sæculorum* in the lives of humble private men.

So much for the metaphysical attributes of God! From the point of view of practical religion, the metaphysical monster which they offer to our worship is an absolutely worthless invention of the scholarly mind.

What shall we now say of the attributes called moral? Pragmatically, they stand on an entirely different footing. They positively determine fear and hope and expectation, and are foundations for the saintly life. It needs but a glance at them to show how great is their significance.

God's holiness, for example: being holy, God can will nothing but the good. Being omnipotent, he can secure its triumph. Being omniscient, he can see us in the dark. Being just, he can punish us for what he sees. Being loving, he can pardon too. Being unalterable, we can count on him securely. These qualities enter into connection with our life, it is highly important that we should be informed concerning them. That God's purpose in creation should be the manifestation of his glory is also an attribute which has definite relations to our practical life. Among other things it has given a definite character to worship in all Christian countries. If dogmatic theology really does prove beyond dispute that a God with characters like these exists, she may well claim to give a solid basis to religious sentiment. But verily, how stands it with her arguments?

It stands with them as ill as with the arguments for his existence. Not only do post-Kantian idealists reject them root and branch, but it is a plain historic fact that they never have converted any one who has found in the moral complexion of the world, as he experienced it, reasons for doubting that a good God can have framed it. To prove God's goodness by the scholastic argument that there is no non-being in his essence would sound to such a witness simply silly.

No! the book of Job went over this whole matter once for all and definitively. Ratiocination is a relatively superficial and unreal path to the deity: "I will lay mine hand upon my mouth; I have heard of Thee by the hearing of the ear, but now mine eye seeth Thee." An intellect perplexed and baffled, yet a trustful sense of presence—such is the situation of the man who is sincere with himself and with the facts, but who remains religious still.[1]

[1] Pragmatically, the most important attribute of God is his punitive justice. But who, in the present state of theological opinion on that point, will dare maintain that hell fire or its equivalent in some shape is rendered certain by pure logic? Theology herself has largely based this doctrine upon revelation; and, in discussing it, has tended more and more to substitute conventional ideas of criminal law for *a priori* principles of reason. But the very notion that this glorious uni-

We must therefore, I think, bid a definitive good-by to dogmatic theology. In all sincerity our faith must do without that warrant. Modern idealism, I repeat, has said good-by to this theology forever. Can modern idealism give faith a better warrant, or must she still rely on her poor self for witness?

The basis of modern idealism is Kant's doctrine of the Transcendental Ego of Apperception. By this formidable term Kant merely meant the fact that the consciousness "I think them" must (potentially or actually) accompany all our objects. Former skeptics had said as much, but the "I" in question had remained for them identified with the personal individual. Kant abstracted and depersonalized it, and made it the most universal of all his categories, although for Kant himself the Transcendental Ego had no theological implications.

It was reserved for his successors to convert Kant's notion of *Bewusstsein überhaupt*, or abstract consciousness, into an infinite concrete self-consciousness which is the soul of the world, and in which our sundry personal self-consciousnesses have their being. It would lead me into technicalities to show you even briefly how this transformation was in point of fact effected. Suffice it to say that in the Hegelian school, which to-day so deeply influences both British and American thinking, two principles have borne the brunt of the operation.

The first of these principles is that the old logic of identity never gives us more than a post-mortem dissection of *disjecta membra*, and that the fullness of life can be construed to thought only by recognizing that every object which our

verse, with planets and winds, and laughing sky and ocean, should have been conceived and had its beams and rafters laid in technicalities of criminality, is incredible to our modern imagination. It weakens a religion to hear it argued upon such a basis.

thought may propose to itself involves the notion of some other object which seems at first to negate the first one.

The second principle is that to be conscious of a negation is already virtually to be beyond it. The mere asking of a question or expression of a dissatisfaction proves that the answer or the satisfaction is already imminent; the finite, realized as such, is already the infinite *in posse*.

Applying these principles, we seem to get a propulsive force into our logic which the ordinary logic of a bare, stark self-identity in each thing never attains to. The objects of our thought now *act* within our thought, act as objects act when given in experience. They change and develop. They introduce something other than themselves along with them; and this other, at first only ideal or potential, presently proves itself also to be actual. It supersedes the thing at first supposed, and both verifies and corrects it, in developing the fullness of its meaning.

The program is excellent; the universe *is* a place where things are followed by other things that both correct and fulfill them; and a logic which gave us something like this movement of fact would express truth far better than the traditional school-logic, which never gets of its own accord from anything to anything else, and registers only predictions and subsumptions, or static resemblances and differences. Nothing could be more unlike the methods of dogmatic theology than those of this new logic. Let me quote in illustration some passages from the Scottish transcendentalist whom I have already named.

"How are we to conceive," Principal Caird writes, "of the reality in which all intelligence rests?" He replies: "Two things may without difficulty be proved, viz., that this reality is an absolute Spirit, and conversely that it is only in communion with this absolute Spirit or Intelligence that the finite Spirit can realize itself. It is absolute; for the faintest movement of human intelligence would be arrested, if it did not presuppose the absolute reality of intelligence, of thought itself. Doubt or denial themselves presuppose and indirectly affirm it. When I pronounce anything to be true, I pronounce it, indeed, to be relative to thought, but not to be relative to my thought, or to the thought of any other individual mind. From the existence of all individual minds as such I can abstract; I can think them away. But that which I cannot think away is thought or self-consciousness itself, in its independence and absoluteness, or, in other words, an Absolute Thought or Self-Consciousness."

Here, you see, Principal Caird makes the transition which Kant did not make: he converts the omnipresence of consciousness in general as a condition of "truth" being anywhere possible, into an omnipresent universal consciousness, which he identifies with God in his concreteness. He next proceeds to use the principle that to acknowledge your limits is in essence to be beyond them; and makes the transition to the religious experience of individuals in the following words:—

"If [Man] were only a creature of transient sensations and impulses, of an ever coming and going succession of intuitions, fancies, feelings, then nothing could ever have for him the character of objective truth or reality. But it is the prerogative of man's spiritual nature that he can yield himself up to a thought and will that are infinitely larger than his own. As a thinking, self-conscious being, indeed, he may be said, by his very nature, to live in the atmosphere of the Universal Life. As a thinking being, it is possible for me to suppress and quell in my consciousness every movement of self-assertion, every notion and opinion that is merely mine, every desire that belongs to me as this particular Self, and to become the pure medium of a thought that is universal—in one word, to live no more my own life, but let my consciousness be possessed and suffused by the Infinite and Eternal life of spirit. And yet it is just in this renunciation of self that I truly gain myself, or realize the highest possibilities of my own nature. For whilst in one sense we give up self to live the universal and absolute life of reason, yet that to which we thus surrender ourselves is in reality our truer self. The life of absolute reason is not a life that is foreign to us."

Nevertheless, Principal Caird goes on to say, so far as we are able outwardly to realize this doctrine, the balm it offers remains incomplete. Whatever we may be *in posse*, the very best of us *in actu* falls very short of being absolutely divine. Social morality, love, and self-sacrifice even, merge our Self only in some other finite self or selves. They do not quite identify it with the Infinite. Man's ideal destiny, infinite in abstract logic, might thus seem in practice forever unrealizable.

"Is there, then," our author continues, "no solution of the contradiction between the ideal and the actual? We answer, There is such a solution, but in order to reach it we are carried beyond the sphere of morality into that of religion. It may be said to be the essential characteristic of religion as contrasted with morality, that it changes aspiration into fruition, anticipation into realization; that instead of leaving man in the interminable pursuit of a vanishing ideal, it makes him the actual partaker of a divine or infinite life. Whether we view religion from the human side or the divine—as the surrender of the soul to God, or as the life of God in the soul—in either aspect it is of its very essence that the Infinite has ceased to be a far-off vision, and has become a present reality. The very first pulsation of the spiritual life, when we rightly apprehend its significance, is the indication that the division between the Spirit and its object has vanished, that the ideal has become real, that the finite has reached its goal and become suffused with the presence and life of the Infinite.

"Oneness of mind and will with the divine mind and will is not the future hope and aim of religion, but its very beginning and birth in the soul. To enter on the religious life is to terminate the struggle. In that act which constitutes the beginning of the religious life—call it faith, or trust, or self-surrender, or by whatever name you will—there is involved the identification of the finite with a life which is eternally realized. It is true indeed that the religious life is progressive; but understood in the light of the foregoing idea, religious progress is not progress *towards*, but *within* the sphere of the Infinite. It is not the vain attempt by endless finite additions or increments to become possessed of infinite wealth, but it is the endeavor, by the constant exercise of spiritual activity, to appropriate that infinite inheritance of which we are already in possession. The whole future of the religious life is given in its beginning, but it is given implicitly. The position of the man who has entered on the religious life is that evil, error, imperfection, do not really belong to him: they are excrescences which have no organic relation to his true nature: they are already virtually, as they will be actually, suppressed and annulled, and in the very process of being annulled they become the means of spiritual progress. Though he is not exempt from temptation and conflict, [yet] in that inner sphere in which his true life lies, the struggle is over, the victory already achieved. It is not a finite but an infinite life which the spirit lives. Every pulse-beat of its [existence] is the expression and realization of the life of God." [1]

You will readily admit that no description of the phenomena of the religious consciousness could be better than these words of your lamented preacher and philosopher. They reproduce the very rapture of those crises of conversion of which we have been hearing; they utter what the mystic felt but was unable to communicate; and the saint, in hearing them, recognizes his own experience. It is indeed gratifying to find the content of religion reported so unanimously. But when all is said and done, has Principal Caird —and I only use him as an example of that whole mode of thinking—transcended the sphere of feeling and of the direct experience of the individual, and laid the foundations of religion in impartial reason? Has he made religion universal by coercive reasoning, transformed it from a private

[1] John Caird: An Introduction to the Philosophy of Religion, London and New York, 1880, pp. 243-250, and 291-299, much abridged.

faith into a public certainty? Has he rescued its affirmations from obscurity and mystery?

I believe that he has done nothing of the kind, but that he has simply reaffirmed the individual's experiences in a more generalized vocabulary. And again, I can be excused from proving technically that the transcendentalist reasonings fail to make religion universal, for I can point to the plain fact that a majority of scholars, even religiously disposed ones, stubbornly refuse to treat them as convincing. The whole of Germany, one may say, has positively rejected the Hegelian argumentation. As for Scotland, I need only mention Professor Fraser's and Professor Pringle-Pattison's memorable criticisms, with which so many of you are familiar.[1] Once more, I ask, if transcendental idealism were

[1] A. C. FRASER: Philosophy of Theism, second edition, Edinburgh and London, 1899, especially part ii, chaps. vii and viii.; A. SETH [PRINGLE-PATTISON]: Hegelianism and Personality, Ibid., 1890, passim.

The most persuasive arguments in favor of a concrete individual Soul of the world, with which I am acquainted, are those of my colleague, Josiah Royce, in his Religious Aspect of Philosophy, Boston, 1885; in his Conception of God, New York and London, 1897; and lately in his Aberdeen Gifford Lectures, The World and the Individual, 2 vols., New York and London, 1901-02. I doubtless seem to some of my readers to evade the philosophic duty which my thesis in this lecture imposes on me, by not even attempting to meet Professor Royce's arguments articulately. I admit the momentary evasion. In the present lectures, which are cast throughout in a popular mould, there seemed no room for subtle metaphysical discussion, and for tactical purposes it was sufficient, the contention of philosophy being what it is (namely, that religion can be transformed into a universally convincing science), to point to the fact that no religious philosophy has actually convinced the mass of thinkers. Meanwhile let me say that I hope that the present volume may be followed by another, if I am spared to write it, in which not only Professor Royce's arguments, but others for monistic absolutism shall be considered with all the technical fullness which their great importance calls for. At present I resign myself to lying passive under the reproach of superficiality.

as objectively and absolutely rational as it pretends to be, could it possibly fail so egregiously to be persuasive?

What religion reports, you must remember, always purports to be a fact of experience: the divine is actually present, religion says, and between it and ourselves relations of give and take are actual. If definite perceptions of fact like this cannot stand upon their own feet, surely abstract reasoning cannot give them the support they are in need of. Conceptual processes can class facts, define them, interpret them; but they do not produce them, nor can they reproduce their individuality. There is always a *plus*, a *thisness*, which feeling alone can answer for. Philosophy in this sphere is thus a secondary function, unable to warrant faith's veracity, and so I revert to the thesis which I announced at the beginning of this lecture.

In all sad sincerity I think we must conclude that the attempt to demonstrate by purely intellectual processes the truth of the deliverances of direct religious experience is absolutely hopeless.

It would be unfair to philosophy, however, to leave her under this negative sentence. Let me close, then, by briefly enumerating what she *can* do for religion. If she will abandon metaphysics and deduction for criticism and induction, and frankly transform herself from theology into science of religions, she can make herself enormously useful.

The spontaneous intellect of man always defines the divine which it feels in ways that harmonize with its temporary intellectual prepossessions. Philosophy can by comparison eliminate the local and the accidental from these definitions. Both from dogma and from worship she can remove historic incrustations. By confronting the spontaneous religious constructions with the results of natural science, philosophy can also eliminate doctrines that are now known to be scientifically absurd or incongruous.

Sifting out in this way unworthy formulations, she can leave a residuum of conceptions that at least are possible. With these she can deal as *hypotheses*, testing them in all the manners, whether negative or positive, by which hypotheses are ever tested. She can reduce their number, as some are found more open to objection. She can perhaps become the champion of one which she picks out as being the most closely verified or verifiable. She can refine upon the definition of this hypothesis, distinguishing between what is innocent over-belief and symbolism in the expression of it, and what is to be literally taken. As a result, she can offer mediation between different believers, and help to bring about consensus of opinion. She can do this the more successfully, the better she discriminates the common and essential from the individual and local elements of the religious beliefs which she compares.

I do not see why a critical Science of Religions of this sort might not eventually command as general a public adhesion as is commanded by a physical science. Even the personally non-religious might accept its conclusions on trust, much as blind persons now accept the facts of optics—it might appear as foolish to refuse them. Yet as the science of optics has to be fed in the first instance, and continually verified later, by facts experienced by seeing persons; so the science of religions would depend for its original material on facts of personal experience, and would have to square itself with personal experience through all its critical reconstructions. It could never get away from concrete life, or work in a conceptual vacuum. It would forever have to confess, as every science confesses, that the subtlety of nature flies beyond it, and that its formulas are but approximations. Philosophy lives in words, but truth and fact well up into our lives in ways that exceed verbal formulation. There is in the living act of perception always something that glimmers and twinkles and will not be caught, and for which reflection comes too late. No one knows this as well as the philosopher. He must fire his volley of new vocables out of his conceptual shotgun, for his profession condemns him to this industry, but he secretly knows the hollowness and irrelevancy. His formulas are like stereoscopic or kinetoscopic photographs seen outside the instrument; they lack the depth, the motion, the vitality. In the religious sphere, in particular, belief that formulas are true can never wholly take the place of personal experience.

In my next lecture I will try to complete my rough description of religious experience; and in the lecture after that, which is the last one, I will try my hand at formulating conceptually the truth to which it is a witness.

## Lecture XX

# CONCLUSIONS

THE material of our study of human nature is now spread before us; and in this parting hour, set free from the duty of description, we can draw our theoretical and practical conclusions. In my first lecture, defending the empirical method, I foretold that whatever conclusions we might come to could be reached by spiritual judgments only, appreciations of the significance for life of religion, taken "on the whole." Our conclusions cannot be as sharp as dogmatic conclusions would be, but I will formulate them, when the time comes, as sharply as I can.

Summing up in the broadest possible way the characteristics of the religious life, as we have found them, it includes the following beliefs:—

1. That the visible world is part of a more spiritual universe from which it draws its chief significance;
2. That union or harmonious relation with that higher universe is our true end;
3. That prayer or inner communion with the spirit thereof—be that spirit "God" or "law"—is a process wherein work is really done, and spiritual energy flows in and produces effects, psychological or material, within the phenomenal world.

Religion includes also the following psychological characteristics:—

4. A new zest which adds itself like a gift to life, and takes the form either of lyrical enchantment or of appeal to earnestness and heroism.

5. An assurance of safety and a temper of peace, and, in relation to others, a preponderance of loving affections.

In illustrating these characteristics by documents, we have been literally bathed in sentiment. In re-reading my manuscript, I am almost appalled at the amount of emotionality which I find in it. After so much of this, we can afford to be dryer and less sympathetic in the rest of the work that lies before us.

The sentimentality of many of my documents is a consequence of the fact that I sought them among the extravagances of the subject. If any of you are enemies of what our ancestors used to brand as enthusiasm, and are, nevertheless, still listening to me now, you have probably felt my selection to have been sometimes almost perverse, and have wished I might have stuck to soberer examples. I reply that I took these extremer examples as yielding the profounder information. To learn the secrets of any science, we go to expert specialists, even though they may be eccentric persons, and not to commonplace pupils. We combine what they tell us with the rest of our wisdom, and form our final judgment independently. Even so with religion. We who have pursued such radical expressions of it may now be sure that we know its secrets as authentically as anyone can know them who learns them from another; and we have next to answer, each of us for himself, the practical question: what are the dangers in this element of life? and in what proportion may it need to be restrained by other elements, to give the proper balance?

But this question suggests another one which I will answer immediately and get it out of the way, for it has more than once already vexed us.[1] Ought it to be assumed that in all men the mixture of religion with other elements should be identical? Ought it, indeed, to be assumed that

[1] For example, on pages 133, 160, 326 above.

the lives of all men should show identical religious elements? In other words, is the existence of so many religious types and sects and creeds regrettable?

To these questions I answer "No" emphatically. And my reason is that I do not see how it is possible that creatures in such different positions and with such different powers as human individuals are, should have exactly the same functions and the same duties. No two of us have identical difficulties, nor should we be expected to work out identical solutions. Each, from his peculiar angle of observation, takes in a certain sphere of fact and trouble, which each must deal with in a unique manner. One of us must soften himself, another must harden himself; one must yield a point, another must stand firm—in order the better to defend the position assigned him. If an Emerson were forced to be a Wesley, or a Moody forced to be a Whitman, the total human consciousness of the divine would suffer. The divine can mean no single quality, it must mean a group of qualities, by being champions of which in alternation, different men may all find worthy missions. Each attitude being a syllable in human nature's total message, it takes the whole of us to spell the meaning out completely. So a "god of battles" must be allowed to be the god for one kind of person, a god of peace and heaven and home, the god for another. We must frankly recognize the fact that we live in partial systems, and that parts are not interchangeable in the spiritual life. If we are peevish and jealous, destruction of the self must be an element of our religion; why need it be one if we are good and sympathetic from the outset? If we are sick souls, we require a religion of deliverance; but why think so much of deliverance, if we are healthy-minded? [1] Unquestionably, some men have the com-

[1] From this point of view, the contrasts between the healthy and the morbid mind, and between the once-born and the twice-born types, of which I spoke in earlier lectures (see pp. 159-164), cease to be

pleter experience and the higher vocation, here just as in the social world; but for each man to stay in his own experience, whate'er it be, and for others to tolerate him there, is surely best.

But, you may now ask, would not this one-sidedness be cured if we should all espouse the science of religions as our own religion? In answering this question I must open again the general relations of the theoretic to the active life.

Knowledge about a thing is not the thing itself. You remember what Al-Ghazzali told us in the Lecture on Mysticism—that to understand the causes of drunkenness, as a physician understands them, is not to be drunk. A science might come to understand everything about the causes and elements of religion, and might even decide which elements were qualified, by their general harmony with other

the radical antagonisms which many think them. The twice-born look down upon the rectilinear consciousness of life of the once-born as being "mere morality," and not properly religion. "Dr. Channing," an orthodox minister is reported to have said, "is excluded from the highest form of religious life by the extraordinary rectitude of his character." It is indeed true that the outlook upon life of the twice-born—holding as it does more of the element of evil in solution—is the wider and completer. The "heroic" or "solemn" way in which life comes to them is a "higher synthesis" into which healthy-mindedness and morbidness both enter and combine. Evil is not evaded, but sublated in the higher religious cheer of these persons (see pp. 47-52, 354-357). But the final consciousness which each type reaches of union with the divine has the same practical significance for the individual; and individuals may well be allowed to get to it by the channels which lie most open to their several temperaments. In the cases which were quoted in Lecture IV, of the mind-cure form of healthy-mindedness, we found abundant examples of regenerative process. The severity of the crisis in this process is a matter of degree. How long one shall continue to drink the consciousness of evil, and when one shall begin to short-circuit and get rid of it, are also matters of amount and degree, so that in many instances it is quite arbitrary whether we class the individual as a once-born or a twice-born subject.

branches of knowledge, to be considered true; and yet the best man at this science might be the man who found it hardest to be personally devout. *Tout savoir c'est tout pardonner.* The name of Renan would doubtless occur to many persons as an example of the way in which breadth of knowledge may make one only a dilettante in possibilities, and blunt the acuteness of one's living faith.[1] If religion be a function by which either God's cause or man's cause is to be really advanced, then he who lives the life of it, however narrowly, is a better servant than he who merely knows about it, however much. Knowledge about life is one thing; effective occupation of a place in life, with its dynamic currents passing through your being, is another.

For this reason, the science of religions may not be an equivalent for living religion; and if we turn to the inner difficulties of such a science, we see that a point comes when she must drop the purely theoretic attitude, and either let her knots remain uncut, or have them cut by active faith. To see this, suppose that we have our science of religions constituted as a matter of fact. Suppose that she has assimilated all the necessary historical material and distilled out of it as its essence the same conclusions which I myself a few moments ago pronounced. Suppose that she agrees that religion, wherever it is an active thing, involves a belief in ideal presences, and a belief that in our prayerful communion with them,[2] work is done, and something real comes to pass. She has now to exert her critical activity, and to decide how far, in the light of other sciences and in that of general philosophy, such beliefs can be considered *true*.

Dogmatically to decide this is an impossible task. Not only are the other sciences and the philosophy still far from

[1] Compare, e. g., the quotation from Renan on p. 37, above.

[2] "Prayerful" taken in the broader sense explained above on pp 453 ff.

being completed, but in their present state we find them full of conflicts. The sciences of nature know nothing of spiritual presences, and on the whole hold no practical commerce whatever with the idealistic conceptions towards which general philosophy inclines. The scientist, so-called, is, during his scientific hours at least, so materialistic that one may well say that on the whole the influence of science goes against the notion that religion should be recognized at all. And this antipathy to religion finds an echo within the very science of religions itself. The cultivator of this science has to become acquainted with so many groveling and horrible superstitions that a presumption easily arises in his mind that any belief that is religious probably is false. In the "prayerful communion" of savages with such mumbo-jumbos of deities as they acknowledge, it is hard for us to see what genuine spiritual work—even though it were work relative only to their dark savage obligations—can possibly be done.

The consequence is that the conclusions of the science of religions are as likely to be adverse as they are to be favorable to the claim that the essence of religion is true. There is a notion in the air about us that religion is probably only an anachronism, a case of "survival," an atavistic relapse into a mode of thought which humanity in its more enlightened examples has outgrown; and this notion our religious anthropologists at present do little to counteract.

This view is so widespread at the present day that I must consider it with some explicitness before I pass to my own conclusions. Let me call it the "Survival theory," for brevity's sake.

The pivot round which the religious life, as we have traced it, revolves, is the interest of the individual in his private personal destiny. Religion, in short, is a monumental chapter in the history of human egotism. The gods believed in—whether by crude savages or by men disciplined intellectually—agree with each other in recognizing personal calls. Religious thought is carried on in terms of personality, this being, in the world of religion, the one fundamental fact. To-day, quite as much as at any previous age, the religious individual tells you that the divine meets him on the basis of his personal concerns.

Science, on the other hand, has ended by utterly repudiating the personal point of view. She catalogues her elements and records her laws indifferent as to what purpose may be shown forth by them, and constructs her theories quite careless of their bearing on human anxieties and fates. Though the scientist may individually nourish a religion, and be a theist in his irresponsible hours, the days are over when it could be said that for Science herself the heavens declare the glory of God and the firmament showeth his handiwork. Our solar system, with its harmonies, is seen now as but one passing case of a certain sort of moving equilibrium in the heavens, realized by a local accident in an appalling wilderness of worlds where no life can exist. In a span of time which as a cosmic interval will count but as an hour, it will have ceased to be. The Darwinian notion of chance production, and subsequent destruction, speedy or deferred, applies to the largest as well as to the smallest facts. It is impossible, in the present temper of the scientific imagination, to find in the driftings of the cosmic atoms, whether they work on the universal or on the particular scale, anything but a kind of aimless weather, doing and undoing, achieving no proper history, and leaving no result. Nature has no one distinguishable ultimate tendency with which it is possible to feel a sympathy. In the vast rhythm of her processes, as the scientific mind now follows them, she appears to cancel herself. The books of natural theology which satisfied the intellects of our grandfathers seem to us quite grotesque,[1] representing, as they did, a

[1] How was it ever conceivable, we ask, that a man like Christian Wolff, in whose dry-as-dust head all the learning of the early eighteenth century was concentrated, should have preserved such a baby-like faith in the personal and human character of Nature as to expound her operations as he did in his work on the uses of natural things? This, for example, is the account he gives of the sun and its utility:—

"We see that God has created the sun to keep the changeable conditions on the earth in such an order that living creatures, men and beasts, may inhabit its surface. Since men are the most reasonable of creatures, and able to infer God's invisible being from the contemplation of the world, the sun in so far forth contributes to the primary purpose of creation: without it the race of man could not be preserved or continued. . . . The sun makes daylight, not only on our earth, but also on the other planets; and daylight is of the utmost utility to us; for by its means we can commodiously carry on those occupations which in the night-time would either be quite impossible, or at any rate impossible without our going to the expense of artificial light. The beasts of the field can find food by day which they would not be able to find at night. Moreover we owe it to the sunlight that we are able to see everything that is on the earth's surface, not only near by, but also at a distance, and to recognize both near and far things according to their species, which again is of manifold use to us not only in the business necessary to human life, and when we are traveling, but also for the scientific knowledge of Nature, which knowledge for the most part depends on observations made with the help of sight, and, without the sunshine, would have been impossible. If any one would rightly impress on his mind the great advantages which he derives from the sun, let him imagine himself living through only one month, and see how it would be with all his undertakings, if it were not day but night. He would then be sufficiently convinced out of his own experience, especially if he had much work to carry on in the street or in the fields. . . . From the sun we learn to recognize when it is midday, and by knowing this point of time exactly, we can set our clocks right, on which account astronomy owes much to the sun. . . . By help of the sun one can find the meridian. . . . But the meridian is the basis of our sun-dials, and generally speaking, we should have no sun-dials if we had no sun." Vernünftige Gedanken von den Absichter der natürlichen Dinge, 1782, pp. 74-84.

Or read the account of God's beneficence in the institution of "the

God who conformed the largest things of nature to the paltriest of our private wants. The God whom science rec-

great variety throughout the world of men's faces, voices, and handwriting," given in Derham's Physico-theology, a book that had much vogue in the eighteenth century. "Had Man's body," says Dr. Derham, "been made according to any of the Atheistical Schemes, or any other Method than that of the infinite Lord of the World, this wise Variety would never have been: but Men's Faces would have been cast in the same, or not a very different Mould, their Organs of Speech would have sounded the same or not so great a Variety of Notes; and the same Structure of Muscles and Nerves would have given the Hand the same Direction in Writing. And in this Case, what Confusion, what Disturbance, what Mischiefs would the world eternally have lain under! No Security could have been to our persons; no Certainty, no Enjoyment of our Possessions; no Justice between Man and Man; no Distinction between Good and Bad, between Friends and Foes, between Father and Child, Husband and Wife, Male or Female; but all would have been turned topsy-turvy, by being exposed to the Malice of the Envious and ill-Natured, to the Fraud and Violence of Knaves and Robbers, to the Forgeries of the crafty Cheat, to the Lusts of the Effeminate and Debauched, and what not! Our Courts of Justice can abundantly testify the dire Effects of Mistaking Men's Faces, of counterfeiting their Hands, and forging Writings. But now as the infinitely wise Creator and Ruler hath ordered the Matter, every man's Face can distinguish him in the Light, and his Voice in the Dark; his Hand-writing can speak for him though absent, and be his Witness, and secure his Contracts in future Generations. A manifest as well as admirable Indication of the divine Superintendence and Management."

A God so careful as to make provision even for the unmistakable signing of bank checks and deeds was a deity truly after the heart of eighteenth century Anglicanism.

I subjoin, omitting the capitals, Derham's "Vindication of God by the Institution of Hills and Valleys," and Wolff's altogether culinary account of the institution of Water:—

"The uses," says Wolff, "which water serves in human life are plain to see and need not be described at length. Water is a universal drink of man and beasts. Even though men have made themselves drinks that are artificial, they could not do this without water. Beer is brewed of water and malt, and it is the water in it which quenches thirst. Wine is prepared from grapes, which could never have grown without the help of water; and the same is true of those drinks which

ognizes must be a God of universal laws exclusively, a God who does a wholesale, not a retail business. He cannot ac-

in England and other places they produce from fruit. . . . Therefore since God so planned the world that men and beasts should live upon it and find there everything required for their necessity and convenience, he also made water as one means whereby to make the earth into so excellent a dwelling. And this is all the more manifest when we consider the advantages which we obtain from this same water for the cleaning of our household utensils, of our clothing, and of other matters. . . . When one goes into a grinding-mill one sees that the grindstone must always be kept wet and then one will get a still greater idea of the use of water."

Of the hills and valleys, Derham, after praising their beauty, discourses as follows: "Some constitutions are indeed of so happy a strength, and so confirmed an health, as to be indifferent to almost any place or temperature of the air. But then others are so weakly and feeble, as not to be able to bear one, but can live comfortably in another place. With some the more subtle and finer air of the hills doth best agree, who are languishing and dying in the feculent and grosser air of great towns, or even the warmer and vaporous air of the valleys and waters. But contrariwise, others languish on the hills, and grow lusty and strong in the warmer air of the valleys.

"So that this opportunity of shifting our abode from the hills to the vales, is an admirable easement, refreshment, and great benefit to the valetudinarian, feeble part of mankind; affording those an easy and comfortable life, who would otherwise live miserably, languish, and pine away.

"To this salutary conformation of the earth we may add another great convenience of the hills, and that is affording commodious places for habitation, serving (as an eminent author wordeth it) as screens to keep off the cold and nipping blasts of the northern and easterly winds, and reflecting the benign and cherishing sunbeams, and so rendering our habitations both more comfortable and more cheerly in winter.

"Lastly, it is to the hills that the fountains owe their rise and the rivers their conveyance, and consequently those vast masses and lofty piles are not, as they are charged, such rude and useless excrescences of our ill-formed globe; but the admirable tools of nature, contrived and ordered by the infinite Creator, to do one of its most useful works. For, was the surface of the earth even and level, and the middle parts of its islands and continents not mountainous and high as now it is, it is most certain there could be no descent for the

commodate his processes to the convenience of individuals. The bubbles on the foam which coats a stormy sea are floating episodes, made and unmade by the forces of the wind and water. Our private selves are like those bubbles—epiphenomena, as Clifford, I believe, ingeniously called them; their destinies weigh nothing and determine nothing in the world's irremediable currents of events.

You see how natural it is, from this point of view, to treat religion as a mere survival, for religion does in fact perpetuate the traditions of the most primeval thought. To coerce the spiritual powers, or to square them and get them on our side, was, during enormous tracts of time, the one great object in our dealings with the natural world. For our ancestors, dreams, hallucinations, revelations, and cock-and-bull stories were inextricably mixed with facts. Up to a comparatively recent date such distinctions as those between what has been verified and what is only conjectured, between the impersonal and the personal aspects of existence, were hardly suspected or conceived. Whatever you imagined in a lively manner, whatever you thought fit to be true, you affirmed confidently; and whatever you affirmed, your comrades believed. Truth was what had not yet been contradicted, most things were taken into the mind from the point of view of their human suggestiveness, and the attention confined itself exclusively to the æsthetic and dramatic aspects of events.[1]

rivers, no conveyance for the waters; but, instead of gliding along those gentle declivities which the higher lands now afford them quite down to the sea, they would stagnate and perhaps stink, and also drown large tracts of land.

"[Thus] the hills and vales, though to a peevish and weary traveler they may seem incommodious and troublesome, yet are a noble work of the great Creator, and wisely appointed by him for the good of our sublunary world."

Until the seventeenth century this mode of thought prevailed. One need only recall the dramatic treatment even of mechanical

How indeed could it be otherwise? The extraordinary value, for explanation and prevision, of those mathemati-

questions by Aristotle, as, for example, his explanation of the power of the lever to make a small weight raise a larger one. This is due, according to Aristotle, to the generally miraculous character of the circle and of all circular movement. The circle is both convex and concave; it is made by a fixed point and a moving line, which contradict each other; and whatever moves in a circle moves in opposite directions. Nevertheless, movement in a circle is the most "natural" movement; and the long arm of the lever, moving, as it does, in the larger circle, has the greater amount of this natural motion, and consequently requires the lesser force. Or recall the explanation by Herodotus of the position of the sun in winter: It moves to the south because of the cold which drives it into the warm parts of the heavens over Libya. Or listen to Saint Augustine's speculations: "Who gave to chaff such power to freeze that it preserves snow buried under it, and such power to warm that it ripens green fruit? Who can explain the strange properties of fire itself, which blackens all that it burns, though itself bright, and which, though of the most beautiful colors, discolors almost all that it touches and feeds upon, and turns blazing fuel into grimy cinders? . . . Then what wonderful properties do we find in charcoal, which is so brittle that a light tap breaks it, and a slight pressure pulverizes it, and yet is so strong that no moisture rots it, nor any time causes it to decay." City of God, book xxi, ch. iv.

Such aspects of things as these, their naturalness and unnaturalness, the sympathies and antipathies of their superficial qualities, their eccentricities, their brightness and strength and destructiveness, were inevitably the ways in which they originally fastened our attention.

If you open early medical books, you will find sympathetic magic invoked on every page. Take, for example, the famous vulnerary ointment attributed to Paracelsus. For this there were a variety of receipts, including usually human fat, the fat of either a bull, a wild boar, or a bear; powdered earthworms, the *usnia,* or mossy growth on the weathered skull of a hanged criminal, and other materials equally unpleasant—the whole prepared under the planet Venus if possible, but never under Mars or Saturn. Then, if a splinter of wood, dipped in the patient's blood, or the bloodstained weapon that wounded him, be immersed in this ointment, the wound itself being tightly bound up, the latter infallibly gets well—I quote now Van Helmont's account—for the blood on the weapon or splinter, containing in it the spirit of the wounded man, is roused to active excite-

cal and mechanical modes of conception which science uses was a result that could not possibly have been expected in

ment by the contact of the ointment, whence there results to it a full commission or power to cure its cousin-german, the blood in the patient's body. This it does by sucking out the dolorous and exotic impression from the wounded part. But to do this it has to implore the aid of the bull's fat, and other portions of the unguent. The reason why bull's fat is so powerful is that the bull at the time of slaughter is full of secret reluctancy and vindictive murmurs, and therefore dies with a higher flame of revenge about him than any other animal. And thus we have made it out, says this author, that the admirable efficacy of the ointment ought to be imputed, not to any auxiliary concurrence of Satan, but simply to the energy of the *posthumous character of Revenge* remaining firmly impressed upon the blood and concreted fat in the unguent. J. B. VAN HELMONT: A Ternary of Paradoxes, translated by WALTER CHARLETON, London, 1650.—I much abridge the original in my citations.

The author goes on to prove by the analogy of many other natural facts that this sympathetic action between things at a distance is the true rationale of the case. "If," he says, "the heart of a horse, slain by a witch, taken out of the yet reeking carcase, be impaled upon an arrow and roasted, immediately the whole witch becomes tormented with the insufferable pains and cruelty of the fire, which could by no means happen unless there preceded a conjunction of the spirit of the witch with the spirit of the horse. In the reeking and yet panting heart, the spirit of the witch is kept captive, and the retreat of it prevented by the arrow transfixed. Similarly hath not many a murdered carcase at the coroner's inquest suffered a fresh hæmorrhage or cruentation at the presence of the assassin?—the blood being, as in a furious fit of anger, enraged and agitated by the impress of revenge conceived against the murderer, at the instant of the soul's compulsive exile from the body. So, if you have dropsy, gout, or jaundice, by including some of your warm blood in the shell and white of an egg, which, exposed to a gentle heat, and mixed with a bait of flesh, you shall give to a hungry dog or hog, the disease shall instantly pass from you into the animal, and leave you entirely. And similarly again, if you burn some of the milk either of a cow or of a woman, the gland from which it issued will dry up. A gentleman at Brussels had his nose mowed off in a combat, but the celebrated surgeon Tagliacozzus digged a new nose for him out of the skin of the arm of a porter at Bologna. About thirteen months after his return to his own country, the engrafted nose

advance. Weight, movement, velocity, direction, position, what thin, pallid, uninteresting ideas! How could the richer animistic aspects of Nature, the peculiarities and oddities that make phenomena picturesquely striking or expressive, fail to have been first singled out and followed by philosophy as the more promising avenue to the knowledge of Nature's life? Well, it is still in these richer animistic and dramatic aspects that religion delights to dwell. It is the terror and beauty of phenomena, the "promise" of the dawn and of the rainbow, the "voice" of the thunder, the "gentleness" of the summer rain, the "sublimity" of the stars, and not the physical laws which these things follow, by which the religious mind still continues to be most impressed; and just as of yore, the devout man tells you that in the solitude of his room or of the fields he still feels the divine presence, that inflowings of help come in reply to his prayers, and that sacrifices to this unseen reality fill him with security and peace.

Pure anachronism! says the survival-theory;—anachronism for which deanthropomorphization of the imagination is the remedy required. The less we mix the private with the cosmic, the more we dwell in universal and impersonal terms, the truer heirs of Science we become.

In spite of the appeal which this impersonality of the scientific attitude makes to a certain magnanimity of temper, I believe it to be shallow, and I can now state my reason in comparatively few words. That reason is that, so long as we deal with the cosmic and the general, we deal only

grew cold, putrefied, and in a few days dropped off, and it was then discovered that the porter had expired, near about the same punctilio of time. There are still at Brussels eye-witnesses of this occurrence," says Van Helmont; and adds, "I pray what is there in this of superstition or of exalted imagination?"

Modern mind-cure literature—the works of Prentice Mulford, for example—is full of sympathetic magic.

with the symbols of reality, but *as soon as we deal with private and personal phenomena as such, we deal with realities in the completest sense of the term.* I think I can easily make clear what I mean by these words.

The world of our experience consists at all times of two parts, an objective and a subjective part, of which the former may be incalculably more extensive than the latter, and yet the latter can never be omitted or suppressed. The objective part is the sum total of whatsoever at any given time we may be thinking of, the subjective part is the inner "state" in which the thinking comes to pass. What we think of may be enormous—the cosmic times and spaces, for example—whereas the inner state may be the most fugitive and paltry activity of mind. Yet the cosmic objects, so far as the experience yields them, are but ideal pictures of something whose existence we do not inwardly possess but only point at outwardly, while the inner state is our very experience itself; its reality and that of our experience are one. A conscious field *plus* its object as felt or thought of *plus* an attitude towards the object *plus* the sense of a self to whom the attitude belongs—such a concrete bit of personal experience may be a small bit, but it is a solid bit as long as it lasts; not hollow, not a mere abstract element of experience, such as the "object" is when taken all alone. It is a *full* fact, even though it be an insignificant fact; it is of the *kind* to which all realities whatsoever must belong; the motor currents of the world run through the like of it; it is on the line connecting real events with real events. That unsharable feeling which each one of us has of the pinch of his individual destiny as he privately feels it rolling out on fortune's wheel may be disparaged for its egotism, may be sneered at as unscientific, but it is the one thing that fills up the measure of our concrete actuality, and any would-be existent that should lack such a feeling, or its analogue, would be a piece of reality only half made up.[1]

If this be true, it is absurd for science to say that the egotistic elements of experience should be suppressed. The axis of reality runs solely through the egotistic places—they are strung upon it like so many beads. To describe the world with all the various feelings of the individual pinch of destiny, all the various spiritual attitudes, left out from the description—they being as describable as anything else—would be something like offering a printed bill of fare as the equivalent for a solid meal. Religion makes no such blunder. The individual's religion may be egotistic, and those private realities which it keeps in touch with may be narrow enough; but at any rate it always remains infinitely less hollow and abstract, as far as it goes, than a science which prides itself on taking no account of anything private at all.

A bill of fare with one real raisin on it instead of the word "raisin," with one real egg instead of the word "egg," might be an inadequate meal, but it would at least be a commencement of reality. The contention of the survival-theory that we ought to stick to non-personal elements exclusively seems like saying that we ought to be satisfied forever with reading the naked bill of fare. I think, therefore, that however particular questions connected with our individual destinies may be answered, it is only by acknowledging them as genuine questions, and living in the sphere of thought which they open up, that we become profound. But to live thus is to be religious; so I unhesitatingly repudiate the survival-theory of religion, as being founded on an egregious mistake. It does not follow, because our ancestors

[1] Compare Lotze's doctrine that the only meaning we can attach to the notion of a thing as it is "in itself" is by conceiving it as it is *for* itself; i. e., as a piece of full experience with a private sense of "pinch" or inner activity of some sort going with it.

made so many errors of fact and mixed them with their religion, that we should therefore leave off being religious at all.[1] By being religious we establish ourselves in possession of ultimate reality at the only points at which reality

[1] Even the errors of fact may possibly turn out not to be as wholesale as the scientist assumes. We saw in Lecture IV how the religious conception of the universe seems to many mind-curers "verified" from day to day by their experience of fact. "Experience of fact" is a field with so many things in it that the sectarian scientist, methodically declining, as he does, to recognize such "facts" as mind-curers and others like them experience, otherwise than by such rude heads of classification as "bosh," "rot," "folly," certainly leaves out a mass of raw fact which, save for the industrious interest of the religious in the more personal aspects of reality, would never have succeeded in getting itself recorded at all. We know this to be true already in certain cases; it may, therefore, be true in others as well. Miraculous healings have always been part of the supernaturalist stock in trade, and have always been dismissed by the scientist as figments of the imagination. But the scientist's tardy education in the facts of hypnotism has recently given him an apperceiving mass for phenomena of this order, and he consequently now allows that the healings may exist, provided you expressly call them effects of "suggestion." Even the stigmata of the cross on Saint Francis's hands and feet may on these terms not be a fable. Similarly, the time-honored phenomenon of diabolical possession is on the point of being admitted by the scientist as a fact, now that he has the name of "hystero-demonopathy" by which to apperceive it. No one can foresee just how far this legitimation of occultist phenomena under newly found scientist titles may proceed—even "prophecy," even "levitation," might creep into the pale.

Thus the divorce between scientist facts and religious facts may not necessarily be as eternal as it at first sight seems, nor the personalism and romanticism of the world, as they appeared to primitive thinking, be matters so irrevocably outgrown. The final human opinion may, in short, in some manner now impossible to foresee, revert to the more personal style, just as any path of progress may follow a spiral rather than a straight line. If this were so, the rigorously impersonal view of science might one day appear as having been a temporarily useful eccentricity rather than the definitively triumphant position which the sectarian scientist at present so confidently announces it to be.

is given us to guard. Our responsible concern is with our private destiny, after all.

You see now why I have been so individualistic throughout these lectures, and why I have seemed so bent on rehabilitating the element of feeling in religion and subordinating its intellectual part. Individuality is founded in feeling; and the recesses of feeling, the darker, blinder strata of character, are the only places in the world in which we catch real fact in the making, and directly perceive how events happen, and how work is actually done.[1] Compared with this world of living individualized feelings, the world of generalized objects which the intellect contemplates is without solidity or life. As in stereoscopic or kinetoscopic pictures seen outside the instrument, the third dimension, the movement, the vital element, are not there. We get a beautiful picture of an express train supposed to be moving, but where in the picture, as I have heard a friend say, is the energy or the fifty miles an hour?[2]

[1] Hume's criticism has banished causation from the world of physical objects, and "Science" is absolutely satisfied to define cause in terms of concomitant change—read Mach, Pearson, Ostwald. The "original" of the notion of causation is in our inner personal experience, and only there can causes in the old-fashioned sense be directly observed and described.

[2] When I read in a religious paper words like these: "Perhaps the best thing we can say of God is that he is *the Inevitable Inference*," I recognize the tendency to let religion evaporate in intellectual terms. Would martyrs have sung in the flames for a mere inference, however inevitable it might be? Original religious men, like Saint Francis, Luther, Behmen, have usually been enemies of the intellect's pretension to meddle with religious things. Yet the intellect, everywhere invasive, shows everywhere its shallowing effect. See how the ancient spirit of Methodism evaporates under those wonderfully able rationalistic booklets (which every one should read) of a philosopher like Professor Bowne (The Christian Revelation, The Christian Life, The Atonement: Cincinnati and New York, 1898, 1899, 1900). See the positively expulsive purpose of philosophy properly so called:—

"Religion," writes M. Vacherot (La Religion, Paris, 1869, pp. 313,

Let us agree, then, that Religion, occupying herself with personal destinies and keeping thus in contact with the only absolute realities which we know, must necessarily play an eternal part in human history. The next thing to decide is what she reveals about those destinies, or whether indeed she reveals anything distinct enough to be considered a general message to mankind. We have done as you see, with our preliminaries, and our final summing up can now begin.

I am well aware that after all the palpitating documents which I have quoted, and all the perspectives of emotion-inspiring institution and belief that my previous lectures have opened, the dry analysis to which I now advance may appear to many of you like an anti-climax, a tapering-off

436, et passim), "answers to a transient state or condition, not to a permanent determination of human nature, being merely an expression of that stage of the human mind which is dominated by the imagination. . . . Christianity has but a single possible final heir to its estate, and that is scientific philosophy."

In a still more radical vein, Professor Ribot (Psychologie des Sentiments, p. 310) describes the evaporation of religion. He sums it up in a single formula—the ever-growing predominance of the rational intellectual element, with the gradual fading out of the emotional element, this latter tending to enter into the group of purely intellectual sentiments. "Of religious sentiment properly so called, nothing survives at last save a vague respect for the unknowable *x* which is a last relic of the fear, and a certain attraction towards the ideal, which is a relic of the love, that characterized the earlier periods of religious growth. To state this more simply, *religion tends to turn into religious philosophy.*—These are psychologically entirely different things, the one being a theoretic construction of ratiocination, whereas the other is the living work of a group of persons, or of a great inspired leader, calling into play the entire thinking and feeling organism of man."

I find the same failure to recognize that the stronghold of religion lies in individuality in attempts like those of Professor Baldwin (Mental Development, Social and Ethical Interpretations, ch. x) and Mr. H. R. Marshall (Instinct and Reason, chaps. viii. to xii.) to make it a purely "conservative social force."

and flattening out of the subject, instead of a crescendo of interest and result. I said awhile ago that the religious attitude of Protestants appears poverty-stricken to the Catholic imagination. Still more poverty-stricken, I fear, may my final summing up of the subject appear at first to some of you. On which account I pray you now to bear this point in mind, that in the present part of it I am expressly trying to reduce religion to its lowest admissible terms, to that minimum, free from individualistic excrescences, which all religions contain as their nucleus, and on which it may be hoped that all religious persons may agree. That established, we should have a result which might be small, but would at least be solid; and on it and round it the ruddier additional beliefs on which the different individuals make their venture might be grafted, and flourish as richly as you please. I shall add my own over-belief (which will be, I confess, of a somewhat pallid kind, as befits a critical philosopher), and you will, I hope, also add your over-beliefs, and we shall soon be in the varied world of concrete religious constructions once more. For the moment, let me dryly pursue the analytic part of the task.

Both thought and feeling are determinants of conduct, and the same conduct may be determined either by feeling or by thought. When we survey the whole field of religion, we find a great variety in the thoughts that have prevailed there; but the feelings on the one hand and the conduct on the other are almost always the same, for Stoic, Christian, and Buddhist saints are practically indistinguishable in their lives. The theories which Religion generates, being thus variable, are secondary; and if you wish to grasp her essence, you must look to the feelings and the conduct as being the more constant elements. It is between these two elements that the short circuit exists on which she carries on her principal business, while the ideas and symbols and other institutions form loop-lines which may be perfections and improvements, and may even some day all be united into one harmonious system, but which are not to be regarded as organs with an indispensable function, necessary at all times for religious life to go on. This seems to me the first conclusion which we are entitled to draw from the phenomena we have passed in review.

The next step is to characterize the feelings. To what psychological order do they belong?

The resultant outcome of them is in any case what Kant calls a "sthenic" affection, an excitement of the cheerful, expansive, "dynamogenic" order which, like any tonic, freshens our vital powers. In almost every lecture, but especially in the lectures on Conversion and on Saintliness, we have seen how this emotion overcomes temperamental melancholy and imparts endurance to the Subject, or a zest, or a meaning, or an enchantment and glory to the common objects of life.[1] The name of "faith-state," by which Professor Leuba designates it, is a good one.[2] It is a biological as well as a psychological condition, and Tolstoy is absolutely accurate in classing faith among the forces *by which men live*.[3] The total absence of it, anhedonia,[4] means collapse.

The faith-state may hold a very minimum of intellectual content. We saw examples of this in those sudden raptures of the divine presence, or in such mystical seizures as Dr. Bucke described.[5] It may be a mere vague enthusiasm, half spiritual, half vital, a courage, and a feeling that great and wondrous things are in the air.[6]

1 Compare, for instance, pages 200, 215, 219, 222, 244-250, 270-273.

2 American Journal of Psychology, vii. 345.

3 Above, p. 181.

4 Above, p. 143.

5 Above, p. 391.

6 Example: Henri Perreyve writes to Gratry: "I do not know how to deal with the happiness which you aroused in me this morning. It overwhelms me; I want to *do* something, yet I can do nothing and

When, however, a positive intellectual content is associated with a faith-state, it gets invincibly stamped in upon belief,[1] and this explains the passionate loyalty of religious persons everywhere to the minutest details of their so widely differing creeds. Taking creeds and faith-state together, as forming "religions," and treating these as purely subjective phenomena, without regard to the question of their "truth," we are obliged, on account of their extraordinary influence upon action and endurance, to class them amongst the most important biological functions of mankind. Their stimulant and anæsthetic effect is so great that Professor Leuba, in a recent article,[2] goes so far as to say

am fit for nothing. . . . I would fain do *great things*." Again, after an inspiring interview, he writes: "I went homewards, intoxicated with joy, hope, and strength. I wanted to feed upon my happiness in solitude, far from all men. It was late; but, unheeding that, I took a mountain path and went on like a madman, looking at the heavens, regardless of earth. Suddenly an instinct made me draw hastily back —I was on the very edge of a precipice, one step more and I must have fallen. I took fright and gave up my nocturnal promenade." A. Gratry: Henri Perreyve, London, 1872, pp. 92, 89.

This primacy, in the faith-state, of vague expansive impulse over direction is well expressed in Walt Whitman's lines (Leaves of Grass, 1872, p. 190):—

"O to confront night, storms, hunger, ridicule, accidents, rebuffs, as
the trees and animals do. . . .
Dear Camerado! I confess I have urged you onward with me, and
still urge you, without the least idea what is our destination,
Or whether we shall be victorious, or utterly quell'd and defeated."

This readiness for great things, and this sense that the world by its importance, wonderfulness, etc., is apt for their production, would seem to be the undifferentiated germ of all the higher faiths. Trust in our own dreams of ambition, or in our country's expansive destinies, and faith in the providence of God, all have their source in that onrush of our sanguine impulses, and in that sense of the exceedingness of the possible over the real.

[1] Compare Leuba: Loc. cit., pp. 346-349.

[2] The Contents of Religious Consciousness, in The Monist, xi. 536, July 1901.

that so long as men can *use* their God, they care very little who he is, or even whether he is at all. "The truth of the matter can be put," says Leuba, "in this way: *God is not known, he is not understood; he is used*—sometimes as meat-purveyor, sometimes as moral support, sometimes as friend, sometimes as an object of love. If he proves himself useful, the religious consciousness asks for no more than that. Does God really exist? How does he exist? What is he? are so many irrelevant questions. Not God, but life, more life, a larger, richer, more satisfying life, is, in the last analysis, the end of religion. The love of life, at any and every level of development, is the religious impulse."[1]

At this purely subjective rating, therefore, Religion must be considered vindicated in a certain way from the attacks of her critics. It would seem that she cannot be a mere anachronism and survival, but must exert a permanent function, whether she be with or without intellectual content, and whether, if she have any, it be true or false.

We must next pass beyond the point of view of merely subjective utility, and make inquiry into the intellectual content itself.

First, is there, under all the discrepancies of the creeds,

[1] Loc. cit., pp. 571, 572, abridged. See, also, this writer's extraordinarily true criticism of the notion that religion primarily seeks to solve the intellectual mystery of the world. Compare what W. Bender says (in his Wesen der Religion, Bonn, 1888, pp. 85, 38): "Not the question about God, and not the inquiry into the origin and purpose of the world is religion, but the question about Man. All religious views of life are anthropocentric." "Religion is that activity of the human impulse towards self-preservation by means of which Man seeks to carry his essential vital purposes through against the adverse pressure of the world by raising himself freely towards the world's ordering and governing powers when the limits of his own strength are reached." The whole book is little more than a development of these words.

a common nucleus to which they bear their testimony unanimously?

And second, ought we to consider the testimony true?

I will take up the first question first, and answer it immediately in the affirmative. The warring gods and formulas of the various religions do indeed cancel each other, but there is a certain uniform deliverance in which religions all appear to meet. It consists of two parts:—

1. An uneasiness; and
2. Its solution.

1. The uneasiness, reduced to its simplest terms, is a sense that there is *something wrong about us* as we naturally stand.

2. The solution is a sense that *we are saved from the wrongness* by making proper connection with the higher powers.

In those more developed minds which alone we are studying, the wrongness takes a moral character, and the salvation takes a mystical tinge. I think we shall keep well within the limits of what is common to all such minds if we formulate the essence of their religious experience in terms like these:—

The individual, so far as he suffers from his wrongness and criticises it, is to that extent consciously beyond it, and in at least possible touch with something higher, if anything higher exist. Along with the wrong part there is thus a better part of him, even though it may be but a most helpless germ. With which part he should identify his real being is by no means obvious at this stage; but when stage 2 (the stage of solution or salvation) arrives,[1] the man identifies his real being with the germinal higher part of himself; and does so in the following way. *He becomes con-*

[1] Remember that for some men it arrives suddenly, for others gradually, whilst others again practically enjoy it all their life.

*scious that this higher part is conterminous and continuous with a* MORE *of the same quality, which is operative in the universe outside of him, and which he can keep in working touch with, and in a fashion get on board of and save himself when all his lower being has gone to pieces in the wreck.*

It seems to me that all the phenomena are accurately describable in these very simple general terms.[1] They allow for the divided self and the struggle; they involve the change of personal centre and the surrender of the lower self; they express the appearance of exteriority of the helping power and yet account for our sense of union with it;[2] and they fully justify our feelings of security and joy. There is probably no autobiographic document, among all those which I have quoted, to which the description will not well apply. One need only add such specific details as will adapt it to various theologies and various personal temperaments, and one will then have the various experiences reconstructed in their individual forms.

So far, however, as this analysis goes, the experiences are only psychological phenomena. They possess, it is true, enormous biological worth. Spiritual strength really increases in the subject when he has them, a new life opens for him, and they seem to him a place of conflux where the forces of two universes meet; and yet this may be nothing but his subjective way of feeling things, a mood of his own fancy, in spite of the effects produced. I now turn to my

[1] The practical difficulties are: 1, to "realize the reality" of one's higher part; 2, to identify one's self with it exclusively; and 3, to identify it with all the rest of ideal being.

[2] "When mystical activity is at its height, we find consciousness possessed by the sense of a being at once *excessive* and *identical* with the self: great enough to be God; interior enough to be *me*. The "objectivity" of it ought in that case to be called *excessivity*, rather, or exceedingness." RÉCÉJAC: Essai sur les fondements de la conscience mystique, 1897, p. 46.

second question: What is the objective "truth" of their content?[1]

The part of the content concerning which the question of truth most pertinently arises is that "MORE of the same quality" with which our own higher self appears in the experience to come into harmonious working relation. Is such a "more" merely our own notion, or does it really exist? If so, in what shape does it exist? Does it act, as well as exist? And in what form should we conceive of that "union" with it of which religious geniuses are so convinced?

It is in answering these questions that the various theologies perform their theoretic work, and that their divergencies most come to light. They all agree that the "more" really exists; though some of them hold it to exist in the shape of a personal god or gods, while others are satisfied to conceive it as a stream of ideal tendency embedded in the eternal structure of the world. They all agree, moreover, that it acts as well as exists, and that something really is effected for the better when you throw your life into its hands. It is when they treat of the experience of "union" with it that their speculative differences appear most clearly. Over this point pantheism and theism, nature and second birth, works and grace and karma, immortality and reincarnation, rationalism and mysticism, carry on inveterate disputes.

At the end of my lecture on Philosophy[2] I held out the notion that an impartial science of religions might sift out from the midst of their discrepancies a common body of doctrine which she might also formulate in terms to which

[1] The word "truth" is here taken to mean something additional to bare value for life, although the natural propensity of man is to believe that whatever has great value for life is thereby certified as true.

[2] Above, p. 445.

physical science need not object. This, I said, she might adopt as her own reconciling hypothesis, and recommend it for general belief. I also said that in my last lecture I should have to try my own hand at framing such an hypothesis.

The time has now come for this attempt. Who says "hypothesis" renounces the ambition to be coercive in his arguments. The most I can do is, accordingly, to offer something that may fit the facts so easily that your scientific logic will find no plausible pretext for vetoing your impulse to welcome it as true.

The "more," as we called it, and the meaning of our "union" with it, form the nucleus of our inquiry. Into what definite description can these words be translated, and for what definite facts do they stand? It would never do for us to place ourselves offhand at the position of a particular theology, the Christian theology, for example, and proceed immediately to define the "more" as Jehovah, and the "union" as his imputation to us of the righteousness of Christ. That would be unfair to other religions, and, from our present standpoint at least, would be an over-belief.

We must begin by using less particularized terms; and, since one of the duties of the science of religions is to keep religion in connection with the rest of science, we shall do well to seek first of all a way of describing the "more," which psychologists may also recognize as real. The *subconscious self* is nowadays a well-accredited psychological entity; and I believe that in it we have exactly the mediating term required. Apart from all religious considerations, there is actually and literally more life in our total soul than we are at any time aware of. The exploration of the transmarginal field has hardly yet been seriously undertaken, but what Mr. Myers said in 1892 in his essay on the Subliminal Consciousness[1] is as true as when it was first written: "Each of us is in reality an abiding psychical entity far more extensive than he knows—an individuality which can never express itself completely through any corporeal manifestation. The Self manifests through the organism; but there is always some part of the Self unmanifested; and always, as it seems, some power of organic expression in abeyance or reserve."[2] Much of the content of this larger background against which our conscious being stands out in relief is insignificant. Imperfect memories, silly jingles, inhibitive timidities, "dissolutive" phenomena of various sorts, as Myers calls them, enters into it for a large part. But in it many of the performances of genius seem also to have their origin; and in our study of conversion, of mystical experiences, and of prayer, we have seen how striking a part invasions from this region play in the religious life.

Let me then propose, as an hypothesis, that whatever it may be on its *farther* side, the "more" with which in religious experience we feel ourselves connected is on its *hither* side the subconscious continuation of our conscious life. Starting thus with a recognized psychological fact as our basis, we seem to preserve a contact with "science" which

[1] Proceedings of the Society for Psychical Research, vol. vii. p. 305. For a full statement of Mr. Myers's views, I may refer to his posthumous work, "Human Personality in the Light of Recent Research," which is already announced by Messrs. Longmans, Green & Co. as being in press. Mr. Myers for the first time proposed as a general psychological problem the exploration of the subliminal region of consciousness throughout its whole extent, and made the first methodical steps in its topography by treating as a natural series a mass of subliminal facts hitherto considered only as curious isolated facts, and subjecting them to a systematized nomenclature. How important this exploration will prove, future work upon the path which Myers has opened can alone show. Compare my paper: "Frederic Myers's Services to Psychology," in the said Proceedings, part xlii., May, 1901.

[2] Compare the inventory given above on pp. 472-4, and also what is said of the subconscious self on pp. 228-231. 235-236.

the ordinary theologian lacks. At the same time the theologian's contention that the religious man is moved by an external power is vindicated, for it is one of the peculiarities of invasions from the subconscious region to take on objective appearances, and to suggest to the Subject an external control. In the religious life the control is felt as "higher"; but since on our hypothesis it is primarily the higher faculties of our own hidden mind which are controlling, the sense of union with the power beyond us is a sense of something, not merely apparently, but literally true.

This doorway into the subject seems to me the best one for a science of religions, for it mediates between a number of different points of view. Yet it is only a doorway, and difficulties present themselves as soon as we step through it, and ask how far our transmarginal consciousness carries us if we follow it on its remoter side. Here the over-beliefs begin: here mysticism and the conversion-rapture and Vedantism and transcendental idealism bring in their monistic interpretations[1] and tell us that the finite self rejoins the absolute self, for it was always one with God and identical with the soul of the world.[2] Here the prophets of all the

[1] Compare above, pp. 410 ff.

[2] One more expression of this belief, to increase the reader's familiarity with the notion of it:—

"If this room is full of darkness for thousands of years, and you come in and begin to weep and wail, 'Oh, the darkness,' will the darkness vanish? Bring the light in, strike a match, and light comes in a moment. So what good will it do you to think all your lives, 'Oh, I have done evil, I have made many mistakes'? It requires no ghost to tell us that. Bring in the light, and the evil goes in a moment. Strengthen the real nature, build up yourselves, the effulgent, the resplendent, the ever pure, call that up in every one whom you see. I wish that every one of us had come to such a state that even when we see the vilest of human beings we can see the God within, and instead of condemning, say, 'Rise, thou effulgent One, rise thou who art always pure, rise thou birthless and deathless, rise almighty, and manifest your nature.' . . . This is the highest prayer that the Advaita

different religions come with their visions, voices, raptures, and other openings, supposed by each to authenticate his own peculiar faith.

Those of us who are not personally favored with such specific revelations must stand outside of them altogether and, for the present at least, decide that, since they corroborate incompatible theological doctrines, they neutralize one another and leave no fixed results. If we follow any one of them, or if we follow philosophical theory and embrace monistic pantheism on non-mystical grounds, we do so in the exercise of our individual freedom, and build out our religion in the way most congruous with our personal susceptibilities. Among these susceptibilities intellectual ones play a decisive part. Although the religious question is primarily a question of life, of living or not living in the higher union which opens itself to us as a gift, yet the spiritual excitement in which the gift appears a real one will often fail to be aroused in an individual until certain particular intellectual beliefs or ideas which, as we say, come home to him, are touched.[1] These ideas will thus be essen-

teaches. This is the one prayer: remembering our nature." . . . "Why does man go out to look for a God? . . . It is your own heart beating, and you did not know, you were mistaking it for something external. He, nearest of the near, my own self, the reality of my own life, my body and my soul.—I am Thee and Thou art Me. That is your own nature. Assert it, manifest it. Not to become pure, you are pure already. You are not to be perfect, you are that already. Every good thought which you think or act upon is simply tearing the veil, as it were, and the purity, the Infinity, the God behind, manifests itself—the eternal Subject of everything, the eternal Witness in this universe, your own Self. Knowledge is, as it were, a lower step, a degradation. We are It already; how to know It?" SWAMI VIVEKANANDA: Addresses, No. XII., Practical Vedanta, part iv. pp. 172, 174, London, 1897; and Lectures, The Real and the Apparent Man, p. 24, abridged.

[1] For instance, here is a case where a person exposed from her birth to Christian ideas had to wait till they came to her clad in spiritistic

tial to that individual's religion;—which is as much as to say that over-beliefs in various directions are absolutely indispensable, and that we should treat them with tenderness and tolerance so long as they are not intolerant themselves. As I have elsewhere written, the most interesting and valuable things about a man are usually his over-beliefs.

Disregarding the over-beliefs, and confining ourselves to what is common and generic, we have in *the fact that the conscious person is continuous with a wider self through which saving experiences come,*[1] a positive content of religious experience which, it seems to me, *is literally and objectively true as far as it goes.* If I now proceed to state my own hypothesis about the farther limits of this extension of our personality, I shall be offering my own over-belief—though I know it will appear a sorry under-belief to some of you—for which I can only bespeak the same indulgence which in a converse case I should accord to yours.

formulas before the saving experience set in:—

"For myself I can say that spiritualism has saved me. It was revealed to me at a critical moment of my life, and without it I don't know what I should have done. It has taught me to detach myself from worldly things and to place my hope in things to come. Through it I have learned to see in all men, even in those most criminal, even in those from whom I have most suffered, undeveloped brothers to whom I owed assistance, love, and forgiveness. I have learned that I must lose my temper over nothing, despise no one, and pray for all. Most of all I have learned to pray! And although I have still much to learn in this domain, prayer ever brings me more strength, consolation, and comfort. I feel more than ever that I have only made a few steps on the long road of progress; but I look at its length without dismay, for I have confidence that the day will come when all my efforts shall be rewarded. So Spiritualism has a great place in my life, indeed it holds the first place there." Flournoy Collection.

[1] "The influence of the Holy Spirit, exquisitely called the Comforter, is a matter of actual experience, as solid a reality as that of electro-magnetism." W. C. Brownell, Scribner's Magazine, vol. xxx. p 112.

The further limits of our being plunge, it seems to me, into an altogether other dimension of existence from the sensible and merely "understandable" world. Name it the mystical region, or the supernatural region, whichever you choose. So far as our ideal impulses originate in this region (and most of them do originate in it, for we find them possessing us in a way for which we cannot articulately account), we belong to it in a more intimate sense than that in which we belong to the visible world, for we belong in the most intimate sense wherever our ideals belong. Yet the unseen region in question is not merely ideal, for it produces effects in this world. When we commune with it, work is actually done upon our finite personality, for we are turned into new men, and consequences in the way of conduct follow in the natural world upon our regenerative change.[1] But that which produces effects within another reality must be termed a reality itself, so I feel as if we had

[1] That the transaction of opening ourselves, otherwise called prayer, is a perfectly definite one for certain persons, appears abundantly in the preceding lectures. I append another concrete example to reinforce the impression on the reader's mind:—

"Man can learn to transcend these limitations [of finite thought] and draw power and wisdom at will. . . . The divine presence is known through experience. The turning to a higher plane is a distinct act of consciousness. It is not a vague, twilight or semi-conscious experience. It is not an ecstasy; it is not a trance. It is not super-consciousness in the Vedantic sense. It is not due to self-hypnotization. It is a perfectly calm, sane, sound, rational, common-sense shifting of consciousness from the phenomena of sense-perception to the phenomena of seership, from the thought of self to a distinctively higher realm. . . . For example, if the lower self be nervous, anxious, tense, one can in a few moments compel it to be calm. This is not done by a word simply. Again I say, it is not hypnotism. It is by the exercise of power. One feels the spirit of peace as definitely as heat is perceived on a hot summer day. The power can be as surely used as the sun's rays can be focused and made to do work, to set fire to wood." The Higher Law, vol. iv. pp. 4, 6, Boston, August, 1901.

no philosophic excuse for calling the unseen or mystical world unreal.

God is the natural appellation, for us Christians at least, for the supreme reality, so I will call this higher part of the universe by the name of God.[1] We and God have business with each other; and in opening ourselves to his influence our deepest destiny is fulfilled. The universe, at those parts of it which our personal being constitutes, takes a turn genuinely for the worse or for the better in proportion as each one of us fulfills or evades God's demands. As far as this goes I probably have you with me, for I only translate into schematic language what I may call the instinctive belief of mankind: God is real since he produces real effects.

The real effects in question, so far as I have as yet admitted them, are exerted on the personal centres of energy of the various subjects, but the spontaneous faith of most of the subjects is that they embrace a wider sphere than this. Most religious men believe (or "know," if they be mystical) that not only they themselves, but the whole universe of beings to whom the God is present, are secure in his parental hands. There is a sense, a dimension, they are sure, in which we are *all* saved, in spite of the gates of hell and all adverse terrestrial appearances. God's existence is the guarantee of an ideal order that shall be permanently preserved. This world may indeed, as science assures us, some day burn up or freeze; but if it is part of his order, the old ideals are sure to be brought elsewhere to fruition, so that where God is, tragedy is only provisional and partial, and shipwreck and dissolution are not the absolutely final things. Only when this farther step of faith concern-

[1] Transcendentalists are fond of the term "Over-soul," but as a rule they use it in an intellectualist sense, as meaning only a medium of communion. "God" is a causal agent as well as a medium of communion, and that is the aspect which I wish to emphasize.

ing God is taken, and remote objective consequences are predicted, does religion, as it seems to me, get wholly free from the first immediate subjective experience, and bring a *real hypothesis* into play. A good hypothesis in science must have other properties than those of the phenomenon it is immediately invoked to explain, otherwise it is not prolific enough. God, meaning only what enters into the religious man's experience of union, falls short of being an hypothesis of this more useful order. He needs to enter into wider cosmic relations in order to justify the subject's absolute confidence and peace.

That the God with whom, starting from the hither side of our own extra-marginal self, we come at its remoter margin into commerce should be the absolute world-ruler, is of course a very considerable over-belief. Over-belief as it is, though, it is an article of almost every one's religion. Most of us pretend in some way to prop it upon our philosophy, but the philosophy itself is really propped upon this faith. What is this but to say that Religion, in her fullest exercise of function, is not a mere illumination of facts already elsewhere given, not a mere passion, like love, which views things in a rosier light. It is indeed that, as we have seen abundantly. But it is something more, namely, a postulator of new *facts* as well. The world interpreted religiously is not the materialistic world over again, with an altered expression; it must have, over and above the altered expression, *a natural constitution* different at some point from that which a materialistic world would have. It must be such that different events can be expected in it, different conduct must be required.

This thoroughly "pragmatic" view of religion has usually been taken as a matter of course by common men. They have interpolated divine miracles into the field of nature, they have built a heaven out beyond the grave. It is only transcendentalist metaphysicians who think that, without adding any concrete details to Nature, or subtracting any, but by simply calling it the expression of absolute spirit, you make it more divine just as it stands. I believe the pragmatic way of taking religion to be the deeper way. It gives it body as well as soul, it makes it claim, as everything real must claim, some characteristic realm of fact as its very own. What the more characteristically divine facts are, apart from the actual inflow of energy in the faith-state and the prayer-state, I know not. But the over-belief on which I am ready to make my personal venture is that they exist. The whole drift of my education goes to persuade me that the world of our present consciousness is only one out of many worlds of consciousness that exist, and that those other worlds must contain experiences which have a meaning for our life also; and that although in the main their experiences and those of this world keep discrete, yet the two become continuous at certain points, and higher energies filter in. By being faithful in my poor measure to this over-belief, I seem to myself to keep more sane and true. I *can*, of course, put myself into the sectarian scientist's attitude, and imagine vividly that the world of sensations and of scientific laws and objects may be all. But whenever I do this, I hear that inward monitor of which W. K. Clifford once wrote, whispering the word "bosh!" Humbug is humbug, even though it bear the scientific name, and the total expression of human experience, as I view it objectively, invincibly urges me beyond the narrow "scientific" bounds. Assuredly, the real world is of a different temperament—more intricately built than physical science allows. So my objective and my subjective conscience both hold me to the over-belief which I express. Who knows whether the faithfulness of individuals here below to their own poor over-beliefs may not actually help God in turn to be more effectively faithful to his own greater tasks?

# POSTSCRIPT

IN writing my concluding lecture I had to aim so much at simplification that I fear that my general philosophic position received so scant a statement as hardly to be intelligible to some of my readers. I therefore add this epilogue, which must also be so brief as possibly to remedy but little the defect. In a later work I may be enabled to state my position more amply and consequently more clearly.

Originality cannot be expected in a field like this, where all the attitudes and tempers that are possible have been exhibited in literature long ago, and where any new writer can immediately be classed under a familiar head. If one should make a division of all thinkers into naturalists and supernaturalists, I should undoubtedly have to go, along with most philosophers, into the supernaturalist branch. But there is a crasser and a more refined supernaturalism, and it is to the refined division that most philosophers at the present day belong. If not regular transcendental idealists, they at least obey the Kantian direction enough to bar out ideal entities from interfering causally in the course of phenomenal events. Refined supernaturalism is universalistic supernaturalism; for the "crasser" variety "piecemeal" supernaturalism would perhaps be the better name. It went with that older theology which to-day is supposed to reign only among uneducated people, or to be found among the few belated professors of the dualisms which Kant is thought to have displaced. It admits miracles and providential leadings, and finds no intellectual difficulty in mixing the ideal and the real worlds together by interpolating influences from the ideal region among the forces that causally determine the real world's details. In this the refined supernaturalists think that it muddles disparate dimensions of existence. For them the world of the ideal has no efficient causality, and never bursts into the world of phenomena at particular points. The ideal world, for them, is not a world of facts, but only of the meaning of facts; it is a point of view for judging facts. It appertains to a different "-ology," and inhabits a different dimension of being altogether from that in which existential propositions obtain. It cannot get down upon the flat level of experience and interpolate itself piecemeal between distinct portions of nature, as those who believe, for example, in divine aid coming in response to prayer, are bound to think it must.

Notwithstanding my own inability to accept either popular Christianity or scholastic theism, I suppose that my belief that in communion with the Ideal new force comes into the world, and new departures are made here below, subjects me to being classed among the supernaturalists of the piecemeal or crasser type. Universalistic supernaturalism surrenders, it seems to me, too easily to naturalism. It takes the facts of physical science at their face-value, and leaves the laws of life just as naturalism finds them, with no hope of remedy, in case their fruits are bad. It confines itself to sentiments about life as a whole, sentiments which may be admiring and adoring, but which need not be so, as the existence of systematic pessimism proves. In this universalistic way of taking the ideal world, the essence of practical religion seems to me to evaporate. Both instinctively and for logical reasons, I find it hard to believe that principles can exist which make no difference in facts.[1] But all facts

[1] Transcendental idealism, of course, insists that its ideal world makes *this* difference, that facts *exist*. We owe it to the Absolute that we have a world of fact at all. "A world" of fact!—that exactly is the trouble. An entire world is the smallest unit with which the Absolute can work, whereas to our finite minds work for the better ought to be

are particular facts, and the whole interest of the question of God's existence seems to me to lie in the consequences for particulars which that existence may be expected to entail. That no concrete particular of experience should alter its complexion in consequence of a God being there seems to me an incredible proposition, and yet it is the thesis to which (implicitly at any rate) refined supernaturalism seems to cling. It is only with experience *en bloc*, it says, that the Absolute maintains relations. It condescends to no transactions of detail.

I am ignorant of Buddhism and speak under correction, and merely in order the better to describe my general point of view; but as I apprehend the Buddhistic doctrine of Karma, I agree in principle with that. All supernaturalists admit that facts are under the judgment of higher law; but for Buddhism as I interpret it, and for religion generally so far as it remains unweakened by transcendentalistic metaphysics, the word "judgment" here means no such bare academic verdict or platonic appreciation as it means in Vedantic or modern absolutist systems; it carries, on the contrary, *execution* with it, is *in rebus* as well as *post rem*, and operates "causally" as partial factor in the total fact. The universe becomes a gnosticism[1] pure and simple on any other terms. But this view that judgment and execution

done within this world, setting in at single points. Our difficulties and our ideals are all piecemeal affairs, but the Absolute can do no piecework for us; so that all the interests which our poor souls compass raise their heads too late. We should have spoken earlier, prayed for another world absolutely, before this world was born. It is strange, I have heard a friend say, to see this blind corner into which Christian thought has worked itself at last, with its God who can raise no particular weight whatever, who can help us with no private burden, and who is on the side of our enemies as much as he is on our own. Odd evolution from the God of David's psalms!

[1] See my Will to Believe and other Essays in popular Philosophy, 1897, p. 165.

go together is that of the crasser supernaturalist way of thinking, so the present volume must on the whole be classed with the other expressions of that creed.

I state the matter thus bluntly, because the current of thought in academic circles runs against me, and I feel like a man who must set his back against an open door quickly if he does not wish to see it closed and locked. In spite of its being so shocking to the reigning intellectual tastes, I believe that a candid consideration of piecemeal supernaturalism and a complete discussion of all its metaphysical bearings will show it to be the hypothesis by which the largest number of legitimate requirements are met. That of course would be a program for other books than this; what I now say sufficiently indicates to the philosophic reader the place where I belong.

If asked just where the differences in fact which are due to God's existence come in, I should have to say that in general I have no hypothesis to offer beyond what the phenomenon of "prayerful communion," especially when certain kinds of incursion from the subconscious region take part in it, immediately suggests. The appearance is that in this phenomenon something ideal, which in one sense is part of ourselves and in another sense is not ourselves, actually exerts an influence, raises our centre of personal energy, and produces regenerative effects unattainable in other ways. If, then, there be a wider world of being than that of our every-day consciousness, if in it there be forces whose effects on us are intermittent, if one facilitating condition of the effects be the openness of the "subliminal" door, we have the elements of a theory to which the phenomena of religious life lend plausibility. I am so impressed by the importance of these phenomena that I adopt the hypothesis which they so naturally suggest. At these places at least, I say, it would seem as though transmundane energies, God, if you will, produced immediate effects within the natural world to which the rest of our experience belongs.

The difference in natural "fact" which most of us would assign as the first difference which the existence of a God ought to make would, I imagine, be personal immortality. Religion, in fact, for the great majority of our own race *means* immortality, and nothing else. God is the producer of immortality; and whoever has doubts of immortality is written down as an atheist without farther trial. I have said nothing in my lectures about immortality or the belief therein, for to me it seems a secondary point. If our ideals are only cared for in "eternity," I do not see why we might not be willing to resign their care to other hands than ours. Yet I sympathize with the urgent impulse to be present ourselves, and in the conflict of impulses, both of them so vague yet both of them noble, I know not how to decide. It seems to me that it is eminently a case for facts to testify. Facts, I think, are yet lacking to prove "spirit-return," though I have the highest respect for the patient labors of Messrs. Myers, Hodgson, and Hyslop, and am somewhat impressed by their favorable conclusions. I consequently leave the matter open, with this brief word to save the reader from a possible perplexity as to why immortality got no mention in the body of this book.

The ideal power with which we feel ourselves in connection, the "God" of ordinary men, is, both by ordinary men and by philosophers, endowed with certain of those metaphysical attributes which in the lecture on philosophy I treated with such disrespect. He is assumed as a matter of course to be "one and only" and to be "infinite"; and the notion of many finite gods is one which hardly any one thinks it worth while to consider, and still less to uphold. Nevertheless, in the interests of intellectual clearness, I feel bound to say that religious experience, as we have studied it, cannot be cited as unequivocally supporting the infinitist belief. The only thing that it unequivocally testifies to is that we can experience union with *something* larger than ourselves and in that union find our greatest peace. Philosophy, with its passion for unity, and mysticism with its monoideistic bent, both "pass to the limit" and identify the something with a unique God who is the all-inclusive soul of the world. Popular opinion, respectful to their authority, follows the example which they set.

Meanwhile the practical needs and experiences of religion seem to me sufficiently met by the belief that beyond each man and in a fashion continuous with him there exists a larger power which is friendly to him and to his ideals. All that the facts require is that the power should be both other and larger than our conscious selves. Anything larger will do, if only it be large enough to trust for the next step. It need not be infinite, it need not be solitary. It might conceivably even be only a larger and more godlike self, of which the present self would then be but the mutilated expression, and the universe might conceivably be a collection of such selves, of different degrees of inclusiveness, with no absolute unity realized in it at all.[1] Thus would a sort of polytheism return upon us—a polytheism which I do not on this occasion defend, for my only aim at present is to keep the testimony of religious experience clearly within its proper bounds. [Compare p. 130 above.]

Upholders of the monistic view will say to such a polytheism (which, by the way, has always been the real religion of common people, and is so still to-day) that unless there be one all-inclusive God, our guarantee of security is left imperfect. In the Absolute, and in the Absolute only, *all* is saved. If there be different gods, each caring for his part, some portion of some of us might not be covered with divine protection, and our religious consolation would thus

[1] Such a notion is suggested in my Ingersoll Lecture On Human Immortality, Boston and London, 1899.

fail to be complete. It goes back to what was said on pages 129-131, about the possibility of there being portions of the universe that may irretrievably be lost. Common sense is less sweeping in its demands than philosophy or mysticism have been wont to be, and can suffer the notion of this world being partly saved and partly lost. The ordinary moralistic state of mind makes the salvation of the world conditional upon the success with which each unit does its part. Partial and conditional salvation is in fact a most familiar notion when taken in the abstract, the only difficulty being to determine the details. Some men are even disinterested enough to be willing to be in the unsaved remnant as far as their persons go, if only they can be persuaded that their cause will prevail—all of us are willing, whenever our activity-excitement rises sufficiently high. I think, in fact, that a final philosophy of religion will have to consider the pluralistic hypothesis more seriously than it has hitherto been willing to consider it. For practical life at any rate, the *chance* of salvation is enough. No fact in human nature is more characteristic than its willingness to live on a chance. The existence of the chance makes the difference, as Edmund Gurney says, between a life of which the keynote is resignation and a life of which the keynote is hope.[1] But all these statements are unsatisfactory from their brevity, and I can only say that I hope to return to the same questions in another book.

[1] Tertium Quid, 1887, p. 99. See also pp. 148, 149.